Sowing
Priceless
Seeds

Sowing Priceless *Seeds*

Treasured Joys *and* Tears *of the* Lighthouse

Sally Sanders

XULON ELITE

Xulon Press Elite
555 Winderley Pl, Suite 225
Maitland, FL 32751
407.339.4217
www.xulonpress.com

© 2024 by Sally Sanders

All rights reserved solely by the author. The author guarantees all contents are original and do not infringe upon the legal rights of any other person or work. No part of this book may be reproduced in any form without the permission of the author.

Due to the changing nature of the Internet, if there are any web addresses, links, or URLs included in this manuscript, these may have been altered and may no longer be accessible. The views and opinions shared in this book belong solely to the author and do not necessarily reflect those of the publisher. The publisher therefore disclaims responsibility for the views or opinions expressed within the work.

Unless otherwise indicated, Scripture quotations taken from the King James Version (KJV) – *public domain.*

Paperback ISBN-13: 979-8-86850-418-1
Ebook ISBN-13: 979-8-86850-419-8

Table of Contents

Acknowledgments ix
Preface xiii
Chapter 1: Molly 1
Chapter 2: Costa Rica 11
Chapter 3: Oodles and Iffies 29
Chapter 4: The Lord Supplies and Protects 51
Chapter 5: 2 More Oodles, a Grandma, and 2 Iffies 63
Chapter 6: A New House 85
Chapter 7: Growing Pains 97
Chapter 8: Betsy 139
Chapter 9: Dito 153
Chapter 10: The Next Generation 179
Chapter 11: Jerry Cornsnapple 221
Chapter 12: And the Family Continues to Grow 241
Chapter 13: Staying Busy 275
Chapter 14: Staying Busy – Part 2 293
Chapter 15: A Little More About Dito 343
Chapter 16: Latest Generation 357
Author's Final Thoughts 391

Acknowledgments

First and foremost, I am ever so grateful to the Lord Jesus Christ for His gift of salvation and hope of heaven; His alone is all the praise and glory. Next, a special thank you to my father and mother, who took me to church every time the doors were opened and taught me to love the Lord through their example. I thank my brothers Don, Dave, and Ed and their families for their financial and prayer support down through the years. Thank you to every pastor and teacher who taught me about Christ during my childhood and teen years at Cielo Vista Park Baptist Church. Thank you to the professors and students who taught and encouraged me during my years of study at Pacific Coast Baptist Bible College. Thank you to the DeVore, Frazier, and Morris families who opened my eyes to missions.

I thank the Lord for the many years of mission work that He has given me as the director of the Lighthouse Children's Home in Costa Rica. I also thank and praise Him for the multitude of co-laborers He has provided without whom this work would not have been possible. No one alone could have accomplished what has been done over the decades; therefore, I want to recognize several others who poured much of their lives into this ministry, laboring faithfully with me through the years to make it all possible.

A special thank you to Maudie Meek, Robert and Francis Heflin, and Larry and Paula Neff for allowing the Lord to use you all in making this dream a reality. A huge thank you to Patricia Neff, the children's aunt and sharer of my dream, who has been instrumental in many areas from running errands, handling legal matters, helping several years with the accounting to occasionally taking care of the children in my absence, as well as loving, praying for, and counseling them through the years.

I thank Maria Gaitan, our weekday, breakfast/lunch cook for over twenty-seven years of service, and Mayra Ramirez who has helped for years with cooking, cleaning, and sewing. Thank you, Teacher Maria Elena Azofeifa, for your many years of service and dedication to the children's education. Many others have taught in the school and helped in the home for shorter periods of time, the Orrs, Tomi, Jim, Gina, Glenda, Andrea, Maria, Adriana, Olga, Cindy, Lorna, Hannia, Brooke, Rachel, Bethany, Rebecca, Belen, Eileen, and Sarita. Thank you, Ryan and Brooke Carter, for your help in numerous ways, on many occasions, and for your sacrificial love for the children. Thank you, Matt Sweet, Danilo Mora, and Dean Medrano for your skills and faithfulness in the area of maintenance. Thank you, Ron and Tara, Lina, and each of the field representatives and staff who faithfully serve on the front lines raising the much-needed support and doing the Stateside office work. It's not possible to name everyone who has helped; God remembers your labor of love.

A very special thank you to my dear husband, Terry Sanders, for his patience, counsel, and generosity in giving his time and money to this ministry over and over again. God Almighty knew how much I needed someone to lean on and brought Terry into my life at just the right time. Thank you to Terry's parents Harland and Rose Sanders and his sister and brother-in-law, Brenda and Bill Lemus, for their prayers and generous financial support through the years, and for housing groups of children several times on trips to the States.

Thank you to each of the children who grew up in the home, have continued serving the Lord, and have given their time and finances to help other generations of children growing up in the home. A very special thank you to Connie Raney, who has been the cheerleader behind the scenes, encouraging me to write this history. Without her help and support, this book would not have been possible.

Last but certainly not least, a big thank you to each one of the churches and individuals who have faithfully supported our home or sponsored children down through the years. It is your offerings that have paid the salaries and bills and bought the food, medicine, clothes, books, toys, and so on. While we know that God is able to accomplish whatever He chooses, I am glad that He has used you to be such a great blessing and an important part of this work. Thank you also for your prayers; they are what have kept us going.

Preface

All the stories in this book are true, as well as I remember them. They are the little anecdotes that we have shared with visitors for years, many of whom have suggested that they be written in a book. These stories have finally been written down. Of course, without the children, there would be no home, so our story is their story. They have been the center of all our dreams, laughter, and trials.

That said, I felt it necessary to introduce you to them, writing a little bit about each child, their strengths, their weaknesses, their little quirks, and how God used them to teach us all. I certainly hope you enjoy getting to know our precious children.

Most of the names, including my own, have been changed to protect both the innocent and the guilty. Kindly enjoy this tiny glimpse into thirty-five-plus years of life in a children's home on a mission field and how it all came to be.

Sally Sanders

Chapter 1

Molly

Some little girls enjoy playing with dolls, carrying them around, and giving them an important place in their hearts and lives. Other young ladies seem to have some kind of special talent for destroying the perfect hairdos with which their doll comes out of the box in a matter of two or three days. This feat is followed by losing all their clothes by day four or five (even when the doll comes complete with several different changes of clothes) and then stuffing them in their closets to live their make-believe lives in solitude and abandonment, with matted hair and no clothes.

Molly was the first type of little girl, although almost all of her future daughters, to her dismay, were the second type of miniature mothers. Molly's dolls were extremely important to her. John was probably the most important since he had been a part of life for as far back as she could remember. His size also made him important. John came into her life when she was just two years old and just a little over a foot taller than she was. That didn't stop her from hauling him everywhere she went. He sat next to her at the dinner table and on the couch as they watched black-and-white TV at night. He watched her color and looked through picture books with her. She would rock him to sleep several times a day in the crib he came with but then pick him up and put him in bed with her at bedtime, hugging him tightly as she fell asleep.

No one knows exactly how many birthday parties John had in his first two years of life, but guessing close to twenty would probably not be much of an exaggeration. Whenever little Molly was bored, she would tell her mother that John was having a birthday. Mother would find some little snack, and Molly would wrap up a few toys in newspaper, then they would sing "Happy Birthday" and poof, instant party. And when Molly had her birthday, there was John sitting in his toy highchair next to the birthday girl, just as happy as any little pretend baby boy could be.

Molly talked to John a lot. She shared with him all the few itsy-bitsy bits of information about life that she had learned. Although she didn't know much—she was quite young herself—she liked to tell him the Bible stories she was learning at Sunday school. But the biggest shock for Molly's mother was the day she stood close by the door to listen in on one of Molly's conversations with John. Molly was telling John that he was a sinner and deserved to go to hell for his sins because sin had to be punished. She said that God had sent His Son, Jesus Christ, to die on the cross, take his punishment, and forgive his sins. Molly told John that if he would believe in Jesus and take Him as his Savior, he would live with Him forever in heaven one day. Molly had been going to church since she was two days old, so why would this simple conversation shock her mother? Molly wasn't even three years old yet.

Yes, God had His eye on little Molly and her tender heart for her baby doll. He had plans for her and grew in her heart that motherly love.

[A LESSON TO LEARN: God has plans for all His dear children. Jeremiah 29:11 says, "For I know the thoughts that I think toward you, saith the Lord, thoughts of peace, and not of evil, to give you an expected end." He has thoughts, plans, and ideas, yes, for your life, and will give you everything you need to be what He would have you become, but He leaves life's choices up to you; choose carefully. And if you, reader, have not yet been adopted into God's family, by faith in the redeeming work of Christ as spoken of in Galatians 4:4–5, "God sent forth His Son, made of a woman, made under the law, to redeem them that were under the law, that we might receive the adoption of sons," God has a plan for you too. Second Peter 3:9 says that God is not willing that any should perish, but that all should come to repentance. God loved you from the foundation of the world and sent Christ to be your Savior. John 3:16–18 clearly tells us,

> For God so loved the world, that he gave his only begotten Son, that whosoever believeth in him should not perish, but have everlasting life. For God sent not his Son into the world to condemn the world; but that the world through him might be saved. He that believeth on him is not condemned: but he that believeth not is condemned already, because he hath not believed in the name of the only begotten Son of God.

God's plan for you is to realize that you are a sinner in need of a Savior, turn from trusting in yourself, religion, or any other person or thing, and put your trust in the finished work of Christ on the cross, dying to pay for your sins, thus accepting Him alone as your Lord and Savior.]

    Molly came from a stable Christian family. Her mother was able to stay home and spend time with the children, and her father held the same job from before Molly was born until he retired. No family is without its problems, and theirs certainly had its share, but both parents loved the Lord and attended church regularly every time the doors were open. Her mother taught in Sunday school and sang in the choir, and her father was the church treasurer.

    Molly was the youngest in her family, and although she had three older siblings, all of them were boys, and two of them were too much older than her to be playmates. Her third brother, Paul, was only fourteen months older than her. They spent lots of time together as long as Molly wanted to play boy games and whenever Paul was willing to accept a little sister tagging along. The fact was that, just like in her own family, there were more boys in the neighborhood than girls, so if Molly wanted to be included, she had to learn boy games. She spent her childhood climbing trees, running obstacle courses, climbing on the house, jumping off the roof of the house, playing army, and engaging in football and baseball games in the middle of the street.

Should Molly whine or complain, which little sisters are well-known for doing, she was told to stop being such a baby, that they, the boys, didn't want a girl around anyway, and she should just go inside and play with her dolls. She would go to her room, crying and praying for a little sister to play with, or several little sisters, then she would place all her dolls in neat little rows on her bed. By this time, she had many more dolls; each one was important, and each one had a name. She would pull out her little toy chalkboard and begin to teach them everything she was learning at school. Now, God was developing in Molly not just a mother's heart but something new, a teacher's heart.

Molly could remember often raising her hand during the invitation at church because she wanted to be saved. She also remembered that her mother would always reach over and put her hand back down, telling her later that she felt she was too young to understand, being not quite five years old. Molly stopped raising her hand, but she continued to worry about her salvation and finally decided to talk to her mother about it. Her mother asked her why she was no longer raising her hand in the invitation, and Molly told her she was waiting for her mother to tell her she was old enough to get saved. It was at that point that her mother felt she should not stand in her way and told her she could get saved when she felt ready.

The following Sunday, Molly tried very hard to walk forward in the invitation, but she was too afraid. She could remember feeling miserable all Sunday afternoon and being afraid of dying without Christ. On Sunday evening, she could put it off no longer and walked down the aisle all by herself to accept Christ as her Savior. She was very young, but she knew she was a sinner and needed a Savior. She simply believed that Christ was the Son of God who died and rose again to pay for her sins. She put her trust in what Christ did on the cross. Molly couldn't remember a whole lot of things from before she was five, but she never forgot that day. She also remembered worrying about her brother and other kids at church who she thought weren't saved yet.

As a grown lady, Molly would one day look back on her childhood and teen years and be able to recognize all the people God had brought into her life to direct her toward the special ministry the Lord would open up for her. There were so many of them, her parents, brothers, pastor, loving church family, youth director and his wife, friends, and missionaries, all of whom took an interest in her and nurtured her with God's Word and wise counsel.

One such friend encouraged her to commit to memory as much Scripture as possible, and memorizing whole chapters of God's Word became her hobby. Oh, how those Scriptures had helped her time and time again. She realized that there was nothing great about her. Christ in her was her only strength. The people He had placed around her were the tools He used to mold her.

Events also shaped her life. Beginning at the age of eight, she would attend a children's camp every summer. The lady who taught the camp had such a talent for working with children. She was funny, dynamic, and had a little girl ventriloquist dummy named, of all names, Molly. Little Molly was awe-stricken. Such a tiny detail, but what an impact it made on her. Molly decided she wanted to be just like that lady someday, telling children about Jesus. There was that teacher's heart again.

Months later, she saw a small ventriloquist dummy in the window of a toy store for eight dollars. Her mother wouldn't buy it for her because she said it wasn't a toy; it was something you had to know how to work. Molly saved up her dimes and quarters from doing chores around the house until she was able to buy the dummy herself. It came with a small instruction booklet on how to be a ventriloquist.

Molly was encouraged when she heard her mother telling everyone that she herself had read the booklet and couldn't do ventriloquism, but Molly read it and could.

Her mother wrote her several little skits, and within months, Molly was doing specials with her dummy in Sunday school. Thus, at the age of nine, shy Molly, who was the quietest one in all her classes and practically hid behind her mother's skirt, when being introduced to anyone, was now doing ventriloquism in front of classes full of people.

Her little dummy, Archie, was Molly's security blanket. Everyone loved Archie and laughed at his jokes. Molly would never have sung a solo, but Archie could sing. And if Archie didn't hit the right note or forgot the words to the song, it was just all the funnier. Nobody was making fun of or laughing at Molly; they were laughing at Archie. Yet, Archie was nothing without Molly, and she was loving the attention. She was on her way to becoming the nice teacher from camp. It was one more piece of the puzzle of God's plan for her life. Archie became a lifelong friend.

Another event that shaped Molly's thinking and destiny involved missions. For many years during her childhood, Molly's mother would go across the border from their home in El Paso, Texas, to a small mission church in Juarez, Mexico. Her mother had told the Lord that if He would give her a van, she would use it for his service. Soon afterward, they were able to purchase a bright red van, and her mother began to cross the border, picking up several families, and taking them up the steep, dirt road to the little church. Her mother would make the trip every other Sunday afternoon, and Molly was the only one in the family who cared to go with her.

In the Sunday school class at the mission, children of all ages were together in one small room, and everyone well-behaved got to pick a brightly-colored piece of Mexican candy out of a huge jar. Since Molly could neither speak nor understand Spanish, she was always very quiet. She just sat there, staring at that larger-than-a-jug glass container full of candy, enjoying listening to the gibberish until it was her turn to pick a piece of candy.

Life went on after the brightly-colored candy. Their family no longer had the van, and the trips to the mission had ended. Molly turned into a teenager and became very involved in multiple ministries in her own church, bus ministry, youth group, visitation, choir, and ultimately, at the age of eighteen, teaching a class of second-grade boys. The little mission was a thing of the past, that is, until two missionary daughters invited her to a youth camp in Mexico. The camp only cost five dollars, and the girls kept going on and on about all the fun they had at the previous year's camp. Molly had taken three years of Spanish in high school, and this sounded like the perfect opportunity to use everything she had learned.

Once at camp, she realized that after three years of Spanish, she knew practically nothing. Everyone spoke so fast and all at the same time. Nevertheless, she had the time of her life, making friends through invented sign language. She soon realized that some of the teens were the same little children her mother had picked up week after week and who had been in her mission Sunday school class, picking candy from the same glass jar. God used that camp to break her and grow in her the heart of a missionary. At the end of the camp, she stood on the hill the church was built on, looking over the city of Juarez and told God that if He would open the door for her to return to the mission field, she would step through.

Less than a month after the camp, Molly was leaving home to begin her first year at Bible college. She took with her a mother's heart, a teacher's heart, and now, a missionary's heart. During her four years at Bible college, she told everyone that she would be a missionary to Mexico. Upon graduation, she returned to El Paso and began teaching in Christian schools and waiting for God to open a door in Mexico.

For three years, Molly taught in El Paso during the week while helping in the church in Mexico on the weekends, but no doors for full-time mission work seemed to be opening. By this time, she was speaking enough Spanish to get by, and although many people told her to wait until she got married, she felt she was ready for the mission field. She did eventually want to get married, but getting to the mission field was at the top of her priority list. What if she never married and ended up waiting so long that she missed the mission field?

Molly got her nerves up and went to talk to her pastor. A close missionary friend had suggested the idea of maybe teaching in a Bible college in Mexico where she could possibly live in the dorms and wouldn't need much support. She bravely explained that she had already graduated college, could speak the Spanish language, had three years of teaching experience, and was ready for the mission field. To her surprise, her pastor said he knew of no place in Mexico but had a good friend in Costa Rica who had a Bible college. Her heart sank. For seven years, she had been talking about Mexico, and she didn't even have any idea where Costa Rica was on the map. After her big "I'm ready" speech, she couldn't exactly say no thank you. They decided to pray about it for two weeks. By the end of that time, God had given her peace about Costa Rica. They called the missionary, and he said to have her get her passport because he could use her immediately; they had just started their school year.

Molly was really excited about the trip until the night before she left. The ladies of the church she had grown up in wanted to give her a going-away party. As each lady drew near to "encourage" her, she listened to their parting words. Several said, "You are so brave," and others said, "I could never do what you are doing." One lady said, "I heard a documentary that said the cockroaches in Costa Rica can grow to five inches long," and yet another said, "I understand that a large part of Costa Rica is jungle, with wild animals, snakes, and poisonous frogs." Molly felt a sick feeling coming over her; she was not a brave person at all. She literally thought for a minute that she would have to be excused and run to the bathroom.

Molly made it through the rest of the party but continued to ask herself for the remainder of the evening what on earth she was getting into. Her only comfort was in the fact that the missionary had suggested an eight-month trial term, so there was a small window of escape. That time frame would take her right up to Christmas, when she would return home and make a final decision as to whether she felt God wanted her in Costa Rica.

And that is how it happened. In less than a month from the time the missionary had said yes, she was getting off a plane in the beautiful country of Costa Rica, a country in which she knew no one. She had a phone number in her pocket in case the people who were supposed to be there holding a small chalkboard with her name on it didn't show. Her support consisted of three churches and her parents and totaled up to about $300 a month. How wonderful that God was willing to use insignificant, unpopular, plain-faced, little Molly Prunewipple. The year was 1985, and she was twenty-six years old. As she stepped through customs, there was the chalkboard, and there was her name; the adventure of a lifetime was about to begin.

Prayer:

Dear heavenly Father, we praise you, for you alone are our strength, our rock, our fortress, our deliverer. Thank you for giving us your Spirit to guide, comfort, and counsel us. Thank you for your Word that lights our path in all wisdom and understanding. Thank you for the precious blood of your own Son that has cleansed and redeemed us. Thank you for your willingness to use us, though we are undeserving and weak. Help us to be willing to be used, and teach us to choose our paths carefully. In Jesus's name, we pray, amen.

Second Corinthians 3:5 says, "Not that we are sufficient of ourselves to think anything as of ourselves; but our sufficiency is of God."

Chapter 2

Costa Rica

Although Costa Rica does have its rainforests and jungle-like areas, Molly was relieved to learn that she would be living in the capital city of San Jose, far away from the poisonous frogs. The church where she would be working had a Sunday attendance of around 700 people and a Bible seminary of about thirty students. Only thirteen of the students lived on campus. Molly and one other teacher lived in one big dorm room with the eight on-campus female students.

It wasn't long before Molly fell in love with Costa Rica and its people. The country was beautiful, with tall, green mountains and colorful flowers. It was a far cry from the flat, hot desert where she had been raised. The people were extra friendly, loved U.S. citizens, and also wanted to be helpful. The year-round seventy-five-degree temperature of the Central Valley was perfect for her. She realized the importance of not only being willing to be used by God but letting Him lead. Costa Rica had definitely been a door that God Himself had opened; she had never considered it herself. Yet, she was so very happy with His choice for her.

Her responsibilities began immediately. She taught four different classes in the Bible seminary, had a Sunday and Wednesday night children's class called "The Followers of Christ," was put in charge of the seminary's singing group, and walked with the students on a visitation program every afternoon, rain or shine, usually rain. In addition, she was told to prepare a VBS program for a mid-year missions tour. Since all of her time was spent with the girls in the dorm, she seldom heard English, and her Spanish began to improve.

Molly never really went through culture shock, but there were a few little foreign field oddities that she thought were funny. In every neighborhood, a family or two had turned the front room of their tiny houses into little stores. In these stores, everything was sold individually. Thus, if you cut your finger, you went to the store and bought one Band-Aid as opposed to a box of Band-Aids. You could also buy just one safety pin, one aspirin, one piece of writing paper, one envelope, one egg, and even one cup of sugar or flour. Cokes came in glass bottles but were poured into plastic bags with a straw sticking out of the top, so the bottles stayed at the store.

Phones were another oddity back in 1985 when Molly arrived in the country. There were plenty of pay phones on street corners throughout every neighborhood, but many people did not have telephones in their houses. The lines at the pay phone could be six or seven people long. It was considered common courtesy to limit your call to five minutes, though some people were not so courteous. In those cases, the entire line of people could be heard tapping their feet, clearing their throats, yawning, and so on. There were also no phones in the dorm or church. Fortunately, the missionaries who lived on the opposite end of the property did have a phone.

About once a month, Molly's mother would call, and they would send someone over to tell her. She would race across the property, calling out, "Make room, make room," knowing that long-distance phone calls weren't cheap, and her mother could only afford about a twenty-minute conversation. Returning to the dorm with a smile on her face after said phone calls, Molly would find all the girls happy for her and eager to listen to her news from home.

The hardest thing to get used to was the campus diet in the first couple of years. The school's kitchen was on a tight budget. The sweet little lady who cooked worked miracles to feed everyone. She provided three meals a day for almost twenty people on only about ten dollars a week. Breakfast every morning was "gallo pinto," which was black beans mixed with rice, a small piece of bread, and sometimes, if they were lucky, a spoonful of something similar to sour cream. Lunch was rice and beans, and supper, to add variety, was beans and rice. With the lunchtime rice and beans, they served cabbage and lemon salad and some kind of "picadillo" (diced potatoes, chopped green beans, or some other vegetable mixed with a tad of ground beef). The food served with the supper beans and rice was not quite so fancy, maybe just fried plantains or the bitter spinach and eggs dish, which they had at least once a week.

Molly liked raw spinach and even canned spinach and couldn't figure out why that particular meal was so bitter. One of the girls told her it was because the cook was chopping the stems up with the leaves in an effort to stretch it out and feed more people. Noticing how many people were throwing it in the trash, Molly was sure that the "use the stems too" theory was actually feeding fewer people.

Molly thought back to her college days when the students would joke about some not-so-favorite meals, saying the college was preparing them for the mission field. One such meal, a not-so-great take on chicken fried steak, had been named the "Dreaded Breaded" by students. Now Molly found herself longing for some Dreaded Breaded and realized that the college cafeteria had failed miserably in preparing her for the mission field. Not only was she eating beans and rice three times a day, but she also found the Costa Rican white rice and black beans to be very bland in comparison to the Spanish rice and pinto beans she had grown up eating from living on the Mexican border.

Sundays were better as the menu rotated between a chicken and rice dish one Sunday and a roast and potatoes dish the next. The roast was cut into one-and-a-half-inch squares; everyone was allowed two squares. An older missionary lady stood guard over the precious morsels, making sure no one took more than two. Once, a third piece fell onto the plate of one of the girls. The roast beef guard's eyes grew big, and Molly imagined seeing steam coming out of her ears as she hurried over to force the offender to return a piece.

Molly's biggest initiation to the country came after she had been in Costa Rica for two months. That is when the seminary ladies left the big city of San Jose in the beautiful Central Valley and set out for a five-week Vacation Bible School (VBS) tour to the remote, jungle-like areas of Costa Rica. They would be staying one week in each of five different churches, doing a VBS for the children during the day and attending revival meetings at night. Molly soon realized why most of Costa Rica's population lived in the Central Valley. The climate was quite different in the remote regions, very, very hot and humid. There was no escaping the heat; it was constant night and day. The people lived in open-air houses, as there was absolutely no such thing as air-conditioning. The windows in the houses were square openings with no glass, just bars to keep out thieves and large animals.

The mosquitos were uncontrollable and seemed to bite right through clothing despite mosquito repellent. By week three, Molly decided to count her mosquito bites by putting a small blue dot next to each one with a writing pen. When she finished counting, she had 120 blue dots on her arms and legs. Neither the heat nor the mosquitos seemed to bother the people who had grown up in the area. Molly was covered with bites, and they had none. They tried to tell her that her blood was sweeter, but she supposed their skin had grown tough, and her skin must have been more sensitive to the bites. Molly had hoped that the afternoon rains, which came every day, would cool things down a tad. She soon found out that things didn't work that way. The rains only drove up the humidity, which made the heat more unbearable and the mosquito bites itch more.

That was also the trip when Molly met up with the feared cockroaches. It all started shortly after entering a large room in a rather run-down empty house. They would all be sleeping on the floor in that room. As they began pulling out the sleeping bags and arranging their things, a girl on the opposite side of the room from Molly started yelling about seeing a cockroach. This was followed by wild screaming from several girls. Molly was curious to see whether or not the cockroach was truly five inches long. She came as close as safety measures would allow, saw that it was no larger than two inches long, and went back to her side of the room. She laughed as she watched the silly girls screaming and throwing their sandals at the surprised bug, trying to kill it. She was glad it was not on her end of the room and, thus, was not a problem she would have to deal with, or so she thought.

About that time the cockroach flew all the way across the room and landed on Molly's skirt. Now she was the silly girl screaming and turning around in circles. One of the girls came to her rescue, batting the cockroach off her skirt and smashing the poor little thing into the ground. Certainly, there must be all kinds of cockroaches in all parts of the world, but where Molly had grown up, none of them knew how to fly. She wasn't sure which was worse, a five-inch cockroach or a flying one.

There were a few embarrassing things that happened during the five-week tour. The first involved the entire group of girls. They had practiced several songs to sing as specials in the evening services. They understood the seriousness of their specials, as they were to glorify the Lord, and the group was representing the Bible seminary. Nevertheless, the only accompaniment they had was a guitar, and the only one who could play it was a somewhat unusual girl who was easily distracted. At practices, she was constantly changing things on them, either the song, the key they were going to sing in, or anything else. They had finally found a handful of songs she could handle, all with a short simple introduction, and had successfully practiced them for weeks before their trip began. They could only hope that the wacky guitarist would not make a fool of herself.

Now it was the first night at the first church, and they were ready to sing their first special. The guitar player was located center stage with the rest of the girls lined up on either side of her. As she began to play, each of the other girls realized they had no idea what she was playing.

It was an introduction they had never heard, and nobody knew when to start singing. First, they began to glance at each other with puzzled looks on their faces. Molly was planning on just jumping in whenever the guitar player started to sing, but the introduction kept going on and on; it was the longest introduction in the history of music. Somewhere in the middle, one of the girls giggled, and boy did that spread fast.

Finally, with no warning, the guitar player started to sing, and although it was indeed the same words as the song they had practiced, she had caught everyone off guard. She was the only one not laughing and sang the whole song, apparently oblivious to what was going on around her. The rest of the girls tried their hardest to get serious. Each of them would come in at different times, sing a few words, and then begin giggling again. The saddest part was, to the unexpected eye, the guitarist was the only one who did not make a fool of herself. She came off as extremely professional, keeping her self-poise while everyone else lost it. The special was a disaster. After the service, the entire group got the bawling out of their lives from the pastor of the church. Molly felt worse than anyone as she was supposed to be in charge of the singing group.

Every night after that, the specials came off without a glitch. They were too scared to mess up again. Everyone did their best to represent the seminary well and, more importantly, honor their Savior. Nevertheless, at odd times during the following weeks, someone might be laughing alone or maybe just smiling at nothing, and they all knew what they were remembering. Molly was sure that God himself had a sense of humor and obviously knew they had not purposed to mess up; it was just one of those things, one of those humbling things that remind all of us that we are only human.

Many years later, at a Bible conference, a pastor's wife approached Molly. She explained that she had accepted Christ as her Savior at the age of nine, in that very church, on that very week of that first stop on their mission tour. She remembered the Bible lessons that Molly taught, Archie, Molly's ventriloquist dummy, and even the verses they had memorized. She reminded her of things that Molly herself had long forgotten. But the lady never mentioned the special. Isn't that just like our God? He had worked that week despite their failure. He was, after all, the one who said, "My grace is sufficient for thee: for my strength is made perfect in weakness." - 2 Corinthians 12:9

The other embarrassing experience during the trip was a little more private, not in front of an entire church congregation. Different families in one of the churches were inviting the girls over for meals. One lady made them a very special delicacy, pig's feet. Molly was aware of two important facts. First, she knew that pig's feet were indeed a meal, even though she had never tried them, and there was absolutely no one else whom she had ever seen eating them in her entire life. She also knew that she had learned in her mission classes at Bible college the importance of accepting and eating anything that was put in front of you on the mission field so as not to offend those whom you had gone to the field to serve.

As Molly held the scrumptious foot in her hand, she could not get her eyes past all the long, black hairs protruding from the tasty treat. This would not be easy. Where was she supposed to bite? Then right smack dab in the middle of her contemplations, a very large bee flew right toward her face and started circling the pig's foot. Molly was just as scared of bees as she was of flying cockroaches and began waving her hand wildly around. To her surprise, the pig's foot, hair, and all flew through the air, across the table, and landed on the floor, leaving her holding a bare bone in her hand. Saved by the bee. The surprised hostess felt so sorry and offered her own pig foot meal to her, but Molly whispered to one of the girls that she would be just as happy eating anything else. The lady, who didn't have much else, suggested frying Molly an egg. That was the most delicious egg Molly ever ate in her entire life. She said a second prayer, an extra, silent prayer to God, thanking Him for the egg and sending the bee. God seemed to care even about her little problems; He had her back.

By the end of the five hot, sticky weeks, Molly's only desire was to get out of the rural communities and back to the much cooler, perfect temperature, big city of San Jose. She was so very tired of the heat and mosquitos. But she had survived her first "jungle" mission trip without being attacked by wild animals, snakes, or poisonous frogs. She had a new appreciation for those who serve the Lord for years in difficult climates and circumstances. Yet, each Christian's calling is different, and God knows what is best for each one and places them exactly where He can use them best. Molly was sure that God had placed her in the right place.

Molly visited each of those five churches many more times through the years, but none of the other visits were as memorable as that first trip. None, that is, except for one that took place about two years later. They were in the small village of Sierpe, the place of the flying cockroach. This time, it was for a combination VBS/youth camp. Probably forty or fifty teens had come from the church in San Jose. They were doing a VBS in the morning and camp activities in the afternoon and evening. On the same property as the old house the girls had stayed in, the church had constructed six thatched-roof, open-air huts to house the teens. The property was next to a river, and they had a system of pulling the water from the river for the showers. It was all quite Robinson Crusoe rustic, but the teens were having a great time.

The teens had a visitation program set up to invite the children of the village to the VBS. Visiting door-to-door, some of the teens found a set of ten-month-old twins, a boy and a girl, literally starving to death. The lady who had the babies said that the twin's grandma had found them in a box in the mountain. She had asked the lady to watch them, promising to return, and the lady had not seen the grandmother for two months. They were skin and bones, with sunken-in eyes and boils on their bodies. The lady said they were eating only a couple of spoonfuls of milk every two hours. She was anxious for the grandma to return because she had her own four children to care for and was very poor herself.

Everyone felt compassion for the babies. They talked about ways to possibly rescue them. On many occasions, Molly had thought about one day starting either a Christian school or a children's home. Her mind raced wildly. If they could rescue these two babies, it could be the start of a home. It was talked about so much that week that it seemed like a reality. Molly was told that a church member had even talked to the children's welfare department when they returned to San Jose and had the necessary paperwork to go into the home and remove the children.

Then, everything suddenly came to a halt. Molly probably never knew all the details, but she was told it was too big of a risk, and it wouldn't be done. She was heartbroken and totally unable to understand. She had already built a future in her mind and opened her heart only to see all her hopes and dreams gone almost as quickly as she had hoped and dreamed them up. She knew she had no power nor authority to change the facts, felt so utterly helpless, and cried for days over the babies. She was told later that the health department went in and rescued the babies, and that was the end of the story.

It wasn't the end of the story for Molly, though. She prayed and told the Lord that if he would open the door with the government, she would open the door of her house for children who needed a permanent place to grow up. This was the third time in her life that God had used a camp to touch her heart. The first was the call to teach children about Jesus, the second was the call to the mission field, and now it was a call to start a children's home. Never underestimate the impact that a youth camp can have on a young person's life.

Polly

Molly would soon see through the years that the Lord was always there to supply what she needed when she needed it. One need He supplied for her was a special friend who also felt a desire to work with abandoned children. Polly was a tender-hearted teen in the church with a deep desire to serve the Lord. When they first met, Molly had no idea that she would become a friend and colleague for life.

Molly continued in that same ministry for two more years, always thinking and talking about a children's home. One of the projects she was put in charge of during that time was summer Bible clubs. The church had eight different bus routes that picked up children for Sunday school. They found sixteen families in those routes willing to loan a space in their house for a Bible club once a week. A group of teens volunteered their three months of school vacation to work in the clubs. Molly's job was to prepare the lessons, the teens, puppet skits, and so on.

It was a thrilling time for Molly and the teens as they learned together and shared God's love and Christ's free gift of salvation with hundreds of children each week. The time had a special impact on the life of Polly, who began to seriously consider her service to the Lord. As she grew close to Molly with her questions, they soon became good friends. Molly opened up to her about wanting to start a children's home, and she said she would be very interested in helping.

During this time, one of Molly's brothers had helped her get a little more support, and she felt it was time to get out on her own. She began renting an extremely small three-room house around the corner from the church for only seventy-five dollars a month. Her new friend Polly and one other girl from the seminary moved in with her to occupy the other two rooms. Since they were at the church all day, they would continue eating lunch in the dining hall but would take care of their own breakfast and supper. This was going to be so exciting. Food, food, food was all Molly could think about. They bought whole pieces of chicken and pork chops and other real foods. They rotated the cooking responsibilities among the three of them with the only rule finally being, "NO RICE AND BEANS." They would still get that for lunch at the seminary.

When her roommates asked Polly what she was going to cook on her night, she was too embarrassed to say she couldn't cook and said she was cooking steaks because it sounded pretty easy. It also sounded very delicious. They weren't big, juicy steaks, more like thin breakfast steaks, but it was MEAT. Maybe it was the meat they bought—they weren't used to buying meat—or maybe it was the way she had cooked them, but the meat was very difficult to cut and even more difficult to chew. As they chewed, and chewed, and chewed some more, they began looking around the table to see if the others were having the same problem. The looks turned into grins, which was when Polly confessed she didn't know how to cook, after which the grins turned into loud laughter. She was willing to help Molly or the other girl but did not want her own night, nor did they want her to have her own night. That worked out great, and they soon had quite a menu, at least better than spinach eggs. Life was great, and the ladies shared many times of spiritual growth and fellowship along with lots of laughter.

Since the church was very large, it seemed like there was always some kind of party going on, either a wedding shower, baby shower, graduation, and so on. Molly and Polly didn't miss a single one because any party meant a good meal. All three girls being so new to cooking meant that a decent meal could never be turned down. One particular party was a fancy wedding reception. The food was fantastic, and Molly and Polly oohed and aahed over every morsel.

After her last bite, Polly announced she was going back for more. Molly, being older and more mature, explained to Polly that would not only be socially unacceptable but was also very embarrassing. Polly said she didn't care; when would she ever get another meal like that? The ladies went back and forth about it for a while, but Polly could not be talked out of it. As Polly got up and started walking toward the serving line, Molly saw that her efforts were useless and called Polly back to the table. On Polly's return, Molly told her that if she was so intent on embarrassing herself, could she please bring a plate back for Molly too? Molly couldn't stand the thought of sitting there watching Polly eat a second plate.

The only tragedy while they lived in the little house was the day that Molly walked into the tiny bathroom to find a large rat in the toilet looking up at her with a not-so-friendly face. As she happened to be alone at the time, she ran from the bathroom, shutting the door tightly, and hurried to the church, looking for help. She returned almost immediately with a chivalrous young man who was willing to help, although he had no idea what the problem was yet.

After sizing up the situation, he entered the bathroom with only a broomstick and a white plastic bag. Molly listened from the other side of the closed door. There were hitting sounds, then human yelling, then more hitting sounds, then animal yelps and squeals, and so on. The battle went on for several minutes. Sometimes, it sounded like the chivalrous young man was winning, and at other times, as though the mean-faced rodent was going to win. Finally, the chivalrous young man emerged from the bathroom with a smile on his face, a blood-stained broomstick, and a bulging white plastic bag. Molly threw the broomstick away. The rest of the cleanup was not much fun.

As time passed on, thoughts of a children's home remained in her mind. Molly had no idea what the first step was in starting a children's home. She did think, however, that it would be nice to raise children in a smaller town, right outside the big city. She wished to be out of the hustle and bustle but close enough to enjoy Central Valley's perfect climate and have modern conveniences close by. With that thought in mind, the ladies began planning little picnics on holidays in various small towns just to "check them out."

On August 15th, Mother's Day in Costa Rica, Molly and three friends decided to visit the lovely town of Palmares, known for its beautiful central park where sloths live in the trees. Molly decided she would add to the holiday by taking her treasured Dr. Pepper that someone had brought her from the States. It was a soft drink that was completely unavailable in Costa Rica, so taking a couple on the picnic was a very special treat. As they sat in the park eating cold chicken and potato salad and drinking Dr. Pepper, they began playing the family-oriented card game called UNO. Not many minutes into the game, it started to rain. They looked around for a dry place to take cover and spotted the Catholic church. There is a Catholic church in front of every central park in Costa Rica, and the one in Palmares had a large, covered area in the front with several sections of steps. One member of the group pointed out the church, and they all grabbed up the picnic things and ran for it. Laughing, they settled down on the dry steps, each with their cards still in their hands, and continued their picnic, happy that the rain had not ruined their plans.

The friends were happy, that is, until ten or fifteen minutes later when Molly felt a rough something on her shoulder and turned her head to see a police officer hovering over and tapping her with his billy club. Two other police officers were standing behind some of the others. They were telling them to gather their things and walk with them to the police station. Dumbfounded, they gathered up their picnic for the second time and walked in silence the two blocks to the police station, oblivious as to what was happening.

Once at the station, both their Dr. Pepper and their UNO cards were confiscated, and they were told that they were being arrested for drinking and gambling on the steps of the Catholic church. The officer in charge was smelling the Dr. Pepper and examining the cards. Polly, the one who could talk her way out of almost any situation, was trying her hardest to explain. The officers quickly realized they had brought the group in under false charges, but the head officer was having a hard time admitting it and continued writing in his little notebook.

Things got more complicated when he asked them for their identification. Costa Rican law requires everyone eighteen and over to carry their I.D. card at all times. Only one of the four had any identification on them, and two of them were foreigners, Molly, and a Nicaraguan girl. They gave them phone numbers to verify their identity, but that wasn't good enough. They talked about someone bringing their identification, but no one could do that. The head officer's suggestion was to leave the three unidentified ladies in the one rustic jail cell overnight and let the one with the I.D. card go and bring back everyone else's I.D. the next day. It became obvious that he was purposely trying to make things difficult for them.

The last bus to San Jose left Palmares at 4:00 p.m. every day. At 4:10 p.m. the officer finally came up with a solution. They would retain the only I.D. card, and all four would have to return the following morning at 8:00 a.m. with their identification to get the one I.D. card back. They were not sure why one person could walk around without a card until the following morning when that was the reason everyone else was in trouble, but it was best not to ask any more questions. Since the last bus had already left for San Jose, they had to catch a different bus to a city farther away that had a later bus leaving for San Jose.

After waiting in long lines everywhere, on account of the holiday, they finally got off the bus in their own neighborhood, which stopped right in front of their church. It was shortly after 9:00 p.m., and to their surprise, they found the "Roast Beef Guard" missionary lady waiting for them. They were told that they should be ashamed of themselves for destroying their Christian testimony by getting arrested. There was no sense in trying to explain; they had already used up enough words for one day. They rounded the corner from the church, crept into the house with their heads hung low, and closed the door.

Once inside, they started to laugh all over again. Molly wondered what the little old lady missionary "guard" would have thought of them had she known that not only were they not ashamed of themselves, but they had also laughed about the experience all the way home. *Who knows*, Molly thought; maybe she would write about it in a book someday. She figured that maybe even the Lord, whom she felt had saved them from having to spend a night in jail, might have chuckled a little that day.

Notwithstanding, Palmares was their favorite little town of the ones they had visited, and Molly felt like it would be the place to open the home. She was serious enough about starting a home, but she really had no idea how to begin. It had been two years since they had found the little twins, and she had still not stepped out in faith. What she really needed was a little push, and Polly gave it to her. One day, she simply asked Molly if she was ever going to open a home because if she wasn't, Polly was going to go work at a children's home she had heard about. Molly got nervous, feeling she would need Polly's help, and she was about to lose her.

Her first step was to talk to the pastor of her sending church, who readily gave her his blessing. Encouraged, she made public her plans and soon found that not everyone was eager to hand out blessings. Some folks told her she was crazy, and others that she was too poor and would starve to death. One missionary threatened to contact her supporting churches and have them cut her off; wow, all seven churches. One pastor asked if she was a missionary or a babysitter. One missionary suggested she just forget the idea, saying it was impossible.

Molly could not forget the idea; in fact, she could think of nothing else. She felt it was what God wanted her to do, and she would not be happy doing anything else. She never expected to make such a stir and never felt so scrutinized by everyone. It seemed there was no one who didn't have an opinion, and most of them were negative. One morning, she even woke up with a rash on her arms. They rushed to the hospital, thinking she was having an allergic reaction to something, only to hear the doctor tell her that the rash was from nerves; she was a nervous wreck.

Right when it seemed like everyone was intent on discouraging her, a girl came to her door with a phone number on a piece of paper and instructions to call the number at 5:00 p.m. It was the number of a missionary and his wife who were very interested in helping her start a home. They set up a time and place to meet and talk. He had a house she could start in immediately. By this time, though, Molly had already put a down payment on a small house in Palmares, the opposite direction from the house this missionary had. He was also in a different missionary group, and though it was a like-minded doctrine and Molly was independent and unattached to any group, she had this idea in her mind that staying with the same missionary group would stir up less controversy. The truth is that everyone had already expressed their opinions, and they weren't going to change. Nevertheless, she thanked him and left.

Soon afterward, the government approved Molly to take in children, and Molly and Polly moved into a little wooden cottage in Palmares, waiting for the government to approve their house and offer them some children. They were only in that house for a few months. Neither of the churches she was hoping they would be able to work with seemed to be working out. Everyone was skeptical about getting involved with a poor missionary with nothing but big dreams.

In the midst of questioning the Lord about what direction they should go, Molly received a letter from the same missionary who had shown interest in a children's home ministry. He was simply asking her to call him and set up a Sunday that she could come to teach in their junior church ministry in San Jose. Molly called and scheduled it for the following Sunday. On Saturday night, she put a roast in the slow cooker so lunch would be ready since the trip back from San Jose would be later than usual.

That was the night the excitement began. The old wooden cottage had holes in the floors, and the delicious smell of cooking meat was attracting an entire community of little mice. Molly hadn't been in bed for fifteen minutes when she heard scratching on the floor. As she reached over and flipped on the light, she saw mice scattering in all directions. Knowing that Polly had mosquito netting hanging over her bed, Molly quickly summed up that any protection was better than no protection and ran to Polly's room, sliding under the netting and tucking it tightly under the mattress on all sides. Although Molly spent most of the night scared of all the little noises in the house, Polly never woke up and was quite surprised in the morning to find an extra person scrunched down in her bed.

The excitement continued all morning long. Molly's little dog, Cherry, was so excited to have new friends to play with and spent all morning barking and chasing mice from room to room and side to side. Molly stood on her bed to get dressed. From there, she ran to a chair in the kitchen to make breakfast, then to another chair in the bathroom to fix her hair. Polly, who was also chair hopping, suggested they leave for church early; after all, they didn't want to be late. On their way out the door, they stopped and reported the problem to their landlord, hoping he would take care of the mice while they were gone.

Molly and Polly enjoyed their day with the missionary couple. They were an older couple, and there was a large number of children in junior church, so large that it seemed a little overwhelming for one elderly missionary lady. They could definitely use some help and seemed eager to find some. So eager, in fact, that at the end of the service, without even asking, the missionary handed Molly the lesson for the following Sunday and invited them to a Bible club during the week to be held in the little house he had previously offered them to begin the children's home.

There was a lot to think about on the bus ride home that day. A nice little cement house in the city sounded a lot better than a wooden cottage in the country. By this time, Molly was eager to see the house the missionary was offering them. She realized that God could speak to her about His will for her life in more ways than in youth camps. There was that sense of humor showing itself again, and she felt that this time, He was using little mice to encourage her to accept this missionary's kind offer. If she thought, however, that this was the end of her battle with mice, she was painfully mistaken. There would be many more battles, but never again so many all-morning races through the house.

A few weeks later, Molly and Polly found themselves packing up again and heading off to Cartago, one step closer to the dream. God was truly blessing. Missionaries Robert and Francis Heflin generously provided them with a small three-bedroom, rent-free house. Months later, they would also supply them with the first car that Molly had driven since arriving in Costa Rica, and months after that, their first phone line. Soon, the sweet couple would become the children's honorary grandparents. The Lord would use the kindness of the Heflins to answer years of Molly's prayers to be able to open her home and heart to children who needed a home they could live in and hearts that would love them.

[A LESSON TO LEARN: Each life is like a book that God is co-writing together with us. It contains our own special stories, and every book is different. There are parts of the book that God decides, such as appearance, abilities, and when and where one is born. There are many, many other parts of the book that God leaves up to us, for He has given us a free will.

Yet, God himself wrote His own book, the greatest book, the Holy Bible, to guide us in writing ours. His book is the story of our Lord and Savior, Jesus Christ. In it, God has written everything that He wanted us to know about His dear Son. Though the Bible is the perfect guide to Christ and a Christlike life, answering any problem we will face, yet the life-changing decisions are left up to us to write in our book. The biggest of those decisions is, of course, what will you do with Christ? Will you accept His finished work on the cross to forgive your sins and offer you an eternal home in heaven? His Word plainly says in Acts 16:31, "Believe on the Lord Jesus Christ, and thou shalt be saved." Christ said in John 10:28, "And I give unto them eternal life; and they shall never perish, neither shall any man pluck them out of my hand."

Having Christ as your Savior guarantees a happy ending to your book. If you have already accepted His free gift, are you allowing His Word and prayer to guide your decisions? How are you responding to God's guidebook as you write the book of your life? One decision can change a life drastically. Each choice is so important; carefully and prayerfully make God-honoring choices.]

Prayer:

Dear heavenly Father, thank you for the lives you have given us and the opportunity that each of us has to write a book with our lives that brings glory to your name. Teach us to make each decision based on the wisdom of your book, the Bible. In Jesus's name, we pray, amen.

Chapter 3

Oodles and Iffies

Molly had asked the government for children who needed a permanent place in which to grow. She did not want to be a stopover for kids going out for adoption. She desired to form a family and raise children to know and serve the Lord. As a result, the government gave her children who were not good candidates for adoption, such as groups of siblings that were hard to place, special needs children, or children over seven years old who were also unlikely to go out in adoption. She wasn't sure how much the Lord would allow her to do, but she felt she could at least help a handful of children.

So it was that the children began to come. There were lots of little boys such as Boodles, Coodles, Doodles, and Floodles, Neddles and Niddles, Raddles, Riddles, Goodles, Loodles, Soodles, Toodles, and Poodles. There were also loads of little girls like Buffy, Biffy, Kiffy, and Fluffy, Miffy, and Muffy, Naffy, Niffy, and Nuffy, and of course, Raffy, Riffy, and Ruffy, not to mention Giffy, Siffy, Laffy, Liffy and Luffy, Piffy and Puffy, Smaffy and Twaffy, and more. There were ninety-one in all. Oh my, but we are getting way ahead of ourselves.

They started with one small group. Once in Cartago, Polly began the three-block walk to the nearest pay phone every day, asking the government for a group of children. This went on for well over a month before they finally offered them a family of three, consisting of two girls, Buffy, age eight; Biffy, almost five; and a little boy, Boodles, three years old.

Buffy, Biffy, and Boodles

Since this was their first group, Molly and Polly had to visit the three siblings in a large government orphanage once a week for a month before they could bring them home. As they sat nervously waiting in the social worker's office to meet the children, two hearts pounded with numerous different emotions, from excitement to anxiety to joy to fear.

All three children came running into the room. The oldest girl, Buffy, immediately ran and hid behind the social worker who sat at her desk. Little Boodles ran straight to the far corner of the room and began pulling toys out of a box, oblivious to the fact that Molly and Polly were even there, much less that they were smiling from ear to ear in an effort to make a good first impression on the little youngsters. As the last one, little Biffy, came running in, Polly grabbed her up in her arms, fixing her firmly on her lap, holding tight and hoping she would not try to escape. Biffy turned out to be the talkative one, answering all the simple questions about her favorite things to do. Buffy whispered to the social worker, asking her which lady was her new mother, but refused to come out of hiding. Boodles played happily in the corner and seemed to neither see nor hear anything that was going on.

The social worker finally suggested that they take a walk outside to get to know the children. Since Buffy was still very reluctant, and Polly had grabbed Biffy's hand, Molly reached down and picked up little Boodles. To her surprise, Boodles clung to her and didn't want to be put down when it was time for them to go. It later occurred to Molly that being in a home with over eighty other children, twenty-some-odd being small babies, three-year-old Boodles probably never got picked up.

The following week when they returned for the second visit, Boodles came running down the long hallway and literally jumped into Molly's arms. He stayed there almost the entire visit, jumping off only when the bread cart came into the room, at which time all the children rushed to get a simple piece of bread and a glass of Kool-Aid. Biffy complained that only Boodles was allowed in Mommy's lap. Boodles scooted over to just sit on one knee and made room for Biffy on Mommy's other knee.

The social workers told Molly and Polly that they originally had some reservations about giving them the children because of Buffy's reluctance, but since then, they had seen such a change in Boodles that they were sure the family was for them. They explained that before, Boodles sat on the floor daily, playing alone without interacting with anyone. If he had nothing to play with, he would just sit, rock, and whistle all day. After their first visit, Boodles had been talking, although he had a very limited vocabulary, and playing with the other children. They were amazed at the change in him.

Finally, on June 5, 1989, the day had arrived to bring the children home. When they arrived at the orphanage, they were told they would have to wait on Boodles, who was out on a morning walk with all the two and three-year-olds. As they finally came onto the property, Molly saw a worker in the middle, holding hands with a whole line of hand-holding children on either side of her. Molly scanned the line with her eyes, looking for little Boodles, but couldn't find him. She finally realized he was the sad little one at the end of the line to the left of the worker. He was covered in mud, from the top of his head to his feet. All that was visible were the whites of his eyes. The worker explained that he had fallen face-first into the mud. Molly could only whisper to herself that he was her son. They soon learned that Boodles seemed to love the ground; indeed, he was constantly throwing himself on the ground, rolling around, and laughing.

They waited while they got Boodles bathed and changed and were soon on the way home with their little charges. They did not yet have a vehicle and so were dependent on the public transportation system. They climbed onto the bus with three little ones and three garbage bags full of clothes, one for each child, and headed for home.

So much anticipation had gone into this big day that Molly's adrenaline was skyrocketing. When night came, and they were tucked into their beds sound asleep, all three in the same small room, Molly got up and stood in the doorway. She was listening to make sure they were still breathing. That night, she got up several times to check on them; she was having a hard time getting to sleep. She had looked forward to this day for so long, and now the impact of it was overwhelming. She was personally responsible for three little people, real people with real souls, and that was a tad bit scary.

Fortunately, after that first night, Molly had no more trouble falling asleep. Biffy, Buffy, and Boodles were not accustomed to living in a house with furniture and things. They kept Molly and Polly hopping. One morning when Molly was preheating the oven, something began to smell like it was burning. Buffy had stuck a plastic-handled knife in the oven just to put it away for safekeeping. Boodles found the hammer and pounded a whole series of little dent marks in the wooden china cabinet with the claw end of the hammer. Biffy was very active and spent a lot of time climbing and jumping off the furniture, thinking, apparently, that the furniture was a jungle gym made specifically for recreation. When Boodles was put in the corner for his behavior, he busied himself by sticking his front teeth into the side of the brand-new bookcase and scrapping them all the way down as low as he could go, leaving long scratch marks. There were several of these sets of marks, probably a new set for every couple of minutes he had been in the corner. When Molly served fried eggs for breakfast, Biffy was confused about how to eat this new food she had never seen. She stretched her hand over the top of it, picked it up, and put the whole egg in her mouth while egg yolk oozed from between her fingers and dripped down her arm.

Oodles and Iffies

There were so many variables about being a mother that Molly had never considered. She loved little Boodles to death, but he was like a little puppy who followed her everywhere with endless questions about what things were, what she was doing, and why. Every once in a while, she just had to escape to the bathroom for some alone time. But that didn't even work very well, as it wouldn't be but thirty seconds before there was the knock on the door, followed by the dreaded question about what she was doing and why. She did get a short break in the afternoon when Boodles laid down for a nap. Many times, Boodles would revert back to his former behavior at nap time. Molly would hear whistling and go in to see him sitting up in bed, rocking back and forth, and whistling. Yet, he was sound asleep, and Molly would simply go over and lay him back down.

Biffy turned out to be multi-talented. Not only was she a bright little girl who learned quickly and had a sharp memory, but she was also very athletic, loving physical activities. She loved to play that she was a gymnast, teaching herself to do cartwheels, walkovers, and other feats. When she was older, she was the only one who ever learned to ride the unicycle that Molly brought back from the States from her childhood days. Biffy was also a talker, made friends easily, and became the leader in the games that were played in front of the house with the neighbors. Even at the breakfast table, she would take the lead in the conversations by sharing all her crazy dreams from the night before. They were all very fantastic and had the others laughing up a storm. Molly was pretty sure that no one could possibly dream so much nor remember so many of the details of the dreams, but Biffy was a people person, and she loved the attention her dreams got her.

Buffy would need to be enrolled in school. Molly was excited when she first saw the school notebooks that Buffy had brought with her from her former school. They contained page after page of perfect, beautiful lettering. Unfortunately, Buffy could not read what she had written. In fact, she only recognized the letter "a" and the number "1," and this was her second time going through first grade. Molly had her work cut out for her. In addition, Buffy cried and complained and begged and pleaded when she found out she was going to have to go to a new school. She did not want to go to any school. Not only was school difficult for her, but she had also been constantly made fun of at her old school for being from the orphanage.

Several things Molly found out about the public school system surprised her. Firstly, the public school was only four hours a day. Oh well, that would give her plenty of time to work with Buffy after school. Secondly, the children had no books. They had a notebook for each subject and spent the day copying everything the teacher wrote on the chalkboard. Thirdly, there were at least forty students in each class with one teacher, and each teacher had a morning session and an afternoon session with a different group of students. That meant that each teacher was responsible for every subject for eighty students and without books.

Molly began to work with Buffy for an hour or so a day, but her progress was slow. Just learning the vowels seemed to take forever. Math was no better. Since she already recognized the number 1, they started with 2, and it took weeks for her to recognize it and be able to write it by herself without copying it. Every day was a struggle since Buffy, with her short attention span, was tired of notebooks by the time she came home. Besides that, no one else had to study. Biffy and Boodles weren't in school, they got to play all day.

During the first week of her new school, Buffy brought home her math notebook with two pages full of simple addition problems. Knowing that Buffy did not even know her numbers yet, much less how to add them together, Molly assumed she had copied it off the board like everything else. However, looking closer, Molly saw that every problem had the wrong answer, and yet there was a great big, beautiful red star at the top of each page. Buffy said the teacher had put the star there when she checked her work.

The following day, when Molly walked to the school to pick Buffy up, she stopped to talk to the teacher. She asked her why she had earned stars when all the answers were wrong. The teacher told her that with forty kids in the class, she didn't have time to grade their work; she only checked to see that it had been done, and for that, the child earned a star. Molly was not impressed, but she knew that Buffy needed to finish the school year.

Homeschooling was unheard of in Costa Rica, and they were just beginning to work with the government. Taking Buffy out of school would be a huge red flag against them. It was shortly before the middle of the school year, but they would just have to make the best of it.

Meanwhile, Polly realized very quickly that she liked helping out in a children's home, but staying home all day with the kids was not her cup of tea. She had earned a degree in accounting in a technical high school and was soon able to find a job. She would come home in the evenings and help with the cleaning. She was also able to run some of the errands and buying on her way home. This arrangement worked well since Molly didn't care for cleaning floors or running errands.

Coodles

Just two months after the first group, five-year-old Coodles came into the home. His feeble great-grandparents had been watching him and were struggling to care for him. Although they were uneducated people who never had the opportunity to learn to read and write, Coodles was extremely intelligent. He had been growing up in an all-adult environment and spoke like a miniature adult, using big words that confused the other children. He didn't even like being with other children, preferring adult company. Coodles hated playing with cars and other toys and loved looking at books.

Both Biffy and Coodles, without even sitting down to study with Molly for more than a couple of rare minutes, were accidentally learning to read faster than Buffy. One day, Coodles asked Polly to see a huge Bible dictionary from the bookcase. As she was getting it down for him, Molly hesitated because it was not a child's book, and she didn't want it torn up. They finally agreed that if he sat perfectly still on the couch, he could look through it for fifteen minutes. Molly was sure he would be bored with it before the fifteen minutes were up. He called out to the other children to come to see the neat book he had. They all came racing, watched as he turned a few pages, then got puzzled looks on their faces, which quickly turned into frowns, and ran off to play. Coodles used up his full fifteen-minute time slot wide-eyed and smiling as he slowly turned the pages. The experiment led to many other fifteen-minute sessions in the same dictionary.

History was Coodles's favorite subject, and he listened attentively to the Bible stories in Sunday school. The flannelgraph Molly used to teach the lessons fascinated him, and he would ask every week if he could play with it. Once again, Molly said that it was not a toy, but remembering that her mother had told her the same thing about the ventriloquist dummy, she finally gave him a chance. It was so important to him, and he was so careful placing each piece in the right place and telling the story perfectly, down to the last details.

On one occasion when Molly needed time to get some things done, she sat all four kids at the dining room table with the plastic container full of Legos. The rule was that you couldn't get up until Mommy said. While Molly did some work, she enjoyed the semi-quietness of having all the kids sitting still at the table working on their individual projects. When she returned to the table, Boodles had made a simple car with two sets of wheels under a stack of Legos, Biffy had made a little house, and Buffy was sitting totally bored, tapping Legos on the table. Coodles had a book opened to one side that he was using as a reference. He was doing a great job constructing Solomon's temple. He was six years old at the time.

The following school year, Molly took a risk and pulled Buffy out of public school to homeschool her. At the same time, she put Biffy and Coodles in public kindergarten. She wasn't worried about their learning. They were both already reading fine but were too young to go into the first grade yet. The only thing the children did at kindergarten in Costa Rica was learn to color and cut out, play, and have story time. The teachers weren't even allowed to start teaching them letters and numbers or writing. Having them out of the house for three or four hours was more about Buffy than it was about them, as it gave Molly some quality one-on-one time to work with her. She was finally learning to read and starting in ACE Paces.

Meanwhile, Boodles was very good at entertaining himself. He had always played by himself and was happy on the floor with a couple of cars for long periods. One day, Molly walked through the living room to find Boodles standing in the corner with a pot on his head, the lid from the pot in one hand, and a broom in the other. She watched him for several minutes, but he never moved. Maybe, she thought, he had misbehaved and was punishing himself by standing in the corner. After another several minutes, she finally asked him what he was doing. He said he was playing guard, and he wasn't allowed to move. Boodles continued playing guard for at least another half hour before he finally decided to go play something else.

One day, Molly rushed back to kindergarten in the middle of the morning because she had forgotten to give Biffy and Coodles the mid-morning snack they were to take with them each day. She entered the room and looked around for the teacher, but she wasn't there. What she found was Coodles sitting on a chair with all the other children on the floor in front of him. He was reading a book to them, and then showing them the pictures, like a good little teacher. None of the children seemed to know where the teacher was. Coodles explained to her later that ever since the teacher accidentally found out that Coodles could read, she would gather the children around him for story time every day and leave the room. Coodles would read until she came back, which, according to him, was often several story books later.

They had a piano, and Molly had taken enough lessons to read the treble clef of the music and chord with her left hand. She taught the kids the little she knew using a couple of beginning piano books she had. Buffy and Boodles didn't show much interest; Biffy did very well, but Coodles really took off. He found a song in the hymn book and began playing it for what seemed like a thousand times a day. They listened to the same song over and over again for several weeks. To the relief of everyone in the home, Coodles finally began a second song, and then a third, and so on. Through mere determination, he basically taught himself to play the piano. Further along, there would be a few others in the home to teach themselves, but none would ever play as well as he. Music would eventually play a major part in the ministry that the Lord would one day give to little Coodles.

Biffy and Coodles became very close friends. No one laughed harder than Coodles at all of Biffy's silly dreams and the funny little things she did. She was a source of continual entertainment to him. He even went along with her silly ideas. One day, they found a cat who they were sure was trapped in a neighbor's front yard. The small garden area had a wall about four feet tall, with another four feet of bars spaced evenly apart rising from the top of the wall. The cat was in the center of the garden. Biffy had the great idea of throwing the poor cat a rope so that he could grab ahold of it, and she could then pull him to safety. They threw the rope repeatedly, but the cat did not take ahold of it, knowing, of course, that he was already in the safest place, far from the reach of the mischievous children.

Suddenly, Biffy came up with a brilliant plan B. If she could just squeeze through the bars and get inside, then Coodles could throw her the rope, and she could grab it and show the cat what he was supposed to do. They found a little stool that she could stand on, and she began by first trying to get her head through the bars. Of course, Molly was oblivious to everything happening out front and kitty-corner to their little house, oblivious until she heard the ear-piercing screams of her younger daughter ringing through the entire neighborhood. Molly darted out the front door and ran toward the screams. She was met there by two other mothers running to the rescue. Realizing that she was not going to fit through the bars, she tried to pull her head back out and found out that it was stuck. She was still standing on the little stool, but Molly's thoughts kept going back to what could have happened if one of the other children had knocked the stool over. Once they had calmed Biffy down, they were able to slowly work her head out. The cat, of course, had darted out of the garden with the sound of the first scream. That must have been, therefore, plan C.

Kiffy

It was a year and four months after Coodles that the fifth child came into the home. That was fine with Molly as becoming an instant mommy to four children had required an adjustment period. Biffy and Buffy had expressed a desire to visit their old orphanage. Molly liked the idea because it would give her a chance to ask about more children. As they walked past the nursery, they could see that there were at least ten cribs with babies in them. The babies stayed in the cribs all day long and would even reach out and hold the hand of the baby in the next crib. Molly was amazed that they all looked rather sad, but none were crying, just standing or sitting there, holding hands from crib to crib. They must have each learned early on that crying didn't help; nobody was going to pick them up. The sight broke their hearts, and Biffy and Buffy begged Mommy to ask for a baby. Molly asked, but they said the babies were perfect for adoption, not a children's home. Nevertheless, Molly told the girls to pray and ask God for a baby. They began praying for a baby girl.

They had only been praying for about four months when God began answering their prayer. By this time, Polly was going two nights a week straight from work to a Bible institute. Although it meant she was away more, it also meant that through her, more missionaries, those from the institute, were becoming aware of their small, newly founded children's home. One of these missionaries who had many works scheduled a different church for every month of the year to take a few groceries by the home. When the church scheduled for November came, the pastor mentioned that he had heard from a church member of a six-month-old baby girl who needed a home. The baby's young, teenage mother was living with a young guy who was not the baby's father. He was mistreating the baby, and the mother was concerned. The pastor set up a meeting between the mother and Molly, but when they met, the mother wasn't yet ready to give up her child. Molly left her phone number and encouraged her to call should the situation become worse. She explained the importance of placing her in a good home before the government found out the baby was in danger and took her away.

A month had passed when Molly got a phone call. The guy had come home drunk and started a fight. In the fight, the baby had gotten cut above her eye. The mother chose to stay with the guy and give up her baby. Molly agreed to meet the mother at the church member's house the following morning. By this time, they had an old Volkswagen van they all piled in, Molly, Polly, who had gotten off work for the event, and four very excited little tikes. And thus, it was that Kiffy became the special, heaven-sent Christmas present they had been praying for. God, in His love, heard their prayers, scanned Costa Rica with His eyes, and chose a little suffering baby, then He miraculously brought her to them just three days before Christmas.

When Molly walked into the room to see the baby, she came face-to-face with the biggest, most beautiful dark eyes she had ever seen. What a precious child! Kiffy was thin, small, and such a sad little baby that it would be some time before they would be able to get a smile out of her and notice her three cute dimples. She had been so neglected that at seven months, she could neither sit up nor roll over but just lie in one spot, wherever she was put. She had a cut above her left eyebrow and several bad-looking marks up and down her skinny legs where she had been pinched so hard that it had broken the skin, leaving terrible scars. She wore a little red, worn-out dress that Molly kept and never gave away. There were a few other items of clothes in a little backpack, none of them worth keeping. The mother went with them to a lawyer known for doing adoptions. It turned out to be a long day, and after waiting for many hours with an impatient, crying baby, and four restless, fidgety children, Molly came out with a paper in her hands stating that she was the child's legal guardian and the promise that the adoption process would begin immediately.

After dropping the mother off in her neighborhood, their first stop was to go directly to Grandma and Grandpa Heflin's house to show them the new addition to the family. They were thrilled. Grandma Heflin was especially fond of babies and, thus, had her in her arms immediately, beginning that day and whenever else they saw Grandma and Grandpa thereafter. Grandpa would be waiting in front of the church every service to lift little Kiffy out of the van and hold her awhile. He would then pass her to Grandma, who could entertain her during the entire preaching service with loads of little surprises she would pull out of her purse. Each service, the purse held new surprises.

They soon realized there were two things that scared Kiffy. Every time the congregation began to sing, Kiffy would begin to cry, and she would cry until the song was finished, starting up again with the first line of the next hymn. The other thing that scared her was teenage boys. She would go into the arms of teenage girls, into the arms of ladies, and even into the arms of little old men. But as soon as a younger man got within a yard of her, she would begin to scream. Molly was fascinated that at the young age of seven months, she could tell the difference between teens and grandpas and associated teens with pain and danger.

It was months before they began to see real changes in Kiffy. Eventually, the smiles came, and then the all-day, everyday hugs and slobbery kisses all over Molly and Polly's cheeks and forehead and even on top of their heads. She became an extremely affectionate child with extremely emotional highs and lows. They referred to her as their drama queen. She could go from exuberant laughter to passionate crying and then back again to laughter faster than the speed of light.

Food became extremely important to little Kiffy. As soon as she learned to hold a spoon, before her first birthday, she wouldn't let anyone else feed her. Nobody was allowed to touch her spoon; it was hers. Is it possible that she remembered what feeling hungry was like and was afraid that whoever had the spoon would eat her food and leave her hungry? Molly didn't know if that was possible, but it was a fact that a good part of life revolved around worrying about food and getting something to eat. One day, when it was not mealtime, Kiffy was chewing on something. Knowing that babies put everything in their mouths, Molly rushed to retrieve the foreign object, but unfortunately, she was too late. She had already swallowed the something and was clutching something else in her little fist. Molly pried her fist open to find half a cockroach. Molly felt sick.

That was only the first of several incidents. Once when Kiffy was still very young, they were invited to another missionary's house to eat. When they stood to leave after the meal, Kiffy blurted out that they hadn't had dessert yet and was very disappointed when she found out there was no dessert. Another day, they were on visitation in a church member's house. As they turned to leave, Kiffy spoke up in an angry voice, complaining that the lady had not given them anything at all to eat. Oh, and then there were the handful of times that Kiffy actually got to ride in airplanes before her fifth birthday. She was under the impression that the airplane was a restaurant. With each plane change, they were no sooner seated when she would begin to ask over and over again in a whiny little voice when they were going to serve the food.

Once when Kiffy was worried that she had no father, Molly told her that God in heaven promised to be a father to the fatherless. Sometime later, Molly announced to the family that one of the older children had accepted Christ as their Savior and would go to heaven. Kiffy immediately wanted to go with him. When Molly explained that she didn't think he was going yet, Kiffy pulled him aside to tell him that when he got to heaven to ask her Father to send back with him some candy for her.

It was certainly no surprise years later that Kiffy became a great cook and baker. Nor was it a surprise that her heart's desire became to open up a little coffee shop with baked goods. But we know that God's plans are always better. Kiffy gave up her coffee shop plans to serve the Lord, and He, in turn, placed her in many different ministries, where she was able to serve the Lord, minister to others, and use her baking talents all at the same time.

Floodles and Fluffy

Only five months after Kiffy's arrival, the government offered Molly and Polly a brother and sister. They were from the same government home as the first group. Floodles was five years old, and little Fluffy was not quite three. She had been in the government since she was only seven months old. It was the only home she could remember and, thus, was where she felt secure. The process went much faster than the first group. One day, they visited the siblings, one day the siblings visited them, and the very next week, the social worker was dropping them off. That was great for Molly and Polly but was probably much too fast for little Fluffy, who had no idea what was happening. Molly tried to hold and comfort Fluffy, but she didn't want anything to do with her. In her little mind, Molly was the mean lady who was tearing her away from her comfort zone.

Molly had purchased a cassette of children's lullabies. Each night, a different child would sit on Molly's lap while she would sing with the tape and rock in the rocking chair. Her plan for the new ones' first night was to put both children in her lap at the same time and sing. Floodles crawled right up and took his place. Fluffy sat against the opposite wall, crying and shaking her head. Floodles, who could not speak clearly, kept calling Fluffy, saying, "Uffy, come to lady; lady good; Uffy, come."

Fluffy did not come but sat pounding her little back against the wall, sobbing, and saying, "No, no, no." Molly sang the lullabies amid the sobs and took the children to bed.

The days that followed were no better. Fluffy would let Molly bathe and dress her, but she would not sit on her lap nor accept any kind of affection from her. Molly backed away to give her time to adjust. The big surprise came on Sunday. Although it was a tad crowded, they were picking up two other families every Sunday to take to church in their Volkswagen van. When the second family, a lady, and her two small grandchildren got in the car, Fluffy climbed from the first seat to the back seat and plopped right down in the lady's lap, laughing and playing with her all the way to church. Molly couldn't believe it, Fluffy was sitting with a total stranger. Every service they went to for about two weeks, Fluffy continued in the same little game.

Then, one Sunday, Fluffy decided she was not going to sit up front with her family but was staying in the back with her newfound friend. Molly told her to come, and she shook her head. Molly decided it was time for a different approach. She took Fluffy to the bathroom for a firm yet gentle discipline session, spoke to her in a serious tone, then prayed with her and hugged her, whether she wanted it or not. They returned to the service and sat with the family. The following day, Fluffy crawled up in Molly's lap several times and even gave her hugs. Fluffy just needed to know who was in charge.

Fluffy was a beautiful little girl with short, thick, silky black hair and bangs that fit perfectly around her little face like a bowling ball with a section cut out for her face and, once brushed, stayed in place all day long. She was a tad bit stubborn at first but quickly decided she didn't care much for punishments and began avoiding trouble. She laughed at any and every silly little thing. Someone falling or bumping into a wall was the funniest thing in the world to her.

She grew up to be a very honest, trustworthy, hard-working ball of energy. As a young adult, she helped in the school, helped with the younger girls, was in charge of the laundry, taught English in the neighborhood, was the captain of the church bus route, graduated from Bible Institute, and still had time for afternoon coffee at any of dozens of different houses of her many neighborhood friends.

Floodles was a stalky, distinguished fellow. His hair, like Fluffy's, combed over perfectly and stayed in place all day. He would stand so straight for pictures, with such a slight, dignified smile, that he gave the impression of being a full-grown man in midget form.

Floodles and Fluffy's mother had been mentally handicapped, and the children had been taken away from her for neglect. At that time, age three or four, Floodles' teeth were so rotted that the government had them removed. He was toothless except for the two bottom-front permanent teeth that had already come in since then. That and the fact that he already had somewhat of a speech impediment made it difficult to understand him. He would repeat himself over and over as Molly and Polly played a guessing game offering him word after word, searching for any word that sounded close to what he was saying. He would shake his head no and sometimes become frustrated and leave. Other times, they would win the game, guessing the right word. Floodles would smile and nod his head, and Molly and Polly would chalk up a point for themselves on their imagination's scoreboard. Soon, they began to understand his language and could translate most of what he said fairly well.

Floodles was very well-behaved, a jewel of a child. Making Mommy happy and being a good little boy was number one on his list of goals. It was also on the list of goals he had for Fluffy, and he was constantly telling her what she should and should not be doing. Fluffy was not a very good student in Floodles's classroom. She did not want him telling her what to do, and poor teacher Floodles spent lots of time rolling his eyes, shaking his head, and throwing his hands up in the air in exasperation after his teaching sessions with Fluffy. This only made Fluffy giggle because driving Floodles crazy was at the top of her list of goals.

Floodles loved to play with cars every bit as much as Coodles hated playing with cars. Floodles had oodles of matchbook-sized cars and would line them all up in a straight line on a little circle-eight track printed on a rug. Then he would advance each car, one by one, about six inches and, thus, take all fifteen or twenty cars round and round the track while talking from car to car between the make-believe drivers. He took very good care of his cars, so much so that he was still playing with the same cars in the same manner when he was eighteen years old.

Molly, who remembered how difficult it had been to teach Buffy to read, wondered if Floodles would ever learn. It was difficult for him, but in the end, he learned faster than Buffy. But the most curious thing about Floodles's reading was that he actually read better than he spoke. This phenomenon was due to the fact that he pronounced the sounds exactly as he had learned them. Molly hoped it would help him understand the pronunciation of words, and he would begin to speak more clearly. Not only did that not happen, but when he began to write, he would also spell the words as he heard them in his head, in his own language. He could write the same ten spelling words twenty times a day for two or three weeks and then, on the test, spell them according to his own pronunciation, getting more than half of them wrong. Art was Floodles's best subject, and he really could draw fairly well, though the perspective in his drawings was not quite right.

Molly could not have begun to imagine at that time what kind of future tenderhearted, simple Floodles would have, but his heavenly Father had him in his hand and would bless his gentle spirit. At nineteen years of age, he was doing school work at about a third or fourth-grade level and getting very frustrated. By that time, the children's home had moved to a larger piece of property. They gave Floodles an option to either keep studying or quit school and take the job of night guard on the property. That was an easy choice for him. He had always wanted to be a policeman, and this was the next best thing. Molly was a little nervous about him running into intruders as he wandered around the property all night long, but she knew it was his best option.

Floodles began his first night of work with a big stick to defend himself, a whistle to scare people away, and a midnight snack. As soon as possible, the home provided him with a nice big flashlight and a set of walkie-talkies to communicate with those who slept inside the house should any danger arise. He took his job so very seriously. With his salary, he slowly began to buy the other things he said he needed to do his job properly. First, he bought a billy club, then two guard uniforms of different colors, then a set of handcuffs, and then a black vest with the word *police* in bold yellow lettering. Later, he was able to get a police hat and a BB gun. Eventually, they constructed a little guard shack, which later grew into his apartment since it was so hard to get any sleep during the day inside the house.

Math had been Floodles's worst subject in school, and he didn't understand how money worked at first. One day, he told Molly that he needed new shoelaces, but he didn't have enough money, only one bill. When Molly asked to see the bill, she realized that it was a large enough bill to buy twenty pairs of shoelaces. In addition, by that time, there were many teenage boys in the home, most of whom were a little envious of Floodles having a real paying job. They began to sell him little things for, you guessed it, only one bill. When he brought one of his prized purchases in to show Molly, and she found out the quantity of the one bill, she made all the little salesmen return 90 percent of the money they had charged and prohibited them from selling anything else to Floodles.

Floodles was so trusting of everyone. When Floodles would go to the local minute market, he would place on the counter the items he wanted, usually snacks, and next to them would empty his pockets of all his bills and change, asking the cashier to take what he needed. Fortunately, he was an honest man and good friend—they gave him plenty of business—and Molly was sure he wouldn't take advantage of Floodles.

Guarding became Floodles's permanent job. As other children would grow up and move on with their lives, he would remind Molly, smiling from ear to ear, that God had chosen him to stay behind to protect Molly and be a good example for the new generations of children. He was indeed a good example.

So it was that two years after opening the home, it had grown from a beginning of three children to seven children, ages one through ten. It would be two more years before any more children came. Molly occupied herself with adjusting to motherhood and readjusting her ideas of what she thought motherhood would be. She had some pretty high and lofty ideas but was now facing reality. Molly thought that she would call all the children to the table for an art project, and they would begin to jump up and down enthusiastically. She did not count on Coodles asking, "Do we HAVE to do this?"

Followed by Buffy saying, "I don't like art projects."

And then Fluffy saying, "Mommy, Floodles is looking at me."

At which point Boodles and Kiffy began fighting over the same crayon, though there were two whole boxes full of crayons on the table. Nor did she count on Biffy declaring, "I'm finished; can I go now?" three minutes into the project, and Floodles doing something totally different than what Molly was trying to instruct them to do.

Molly also had a different concept of what instruction, rules, and discipline would be. Molly had been a phlegmatic mommy pleaser growing up. Her mother always told everyone that she had been the easiest of the four children to raise. Molly thought all children wanted to please their mothers. When she got into trouble and was disciplined for something, she tried to avoid repeating the same mistake, not wanting to get in trouble again. She felt that after she set down the rules, they would test the rules a time or two, and she would have to give further instruction and discipline, and "poof," they would understand and strive to please Mommy from there on out. She did not count on telling Boodles not to touch something, only to have him stare her down as his little hand crept closer and closer to the forbidden object and then snatch it up. Oh my, what was that? She never would have even thought of doing something like that to her mother. Nor did she expect, after having disciplined him, to repeat the same scene over and over again, day after day, with different objects and in different circumstances, but with the same defiant look and creeping hands for more than two months until he finally decided that challenging authority wasn't the best idea. Things were definitely not as easy as she had thought they would be.

[A LESSON TO LEARN: Molly came to understand that she and Polly were simply helping a lot of little sinners understand the gospel of Jesus Christ and truly give their tiny hearts and lives to Him. It was an easy thing to explain to them who Christ was and how, in His great love, He had given His own life to save them from their sins. It was quite another thing, though, for Molly and Polly to let Christ's light shine through them on a 24/7 basis, thriving to make thousands of right decisions daily, for they, too, were simply unworthy sinners saved by grace. Yet, each little sinner in their care was so unique, with his or her special fingerprints, DNA, strengths, and weaknesses, and so full of potential that God Almighty could use should they allow the Lord to work in their heart and life. Each one of them had thousands of temptations and choices ahead of them that would either make them or break them. What a tremendous responsibility to patiently guide them and lovingly show them the light of Christ. It was all becoming quite overwhelming.

Who are the people God has brought into your life? He has put them in your life for a reason, for God is incapable of error. How would He have you reach out to them? How would He have you show His love to them? John 13:34–35 says, "A new commandment I give unto you, That ye love one another; as I have loved you, that ye also love one another. By this shall all men know that ye are my disciples, if ye have love one to another."]

Chapter 4

The Lord Supplies and Protects

Although many people had tried to discourage Molly, telling her she would starve to death, the Lord was faithful. They very quickly realized the truth of Psalm 68:5, where God says that He is the father to the fatherless. Though some felt Molly would lose support by starting a children's home, their support actually more than doubled. That was not to say they were rich since $300 to $400 doubled is still not very much. Nevertheless, they learned to live frugally and trusted in God's provisions.

A lot of decisions had to be made at the grocery store. One week, they would buy a block of cheese, and the next week, some sour cream; both items couldn't be purchased at the same time. When there was money for cookies, the packages were shared between two; no child got a whole little pack of four cookies for himself. Molly and Polly had one little splurge a week that became like a ritual. They would buy one half-liter Coke every week. One night during the week, after the kids were in bed, they would pull out two glasses and divide the coke up, each one making sure the other didn't have more. When they were sure the glasses were even, they would drink their ration slowly, making funny yummy sounds, and laugh about their silliness.

Speaking of frugality, there were also several silly restaurant situations during the early struggling years. The first was late at night after a graduation. At the time, they only had the first four kids. Everyone was starved, but they were having a hard time finding an eating joint open. Finally, they found a little place that was not closed. They planned to just get a Tico taco for each person and maybe some fries. When they got the menu, Molly noticed the tacos were more than three times the price they would have paid at the little snack bar up by their house in Cartago. They asked the waiter to give them a minute to decide, and Molly and Polly argued over the price for a while. Polly said they had no choice; the snack bar in Cartago would be closed. When the waiter came back, Molly asked how much it was for an order of fries, but when he told her, her eyes grew big, and she asked if it was a huge platter full of fries. No, it was a regular order for one person. They asked the waiter to give them a minute, and Molly and Polly had a second discussion. They were too hungry and too embarrassed to leave without ordering anything, and there was nothing at home that could be whipped up quickly. When the waiter came back for the third time, they ordered two Cokes, six straws, and an order of fries. With three people on each side of the booth, it meant a Coke for each side. When the man brought the fries, it was indeed a huge platter, which seemed strange. They put it in the center of the table and dug into it after saying a blessing. The Coke rule was always the same: take five sips and pass it down. When they finished, Molly took Boodles to the bathroom while Polly went to pay. The man refused to take their money. Polly explained that they had money to pay, but he would not accept anything. That explained the huge platter of fries; he was just being nice. Even though Molly didn't know what had happened until they were in the car, she was still embarrassed. She said she was so embarrassed that she would never go back there again. The truth is that with those prices, they would never have returned anyway.

Many a time, Molly would need to take all the children with her to run errands in San Jose. They would park the car, all hold hands, and work their way from store to store, dodging people through the crowded downtown streets. Every week, at some point in time, Kiffy needed a bathroom, but very few stores had public bathrooms. One week, when Kiffy made her weekly announcement, Molly knew the kids were hot and tired, and since McDonalds had the nicest bathrooms in all downtown, Molly decided to splurge on an afternoon snack. She sat all seven children down on a line of stools toward the back of the restaurant and ordered, of course, two Cokes, eight straws, and a large order of fries. There were four girls and only three boys, so Molly would drink from the boy's coke, five sips, and pass it down. Then she began passing out the fries, three for you, three for you, three for you, and so on.

Molly was honestly not trying to draw attention to herself or her children; she had tried to pick a remote corner, especially after the last incident. Nevertheless, one little man sitting by himself, apparently with nothing to do but watch everyone else, saw them. He came near and held out a bill that was equivalent to almost ten dollars. She tried not to accept it, but he insisted, gave her the money, and left. He was probably hoping that she would go buy a couple more orders of fries, but times were hard. Molly put the money in her pocket, finished passing out the fries, and gathered her children together to continue the errands. That was one bathroom break, thanks to Kiffy, that Molly could not complain about.

The third restaurant situation was less dramatic. One Sunday after church, tired of cooking, Molly suggested they go out for pizza. They ordered two large pizzas, enough for the littlest ones to get one piece and the bigger ones two pieces. When the waitress asked what they wanted to drink, Molly told her that water was fine. There must have been some unwritten rule in Costa Rica that when one went out to eat, water was not an option for a drink. Molly herself could not remember anyone drinking just water at a restaurant. The waitress was dumbfounded and, with a puzzled look on her face, kept pressing for a drink order. When she finally realized that water was the only drink order she would receive, she left and returned about five minutes later with the manager. The manager tried to explain that they needed to drink something. Molly said they would drink water. The manager said they needed to choose something else. Molly said there was nothing wrong with water, and she didn't have enough money to buy drinks for everyone. The manager told them to buy cheaper pizzas. Molly explained that she was purchasing the cheapest offer on the menu. The manager said she needed to purchase fewer pizzas. The family had grown by that time, so Molly, with a puzzled look on her face, made one long sweep of her hand around the table and explained that if she bought fewer pizzas, not everyone would get a piece. The manager walked away frustrated. When the pizzas came, Cokes came with them. Molly was about to protest when the waitress explained they were on the house. Once again, they were all embarrassed, but not so much that they didn't enjoy the drinks.

Through it all, it became exciting to watch God supply their needs. They found that He was concerned not only about the big needs but even the tiny needs. Of course, that makes sense since He is the Creator not only of the massive universe full of enormous stars but also of microscopic organisms.

One day, Molly was musing about the fact that all of Boodle's socks had holes, but there was no extra money even for socks. Within days, a sweet lady gave them a package of three or four pairs of socks for each child. It had only been a tiny thought in her head, and God had heard and answered. Her next thought was that she should have prayed for it and could have said that God answered her prayer. Weeks later, she was wondering how they were going to buy school uniforms, and, poof, you guessed it, someone gave them uniforms. Once again, she had the thought that she should have prayed.

The fact of the matter was that one time as a teenager, Molly had been discouraged when God had not answered a very important prayer in the way she felt He should have answered. At that time, she very erroneously concluded that praying for specific things didn't much matter since God would do what He wanted to do. Oh, how wrong she had been. Though she had gotten right with the Lord months later, it still seemed like ever since then, she was reluctant to ask the Lord for specific things. Now she was watching God answering needs she had not even prayed about (Isa. 65:24, "And it shall come to pass, that before they call, I will answer; and while they are yet speaking, I will hear"). She decided to start praying and witnessed answers to prayers as she had never seen before. God indeed was the very best Father and ever so faithfully met all their needs, large and small. Time after time they would have a specific need, and God would supply. Some of them were small needs, food or clothing, and others were large, vehicles, plane tickets, and houses; in all of them, the Lord was faithful. Some of them were needs that they had prayed for, and others were clear needs that God just wanted to bless them with when they least expected it.

Once when giving their missions offering meant that they would literally have no money left to eat with for several weeks, Molly and Polly considered skipping the offering they had promised and making it up later. They knew they had always put God first in their finances and decided to put the money in the offering. Polly put the offering in at the beginning of the service, and at the end of the service, Grandpa Heflin said he knew they had extra expenses that month, and he wanted to help them out. He gave Molly the exact same amount they had put in the offering.

Another huge need that God used Grandpa Heflin to supply was when he approached them about an offering he had to build an addition on the back of their house. This took place shortly before Kiffy came into their lives. At that time, there were four kids and two adults living in a small Costa Rican 500-square-foot house. By constructing on most of the backyard, they would be able to almost double the size, making a huge 960 square-foot house. Molly, who had studied architecture in high school, drew up the plans as she wanted them, and construction began.

This was an especially stressful time for everyone. First, it meant that all the clothes on the lines in the backyard needed to be hung to dry in the covered patio at the front of the house, the clothes for six people. Secondly, since all the houses on the block were connected, sharing their side walls on either side, the only way to get all building materials to the backyard was to take them straight through the house. So, foot-wide wooden planks extended up the three steps at the front of the house, through the porch, living room, kitchen, and into the backyard. Then for months, rebar, wheelbarrows of cinder blocks, paint, tin roofing, tools, and everything else that comes with building were all carried through the house. Workers tried their hardest to balance themselves on the planks to not destroy the floor. Cement bags were piled on the covered porch, wherever there were no clotheslines. There was a pile of sand and a pile of rocks in the street in front of the house. There the cement was mixed manually, shoveled into the wheelbarrow, pushed up the steps through three lines of drying clothes, through the living room, and past Molly, who was constantly stepping aside to let it pass while she stood cooking meals at the stove in the tiny kitchen. It was then dumped in the backyard, followed by stepping aside again to allow the empty wheelbarrow to pass by, returning to the street to be loaded with more cement, and so forth all day long. The washer was also in the tiny kitchen, so when Molly wasn't cooking, she was dodging the wheelbarrow to get clothes in or out of the washer or dodging the wheelbarrow to hang the clothes on one of the lines on the porch amidst the bags of cement.

As for the children, they played in the street as much as possible and stayed in their room or any out-of-the-way corner when they couldn't be outside. The kids helped a little by carrying blocks and materials, but they were all still fairly small and couldn't do much. Most of what they did was just to say they had a part in the construction. Molly and Polly also slapped some cement hither and yon, setting blocks on blocks just to say they helped. By the time they finished, several months later, Molly hoped she would never see another construction. Boy was she in for a surprise.

With the new addition, though the house was still under 1,000 square feet, they felt like they were living in a mansion, especially now

The Lord Supplies and Protects

that there were no piled-up bags of cement, wheelbarrows, planks, or endless sand and dust on every piece of furniture. They moved the stove into the new addition and bought a dryer to put in its place, next to the washer, turning the old kitchen into a laundry room and removing the clotheslines from the patio. How blissful it was to spread out a little!

Another very special, very large love offering came the following year after the construction. They used it to buy the 500-square-foot house next door and converted it into a school. Since the houses were connected, they broke open a doorway between the two. It was just big enough for a learning center, a kindergarten room, and two small rooms for storage. They ran into a lady named Lolly from the first church that Molly had worked in, who lived nearby and was willing to come help for a couple of hours in the morning. She took the kindergarten class of Floodles, Fluffy, and Kiffy, leaving Molly to work with the older kids, Biffy, Buffy, Boodles, and Coodles. Molly also took in five other kids from their church, all of whom were in first and second grade. Thus, Molly officially opened the Christian school with twelve students.

They had a good school year, but by the end of the year, Molly realized it was very, very difficult and costly to get a private Christian school approved by the government. She would have to let go of the five children from outside the home. All of them had come to Molly because they were struggling to learn reading in the public school. They were now reading fine, and the parents were questioning whether or not their children could get their sixth-grade diploma, which was very important in Costa Rica, through Molly's school. Since they were not approved, she could not promise them a diploma. As for her own children, they would cross the sixth-grade bridge when they came to it. She felt that God would provide a way, and years later, He did.

God not only supplied their needs but also protected them. The same year they began the school, but fortunately not during class time, Costa Rica had the worst earthquake of its history. It was the earthquake of 1991, registered 7.7 on the Richter scale, started close to 4:00 p.m., and lasted for almost an entire minute. It was the longest minute of Molly's life. She was very glad that Polly was home at the time, preparing for an activity they were supposed to have in the evening at the Bible seminary, and she was also glad that the activity was immediately canceled. Molly was so thankful she did not have to deal with the situation by herself.

The whole family was in the front part of the house when the quake started, except for Kiffy, who was asleep in her crib in the back addition. Polly ran to the front porch with everyone else, and Molly dashed through the moving house, rushing to rescue Kiffy, not knowing whether or not the whole house would come down on top of them. She grabbed the baby and hurried to the front door while listening to shouts of fear ringing out from each house throughout the neighborhood. Everything just kept shaking and shaking; they thought it would never stop.

It did stop, but the aftermath brought many more tremors throughout the night and during the next week. Each time a little tremor started, they were afraid it would go into another big earthquake. For weeks, Molly kept the kids' shoes and sweaters, along with water and snacks, by the door. The kids would go to bed at about 8:30 p.m., and Polly wouldn't get home from her institute classes until 10:00 p.m. The gap between the two events had always been a little quiet time to read and relax that Molly looked forward to enjoying. Now it was a scary time. Molly's mind went wild, questioning how she would wake up seven sleeping children and get them out the front door before the house collapsed should they have another earthquake.

Although nothing had happened to their house except a few things falling off shelves to the ground, thousands of other people closer to the epicenter had lost their homes and some their lives. Molly was not a brave person, and she practically made herself sick thinking about something that never happened instead of trusting God's sovereignty and protection over their family. With time, life finally settled down again.

Larry and Paula Neff

It was January 1993. They had not received any new children since Floodles and Fluffy almost a year and a half prior to this time. Although they were enjoying their larger house, it was rather obvious they would not be able to take in many more children without becoming cramped again.

Molly expressed her concern to Polly, and they began to pray for a larger house, closer to the capital city. The forty-minute up-hill journey from San Jose to Cartago they were making at least four times a week was taking its toll on their twenty-year-old van, and Molly longed to live closer to San Jose. Less than two months after they began to pray, God answered.

Larry and Paula Neff, founders of the Lighthouse Children's Home of Mississippi, were visiting in Costa Rica. They had several missionary friends, and as they visited in their different homes, they expressed a desire to start a children's home in Costa Rica. Each one told them they should talk to Molly; she already had a home. Finally, Brother Neff asked one of the missionaries to take him to meet Molly. It was one of the missionaries Polly had met at Bible Institute. They came and saw the house and the kids. The Neffs invited them to McDonald's and an evening revival meeting he was preaching. After the meeting, Brother Neff called Molly aside and asked her to consider partnering with them. He liked how she was working with the children; that would be her part. His part would be to help raise badly needed support for the home in the States. He told her that he had a goal to have a larger house closer to San Jose. It was exactly what they had started praying for less than a month earlier.

The Neffs visited them one more time to take them grocery shopping before going back to the States. Brother Neff pushed the cart down every aisle, piling into it things that Molly and Polly never purchased because funds were pretty tight. He stopped in front of the cereal and asked whether or not the children liked it. They replied that they weren't sure since they had never bought it before. Molly sheepishly picked out a box of cereal and put it in the cart. Brother Neff reached over, grabbing three more different boxes, and put them in the cart. Molly and Polly's eyes grew big like saucers. That was the day they bought both a block of cheese and sour cream in the same grocery store run. When they finished, they had not one but two carts full of food. What a blessing!

Here we pause to make mention that only two weeks after meeting the Neffs, Molly's father died. Rather than rushing to the States for the funeral and coming straight back, Molly's mother asked her to make arrangements for the children so she could spend a couple of weeks in the States with her. Although Polly's schedule was fairly full between work and Bible Institute, her little old grandparents volunteered to watch the kids at their house. It was very kind of them, and Polly would be there as often as possible, but Molly knew seven children for three weeks would be too much for them.

It was decided they would watch the five older children, and Molly would take the two youngest. All of this was, of course, an unexpected expense, but once again, God came through for them, supplying the necessary funds through several people. Molly got passports and plane tickets for Kiffy, age two, and Fluffy, age four. That was the trip when Kiffy kept demanding that the food be served. Meanwhile, Fluffy entertained herself by looking out the window. What she saw was a long wing with a round motor hanging down in the middle. She thought it was another smaller plane and hollered out that the airplane had a baby. When the plane turned to the right, she would inform her mother that the baby was going up and needed to be told to come back down. And naturally, when the plane turned left, she was concerned that the baby was escaping downward and once again needed someone to correct it and call it back to its mother's side.

When they finally arrived, Molly pointed their grandma out to the girls, and oh, was Grandma ever so pleased and pleasantly surprised when both little girls yelled, "Grandma," and ran into her arms. For two weeks, they had a very refreshing, blessed time with Grandma.

When Brother Neff heard Molly would be in the States, he invited her to stop by the home in Mississippi for a week before returning to Costa Rica. This gave them more time to talk and plan. He asked Molly to draw up the floor plan for the house that would be best for her. She presented him with a plan that would house up to six boys and six girls. He gave it back and asked her to think a little bigger, like twice as big. Molly had never thought any bigger. Twelve children sounded plenty big to her, but she rethought her thinking and began on a plan that would house up to twenty-four children.

She thought back to their beginning. They had truly stepped out in faith. Their limited finances had not been an issue for them. Though many had been skeptical, Molly had said she was sure she had enough to help three or four children. Both Molly and Polly agreed that by starting with nothing, God's provisions and power would be more evident. They had nothing; every milestone, every accomplishment, would have to come straight from God's hand. And now His faithfulness to provide was more evident than ever before. They lived in a small neighborhood in the small town of Cartago, thousands of miles from the Neffs, who lived in the small town of Kosciusko, Mississippi. Yet, Almighty God saw that both they and the Neffs shared the same burden of James 1:27, "Pure religion and undefiled before God and the Father is this, To visit the fatherless and widows in their affliction . . ." The Lord had lovingly understood their hearts and passions and had orchestrated all the events that would bring them together to further their dreams. God's working and the miraculous way He chose to answer their prayers were glorious.

[A LESSON TO LEARN: Psalm 19:1 says, "The heavens declare the glory of God; and the firmament sheweth his handywork." When we consider all of creation from outer space to the earth with its plants, animals, marine life, the complexity of the human body, and on and on, and on, and the words of Luke 1:37, "For with God nothing shall be impossible," are easy to believe and understand. Our Father's power has no limits, and thus, our service to Him knows no limits. There is nothing more wonderful than serving the Lord.

Will you step out in the corner of the world where God has placed you and give your service to Him? Take the step of faith and sit back and watch the intricate avenues He will lead you down and the multiple dead ends where He will miraculously build bridges for His glory.]

Chapter 5

2 More Oodles, a Grandma, and 2 Iffies

Just two months after Molly's trip, child number eight came into the home, a seven-year-old boy called Moodles. He was the grandson of a lady who attended one of the local Baptist churches. Both parents were drug addicts, and the father was in jail at the time. With so little parental control in his life, Moodles was escaping from first grade every day and spending his time playing down by the train tracks. The grandmother was attempting to step into the situation and rescue the child. Things weren't going well for Granny, though, since both the elderly lady and her husband had several health issues, and the young boy had several disciplinary issues. They agreed on a time to pick him up at the grandmother's house and made it a family outing.

Once there, Molly and Polly were invited to step into the living room for a short conversation. Meanwhile, with the house being rather small, six little faces stood at the front door looking in, their eyes wide with wonder. Grandma had called for the child several times when, suddenly, a smiling burst of energy darted in, jumped over several chairs, made a full circle of the room, and returned down the hallway from where he had first appeared. Granny looked extremely flustered and, stepping over to the hallway he had disappeared down, encouraged him in a soft, mousy voice to come back out and meet the nice ladies. Through much coaxing, Moodles finally made a second appearance, which, unfortunately, followed the same path as the first, jumping over the same chairs and disappearing at the same speed.

Molly glanced over at Polly with raised eyebrows and a look of, "This one's going to be a handful." In between Moodles's appearances and disappearances, Molly and Polly learned that the young charge had already been explained what was going on, had helped pack his own bags, and was looking forward to going to live in a house with other children. After more stepping into the hallway on the part of the Grandma and more coaxing in a soft voice, Moodles finally came out and stood by his bags at the front door. Though he was a live wire, when he finally stood still for a second, they saw that he was a cute little boy with an adorable smile. What followed were hugs, kisses, goodbyes, and "be goods," and more hugs and kisses, bigger kids grabbing bags to help, and Molly and Polly smiling and walking out the front door acting as if this were the most run of the mill normal situation in the world.

If the thought had occurred to Molly that being out of his normal environment, Moodles would settle down once they got to his new unfamiliar home, that thought would have been completely wrong. It was evening by the time they got home, so they got his stuff into his room as quickly as possible and sat down at the table for supper. Moodles did sit still for the prayer and continued to sit for the first two bites of food. After those bites, though, he got up, ran all the way around the table and back to his own place, stuffed another bite in his mouth, and took off running around the table in the opposite direction. This became his normal routine at mealtime. He seemed to be unable to eat a whole meal in one sitting. Every meal was a bite, and a sprint, a bite and a sprint. It is not that Molly never tried to teach him to sit still and eat a full meal but rather that Moodles was one of those, "choose your battles" type of kids, and she chose to give him some leeway, having many other more important battles to try to conquer. At least he was eating, and he was happy at mealtimes. Molly felt like nothing would stop his silly mantic short of plopping herself down on his lap to the point that he could not move at all, and that probably would not have helped his digestion.

On his first morning, the family was heading out the door to go to Saturday morning church visitation when Moodles saw in the front patio the used bicycle the kids had been given. He asked if he could ride it, and Molly explained that they needed to leave, but he could ride it in the afternoon when they came back. Yet, no sooner had she turned around from locking the front door, not fifteen seconds after she had told him no, and he was gone, bike and all. A few of the kids were pointing down the street in the direction he had disappeared. *Perfect*, thought Molly; that direction was a dead-end, he would be back soon, and she'd catch him. Catch him, she did, leaving the bike in the middle of the street for one of the others to put away, and she marched her catch straight back into the house. That was the day that Moodles became the only child in the history of the children's home to be disciplined before he had even been there for twenty-four hours.

Dealing with Moodles was like riding a rollercoaster while wearing a blindfold. There were times when you were going slowly but steadily upward, only to be suddenly dropping at high speeds, not knowing if at the bottom of the drop, you would be jerked to the right or the left or be sent into a spiral or loop, but then, once again, you were slowly going upward. The big difference between the two was, of course, that on a roller coaster, the exciting parts were the quick drops, but with Moodles, the excitement was the slow ascensions. He never did quite settle down and was always a ball of energy. It was his anger, moods, and often, cruelty, more than anything, that kept him on the rollercoaster of ups and downs.

On the positive side, he was an intelligent young fellow and had no problem at school. He actually enjoyed learning. He was also a very talented musician. As a teenager, with no formal music lessons and only a little coaching from others, he taught himself to play both the piano and an old saxophone someone had given the home. He did extremely well on both instruments, played the saxophone in several Christmas dramas, and was even the church pianist for a short period of time.

After only a few months in the home, Moodles and Boodles shared a very unique experience, at ages seven and eight. It all started around 5:30 a.m. when Molly was awakened by the front patio metal door closing rather loudly. Molly knew that Polly had to leave early in the morning, but Polly usually snuck out quietly so as not to wake everyone. Oh well, maybe the wind caught the door; it didn't really matter because Molly fell right back to sleep and was out for over an hour. When she finally got up, she was surprised to see Polly in her room fast asleep and more surprised when Boodles and Moodles were missing from their rooms. She began searching the house frantically and soon had everyone else up helping in the search. Molly asked Polly why she was still at home, and Polly reminded her that it was a holiday in Costa Rica, and she had off from work. Immediately, Molly realized that the slamming door had been the boys, not Polly.

Nobody in the home seemed to have any idea where the boys were. Molly took to the street to ask if anyone in the neighborhood had seen them. One man had seen them rather early walking down the street in their pajamas and with backpacks. He had thought it was a tad bit strange but didn't even bother to ask them where they were going. Boodles was such a good kid, thought Molly. How on earth could he have let Moodles talk him into running away? Where on earth would they go? Was Moodles trying to get back to his grandma's house? Molly rushed back to the house to get the car and comb the streets. She took Coodles and Buffy, the two oldest children, with her to help search. Polly stayed behind making phone calls.

After going up and down streets for about fifteen minutes with no luck, they returned home to rethink the problem. Molly called all the kids together. Someone must have heard them say something, seen them packing, or have some idea what was going on. Coodles, who had just spent fifteen minutes in the car with Molly and hadn't mentioned a thing, slowly raised his hand.

"They might possibly be heading toward the airport," he said. "At least that is what they were talking about." Molly's jaw dropped as Coodles gave her a brief explanation for the sudden disappearance. Now she had a direction to go in and was off in the car again, heading toward the airport, a little more than a two-hour drive from their home. Fortunately, the boys had only had enough time to walk a couple of miles. As the loud Volkswagen van began chugging its way up a steep portion of the Pan-American Highway, the only route they knew of to leave Cartago, the noise attracted the attention of the two little figures halfway up the hill trudging slowly along. They glanced back, recognized Molly, and ran up an embankment to hide behind a huge rock. Molly pulled up to the spot, got out, and hollered up to the boys to come out immediately and get in the car. They lost no time in doing so, and it was a quiet ride back home with tensions high.

Once at home, Molly, Boodles, and Moodles had a very long, private talk. To Molly's absolute, complete surprise, it was Boodles, not Moodles, who had come up with the plan. Moodles had only agreed to accompany Boodles so he wouldn't have to go by himself. Everything had started a little over a week earlier when they had all sung at a missions conference in a supporting church where a visiting pastor from the States was preaching. The missionary had invited the children's home, along with the pastor and his wife, out for a hamburger after the service. The group occupied several small tables, and the nice pastor's wife sat down at Boodles's table. Boodles said she was the prettiest and nicest lady he had ever met. Their friendly conversation covered many topics. At a certain point, Boodles had asked her where she lived and what her house was like. After answering, she told Boodles that maybe he could come to visit her sometime. Boodles had decided to take her up on her invitation.

He knew that the couple wasn't leaving Costa Rica for another week and a half, so he had plenty of time to think it through. He would leave two days before their plane departed because he wasn't sure how long it would take to walk to the airport. Once there, they would sneak past all the guards, get on the same plane the nice lady and her husband got on, and hide under the seats all the way to the States. When they got there, they would pay attention to what car they got in, then grab a taxi and tell him to follow that car. Once they got to her house, they would knock on the door, yell, "Surprise," when she answered, and ask her if she could pay the taxi driver. Boodles planned on staying only a few days, from Tuesday evening to Saturday morning, because he didn't want Mommy to get upset with him. On Saturday morning, he would ask the nice lady to take them back to the airport, and they would return the same way they had gone, getting back on time for church on Sunday.

Molly was shocked, to say the least. She checked their backpacks, and they both had the same things, one extra pair of clothes, their toothbrushes, and their Bibles. The pajamas they had been wearing in the morning were also in the backpacks. They had put them on over the clothes they were then wearing and had peeled them off when the sun got too hot. They also had one blanket between the two of them so they could sleep somewhere under the stars on Monday night.

Molly found out that the older kids knew about the plan and had actually pitched in a few ideas. Everyone had felt it was safer for Moodles to go with Boodles. Coodles had suggested that Boodles grab the money out of the little box Molly had for loose change, just in case they needed to buy food or something. Boodles refused to steal from Mommy. They would eat when they got there. They didn't take more clothes because that would weigh down their backpacks, and anyway, the nice lady, of course, would wash their clothes for them. The kids who knew about the plan said they went along with it because they really didn't believe they would go through with it. When they did, they were afraid to admit they knew.

Molly's heart melted after hearing the whole story and realizing that the boys had not, indeed, run away. Boodles, in his innocence, had simply planned a short vacation without letting her know. In his mind, he had taken every precaution to make sure Mommy did not get upset, although he now understood that somewhere along the line, those precautions were not quite enough. Those who had known about the plan were punished together with the two offenders. Molly knew that deep down, Boodles knew that Mommy would not have approved of the vacation; that's why he didn't tell her. Nevertheless, given the circumstances and Molly's melted heart, the punishment was small and symbolic, nothing in comparison to all the neat punishments Molly had been pondering in her irritation while she was bringing the boys back home in the car.

During this time Brother Neff was in and out of the country at different times, looking for a piece of land. On one such trip, he brought the director from the home in Mississippi, who was excited about meeting the kids. They agreed to meet on the lot they would be looking at that day. The director wanted to get something for the kids and had a can of Coke for each one. He passed out the cans, and Molly asked them to wait in the car for a minute while the adults looked at the piece of property. She figured the Coke would keep them occupied. When she returned, the children all still held their unopened cans on their laps. She asked them why they hadn't opened them. Coodles spoke up for the group and informed her that she had not told them how much they were allowed to drink. When she told them it was theirs and they could drink all of it, they repeated to her in unison and with wide eyes, "All of it?" For years afterward, whenever the director from the States came up in conversation, they would say, "Oh, the Coke man." Finally, land was purchased, and the plans for the house were turned in to the architect. They were one step closer to a new home.

Doodles

Shortly after the vacation that got cut short, Doodles came into their lives. It was a quiet Saturday afternoon, all the children were accounted for and healthy, and Polly had gone to town to get her nails done. Suddenly, there was a knock on the big metal door; anyone knocking on their door was a rarity. Molly opened the door to find the secretary who worked at the same place Polly worked standing on the sidewalk with a bundle in her arms. Molly invited her in, and the first thing she did was ask Molly if she could do her a favor. When Molly asked her what it might be, she stretched her arms out, bundle and all, and asked her if she would take the baby she held. Molly was flabbergasted; this lady just knocked on her door and was asking her to take, as in to keep, as in to rear, this baby. Molly took the baby from her arms, and they sat down to talk.

The secretary's story was that she had found the baby in a basket on her doorstep two days earlier. She did not know who had abandoned him and had no papers for him. She was sure, though, that she couldn't keep him and didn't want to turn him over to the government. A few minutes into the visit, Polly came home and was as flabbergasted to see a baby in Molly's arms as Molly was to have a baby in her arms. Certainly, neither of them had thought when they woke up that morning that maybe someone would just drop off a newborn baby at their front door, but that is exactly what happened. Polly immediately joined in the conversation, and the lady repeated what she had just told Molly. As they talked, the baby began to cry, and Molly stood and began to rock and cuddle and pat and shush, doing everything possible to quiet the baby. The secretary walked over and took the baby back from Molly. He calmed down being in her arms and hearing her voice, and he immediately stopped crying. Molly and Polly glanced at each other. This baby was not acting as though he had known the secretary for only the last two days, but more like for the last nine months. He knew exactly who she was.

Several other things made Molly and Polly suspicious of her story. Knowing that newborns needed to eat quite often, Molly asked the secretary if she had some bottles for the baby, to which she responded in the negative. How could she have had the baby for two days now and not have purchased bottles? Soon afterward, realizing the baby needed to be changed, Molly asked about diapers. She had none of those either. Really, how could that be? But the biggest surprise came when Molly said she would use one of Kiffy's old cloth diapers. When she took off the newborn's pajamas to change him, she found black ink on the bottom of one foot. She touched his foot, and the ink rubbed off on her hand; it was still fresh. This baby had come to them straight from the hospital.

The clencher of the theory that was formulating in Molly's mind was when the time drew near for the secretary to leave, and she began to cry. Why would she be so emotional for this random baby she had supposedly just found on her doorstep less than forty-eight hours ago, a baby she had no interest in keeping and in whom she had not even invested money for simple things like bottles or diapers? Something seemed seriously suspicious. Molly and Polly assured her that they would care for the infant to the best of their ability, and after finally calming herself, she left.

By the end of the next week, Polly came home with all the latest rumors from work. Some whispered that the secretary had suddenly added several new outfits to her wardrobe and that they happened to be quite a bit tighter than the clothes she had been wearing. Other whisperers confirmed that she indeed had previously only been wearing two or three very baggy outfits. Still others whispered about the secretary having called in sick on Friday. Apparently, everyone at work wanted to meet the mystery baby, so one afternoon, Molly piled the crew in the van and made the trip into San Jose to pick up Polly and show off Baby Doodles. The whisperers loved this meeting as it gave them new ammunition. They whispered about how much the baby looked like the secretary and how quickly the secretary had jumped up from her desk and ran to hold him. Nevertheless, the secretary stuck to her story of having found the baby on her doorstep.

To get the paperwork started, Molly and Polly took the baby to the same lawyer they had taken Kiffy to but were disappointed when they were told that without a birth certificate or a mother, she could not even begin to process an adoption. The baby had to be turned over to the government. Their hearts sank; they knew the government would not let them keep the baby. He was perfect for an adoption, and they had a long list of people who had filed papers and were waiting for an adoption. It was the government's decision whom the baby would go to.

Suddenly, Molly remembered a young girl who had spoken to her just recently in one of the supporting Costa Rican churches. She had mentioned to Molly that if she ever needed any help with the government to let her know as her family was personal friends with the chief director of the child's welfare department. Molly took her number and thanked her but said she didn't believe she would need anything since they had never had a problem with the government. Now Molly found herself frantically looking for the number and having Polly call the young lady whose services she thought she would never need.

An appointment was set up at the director's private residence. He was a friendly man and listened attentively to Molly's story and her dread that the baby would be taken away from her. When she finished her explanation, she was surprised to hear him say that he remembered her. She had no memory of ever having seen him and was eager to hear how he knew her. He had seen her one day in the office on business. He asked her if she had been the lady who had all the little kids lined up against the wall doing schoolwork one day. The memory returned. Molly had no choice but to take the children with her that day. She knew government offices usually meant standing in long lines for long periods of time in rooms with very few chairs. In order to keep the children occupied, she had opted to make it a school field trip of sorts. Everyone had their three main ACE school Paces (booklets) and were instructed to do four pages in each book. The little ones all had coloring books. She then lined them up against the wall, sitting on the floor for a lack of chairs, and promised a snack for everyone who was well-behaved. The director said he had been amazed at how they all just sat there the whole time, each one quietly doing his or her own work. He then went on to tell her that she was doing a fantastic job, and nobody was going to take that baby away from her. He asked Molly to go to the regional office on Monday morning and promised that he would contact them that very morning, instructing them to begin the adoption process.

So, as it turned out, it was the children's good behavior that had drawn the director's attention to Molly. Her business that day was not even with him, but he had made a mental note of her. Molly was so grateful that the kids had behaved that day, grateful that Kiffy and Fluffy had not been in one of their arguing moods, grateful that Biffy and Coodles had not been in one of their silly moods, and she was especially grateful that the whole incident had transpired before Moodles had come into their family. How many things could have happened that would have given him a different impression? But God had his hands on the situation, as he always did.

On Monday morning, the regional lawyer couldn't believe what she was being asked to do but obediently began the process. She told Molly the baby could not have her last name until the adoption was complete. She allowed Molly, however, to decide on his first and middle names and then just made up a temporary last name for little Doodles so they could get him a birth certificate. He became the only child that Molly named herself. On the birth certificate, it stated his birthday to be August 26, according to the testimony of the secretary. Molly and Polly knew that couldn't be right; he had to have been born on either the night of the 27th or early in the morning of the 28th. For the rest of his life, when asked about his birthday, they would answer the 26th, 27th, and 28th of August.

The lawyer set up an interview with the secretary, whose story never changed. They made no effort to check her story out or investigate in any way. Interestingly enough, though, the government never bothered them over Doodles; they also never finished his adoption. As young adults, Doodles, as well as Kiffy, Fluffy, and Boodles, signed their own adoption papers and became Molly's legally adopted children.

The nice director who allowed Molly to keep Doodles was only in the position of director for about a year, six months before Doodles' birth, and six months after Doodles' birth. Molly remembered how Queen Esther was able to save her people and how Mordecai had said to her, "Who knoweth whether thou art come to the kingdom for such a time as this." Now she wondered if maybe God had placed this man in his position of authority for such a time as this little baby.

On Doodles's first Sunday morning, Molly got him ready, and then, since they did not yet have any kind of infant seat for him, she placed him ever so gently and carefully on their small couch, surrounded with pillows. As she turned around, she saw Boodles charging toward the couch and leaping into the air, heading directly toward the soft cushion of pillows. Molly reached out with both hands, grabbed Boodles in the air, twirled him around to change his direction, and set him back down, glad that he was a thin little fellow.

"Boodles, what are you doing? The baby! Don't you see the baby? You can't just be jumping onto couches without paying attention," scolded Molly.

Realizing what he had almost done, poor Boodles had a look of surprise, fear, and remorse all at the same time. Molly had an overwhelming look of irritation, shock, and relief all at the same time. *How on earth*, she wondered, *would this tiny baby ever survive having eight older brothers and sisters?* Fortunately, though there were several other close calls, Doodles did survive his childhood.

That same first Sunday, Molly arrived at church eager to show off her new baby. She was trying her hardest to hold him sweetly cuddled in her arms, like every other new mother she had ever seen. It wasn't that easy, though, as two to four-day-old Doodles would not stay still. Maybe it was because he was so happy to be out of the cramped quarters of a birth mother who was successfully hiding her pregnancy. Whatever the reason, he would stretch his arms, kick with his feet, and twist this way and that way, and his moving made Molly move and twist and struggle, and in short, it was becoming impossible for Molly to look dignified and under control. The truth is, only three of Molly's children had come to her as babies, and none of the three was one of those calm babies who just lie there and look cute.

A couple of days later, they realized that Doodles's favorite position was being held upright, looking outward, with Molly's or Polly's arm around his stomach as though they were carrying a sack of potatoes. It seemed to calm him as well as allow him to look around and see everything that was going on around him.

To say that Molly was nervous about the sudden arrival of a newborn would be an understatement. He was so tiny, so defenseless, and they had never prepared in any way for a newborn. With each little unexplainable thing Molly saw in her baby, she was running off to the doctor to ask questions. She opted to take Doodles to a private doctor rather than depend on the free socialized medicine. The appointment would cost her about twenty-five dollars, but she decided it was well worth it.

As Molly sat waiting in a comfortable chair for the doctor to see her, her thoughts went back to an extremely unpleasant experience she had in the socialized medicine hospital when Kiffy was not yet a year old. Kiffy had gotten sick with a high fever. Molly had rushed her to the hospital only to find herself standing in a line, in a room with no chairs, for what seemed like an hour. Molly had been so concerned about Kiffy that she had rushed out without any kind of diaper bag or any kind of stroller in which to put her. Kiffy was not a happy camper; she was very sick and seemed to be gaining weight with each passing minute, feeling heavier and heavier. When it was finally their turn to talk to the doctor, he was sitting behind a desk in a hallway. He asked

Molly what the problem was. When she told him she had a fever, he touched Kiffy's forehead and said it wasn't so bad. Then he squeezed her throat, and she began to cry.

"Throat infection," the doctor exclaimed, and then he wrote out a prescription, told Molly which way to go to get into the next line, and hollered for the next patient to approach the desk. Molly obediently found the next line and began waiting again. In the middle of that line, Kiffy got sick to her stomach. Nobody came, nobody offered a towel to clean up the mess, and Molly felt invisible. When they got to the front of that line, the nurse also seemed blind to Molly's predicament. Molly was trying to explain, but in less than a minute, she had pointed Molly to set the baby on a table, put an injection in her, wrote something on the paper Molly was carrying from station to station, and told Molly where to find the line to turn in the papers. That line was the pharmacy line, where they took the papers and told Molly to return in two to three hours to pick up her medicines. As Molly walked out with her crying baby, she wished she could join in and cry with her but didn't think that would improve the situation.

Within a few short minutes, Molly was brought out of her stroll down memory lane when she heard Doodles's name being called. She walked into what she recognized as a normal doctor's office. Oh her joy, after laying Doodles on the examination table, to see the doctor actually taking his temperature, weighing him, looking into his ears, eyes, and throat, and gently pushing here and there on his pudgy little stomach. She explained her concerns, and he listened and answered every question. Doodles was fine, and Molly took him home with a smile on her face and blissful peace in her heart. The visit had been well worth the twenty-five dollars.

Unfortunately, that was not the only visit to the doctor. It was followed by a second visit and possibly even a third that ended in the same way: everything was fine; there was nothing to worry about. Then it happened that Molly felt something was wrong right in the middle of the night when the doctor's office, obviously, was closed.

2 More Oodles, a Grandma, and 2 Iffies

Polly happened to be spending the night with a friend from Bible college. Molly was so worried about Doodles that she convinced herself into believing she needed to take him to the private hospital in San Jose. To do that, she would have to take everyone with her. Molly woke up the whole gang, stuffed them in the van, pajamas, blankets, pillows, and all, and made the forty-five-minute drive to the hospital. In they walked, Molly in front, holding her little sack of potatoes, and eight little ones filing in behind her, like little ducklings following the mother duck, some with pillows, some with teddy bears, Coodles with a stack of books, and all in their pajamas. They were out rather quickly, as no one was in the emergency waiting room at that time of night. The diagnosis was, of course, the baby was fine, and they could all go home. After that, there was only one more visit to the caring, twenty-five-dollars-a-visit doctor. On that day, he said to Molly, "You have a perfectly healthy baby. He is not the problem; you are. You need to relax; he will be fine." That was a good thing, thought Molly, as she was running out of money anyway.

When the nerves started settling, they saw, just as they had seen with Kiffy, that babies had a way of bringing a lot of joy into the home. Molly was so pleased that the Lord had blessed her with a newborn and the privilege of having one child from day one. She cherished the joy of holding him in her arms and rocking him to sleep. Three-year-old Kiffy loved her baby brother and would stand next to the rocker singing all the lullabies with Mommy. There were the joys of watching him when he started solid foods, seeing the mushy mix come right back out, and pushing it back in with the spoon two or sometimes three times. When Doodles finally learned to swallow well, Boodles enjoyed feeding him more than anyone but usually left a mess all over Doodles's face.

Together as a family, they got to see all of Doodles's firsts. They enjoyed the first smiles, rolling over, holding his own bottle, crawling, walking, and talking. Every new feat was met by a room full of witnesses all jumping up and down and clapping their hands. As he grew, every new word was written down on the Doodles's vocabulary list Molly had started. With a teacher for a mother, he was able to recognize and say all five vowels before he turned two years old. Shortly after that were the first Scripture verses and the first songs; every first was special.

To Molly, Doodles was the cutest baby boy she had ever seen. The standing family joke, however, was that Molly was seeing him through a mother's eye. Kiffy had been such a beautiful baby that everywhere they went, people had to comment on how cute she was. Molly expected the same comments about Doodles, but the comments were always about how chubby he was or how big he was getting. Every time they heard the comments, Polly would laugh, and Molly would just smile and nod but hoped to hear the "so cute" comment someday.

When Doodles was about two months old, Molly decided to sell the little house they had purchased to be their school. It was in serious need of various repairs, especially on the roof. They were in the middle of the rainy season, and every room had buckets and pans to catch the rainwater from all the leaks. Molly was going to miss the playroom they had set up in that house, but even in that room, the children played among the buckets of water. They had no money for repairs and decided to just sell it like it was and let the new owners fix it. After all, they would need the money from the sale for the new house they would soon be moving into. The house sold fast, but Molly's timing was slightly off. She was thinking they would be in their new home within months, but they would actually not move for more than two years.

Grandma

With nine children ranging in ages from newborn to twelve years old and Polly working and going to Bible seminary, Molly was beginning to feel overwhelmed. At one especially tiring time, she said in a letter she wrote home to her mother that although she was surrounded by children all day long, she often felt lonely. Molly mentioned that talking to children and having an adult conversation were two different things. On top of the feeling of loneliness, the family had grown faster than Molly's organization skills, which were never her strong quality. She was struggling to get meals done, clothes washed, and deal with normal household problems and normal children problems, in addition to abnormal household problems and abnormal children problems and still keep up with their homeschool education and a baby.

Shortly after the letter, Molly got a phone call from her mother in the States. She, too, had felt lonely ever since Molly's father had died some ten months earlier, even though she was renting rooms to a few boarders. She told Molly that she had prayed earnestly and felt that God would have her go to Costa Rica as a missionary. She planned to move there in about three months, arriving in January.

This sudden news flash caught Molly totally off guard. She had simply been venting her emotions; she had not been hinting that she wanted her mother to come to Costa Rica. She tried to convince her to at least wait until they were in the new house, but her mother's heart had already decided it was time, and there was no changing it.

Molly was not sure how well her mother would do in her world. There would be so many adjustments. Her mother was in her seventies. The food would be different, and the language, the customs, the house full of kids, and the cramped living quarters—Molly could not imagine how this would all work out. Yet, true to schedule, Grandma arrived in mid-January. Everyone scooted over a bit, rooms were rearranged, and Grandma was given a 9 x 7 room with no closet space but, to her advantage, the only room with a window. The view wasn't that great as it looked out on a 4 x 7 backyard and a block wall, but at least it let in some fresh air.

To Molly's surprise, Grandma adjusted incredibly well. Most of the time, she would sit in the rocker in the small living room. Her arms provided the perfect spot to place a little baby who just wanted to be held. She was also good at reading books to the little ones and answering questions. Molly was afraid she would miss watching TV—they had no television service—but she was content with the same twenty or so VHS tapes the children watched in the evenings. They had all seen the tapes many times but always laughed as if it were the first time to see the silly parts and rooted the heroes on to victory as though the video might end differently and they might not win this time.

Molly grew to be glad that Grandma had come when she had. She was there for most of Doodles's firsts, cheering on with the whole gang. Being confined to such limited spaces drew everyone close together in more ways than one. There were days of lots of conversation and lots of laughter. There was, of course, also plenty of arguing between the children, but whenever things became too much for Grandma to bear, she would slip off to her room and breathe in the fresh air.

Grandma spent the rest of her life in Costa Rica, living to the ripe old age of ninety-seven. She returned to the States on only two or three occasions to visit her sons, grandchildren, and sister. Neither Molly nor her mother ever regretted her decision to move to Costa Rica. Although she wasn't involved in any of the physical labor of working in the home, she could handle babysitting for short periods of time, listened to the kids' school reading, helped financially in a multitude of ways, provided great moral support, and was loved by everyone who knew her.

2 Iffies

Almost a year after Grandma's arrival, Miffy, almost five, and Muffy, age three, came into their lives. From the time they had met Moodles, his grandmother had asked them to pray for his two little sisters. They had been with the mother when Moodles first came but had since been taken from her by social services. Moodles's grandmother was doing everything possible to have the girls moved so they could be with Moodles. When permission was finally granted, Moodles had been with Molly for over a year and a half and hadn't seen his sisters for over two years.

As was the custom with all the children who came from the government, they would visit the home first. It was planned that they would spend an entire Saturday afternoon at the home. Moodles was so excited. He made his sisters little welcome cards and even had some balloons for them that he had kept from a party. Molly had never seen him show so much care for anyone.

Just like Moodles, Miffy and Muffy came through the front door running. They were two cute little chubby girls with miniature ponytails that stood straight up on the top of their heads. They looked very much alike except for one being quite a bit bigger. They immediately wanted to see everything, touch everything, and play with everything. Miffy, the older one, was especially attentive to Moodles. From the time she came in, it was, "Moodles, show me this," "Moodles, show me that," "Moodles, come here," "Moodles, go there," "Moodles, let's play this," and "Moodles, help me with that." Muffy, on the other hand, was quite independent. In a small, high-pitched voice, she went from person to person, talking in what everyone presumed to be Chinese because it certainly did not sound like Spanish. She immediately won everyone's hearts. Kiffy had to hug her every three minutes, and even Coodles, who didn't care for kids in general, was found squeezing Muffy's cheeks on a number of occasions. All in all, the first visit went very well, and everyone was all smiles when the girls left.

Later that day, Coodles, who usually kept to himself and his books, was being a gentleman and extra helpful. When Polly asked him what had gotten into him, he replied that the chubby little girl had transformed him.

The children all waited excitedly for the arrival of the new family members, and Molly was just as excited as the children. She had been having problems with Kiffy and Fluffy, who were both strong-willed and had been doing a lot of fighting lately. Molly calculated that if the girls had more options of playmates instead of fighting, they could play with someone else. After all, Kiffy had taken so kindly to chubby little Muffy that she would be ever so gentle if she were to have a little sister. Moodles himself was jumping and skipping and running through the house more but always with a smile in a happy, carefree manner.

A week or so later, the chubby little girl and her not quite as chubby but taller sister came to live in their home. The arrival honeymoon of the two new family members might have lasted four or five days. What was Molly thinking? How could she possibly have believed that more children would mean less fighting? Where was her brain? As it turned out, chubby little Chinese-speaking Muffy had the strongest will of any of them. Worse than that, anytime a war broke out between Muffy and Kiffy, who was struggling to hold her ground, Muffy called for reinforcements from Miffy, making it two against one. Fluffy, sizing up the situation, tried to steer clear of confrontation most of the time, but sometimes it was inevitable as the fearsome twosome were pushing her buttons as well. To make matters worse, there were now five girls all living together in a 10 x 8 room with two sets of bunk beds, with Miffy and Muffy sharing a bed. Biffy was sleeping on a cot in their little 5 x 10 office area, but her things were still kept in the girl's room, so she basically was still in that room more often than not. Molly was not sure what they would have done if they had not had the covered front patio area to play in during the day. How quickly the huge house they felt they had after the construction seemed to be shrinking. Fourteen people were undoubtedly too many for a 960 square-foot house.

The boys weren't doing much better. Moodles very quickly got tired of being followed around all day long and hearing Muffy calling for him constantly. In addition, though they also called on him to help them in quarrels, he had no interest in getting involved in fights between four screaming, scratching, biting, hair-pulling little "angels." As for Coodles, he once again lost his interest in children. In one of his particularly rude moments, Molly reminded him that he had been transformed by the little chubby girl, to which he only replied, "Not anymore." Even Grandma, who had been so patient up until this time, was often losing it, grumbling under her breath, and hurrying off to her room. She seemed to be in dire need of much more fresh air as she was spending quite a bit more time in her own room with the door closed and her window opened.

Molly's heart went out to Kiffy and Fluffy. She was trying so hard to give all her kids a normal family life. Now, watching these two, she realized that their entire lives would be a series of scooting over and making room for new ones. That was especially difficult right now when there was literally nowhere to move over. The saddest part is that they had not even begun the construction of the new house yet. Once the construction started, it took longer than they expected. All in all, the fourteen of them lived together for eleven months in the little house. Little Kiffy, who had so looked forward to the new arrivals, came to Molly and told her that she wanted to be like Jesus, but she just didn't know how. Bless her heart, such a profound statement for a four-year-old. Molly gave her some words of encouragement, but the truth of the matter was that even the adults were fighting the same battle.

The bickering among the kids was not the only trial they faced. Around three months after the arrival of the new girls, Coodles came down with chicken pox. They were watching the other children carefully and thought the danger had passed when four more cases of chicken pox broke out, exactly two weeks after the first one. Two weeks later, thinking for sure that everyone else must have already had them previously, four more cases broke out, one of which was Polly. Two weeks later, Molly and Grandma found themselves holding their breath, but finally, there were no new cases. What was so curious was that besides the nine cases of chicken pox, during the same six weeks, they also had five cases of vomiting, four cases of diarrhea, three cases of asthma, one mouth infection, and God alone remembers how many coughs and colds. For someone who had said she would never want to be a nurse, Molly sure was getting a chance to try her hand at a nursing career.

Finally, the time was drawing near to leave the old house behind and move on to the new one. Yet, we will not quite shut that door yet without first opening the next, and thereby having the two doors opened simultaneously for a short time. Years later, Molly doubted they were even conscious, as they lived the last months in that small cracker box house of all the sweet memories they would leave behind. Did they know that the sun was going down on a bittersweet chapter of their lives, a chapter in which the precious memories would always outshine the trials?

[A LESSON TO LEARN: The Bible says in Psalm 68:6, "God setteth the solitary in families . . ." That is exactly what he was doing. God was putting together a puzzle. He was taking individual pieces and linking them side by side to form one big, beautiful picture. At the same time, in God's intricacy, each puzzle piece held within itself another puzzle, its own puzzle made of puzzle pieces unlike anyone else's.

Who are the puzzle pieces that God has placed close to your piece? Are you doing your part to allow Him to link each of you into a beautiful picture? What can you do, and how can you reach out to them to make the picture even more lovely? And what about the separate puzzle hidden within your individual piece, the puzzle that only you and your Savior share? Are you allowing God to put that puzzle together? Or are you trying to put pieces together that don't quite fit? Let God work; let Him lead. He knows what the whole picture will look like. Sometimes we can't quite see the form, and sometimes it doesn't even make sense, but rest in Him; it makes perfect sense to Him.]

Chapter 6

A New House

Molly was glad that Brother Neff had asked her to make the floor plan plenty big because he said children needed a lot of room to play. He had that right, but adults needed space too, and they all looked forward to having some. In the new house, instead of having one room apiece, measuring 10' x 8' for the girls and the boys, they would have two rooms apiece, measuring 16' x 14'. The huge living room/dining room combination measured 20' x 55', and the covered porch was 20' x 38'.

The property they had decided to purchase was two and a half acres at the dead end of a new neighborhood. There weren't a lot of houses built yet close to their property; in fact, there was only one. The lady who lived there was very friendly and helped them on many occasions. Her most extraordinary act of kindness was to allow their construction workers to hook a long hose into her water spigot. The area was so new that the water line did not yet extend all the way to their property, and she kindly shared her water for several weeks until they got the water line extended.

The construction finally started right about the time that everyone was getting sick. Polly, who had a worse case of chicken pox than anyone else, happened to be in charge of the construction. By this time, she had graduated from Bible seminary and was no longer working either. Business and accounting were right down her alley. She had already overseen the permissions and had met many times with the architect, engineer, and contractor. The starting date had already been set, the workers contracted to start, and materials purchased to be delivered on said date. Polly got sick days earlier. Canceling meant losing money and was out of the question. Molly planned on going, but Polly insisted on going too. Though she felt terrible, she refused to stay home. She felt like there were too many details that only she knew about. She took painkillers, wrapped up like a leper, and out the door they went.

The construction officially started. Polly would spend the next nine months going here and there, negotiating prices, buying materials, looking for donations, and paying salaries. Although the expenses went way above the budget they had calculated, people stepped up from all directions to have a part in the biggest project of their lives. Brother Neff had raised what they felt would cover the shell of a building, but it seemed that there were constant new expenses and constant problems that slowed them down.

On one particular week, they were really scraping the bottom of the barrel. Polly had $4,000 worth of expenses, $2,000 for badly needed cement, and $2,000 to pay the workers. But she only had $2,000 left. If she paid the workers, they would have no cement to work with, and if she bought the cement, she would have no workers to use it. While driving down the street toward the bank and pondering the predicament, she received a beeper message from Brother Heflin, asking her to drop by the house. She quickly turned the car around, hoping he had some good news. The offering he had for her when she arrived was exactly $2,000. They knew it had been the Lord who had shared that amount with Brother Heflin because they had not shared that need. It was just like their wonderful, mighty Father God to be answering prayers once again before they had even prayed them.

They were amazed at how God used people from all walks of life and every direction to provide. Of course, most of the donations were from churches in the States, but the Lord was so good at surprising them with donations from unexpected places and at just the right times. They received donations from missionaries, tourists, and people they didn't even know but who had heard of their construction. The Costa Rican churches also wanted to have a part in the project, and though they were churches who struggled in the area of finances, Molly and Polly were surprised when their offerings totaled up to over $3,000.

When it became obvious they would not have enough to finish the house, they made three lists. There was the list of what was absolutely essential to move into the house, the list of what would be nice to have, and the list of the things that could wait. The "essential for moving in list" included finishing the roof, plumbing, bathroom sinks and toilets, kitchen sink, windows, and exterior doors. The "sure would be nice but not essential list" included a ceiling, a no-wax floor, and bars on the windows. The "can wait until later list" included painting, closets, most shelves, interior doors, bathroom tiles, countertops, and a kitchen island.

Polly worked very hard on making lists, asking for discounts, comparing prices, crossing things off her lists, and adding new things to her lists. She kept very accurate records of everything spent, every offering received, and every discount obtained. One day, while negotiating with the glass company, the owner decided to donate all the windows and the labor to install them. Well, well, that could be crossed off the list. A few weeks later, an American Christian man who had done several constructions in Costa Rica donated bars for all the windows. That was not even on the essential list but was a big plus since their property was only about 700 meters away from a rough neighborhood. Just between the two donations of windows and bars, they saved $9,500. In addition to that, Polly got other discounts on all kinds of materials totaling up to almost $7,000. The front doors were also donated, as was the electrical installation.

While Polly hurried from place to place each day with all her complicated lists, Molly was busy struggling to hold down the tiny little fort in Cartago. The dream house being built in Tres Rios was suddenly obtaining superpowers and seemed to be the solution to all their problems. Molly's favorite phrase became, "When we get into the new house, that is going to change." According to Molly, if the water went out in Cartago, which it often would for hours at a time, it would never go out in the new house. If there were fights, they wouldn't have them once they got to the new house. If they had mice, which still happened occasionally, there would be none in the new house. In the old house, you could not take a shower, which was heated by an electric coil, at the same time the dryer was running because it would burn out the fuse and would leave you standing in a cold shower. They would never again have a cold shower in the new house. That very special house was going to solve every one of their problems, hundreds of problems. And though her dreaming was totally unrealistic, at least the dream allowed her to maintain some level of sanity.

Taking the kids to visit the construction site also helped keep spirits up. They were really building. It was true and tangible. She explained each room to them. The kids stood in their bedrooms for pictures when they were just barely marked out by foundation ditches. They stood again when the walls were halfway up. It was exciting to see the progress.

Sometime about halfway through the construction, the "Coke man" called and said that he and four others were coming down to work for a week on the house. This was somewhat of a surprise since construction in Costa Rica was different from the States. It was even a bigger surprise when Molly asked where they would be staying and he said they would be staying with them. Molly explained they had no room, but he insisted they didn't need much room and would be at the construction all day. They did come and were actually a huge blessing, doing anything they were asked to do, the Costa Rican way. As far as sleeping arrangements went, they slept in sleeping bags on the covered front porch. Molly was very impressed with their willingness to sacrifice.

Then came the boxes, boxes, and more boxes. Molly certainly did not want to find herself unprepared when it was time to move and had started to pack months before the proposed completion date, which, of course, was moved to a later date, and a later date, and a later date. There were boxes stacked in every corner and against every wall. Maneuvering through the house was an obstacle course of tiny tots and boxes. Of course, they only put in boxes the things they were sure they would not need until they got to the new house.

Unfortunately, when the moving delays kept growing from a one-month delay to a two-month delay to a three-month delay, Molly found herself daily needing things that were already packed. The boxes were kind of labeled but not with much detail. And so began the daily treasure hunts. If there were three stacked boxes labeled kitchen, the item she wanted was inevitably in the bottom box. Other days were worse. The item couldn't be found in any of the boxes, and on careful reinspection of the utensil drawer, Molly would realize after having looked in boxes for thirty minutes that the item was actually right in front of her nose and hadn't even been packed yet.

Finally, moving day arrived. They found a very nice, very brave lady who was willing to keep the four little girls for the day. That in itself was a tremendous relief. Early in the morning, Polly took the first load in the old VW van. It consisted mostly of bunkbeds and bed frames, which were to be set up early so they wouldn't have to worry about putting beds together late at night. In the first load, there were also two doors. They were headed to a house in which "doors" were still on the "future purchases" list. Molly still had the back door they had removed when they had constructed almost their entire backyard. She also had the door that had divided the house from the schoolroom. She wasn't about to leave the doors behind. Their old back door would be the back door of the new house for now. The other door was for the bathroom that the adults would share; the kids' bathrooms already had stalls built. The two doors from the old house always remained in use in the new house. They became nostalgic for Molly, two relics from their past, a reminder of their humble beginnings.

The older kids stayed and helped with the packing. Two-year-old Doodles was very sick and spent his day lying on a mattress in an empty room sleeping. Every once in a while, he would raise his little head to watch furniture being carried down the hall and then off to sleep again. The goal was to be packed and heading out by about 1:00 p.m. As with all the other goals so far, things took longer than they expected, and they were late. It was around 7:00 p.m. when they were finally pulling away from the old home. Not everything fit into the medium-sized moving van, and they squeezed the last boxes into their VW van together with Grandma, the remaining seven children, Molly, and the dog. Polly went with the movers. Cherry, the little Pekinese-Chihuahua, was supposed to sit on Coodles's lap, but she was all over, very excitedly running between the boxes. Little Doodles was in Buffy's lap very, very still, with no interest in chasing Cherry through the maze of boxes, which is exactly what he would have done at any other time.

Pulling away from the house was a very touching moment for Molly. She looked around the empty living room, then closed the door and turned the key ever so slowly. She placed her hand on the door one last time and gave it a little pat. Bless its little heart; it had done its job for six and a half years. If its walls could talk, they would have more memories to share than any of its inhabitants could possibly have remembered.

Thirty minutes later, they pulled up to the new house, a house almost five times bigger than the house they had just left. At long last, they had their house. Things were already being taken off the moving van that had left shortly before them. Molly paused to look at the house in front of her. It was another touching moment. They really made it. As she walked in, once again, there were boxes everywhere and quite a bit of activity. The little girls showed up within minutes. Two men were still working to put the front doors on, one was working on the electricity, a few more on the plumbing, and one on shelves. There were boxes and furniture all over the big living room and dining room area, children running here and there looking for sheets and pajamas, and adults pushing things in every direction. What a mess! Little Doodles lay still on the couch, watching the excitement. At about 9:30 p.m., his fever started going down, and he was up and wandering from room to room.

Molly thought the workers would never leave, but finally, the last nail was nailed, the last hammer heard, and the workers were gone. At 11:00 p.m., after sending everyone to bed, she plopped down on her bed totally exhausted; they had been on their feet all day long. One of the longest days of her life had finally come to an end. Little Doodles lay on a small bed next to her. He was feeling much better, too much better. He was well rested from having slept all day and seemed to suddenly be wide awake. He was used to sleeping in a pitch-black room without windows. Now he was in a room with a big window, and although it was night, there were no curtains, and the moonlight brightened the room.

"Mommy," he said, "Turn out the light." Molly tried to explain that the light was already turned off, but he just kept asking for the light to be turned off. When he finally gave up on his request, his mind wandered to other topics, "Mommy, window, Mommy house, Coodles, Buffy, Kiffy, Mommy, cookie . . ."

Things didn't go much better for Polly, whose room was on the girls' side of the house. Little Muffy, who was also used to sleeping in a dark room, got out of bed and began wandering around. The moonlight shining in the huge windows was casting scary shadows all around the room. She went from room to room for some time while the other girls kept telling her to go back to bed. When she finally found her way into Polly's room, she woke her up. In her high-pitched voice, which was finally starting to sound more like Spanish and less like Chinese, she told her that she didn't like the new house and asked Polly to take her back to the old house. With weary eyes and an aching body, Polly simply scooted over and scooped her into her bed, leaving the house quiet at last.

Apparently, there were mixed emotions about having a large house. Molly would walk out into the spacious living room area in the morning, hold her hands up high, take a slow deep breath of fresh air, and thank the Lord multiple times. She would repeat the process at odd times during the day when the kids were dispersed among the large bedrooms or massive front porch and Molly was alone and noticing the silence. The smallest ones, though, weren't as happy as the adults. Suddenly, the silence would be broken by a child's cry and the words, "Mommy," and it would be Doodles or Muffy, upset and crying because they could not find Mommy in this much too big of a house. As the days passed, boxes were emptied, and things set right, the little ones began to learn in what places or rooms they might find their mother, and the crying for the old house ended forevermore.

Of course, they found that the new house wasn't the answer to all their problems. They were still without water at times or without electricity at other times. They were also without a telephone for more than four months because the lines didn't extend out that far yet. If anyone had to communicate with them, they left a short message or phone number on their beeper. Then one of them, usually Polly, would walk the four blocks to the nearest pay phone to make the call. The new house had more mice, scorpions, and other creatures than the little house, as it was set smack dab in the middle of an open field in an undeveloped neighborhood. They were also very close to an extremely dangerous area full of crime and drugs. They heard the local rumors that the gangs were just waiting for the rich people to move into their big new house to see what treasures they could steal. Little did the bad guys know that all their most valuable treasures were eternal, safeguarded in heaven and not earthly. They would be more than happy to share with them the treasure of a loving Savior named Jesus Christ, who would save them and change their lives.

Though Molly knew these things just the same, having the house broken into was a scary thought about which she spent too much time worrying. At night, she imagined thieves looking through all their curtainless windows, watching them sleep, and planning their attack. Such silliness! How was it even possible that after watching God do so many miracles to provide them with a nice house, Molly could doubt his power to protect them? As so often happens when we worry instead of trusting the Lord, all the worrying was wasted time and emotions. Apparently, even thieves respected a home for abandoned children, and they never had any problems in that respect.

Yet, without a doubt, the blessings of the new house far outweighed the handful of unsolved problems. Having space to move around was the biggest blessing. It actually did cut the fighting down considerably simply because not everyone was occupying the same space all the time. They all had two big bedrooms in which to choose to play, plus a huge living room, the dining room tables, or the big front porch.

Another blessing was that living close to San Jose made it easier to find extra help, and within a week, they added Dolly to the staff. Dolly was a hardworking Christian lady who began helping with breakfast, lunch, and the laundry. Only Molly knew what a lifesaver and blessing Dolly was as she lifted two big responsibilities off of Molly and freed her up to breathe a little and concentrate more on the schooling. She helped in the home Monday to Friday from 7:00 a.m. to 1:00 p.m. She had a sweet, happy disposition, and all the kids and adults loved her.

Later, as the home grew, the older girls took over the laundry, and Dolly stayed in the kitchen. She stayed with them until well past retirement age. When she could no longer handle a full week, she continued working three days a week, and they added Holly to cover the last two days. Holly was as well-loved as Dolly and a very hard worker who helped out in the area of cleaning as well as in the kitchen. Molly felt blessed to have such wonderful, faithful helpers.

Living closer to San Jose also made traveling easier. It more than cut the trip in half that they were making to church four times a week. It also gave them lots of better shopping options and made errands go twice as fast. Molly was sure that even their old VW van that no longer had to constantly climb the steep hill to Cartago was happy.

Another blessing was the simple fact of becoming better known. They were no longer tucked away in a small community in Cartago but on the outskirts of the capital city. So many people and churches, both in Costa Rica and the States, heard about them through the construction and because of their closer location to the city. It became more common for people to show up on their doorstep with bags full of groceries. Although this meant that they became an open book with people constantly in and out, it also meant for them, as groups began to come and help, hundreds of new forever friends, supporters, and prayer warriors. With new support, children could often have a whole pack of four cookies instead of having to share with someone else. The "five sips and pass it on" rule for Coke became a thing of the past, a story that the first generation would tell whenever they came to visit each succeeding generation, especially when they heard a child complaining.

Nevertheless, finances were still tight. Firstly, there was still the list of doors, painting, shelves, counters, and so on that needed to be finished. Then in 1999, they finally built the badly needed cement wall around the property to protect them from intruders. In 2000 and 2001, they built an open-air gym, and in 2003, the school building and visitors' apartments. Somewhere in there was also the construction of a workshop and guard house. For someone who never wanted to see another construction, Molly sure was getting an eyeful of them; it seemed like they would never end.

In addition to constantly saving up for constructions, there were also many new expenses they had not really considered. There were new salaries to consider, like Dolly and a maintenance man they hired. Both the electric and water bills were very much higher than in the small house. Yes, it would be another ten years before they would begin feeling like they were able to make ends meet, buy a few nice "extras" like special meals, and still have a little left in savings, but the day did indeed come.

Yet, as Molly stood in her new house, breathing deeply and admiring the space, and on and off the peace and quiet, all those other constructions had not yet begun. They were all far in the future together with hundreds of other challenges. Today was for basking in the sheer enjoyment of a spacious house, of windows, of fresh air, of new adventures every day, and of looking forward to seeing what God was going to do next.

[A LESSON TO LEARN: Being in the new house reminded Molly of two verses, one in Psalm 31:8 "Thou hast set my feet in a large room," and the prayer of Jabez in 1 Chronicles 4:10, "Oh that thou wouldest bless me indeed, and enlarge my coast, and that thine hand might be with me, and that thou wouldest keep me from evil, that it may not grieve me!" She realized that as God had enlarged His blessings, He had also entrusted her with greater responsibilities. There would be new challenges that Christ alone would enable her to confront. It would be a day-by-day process, God's grace would always be sufficient, and she would be able to do all that God would give her to do through Christ, who would strengthen her.

Oh, the wisdom of God to have us live our lives on a day-by-day basis. Had Molly been able to see all the trials ahead, it would have overwhelmed her. Christ himself said, "Take therefore no thought for the morrow: for the morrow shall take thought for the things of itself. Sufficient unto the day is the evil thereof." – Matthew 6:34

Are there times when you feel overwhelmed? If you contemplate the future, are there things that worry you? Are you afraid that God will ask for more than you are able to give? Be reminded of God's amazing love for you. He sacrificed His only Son to purchase your redemption. He promises to never put on you more than you will be able to bear as you lean on Him for strength. May God bless each dear reader who is testifying of God's saving grace, His love, and His power through the individual life He has given you to live. Carry on, one day at a time.]

Chapter 7

Growing Pains

Filling the spacious rooms of their big house with new family members would, naturally, be their next mission. Eventually, there would be a total of forty-seven kids through the years who would be considered a permanent part of the family, having spent a good deal of their childhood in the home. In addition, they would house forty-four temporary children for any amount of time from just days to less than four years. The most they would ever have at any given time would be twenty-eight, far too many for Molly to manage comfortably and still try to maintain a family atmosphere versus being simply an institution. They all needed a home environment and special attention. After all, each of these children had a precious soul that needed to learn about God's love for them and Christ's great sacrifice and gift of salvation. Each of them also brought with them their own history of baggage and sorrow, of broken homes and physical and mental sorrow. Oh, that they would understand that Christ was both the answer for their pain and their sins.

Thankfully, the Lord gave them five months to settle in before starting to fill the house, sending them the first new one, a nine-year-old boy named Goodles.

Goodles

A school teacher from Molly's church became concerned about a little boy in her class. She had already bought him a pair of shoes because the worn-out pair he was wearing to school was quite a bit too small. Now the little fellow was coming to school with stories that his grandma was going to give him away. Molly and Polly agreed to go with the teacher on a Saturday afternoon to the child's home and find out what was happening.

When they arrived, the shy little Goodles was sitting on a chair against a faraway wall. He sat very still and quiet, listening as the grandmother explained how difficult he was to deal with and how it was certainly true that they needed a place for him. The child was the son of an illegitimate daughter whom the grandmother had given birth to years before she had married. Now she was married and had a family of four children. Goodles's mother had been the source of years and years of fights between his great-grandmother, who had raised the girl, and his grandmother, who was the birth mother. The girl grew up to be a troubled young adult who had three children, one after another, never took care of them, and eventually ran off and left the children. The family divided the three children amongst themselves, and the grandmother ended up with Goodles.

Though he was the son of their half-sister, the grandmother's other children completely rejected Goodles. They rejected his mother and resented this innocent child for barging into their happy family and expecting to feel welcomed. They refused to make room for him in the house, and thus, he slept on the cement floor in the living room. No matter where he happened to be, he was in the way. All the grandmother's children treated him terribly and wanted him gone. His earthly possessions consisted of a few clothes and two Matchbox cars. They had actually already found a new home for him and had talked him into believing it would be great because they had a swimming pool. He was already packed and was to leave on Monday morning for a large boy's home of close to one hundred children and teens who lived in two large dorms and were cared for by Catholic priests.

The teacher explained to the grandmother all the advantages that Goodles would have at Molly's place, especially the advantage of growing up in something closer to a home environment. They didn't mention it, but they all knew and were thinking that the true biggest advantage would be the opportunity to learn who Christ is, what he did for us, and put his faith in him for salvation as opposed to Goodles's own good works, which were like filthy rags in God's eyes.

When they asked Goodles which home he would like to go to, he said that he supposed the one with the swimming pool would be just fine. Molly spoke up and told him that he shouldn't choose until he had seen their home too and offered to take him right then to see it. When they got home, they made a point to show him the rooms and the children and had the boys pull out their toys to share with him. He was sold. He not only told his grandmother that he chose this home, but he also said he wanted to stay right then, he did not want to go back home with her. Goodles did stay while Polly took the grandmother and grandfather home and brought back the already packed backpack and two Matchbox cars.

Goodles was a very likable, friendly child, not at all difficult to deal with like the grandmother had made them believe. He was also so polite that he left the other children staring at him wide-eyed and with their mouths hanging open. Everything was, "Yes, ma'am," "If you please, ma'am," "Excuse me, ma'am," "Thank you very much, ma'am," and "Can I help you, ma'am?" Molly was so pleased with her miniature gentleman.

After about a week, Molly found his weakness. Goodles was a tattletale, but to his credit, a very polite tattletale. He would say, "Excuse me, but so and so touched such and such," or "Pardon me, but could you please tell so and so not to do such and such because that is dangerous?" It seemed like there was not an hour that passed without some kind of accusation. It must have been his way of squeezing into the family, getting Molly's attention, and letting her know that he was not the bad kid doing the wrong things. Several more weeks later, when he had adapted to his new home and was feeling more comfortable, the tattletales subsided greatly.

Goodles became the most curious of the boys. He liked to take things apart to see how they worked. Sometimes, he could put them back together, and sometimes, he could not. One attempt at dissecting a stuffed toy cow that belonged to one of the little ones did not come out favorably. Goodles was fascinated by the fact that a tiny squeeze of the cow made it moo and vibrate at the same time. He absolutely had to know how it could do that. Unfortunately, it was one of those experiments that he was unable to put back together, and even more unfortunately, it was a favorite toy of both the child and of Molly. It was a failed experiment that was only outdone by his watch experiment.

Goodles got a watch for his tenth birthday. He asked if it was waterproof, and Molly told him that she was sure it was not and that he mustn't get it wet. Goodles was not too sure she was correct and felt that he needed to be sure of that. Less than half an hour after the birthday party, he had filled the bathroom sink with water and tested his hypothesis. As it turned out, Mommy was right; it was not waterproof, and his new watch was ruined.

On the following birthday, understanding who her son was, Molly took the broken radio out of their old VW van and wrapped it up as a gift. Goodles loved it and loved taking it apart without fear of getting in trouble. Some of the parts from the radio helped him build the make-believe cockpit he constructed when he decided he wanted to be a pilot—that was only one of his future plans. At another time, he walked around for days in a suit and tie with a briefcase because he wanted to be a businessman. But the future aspiration that floored everyone was when he decided he wanted to be a soldier in the Nicaraguan army. Molly was sure he was the only Costa Rican in history who wanted to be a Nicaraguan soldier. Nicaragua is one of the most politically and economically troubled and unstable countries in Central America. It was, though, his only "soldier" option since Costa Rica doesn't have an army.

Goodles had a strange streak of bad luck with Easter holidays. It all started the year he wanted to be a farmer and decided to plant beans during his holiday weekend. How was he to know that the home's main waterline was right under the spot he chose to thrust his shovel? A nice big water fountain suddenly burst up out of the ground. Now the curious thing about Costa Rica is that in those days, they took very seriously their Holy Week celebration. Everything, literally everything, closed from 12:00 noon on Thursday until Saturday morning. Oddly enough, the guilty shovel cut the PVC pipe in two on Thursday at approximately 12:15 p.m. Molly got in the car and rushed hither and yon, from hardware store to hardware store, looking for a place that could explain to her what to do and sell her the products to do it. After an unsuccessful hour to find something opened, she returned home and began looking through the workshop they had recently built. She found enough things she had seen others use on pipe repairs and was finally able to complete a temporary fix.

The following year, Molly was very careful to explain to Goodles that he was not to plant anything over the holiday weekend. Oh, for sure, he had learned his lesson, no experiments this year. Goodles decided, instead, to play in the backyard. Well, of course, everyone knows that when a kid plays hard outside for a while, he gets plenty thirsty. But how was a kid to know that he was not to put his full weight on the PVC pipe sticking up out of the ground as he drank from the faucet at the top of the pipe? Molly herself had always thought that pipe was not the best idea ever since the maintenance man had put it in so awkwardly. Snap went the pipe, and swoosh went the water, forming a nice little fountain very similar in size to the one they had seen a year ago. Molly could not believe her eyes. Incredibly, the timing was once again perfect; it was Thursday afternoon.

The break was much more complicated than the former one, and Molly was sure she could not fix it, but she had an idea. First, they turned off the main water valve. Then, she found a long garden hose and screwed it into an old faucet they had used during the construction that was located before the main valve. Next, they unwound the hose across the lawn and then the driveway, onto the porch, through the kitchen window, and into the sink. If anyone needed to shower, they would bring their bucket to the kitchen sink, send someone out to turn on the faucet, and fill up their bucket. The same was true for flushing toilets. There were large plastic bowls in the bathroom for washing hands and pitchers of water in the kitchen for drinking. Washing dishes was easiest of all, straight from the hose. The garden hose helped them throughout the weekend until Monday when Molly could find someone to fix the broken pipe.

The following year, Molly told Goodles he was not allowed to play outside on Easter break, then she added in jest, nor the bathroom, nor at the kitchen sink, and better yet, if he needed a glass of water, he should ask someone to get it for him. There was no problem that year.

Goodles stayed in the home until he was grown and working. In all that time, the grandmother never came to visit and might have called twice because the great-grandmother was calling for Goodles from her sick bed. They were surprised to see the grandmother at their front door shortly after Goodles turned eighteen and began working his first job. That was a pattern they would see quite often, family members searching for abandoned children as soon as they were old enough to work and earn money.

Temporary Teens

After Goodles, there was a host of other children. Although Molly had specified that they wanted children who needed a permanent place to grow up, she found herself accepting special cases. There was an array of different situations, all from desperate people with emergency cases, and all sure that Molly was the answer. There was a time when they were being offered a number of teenage kids. Molly had never considered older children because she felt it was easier to take them in at a young age and have time to work with them. Yet, each teen's story seemed so sad. Molly wanted to help all of them, felt like she could make a difference in their lives, and was so determined to reach out to them with the love of Christ.

One young teenage girl's mother had gotten so mad that she threw a knife at her daughter that stuck in the wall inches from where the daughter was standing. How could Molly turn down a situation like that? Several other teen girls came from similar, though not such drastic, situations. There were also several teenage boys who needed homes. Each teen had a sad story about how they had suffered. It was true that they all came from fairly dysfunctional families, but Molly soon learned that there were always two sides to a story. In most cases, when the truth was finally known, they were rebellious teens who were making life impossible for their single mothers. Of course, it made sense that mothers are not going to willingly hand over an exemplary child who was always ready to lend a hand in the home. In some cases, the mother was trying to teach their child a lesson by giving them away but was usually planning to get them back when they had learned their lessons. In other cases, the teen wanted to leave in search of more freedom or maybe just to hurt the mother's feelings. Rarely did these teens last more than a month or two. Usually, they realized in just a few days that there were more rules in their new situation than they had with their mother. A few weeks later, they were crying and begging for permission to call home. After said phone call, Molly was receiving more phone calls from the mother, followed by negotiations, meetings, more negotiations, packing, tears, and waving goodbye.

Molly would refocus. Their home was for abandoned children, not rebellious teenagers. Certainly, there was a need for homes for rebellious teens, but it was not their ministry. Once refocused, life would return to normal, and suddenly, another phone call, another desperate mother pleading for a chance, promising that this case would be different, and then Molly's decision that it would indeed be different. In would come the teen, and within weeks, there would be the calls, negotiations, packing, tears, and goodbyes. Every single case of teen vs. parent only ended up hurting both Molly and her children. Molly soon realized she did not have the gift of working with troubled teens. None of the ones who came to her were interested in spiritual things. They were interested, though, in sharing tidbits of evil information with Molly's children of what they had done, where they had been, and what they had seen.

One young man decided to teach Molly's boys to steal. They actually didn't need the lesson; they already knew how to steal. Nevertheless, up until this time, the stealing had been limited mostly to stealing someone's candy. Now they were taking it to the next level, stealing food from the pantry, canned goods, mostly cans of tuna fish, crackers, cookies, fruits, anything that looked good. Since they were buying in bulk, the food wasn't missed. Molly did think it strange that her teen boys were not hungry at supper time.

It was Goodles, now a preteen, who finally came to Mommy. His conscious was really bothering him. He asked Mommy to walk around the side of the building and check out the ground outside the boy's windows. In doing so, she found a variety of empty cans and plastic packages of food that had been thrown out of the windows into the rain gutter. There was also something else that really hurt and discouraged Molly, empty cans of Dr. Pepper. Some friends had brought her six cans of the precious commodity that was completely unavailable in Costa Rica. They belonged to Molly and had been hidden in her closet for her to enjoy in private. Apparently, the teens had found them. She counted five cans, and sure enough, there was only one can left in her closet.

Goodles wasn't finished. He took her into Grandma's room, stood on her bed, and reached his hand up to the top of one of the ceiling fan blades. There, taped to the top was a large bill of money. Goodles explained that they were stealing the money from Grandma's purse and taping it to fan blades all over the house so as not to be caught with the money. Once again, there were phone calls, discussions, packing, and goodbyes. The mother admitted she was having serious problems with her sixteen-year-old son. Molly felt they were much too serious for him to be placed in a children's home with young kids, and he returned to his family. In the end, all of the troubled teens who had parents needed to be with their own parents.

That was not the only time, though, that things and money disappeared. Molly found that many kids, though not all of them, had problems with stealing. When they had come into the new house, Molly carried two keys, one to the garage gate and one to the back door. Through the years, more and more things needed to be locked up, and her key ring got heavier and heavier. Adults and kids alike needed locked closets. Money could not be left lying around; it was kept in a safe. The food pantry had to be locked. After constructing the school building, the school classroom of the main house was turned into an even larger pantry and supply room as more and more things were placed under lock and key. This room included a second refrigerator, where they kept anything they didn't want to suddenly disappear. The refrigerator in the kitchen was left with the things they felt sure no one would steal or that the kids were free to take, such as fresh vegetables and leftovers. Eventually, even cameras had to be added.

[A LESSON TO LEARN: All these things depressed Molly. She wanted a family in which everyone could trust everyone else. With each new key, she felt they were becoming more like an institution. The more she thought about it, the more it bothered her. She was falling into the unwise practice that so many parents fall into of comparing—comparing their children to their own childhood. All those thoughts of, "I would never have done that" and "My parents didn't have to lock everything up" flooded her mind. They were wrong thoughts, and the

Bible clearly warns us that comparing is unwise. We have no merits of our own with which to compare ourselves to others. Romans 3:23 describes all of us perfectly when it states, "For all have sinned, and come short of the glory of God." Also, in Romans 3:10, we read, "As it is written, There is none righteous, no, not one." We are all sinners, completely unworthy of God's mercy, lost, and deserving of eternal punishment in hell. Yet the only Worthy One, the sinless, perfect Son of God, superior to all others, took upon Himself the punishment for our sins. Only on His merits and through His blood and finished work on the cross are we made worthy to become sons and daughters of God and inherit eternal life.

Molly was just as guilty of breaking God's laws as were those she condemned in her thoughts. Only her choice to accept Christ's forgiveness and His righteousness gave her Christ's power to live for Him. Her responsibility was not to judge but to pray that others would not only accept Christ but also have the desire to allow Him to live through them. It is a choice that is available to all because Christ died for the whole world. Have you recognized your own unworthiness and lost, sinful condition? Have you put your trust in Christ and His finished work on the cross, making Him your Savior and His righteousness yours? It is all about Christ, not about us. May He shine through our lives!]

Gladdles and Gliddles

In the midst of the teens who were coming and going, Gladdles and Gliddles showed up. They were two brothers, ages four and five, who Molly accepted because of their drastic situation. Their mother was a live-in maid and nanny. She was not allowed to have her children at work with her, so she could only be with them on the weekends. During the week, the children lived with their aunt. The mother never imagined that the boys' older cousin would be abusing them. When she found out, she needed a new place for them immediately.

They were funny little boys who brought joy into the home for two years. The younger one, who was the funniest for a number of little quirks he had, became good friends with Doodles, who was only one year younger. While Molly taught school to the others, Doodles and Gliddles would entertain themselves for hours, running in circles around the living room, chasing each other. Gliddles found that to be ever so funny. Gladdles did not find it at all amusing from his front-row seat in the schoolroom. He wished he could run around with them and was frustrated that he was forced to sit in school studying first-grade materials while others enjoyed life. Doodles and Gliddles did have a few kindergarten materials to study as well but finished quickly.

Gliddles was not really smart at figuring things out, but he was great at memorizing Bible verses. He quoted his verses in the same fashion he spoke in, very slowly and pronouncing each word clearly. The fastest anyone ever heard him speak was the day they drove off and left him at the mall. Molly had a system set up to avoid such accidents, but it failed them that day. Each child had a number. When they got on the bus, Molly was number 1 and would holler out her number to get the count started. Then each kid, in numerical order, would shout out the number assigned to them. It was supposed to be done before starting the car and driving off, but they must have been in a hurry that day. Molly had already pulled out onto the street by the time she bellowed her number one. The counting continued, 2, 3, 4, 5, 6, 7, and silence. Molly repeated 7 . . . but nothing, she yelled louder 7. When no one continued with the number 8, everyone started asking among themselves who the number 8 was. When they finally realized that 8 was little five-year-old Gliddles, Molly was horrified. How could that have happened? They had all left together. She was sure she had just seen him. They turned around as fast as possible, hurrying back. Molly envisioned her small innocent child crotched down somewhere in the mall, bawling his eyes out, scared to death.

As they pulled up to the entrance, they soon saw Gliddles, mad as a hornet, legs spread apart in a firm stance and his hands on his hips. When the door was opened, he stomped on the bus and started bawling everyone out for leaving him. He never even realized that he was supposed to be scared. Molly breathed a sigh of relief; he did not know enough to be scared to death. He was not the only child to ever be left somewhere; there were at least six other occasions when youngsters got left behind.

The boys' mother would come to church once a week to visit with them. After the service, she would go with them to the children's home for lunch and spend the afternoon visiting. Molly was thankful that she opened her heart to the gospel during that time and accepted Christ as her Savior. Unfortunately, toward the end of their two-year stay at the home, their estranged father, who had never been responsible for his boys, showed up and began coming with her. He refused to go into the church but waited for them outside during the entire service. He also refused to go home with them for Sunday dinner. He only wanted to take the kids for the day, bringing them back late at night. Soon, he wanted the boys for the entire weekend and questioned Molly's convictions on raising children, the discipline, the schooling, the rules, and so on.

The situation with Gliddles and Gladdles's father was becoming dangerous. These boys had parents who cared about them; they were not abandoned, and they needed to be with their parents. Then, at the same time, the other kids, who really were abandoned and whose parents had not been in the picture for years, began talking about their parents coming to visit and about going places with them. Doodles asked why they got to have two mothers and if he could too. When Molly encouraged the mother to look for a different job that would allow her to raise her own children, she found that she, too, had been thinking along those lines. A few months later, when she had a new job and a place to live, the boys went back to their mother. The move hit Doodles hardest of all. Gliddles had been his chum for two years; they spent all day long playing together. Doodles had the worst asthma attack of his life days later. Molly felt it was emotional.

With Gladdles and Gliddles gone, there were no more little boys for Doodles to play with. All the other boys were six to twelve years older than Doodles. And that is how it happened that young Doodles skipped several years of childhood and went from being a five-year-old boy to thinking he was a teenager overnight. He was quite the athlete anyway and jumped right into competing side by side with the teens in basketball and soccer, the two prominent sports played in their newly constructed gymnasium. Molly found herself gasping over and over as she watched out the window at tiny Doodles running in and out between the legs of the older kids. Some of the boys were conscious of his small size and would try to protect him. Others felt that if he wanted to play, he'd have to be tough.

Once, Molly glanced out in the middle of a basketball game. Doodles was attempting to guard a boy twice his size, a boy who was not known for his kindness. Suddenly, the boy lurched forward, knocking Doodles flat on his back, and then ran right over him, dragging him several feet before shooting the ball. Molly let out the biggest gasp ever and began running to the rescue, thinking she would have to scrape her precious, crying baby up off the gym floor. Certainly, he must have broken something, and certainly, this was one of those trips to the emergency room. By the time she made it to the gym, he was up and running once again, in and out among the legs of the other boys. They must have warned him that if he wasn't tough, he couldn't play with them.

Joodles and Jiffy

After all the other teens who had come and gone, Molly was a little nervous about bringing Joodles, age twelve, and his sister Jiffy, age eleven, into the home. Nevertheless, their wayward mother had definitely not been involved in their lives for many years, qualifying them as abandoned children. Each child had been living for some time with a different aunt, and each aunt had their own lives and children. They had a much older brother who had been placed in a boy's home long before, and they were eager to find a place for the other two siblings.

The relatives who had Joodles found the home first. That their own flesh and blood were looking for a place for them should have been a red flag to Molly, but Goodles's grandmother hadn't wanted him either, and Molly found him to be an obedient and delightful child despite the curiosity that sometimes got him into predicaments. If Molly had felt any reluctance, it was short-lived. Soon, her heart gave in to Joodles's story of the mean aunt who often left him without food, and he joined their household. Some two months later, as soon as they had shared their finding with the other set of relatives, Molly received a call, and Jiffy was finally reunited with her brother under one roof after having been separated for years.

Joodles came into the house eager to please. He was up early, bathed and dressed, and washing his dirty clothes out in the laundry room utility sink. Molly explained to him that they had washers, and he didn't have to wash his clothes out by hand. He had no idea what a washer was and said he preferred to take care of his own things. After washing his clothes, he swept and mopped his bedroom. Molly was extremely pleased, but she only had that Joodles for about a week or so before he somehow got swapped out for a different Joodles. Soon he was dragging out of bed at the same time as everyone else, and Molly found herself asking him to pick up his dirty clothes and put them in the laundry hamper. She asked him what happened to the Joodles who preferred to take care of his own things, but he just smiled and shrugged his shoulders.

Joodles was an active fellow. By the time he came, Molly had started two hours of traditional teaching time with all the students before they started their regular individual workbooks. Joodles would eagerly offer an answer to any question. His answers were always very long but very wrong, detailed explanations that made Jiffy laugh and everyone else scratch their heads in confusion. He would go around and around with his answer, trying to say something that was somewhat correct and might get a "now you got it" look from Molly, but he seldom ever received that look. He had a happy-go-lucky attitude at school and was getting the lowest grades in the class, probably solely from his lack of effort.

Joodles and Moodles soon became close friends, which really didn't surprise anyone. Sometimes Molly had more hope for Moodles and felt like Joodles was a bad influence, and at other times, she had more hope for Joodles and felt that Moodles was the bad influence. Sometimes, they'd go for days without causing problems, and then they'd get caught in some mischievous plan. The kids now had several bikes, and Moodles and Joodles claimed two of them for themselves. Soon, kids would come in complaining that their bikes weren't working while Moodles and Joodles's bikes were always in tip-top shape. Joodles said it was because they took better care of their bikes.

One day, Coodles pointed out how strange it was that they were fixing up their bikes with lots of neat things they obviously didn't have money to buy. That comment opened up a secret investigation, and Molly soon learned that the pair were hoisting parts off the other kids' bikes and taking them down to the bike shop to exchange for nifty additions to put on their own bikes. Moodles and Joodles also became well known for being mean to everyone else, both boys and girls. Then, right about the time Molly was at her wits' end with them, they would do something kind, something gentlemanly, indeed; they would demonstrate Christian character in such a way that would make Molly reprimand herself for giving up hope on them.

The aunt Jiffy lived with had cared for her for five years. Nevertheless, her husband had been putting on the pressure to find a new place for her because she was giving them problems with lying and stealing. That was nothing new that they had never dealt with; indeed, it was normal human behavior. Jiffy's parents were completely out of the picture, and her aunt could not continue caring for her; she had not had a chance to live with her brother in years, and most importantly, she needed to meet the Savior who could change her life. Molly accepted her.

Jiffy was very friendly and talkative. She completed her chores and responsibilities with no signs of rebellion. She was an intelligent girl and did well in school, though she could have done even better with a little effort. Unfortunately, school was not at the top of her priority list. She was one of those students who believed in doing only as much as was totally necessary to get fairly good grades. She was a great negotiator and knew exactly how to manipulate Molly into getting what she wanted. Molly was happy to please her since she was kind and loving and didn't cause problems. Overall, Molly was happy that God had brought her into the home. Jiffy received Christ as her Savior within weeks of her arrival.

As time went by, though, it was the other kids who taught Molly to take caution in trusting Jiffy. Something would go wrong, and Jiffy would give a long, detailed explanation of what had happened in her sweet, innocent voice. Yet in the midst of her confident story, there would be three or four children standing behind Jiffy, shaking their heads so as to tell Molly that what Jiffy was saying was not true.

Polly Pause

About this time, Polly's life began to take several different directions. The first was due to a love Polly had always had with the idea of traveling. She enjoyed listening to Larry and Paula Neff talk about their different adventures to countries abroad. Finally, when the opportunity arose for her to travel with them to the country of Hungary, she immediately took advantage of it. It turned out to be a life-changing trip. Polly had never known her own father, and her biological mother had died when she was only nine years old, leaving a parental void in her life. During the trip, the three of them bonded to the point of becoming like family. Many years later, the Neffs legally adopted Polly as their daughter.

The second new direction took place when Polly felt, for a number of reasons, that she needed to get away and took a six-month trip to visit some friends in the States. Upon her return, she moved in with her sister who lived in a different area of Costa Rica's Central Valley. There she soon met a wonderful man. They were married in 2001.

The third new direction was after marriage when she opened up her own little five-and-dime type store. Managing the store kept her very busy for seventeen years, but she still found time to dedicate a day or two each week to help the home with grocery shopping and the never-ending list of errands.

Though Polly only lived in the home for approximately ten years, she never stopped being a part of it. After selling her store, she had more time to help in other ways such as keeping the books, looking into legal matters, being a tour guide to visiting groups, and watching the kids whenever Molly needed to make trips to the States. She never stopped caring for the kids individually, giving them spiritual counsel, and doing everything possible to be the best aunt in the world. Molly and Polly, united through Christ, continued to share ups and downs, laughs and fights, likes and dislikes, similarities and differences, and struggles and joys, as dear friends should, for the duration of their ministries in the children's home.

Giffy

Giffy came into the home at eleven years of age. She had been in a government home since age three and had never gone out into adoption. One time, a family had taken her in with plans to adopt her but then returned her to the government only two months later. As she grew older, the social workers were eager to find a place for her and thus offered her to Molly.

At age eleven, the public school system had placed Giffy in a third-grade special education classroom and had labeled her as mentally retarded. Her notebooks were full of line after line of the same simple sounds of ma, me, mi, mo, mu, and nothing more. Molly thought for sure she would have to start from zero with her, but after only a few days of classes, she realized that Giffy already knew how to read, although very, very slowly. Within months, she was reading at a normal pace and had good spelling.

It was soon obvious that though she struggled in some subjects, especially math, there were several areas in which Giffy seemed to be especially gifted. She learned English very quickly, faster than the majority of the children. Also, she could easily memorize the words to verses, songs, poems, and even test questions and answers perfectly. She was extremely talented in the area of music, not only having a beautiful singing voice but was soon playing the piano by ear. She could watch a new video, and within thirty minutes after the video had finished, she would be playing the theme song on the piano.

Eventually, after many years of playing, Giffy volunteered to play the piano at church. There was a small catch, however, to her piano talent. She played everything in the key of C, and unfortunately, not all hymns are written in the key of C. Quite often, the congregation found themselves singing so high they would have to stretch their necks upward just to get a squeak of a note out or so low it seemed they had no neck at all, but that their chins were directly attached to their torso. Nevertheless, she was using her talent, and it made her happy to do so.

It amazed Molly that for years, this child had been labeled and put in a classroom coloring and copying letters with children much younger than herself. Yet, she was very capable of learning. Molly never subjected her to countless tests to determine a proper diagnosis; she felt the social system had already done enough testing and had already failed her with their labels. Now, God had put her in a place where she could develop the talents He had given her as best as she could and work through her weaknesses with the help of her loving Savior and the Word of God.

Despite her talents, it was not very long before everyone realized that there was something different about Giffy. She was very talkative and tried hard to make friends with everyone around her. But the other girls found all the little games she suggested to be quite childish for her age and thus began to push her away. This, though it hurt Molly, didn't seem to faze Giffy; she just kept right on talking. They also found out soon enough that she lacked common sense and was constantly saying and doing silly things. She especially could not stop talking about any certain activity that she knew of ahead of time. If a picnic were in the plans, she would talk about it constantly every day, right up until the day before the picnic. At that point in time, she would suddenly begin to question whether or not there was indeed a picnic in the plans; maybe she had invented it or dreamed it up. She would ask if there was anything interesting planned for the following day, which day would be a good day for a picnic, or ask Molly what she was going to do tomorrow. She seemed to love asking questions to which she already knew the answer. If Molly were cutting up chicken in the kitchen, she would come in several times and ask what was for dinner while staring at the chicken on the cutting board.

Giffy had a knack for remembering birthdays as well. If she ever learned of anyone's birthday, the file was automatically etched on the hard drive of her brain, never to be erased for all eternity. They would sit down for morning devotions, and she would ask Molly if she remembered whose birthday it was. Molly would think for a minute to no avail, and then Giffy would name some visitor who had come to the home for a week several years ago. Molly would be lucky if she could even recognize the name of the visitor, much less the visitor's birthday. Yet, all the dates were in Giffy's brain, and the birthday guessing game was played many times a month, each month of the year.

Besides playing the piano and singing, another favorite thing to do was watching videos. Most of Giffy's conversations were about videos she had seen, explained in great detail. She also enjoyed rocking and would spend hours just rocking in the rocking chair or swinging on the swings in the backyard. At night, she would rock herself to sleep holding tight to a stuffed animal and making little purring noises that bothered everyone else in her room.

Although she refused to help with a meal because she was afraid of knives, Giffy proved to be a good, responsible helper in the kitchen cleanup. She was actually their best kitchen helper unless she was specifically told to be very careful with an object, at which point the object would suddenly slip itself out of her hands or outright jump from her hands, dropping straight to the floor.

One time, the cook sent Giffy to the local minute market to buy eggs, which were sold by weight and put in clear plastic bags to carry home. Giffy tarried to the point that the cook asked Molly what could be keeping her. Molly glanced out the window to find Giffy on the front driveway engaged in a long conversation with someone. When she called out the window for her to hurry because Mrs. Dolly needed the eggs, two pounds of eggs plummeted to the ground.

On another occasion, Molly took Giffy and several other kids with her to the open-air farmer's market to help carry the fruits and vegetables. Molly figured Giffy could handle carrying a bag of tomatoes; that wouldn't weigh too much. She made the mistake, though, of telling Giffy to be extra careful with the tomatoes because they were for Mrs. Neff. Giffy was as careful as could be for about ten seconds, and then plop, the bag was on the ground. Molly, with an exasperated look, picked up the bag of tomatoes, repeated her instructions, and without even pausing to think, handed her the bag a second time. Giffy did better; it was a good twenty seconds before the "plop" sound that announced that the tomatoes were once again on the ground. Molly handed the tomatoes to another child and gave Giffy the lettuce, telling her it was fine if she dropped it, but, of course, she never did.

Giffy did not like change. She believed there was only one place for her to sit while watching videos. Once, someone sat in her place, saying they were there first, and Giffy stormed off to her room, preferring not to watch anything, even though it was one of her favorite pastimes. Molly made the child move, but Giffy would still not come out. Molly made it a rule that nobody could sit in Giffy's "place" anymore. She also picked out one place in the dining room to sit and eat. Everyone knew it was her place, but with the passing of time, one know-it-all child finally took it upon himself to sit in the forbidden spot and was stabbed in the cheek with Giffy's fork. He didn't do it again.

Speaking of Giffy's fork, she would set it out to the left of where her plate would eventually be, hours before a meal. She would also place her empty cup directly above where her plate would go, with the handle pointing toward the invisible plate. The kids soon caught on to the perfect placement plan. They would sneak by and quietly move the fork to the right side of the imaginary plate and turn the cup handle in any other direction. When Giffy walked by, she would look surprised and then quickly put things back in order without ever getting mad or upset. Heaven only knows how long the little game went on before someone finally confessed it to Molly and urged her to try it. Out of unbelief, Molly tried it, found it to be true, and asked the kids to stop their little game. She was saddened that the children were so prone to be cruel to one another, even those they knew were special and needed their patience and understanding.

Soodles and Siffy

During these same years, there were two groups of temporary children who really need to be mentioned as they both left an indelible mark on Molly's memory.

The first of the two groups consisted of a young man named Soodles, age nine, and a teen girl named Siffy, age sixteen. They were street kids who the police had picked up. One of the officers had heard about the Lighthouse Home and was absolutely sure that it would be the best place in the world for the young runaways. Molly had her doubts. The two didn't really know each other; they had just happened to choose the same park to sleep in, and the officers had picked them up together.

Most street kids had drug-addicted parents who would send them out to sell things on the streets instead of sending them to school. That was not the case with Soodles. He did not know who his father was, and his mother had died when he was a baby. His grandparents were raising him, who were old and struggled to keep up with him. They sent him to school on a city bus, which was not uncommon at the time, and trusted that he was attending every day, like every other child would.

One day, however, when Soodles was seven years old, instead of getting off at school, he stayed on the bus and went all the way downtown. He spent all day wandering through the city streets and discovered it was more fun than going to school, so he began to do the same thing every day. After doing this for a while, one night, he didn't return home. Apparently, the grandparents contacted the authorities, but nothing was ever done. Soodles just showed up on his own two weeks later. When he returned, once again they did what they could, but he was a different child now and even harder to control. They even enrolled him in a private Christian school in hopes that they could help him. Unfortunately, Soodles had learned the ropes of living on the streets, and he no longer needed his grandparents or any other adult. He soon found his way back to the streets and would only visit the grandparents every once in a while.

Soodles was a cute, little, dimple-faced fellow. He would roam the street begging for money during the day. He could step through the door of a city bus at any bus stop very cheaply or even for free if the driver let him, walk down the aisle collecting money while the bus was moving, and get off at the back door on the very next stop. At that stop, he would wait for the next bus and do the exact same thing. Many people used the buses, and thus, buses stopped every five to ten minutes. He could quickly collect enough money to go to McDonald's, skating, swimming, or, according to him, even for a day at the amusement park. He thought his life was great. He didn't have to go to school and, more importantly, didn't have to obey anyone. Soodles was his own boss; he had no fear of the streets.

Soodles knew of a popular street ministry where he could get one hot meal a day, and if he made it to their dormitory before the doors closed at 9:00 p.m., he had a bed to sleep in at night. The dormitory was a big room with probably close to one hundred beds. Everyone slept together in one room, homeless men and women, boys, and girls, with a guard on duty and the lights on all night long. Weekends were more difficult because the dormitory was closed on Saturday and Sunday. Everyone was on their own. They would find large pieces of cardboard to cover up with and sleep under the eaves of storefronts, curled tightly in little balls. Soodles said he usually looked for a park with a guard he would convince to keep an eye on him during the night.

Molly tried as hard as she could to understand but just couldn't. How could any young child give up a closet full of clothes, a warm bed, the care-free life of a child, toys, three meals a day, a feeling of belonging, love, and a good education to live with only the clothes on his back under a piece of cardboard in a cold park? But that is exactly what he was doing, and there were countless other street children doing the exact same thing. On top of that, this street ministry that should have been encouraging them to get off the street and helping them look for ways of doing so were actually providing the means for them to remain on the street.

Social services claimed they had taken Soodles and other children off the streets several times and even placed them in homes, but they always escaped and went back to the street. It was the law of the street kid, and their motivation was the freedom they felt. What those children failed to understand was that although guards and older homeless people might look out for the dimple-faced street children now, those same kids would soon be teenagers in an "every man for himself" cruel environment. As a teen, Soodles wouldn't be able to earn his money smiling at folks as he walked down the aisles of public buses because they would just yell at him to get a job, and without schooling, that wasn't going to be easy. He would most likely have to get involved in dangerous and terrible things to earn money, and even then, he would live with the fear of being jumped and having his money stolen from him.

Molly hoped and prayed that Soodles would settle down and stay with them. The government had told her that he had never stayed in any home for more than two weeks. Soodles and Siffy had arrived at the home shortly before Christmas, and Molly used the excitement of the season and the anticipation of Christmas to encourage Soodles to stay. Nevertheless, after only a week, he said he wanted to escape. Molly explained that he was not locked in, they were not a jail, and thus, there was no reason to escape; the front gate was opened, and he could leave whenever he wanted. She did not like the idea of the other children hearing the word *escape*. She added that he needed to think really hard about leaving because the rule was that once you left, you couldn't come back.

Soodles continued insisting on leaving. Feeling sorry for letting him go with no money in his pocket, Molly quietly snuck about three dollars in his hand on his way out, explaining to him that it was his inheritance, and he was never to expect any more. She called a family meeting and explained his decision and why it was a wrong decision. At 12:00 midnight, he was knocking on the front gate, wanting to come back. Molly was torn between two thoughts. She had very clearly told him to think things through because he could not come back. On the other hand, he was just a nine-year-old boy and one who was accustomed to running away at that. How much maturity could she expect from him, and how capable was he of making wise decisions? She was reminded of the story of the prodigal son and how his Father welcomed him home. What if taking him back were to save him from a life of ruin?

After thinking for several minutes, while being stared down by pleading little puppy dog eyes, Molly spoke. She would let him back in if he were willing to receive the discipline for running away, but if it ever happened again, he could definitely not come back. Molly was very serious; thoughts raced in her head of all the children thinking that whenever they wanted, they could just take off, have a good time till midnight, come home, and everything would be fine.

Some days later, Molly learned the whole truth of Soodles's escapade. He was not exactly leaving empty-handed. In addition to the money Molly had given him, he had stolen a necklace from a girl who was coming to help in the home. He had eaten with the money Molly had given him, then sold the necklace and spent the money playing video games all evening.

After that night, it seemed like Soodles was settling into the routine. He made it through Christmas, and it was undoubtedly the best Christmas of his life. He received everything he had asked for and more. His empty closet was suddenly full.

Although Soodles had his moments, he was still a child and much easier to handle than sixteen-year-old Siffy. Her first problem was with lice; she was completely infested with them. Many of the other kids had come to the home with serious problems of all kinds of parasites and lice, but Siffy won the grand prize for the worst case of all. They took her outside to cut her hair as short as possible and then began using every remedy they knew to solve the problem. Even with daily washings and applying solution after solution, it was two weeks before they felt they had conquered the foe.

Besides the lice problem, Siffy was a rough, tough, gangster-looking girl who wore all black and walked, or better yet, stomped along all humped over with her hands in her pockets. All of Molly's other children were afraid of her, and Coodles, who was a teenager by this time, began sleeping with a baseball bat under his bed in case he had to defend himself in the middle of the night.

Of course, Siffy was seriously out of place at church. Since the other girls avoided her and Molly taught Sunday school, she was basically on her own in the teen/adult class. Molly required her children to sit anywhere on the first four rows of the auditorium. Knowing the routine, her other teens had run to occupy the third and fourth rows, which left Molly to guide Siffy to the second row and leave her there by herself.

Halfway through Sunday school, Molly snuck out of her class for a minute to check on Siffy. Searching from the back of the auditorium, she could not see her anywhere. Surprised and worried, Molly made her way down the aisle, frantically searching for her new daughter. She found her right where she had left her, but laying completely stretched out on the second pew, sound asleep. That wasn't the only strange-looking church situation. If the family sang a special in church, all the girls would be fixed up nice, and then there was Siffy at the end of the line, humped over with her hands in her black leather jacket. Sometimes she would kind of move her mouth, but most of the time, she would just stand there as serious as could be.

Within days of arriving at the home, with tears in her eyes, she shared her life story with Molly. It was a terrible story almost too terrible to believe, but Molly did believe it. She believed it partly because of the pain she could clearly see it brought to her, and partly because the story was always the same. She repeated it several other times, but the events never changed like the events did in so many of the made-up stories and lies Molly had so often heard. If Molly tried to ask a question to discredit the story, she always had a reasonable answer.

The government had taken Siffy away from her mother for neglect, and for a number of years, she had been passed from one government home to another. For a while, she was even placed with an aunt but was soon back with the government. When she was twelve years old, she escaped and made it back to her mother to find that she had a three-year-old sister. Though it was not uncommon for her to see her mother drunk, shortly after returning, she witnessed a drunken scene that left a terrible scar on her life. Her mother and a neighbor were sitting at a kitchen table, both very drunk. Two small children, Siffy's sister and the neighbor's child, were playing close by. Somehow, a flimsy cabinet where the children were playing got tipped over, knocking a good number of plates onto the floor and breaking them. The two drunken women began to fight over which child was to blame. As the yelling fight turned into a physical battle between them, Siffy's mother yelled, "Okay, it is my kid's fault," reached for a knife, and plunged it into her poor three-year-old baby girl. Siffy watched her die on the floor.

According to Siffy, her mother was never arrested or tried, but Siffy was immediately sent to live with her father. Two years later, in the middle of a number of family problems, Siffy ran away and began living on the streets. In an effort to survive, she had been in several different gangs, had fought policemen, was an expert thief, and had basically done a little bit of everything wrong and illegal imaginable to earn a little money.

If Siffy's story was not true, being an excellent con artist could be added to her list of accomplishments because Molly's heart went out to her. In Molly's eyes, she should have been so much worse, but though all the kids feared her, she never seemed to pose a threat to them. She herself said that whenever she was in someone's house, she was always grateful and would never steal or fight with them. Sure enough, nothing ever showed up missing that she had taken, and she never hurt anyone.

Truth be known, Siffy would help the little ones whenever she could and, on one occasion, actually protected the teens. It all came about the night Molly's teens asked to go with a group from church to an annual Christmas parade of lights downtown. Molly wasn't too excited about them going downtown at night but consented since they would be in a group with other Christian teens. The streets were packed with people, everyone pushing and shoving. The kids said that Siffy felt right at home, like they had never seen her before, pushing, shoving, and cussing out anyone who got near Molly's teens. They had their own personal bodyguard. Suddenly, Buffy began screaming at the top of her lungs, and everyone turned to see an old homeless man, dirty and drunken, leaning on her shoulder. The poor man never knew what hit him, but everyone else clearly saw Siffy grab him with both hands and fling him to the ground. Siffy came home all excited, her adrenaline touching the ceiling. Everyone else was wide-eyed and shaking. Each one said they never wanted to go to the light parade again.

Although Siffy never hurt anyone, she followed Molly around the house like a little puppy. She wanted to be with her constantly. Molly didn't have a moment to herself, and all her other work began piling up. Her story had touched Molly. She was convinced that she had never been shown the love of God, and Molly was determined to show her that a life with Christ in it was different. That was not to be an easy task. It would require Molly to develop, almost overnight, more patience than she had ever shown in her entire life. All of Molly's other children shook their heads in unbelief at Molly's patience with her. Dolly, the cook, told Molly that if there were a crown in heaven for patience, she had won it with only this teen.

Siffy constantly bothered Molly with her teasing. If Molly were bringing a cup to her mouth to take a drink, Siffy would grab the glass and hang on to it, preventing Molly from taking a drink. In the same way, she would grab her fork and prevent her from taking a bite of food. If Molly were ironing, she would take the iron away from her and act like she was going to burn her. If she were cutting something up in the kitchen, she would grab both the knife and Molly's hand and start forcing them toward Molly's throat. Although these little games worried Molly a tad, she never showed fear, not because she wasn't afraid but because she had heard that showing fear in such situations was the worst thing you could do. Instead, Molly would laugh it off and tell Siffy to stop goofing off.

Siffy also seemed determined to break things. Any time that Molly was on the telephone, Siffy would begin tickling her, preventing Molly from carrying on a normal conversation. Once, the telephone battle became so intense that the entire huge telephone/fax machine fell off the desk and broke. She would grab Molly's camera out of her drawer and begin snapping picture after picture of absolutely nothing, touching every button and turning every dial. She would sit down at the computer and begin hitting keys like crazy with all ten fingers at the same time. At evening devotions, she would wait until Molly began talking and then start banging on the piano. Molly would call her down, she would stop, then Molly would start over, and Siffy would begin banging again up to four or five times a night.

Their thirty-passenger bus was another of Siffy's favorite toys. Oftentimes, Molly would have no other choice than to take the whole gang with her on errands. On such occasions, and especially with quick errands, it was easier and faster to leave the kids waiting on the bus rather than to have seventeen kids traipsing behind Molly. But Siffy found sitting still in the bus for more than thirty seconds quite boring and would seize the opportunity to familiarize herself with all the cute little gadgets with which drivers get to play. Molly returned to the bus minutes later to find all her children lined up against the side of the bus, eyes wide in panic, with the bigger kids protectively clutching the younger ones. Apparently, even though Molly had been careful to take the keys with her and put the emergency brake on, as soon as Siffy sat in the driver's seat, everyone bailed in fear. Molly warned Siffy about it several times and added not parking on a hill to her list of precautions, and yet Siffy continued taking the driver's seat and playing with lights, blinkers, horns, steering wheels, and windshield wipers. Likewise, the other children continued to bail out of the bus and line up along the side of the bus, afraid of its rolling off with Siffy in the driver's seat.

Then it happened. One Sunday morning shortly before leaving for church, Siffy must have felt that she was ready for her first driver's lesson. Fortunately, the bus was tightly parked in the carport, and no children were on board or standing in front of the bus. Siffy snuck the keys out of Molly's room and climbed on board. She claimed that all she was trying to do was to start the bus up, certainly to save Molly the trouble. Unfortunately, she knew nothing about pushing the clutch in on a manual transmission, so when she turned the key, the bus lurched forward, hitting the front wall of the house and leaving nice little dents in both the wall and the front of the bus. That was the first and only time Molly ever saw a look of shock on Siffy's face, but at least that was the last time she messed with the bus.

Things finally came to a point where Molly felt she had to discipline her. It all came about when Molly was passing out the clean clothes. The routine was to fold the clothes and stack them neatly on the couch, then call everyone together and pass them out to the owners to be placed in their drawers and closets. Siffy was grabbing the nicely folded clothes, messing them up, and throwing them on the ground. Kids were picking up the clothes, folding them a second time, and putting them back on the couch to be flung to the floor again. Molly spoke several times, warning her that she would be punished. No amount of reasoning was getting through to her.

Molly knew she could not allow this kind of behavior to continue. She had to follow through with the discipline, but neither one of them was going to enjoy it. There were several forms of discipline, and Molly mentally checked off her options. If she sent her to the corner, she was not going to go or stay there. There were no privileges or activities Siffy enjoyed that she could take away from her. She was not going to cooperate with writing one hundred sentences on obedience. Molly opted for a form of discipline that the government allowed at that time, corporal punishment without physical abuse. It is a form of discipline approved by God in Proverbs 23:13–14, "Withhold not correction from the child: for if thou beatest him with the rod, he shall not die. Thou shalt beat him with the rod, and shalt deliver his soul from hell." Also, Proverbs 29:15 says, "The rod and reproof give wisdom: but a child left to himself bringeth his mother to shame."

Siffy followed Molly into the bedroom, but of course, refused to cooperate. Molly wanted to be firm but knew that letting Christ be in control was the most important. She wanted Siffy to see that godly discipline did not include out-of-control abusive anger. Molly talked, explained the discipline procedure, and asked her to lean over the bed. Of course, that did not happen. Molly felt it was important to win this particular battle and asked some boys to help hold her still. It took three teenage boys to hold her down just long enough for two little swats. It looked like a police fight going on right there on the bed.

After the discipline, Molly immediately told the boys to let her go but to remain in the room with Molly. Siffy jumped to the floor on the opposite side of the bed, crying. Molly gave her time to settle down. While she wept softly, Molly explained that obedience was important but that the punishment was over, and she just wanted to pray with her, and they could go finish passing out the clothes. Siffy said nothing but seemed to have calmed down. Molly climbed over the ruffled covers, sat on the bed right next to where Siffy sat on the floor, and put her arm around her. Suddenly, Siffy reared up and, with the back of her hand, whacked Molly so hard in the chest that she fell back on the bed. Molly scurried to get up, moved to the other side of the room, and told her that maybe it would be better to pray from there. She had obviously failed to establish herself as an authority to be respected, but she felt she had made her obedience point in a God-honoring fashion, and that was what most mattered. She prayed and started to leave the room.

When Molly opened the door, Soodles met her and asked if he could talk to Siffy. Molly nodded and motioned him into the room. That little nine-year-old boy began bawling her out, telling her that she had gotten what she deserved and to stop being such a bully and such a crybaby. Then he proceeded to preach to her. Molly had been giving simple salvation stories in the evening devotions, and Soodles began retelling the same stories, telling her that they both needed Christ in their hearts. To Molly's surprise, Siffy agreed with him. Though only

God knows their hearts, both of them recognized their sinful condition and claimed to have taken Christ as their Savior that night. Molly was pleased with the sudden turn of events the first discipline attempt had taken. Siffy never played the clean clothes on the floor trick again, but all the other constant teasing continued.

It was quite remarkable, though, that as rough as Siffy was, every single night she would wait until everyone else was in bed and then go to Molly's room and ask her to pray for her. The night of her discipline was no exception to the rule; there she was, faithful to the habit that she herself had started. On two separate occasions, she had even taken a turn to pray, and both prayers had been quite touching. After the prayer, she insisted that Molly walk her to her room. At the door, Siffy would turn and give Molly a big hug and tell her she loved her before disappearing into the dark room.

It must have been these small gestures of tenderness that gave Molly patience with Siffy, or maybe Molly just knew in her heart that she would probably not be with them for long and wanted her to take happy memories with her of her stay in a Christian home. One thing for sure, Siffy was starving for attention, and since she was looking for it in Molly, Molly was determined to direct her attention toward Christ as often as possible, and that included being patient.

One evening, Siffy even told Molly that the reason she was so mean and teased her so much was because she was too nice. She said that if Molly would only cuss her out and slap her in the face as her mother had always done, she would be good and leave her alone. Molly could never treat her like that, but she was glad that Siffy had noticed a difference in her. Molly's goal was to show Siffy that Christ loved her, and she hoped to demonstrate that love through her own actions of patience and concern. Siffy also told Molly that she had no business taking in street kids; she wasn't "street kid material." It was very dangerous, and she never wanted Molly to take in another kid off the street. Molly was inclined to agree.

Then, amid the Siffy chaos and while Molly was struggling to stay afloat with this new, far-from-normal situation, a second situation unexpectedly raised its ugly head. As it turned out, Molly's first generation of teens were enjoying a little too much their new freedom of riding the city bus to young people's meetings. Molly had thought of it as a win-win situation. It saved Molly from having to drive them to and from the meeting, and it gave them a little independence. It didn't seem dangerous in any way since they were instructed to stay together, being a group of nine by this time. In Molly's mind, if anyone were doing anything wrong, certainly one of the others would let her know about that. Nevertheless, this was, after all, her first generation of teens, and she was unaware of the shift in tattling that occurred when passing from childhood years to teenage years. Most teens were not only too self-conscious to be the bad guy telling on his siblings, but they also maintained an "I won't tell what you're doing if you won't tell what I'm doing" policy among themselves. Thus, it might not have been the win-win situation that Molly thought it to be.

Fortunately, church members who cared about Molly's teens and knew that they did not have permission for girlfriend/boyfriend relationships before the age of eighteen became Molly's long-distance eyes. After catching a couple of her teens on street corners in scenes that were obviously more than friendly conversation, one man reported his sightings to the pastor of the church. Thus, it happened that Molly got on the bus to drive home from church only to find a group of serious, disgruntled teens mumbling and whispering among themselves all the way home. What on earth was going on? Everyone had been fine on the drive to church; why the sudden change? Apparently, the pastor had warned them strongly through the window right before Molly boarded the bus.

By the time they arrived home, a group of four teens were calling a family meeting, a privilege that normally belonged to Molly. In the meeting, they told Molly that they were tired of the pressure of being called "Molly's kids," with everyone expecting them to be so much better than the other teens for being missionary kids. They were also tired of the rules. If Molly didn't change the rules, they were running away from home. There were only two rules they wanted to change. They wanted to have boyfriends and girlfriends, two of them were thirteen years old, and two of them had just turned sixteen years old. Molly had a house full of children whose parents were mommies and daddies at ages fifteen or sixteen, and she wasn't willing to start trying to control childhood romances. The other rule they wanted to change was they wanted freedom to come and go as they pleased, staying out late with their friends if they wanted to, and going places without Molly's having to know where they were and what they were doing. To Molly, their logic that all the other teens had their freedom didn't seem very logical and was probably not totally true.

Molly was absolutely devastated. What was happening to their family? It was a bomb that had exploded out of nowhere and without warning. In Molly's heart, they had always been a family. They had their ups and downs like any family, but families stuck together. Now she found out that they apparently felt no family loyalty to her; she was not their mother. They even let her know, in no uncertain terms, that although she might have thought she was or might have wanted to be, she was not. She was simply someone who was taking care of them for a while. Their timing also devastated Molly. Here she was trying so hard to show Siffy the love there was in a Christian home; how could they be so insensitive?

Molly just couldn't speak to them like she had spoken to Soodles, telling them they were free to go. Soodles was a street boy who had only been with them for weeks and was known for not staying anywhere for very long. These children had been with her for years; they were part of the family, and they absolutely didn't have anywhere to go, even though they might have thought they did. The people they thought they could go live with were the very people who had turned them over to Molly because they couldn't keep them. Molly talked and cried and talked and cried for a long time. The talks and the attitudes carried on into the next day as they awaited Molly's answer as to the rules. She assured them that she loved them and spoke of the importance of loyalty, but in every meeting, the four rebels sat on the sofa side by side with their arms crossed and a cold expression on their faces. When she made some phone calls seeking Christian counsel, she was told that if she didn't change her rules, she was probably going to lose her whole family. Yet, God's Spirit in her told her that if she DID change the rules, she would probably lose her whole family.

Nothing was decided on the second night, and everyone finally went off to bed—everyone except Molly, who stayed up well into the night and early morning, praying and crying. She remembered a resource she had read of analogies between raising children and lion training. God used it to strengthen and guide her. He spoke to her heart, and she dried her tears. She knew she had to at least act strong and do what was right, even if she didn't feel strong.

The next morning at devotions, there were neither tears nor fear shown. Molly walked out with her only two but most faithful "lion training" tools, an old-fashioned paddle and her Bible. The paddle was set on the table, but the Bible was kept in her hand. She told her precious children that though she was very tired, she still held her sword in her hand and would not give up fighting for them; God's Word would rule. She said that she had prayed about changing the rules, but God had not given her a feeling of peace about it, and if it were between pleasing them or God, she must please God. She had never been a better actress. She was still more torn up inside than they could possibly imagine, yet she continued on with their morning devotions and prayer. Molly waited throughout the day to see what the teenagers would do. Yet, they never did anything; the whole issue just ended there, vanished into thin air as though it had been a bad dream.

Unfortunately, the entire episode hardened Molly's heart in some strange way and made her quite skeptical. How could they turn on her so quickly, so harshly? Molly's consolation was that she never felt outnumbered or lonely throughout the incident. Not only did she feel that the Lord helped and comforted her, but all the other children also rallied around her with notes, hugs, and words of kindness; they recognized she needed it. Surprisingly, Siffy, the girl who had received less at Molly's hand and had more motives for becoming rebellious, was one of the kids who came to her side with kind words and a hug. Siffy even wrote her a letter, telling her what a great mom she was and thanking her for all she had done, go figure.

Yet, Siffy was only with them for a week or so longer when she came to Molly and told her she wanted to go back to the street ministry where she had been living in one of their permanent homes. There she had been allowed to come and go as she pleased but had been kicked out for coming home drunk and told that she could return in a month. The month was over, and she was eager to get back. It was that craving for freedom—she had been her own boss for years now—and it was time for her to move on with her life once again. She wasn't rebellious; she just knew she would never fit in, and Molly knew she needed to let her go. Molly agreed to take her to the ministry's main office the following morning.

The next morning, Molly called her into her room for a last prayer. But Siffy was in a teasing mood, and it was not to be a good prayer meeting. Siffy picked up a pair of scissors and made button marks at perfect intervals with one of the sharp points of the scissors where buttons didn't exist from Molly's throat down to her stomach and back up again. Molly opted to make it a short prayer and took Siffy to where she wanted to go.

When Molly returned home, she spent a good number of hours trying to catch up on all the work in which she had fallen behind. When she finished, she glanced at her watch. The kids were watching a video, it was only 7:00 p.m., and Molly didn't know what else to do with herself. She sat down, took a deep breath, and lingered in the marvelous feeling of having nothing urgent to do. With all kinds of time on her hands before bedtime, she just sat and sat, did nothing, and enjoyed every minute of it.

Sadly, Molly never saw Siffy again, but she felt like she had done everything that she could possibly do for her. She was sure that the seed of the Word of God had been planted and prayed that it might someday bear fruit. She had been with them for only a month, but it had seemed like a year.

Soodles stayed with them for two more weeks after Siffy left. On the day he disappeared, the kids had been playing hide-n-seek outside. Soodles hid so well that they never found him. He left all his new clothes and toys behind and took with him only the clothes he was wearing and about ten dollars he had stolen.

Close to two years later, Molly received a phone call from a social worker. She had a young drug addict by the name of Soodles who said he wanted to be placed in Molly's drug rehabilitation center. Molly explained that they were not a drug rehab center. Shortly afterward, some missionaries who visited the home were actively working in one of the many street ministries that Soodles had named and talked about. Molly asked them if they had ever heard of a boy named Soodles. The Soodles they knew fit the description perfectly. They said he had given a very large sum of money to one of the missionary ladies to keep for him. When they questioned him as to where he got it, he confessed that some women who prostitute little boys had given it to him. They told Molly that the things he said he had done to earn the money were too embarrassing to explain.

Strangely enough, Soodles showed up at Molly's front door one more time. He was serious; he would do anything to stay with them, and he was willing to change. Molly confronted him about the things she had heard and felt he was lying when he denied it all. She told him she could not give him an answer without her pastor's approval, but he could stay for a few days until she could talk to the pastor. He stayed in the house for two days, but even in that short time, he had caused several problems among the other children, and Molly really did not feel good about his being there.

By this time, Soodles was almost fourteen years old and knew too much about the street. Molly knew he was a huge risk for the other children; he could hurt them in a number of ways. Molly liked her pastor's decision. He told Soodles that the church would need a month to pray about his return to the home. Meanwhile, Soodles was to be in church every Sunday morning. The pastor drove him back to the street ministry where he had been staying. He came to church for three weeks in a row. Molly was getting nervous. She still didn't have peace about him, but then he didn't return on the fourth Sunday, and they never saw him again. Molly never knew and never asked anyone if he quit coming because the pastor had given him a negative answer or if he just got tired of waiting for an answer and moved on with his hobo lifestyle. Either way, she felt relieved with the way the Lord had worked things out; He knew what she could and could not handle.

Laffy, Liffy, Luffy, and Loodles

The second indelible mark was through another grandmother in another local church. The mother had run off for the umpteenth time and left her children. This time, she had left them at the daycare; she simply never picked them up. The daycare turned the children over to the government, and the government, which by now was quite familiar with their case, took them to the grandmother. Now the grandmother was asking Molly to take them. The siblings consisted of three girls, Laffy, age eleven; Liffy, age five; and little Luffy, age four; and one boy, Loodles, who was nine years old. They were the wildest group of youngsters Molly had ever seen. Their arrival only two days after Soodles left didn't leave Molly very long to recuperate. Adding four new kids to the home took their number up to twenty-one children.

Laffy was a chubby little girl who would steal food off her little sisters' plates after finishing off her own piled-high plate. She was constantly fighting with all the other children. A minimum of four times a day, she would tell Molly she needed to talk to her in private. The private meetings were always the same. She was trying so hard to get along with everyone, but they were constantly fighting and all hated her. Every Sunday, she would corner a different unsuspecting adult and begin to literally cry, with real tears, as she told them what a terrible life she had and how everyone in the children's home was mean to her. After finishing her little drama, she would blatantly invite herself over to their house for Sunday dinner.

One Sunday morning, without Molly's knowledge, she asked the pastor of the church if she could give a testimony. Molly's heart began to race as she watched her newest young charge climb the stairs of the platform. This was probably not going to be good. She asked the church to pray for her because her life was so difficult, and everyone in the home was so mean and unfair to her. She went on to say that she was trying so very hard to be good and please everyone. She felt like she might be improving because she had only been disciplined by "Mommy Molly" on two occasions that week, which was a huge improvement. Needless to say, "Mommy Molly" wanted to crawl under the pew and disappear. Molly, who had been feeling pretty good about herself and how patient she had been with Siffy, had an abrupt awakening of how miserably impatient she really was. She could not handle her "poor me" attitude and brushed off her complaints without an ounce of sympathy or compassion. Laffy was, without a doubt, a failed lesson in patience.

Laffy's little brother, Loodles, was a tad bit easier to handle. Unlike his sister, he was a happy little boy who, like most boys, loved to play in an active sort of way. He was, however, the loudest kid Molly had ever heard. It seemed impossible for his vocal cords to restrain themselves. The child was a human megaphone and must have heard the words "keep it down" one hundred times a day from everyone around him. Even the other children, who were normally oblivious to loud noises around them, were shushing him all day long.

Loodles had two other annoying habits. The first was walking down the aisle at church begging for money. The second, even more annoying, was snatching cell phones off men's belts, where they hung in those days, and running off with them. Molly found herself searching through Sunday school classrooms for the little culprit only to march him to the victim, have him apologize, and five minutes later, start the hunt again when another victim came complaining to her. Sometimes he would hit up the same victim two or three times on the same Sunday morning. Apparently, the thrill of a successful steal outweighed the pain of the consequences because the problem continued.

Liffy, the five-year-old sibling, loved to color. She colored on the walls almost every day, except on the days she chose to color on the floor, or the day she scribbled all over the sofa with a black permanent magic marker. And then there was tiny four-year-old Luffy, who was the quietest and best behaved of the group. Unfortunately, in a sweet little voice, she was a walking dictionary of dirty words and their definitions. Molly learned a few new Spanish words from her, as did all the younger children.

The group had been with Molly for eight long, difficult months when she received a phone call from the mother. She wanted to get her life right and desperately needed her children back. Molly encouraged her in that decision, as she also desperately needed for her to take her children back. The children talked about their mother often and expected her to come back since she had been pulling the disappearing and reappearing act on them for some time. Within days, she came to pick them up, and Molly sighed a sigh of relief.

A few months later, the mother called, wanting Molly to take Laffy, Liffy, Luffy, and Loodles back again. Molly refused to have a part in her selfish back-and-forth games that were destroying her children. After several more phone calls, Molly referred her to her pastor for his approval, but not without first letting her pastor know she didn't want to be involved. Finally, the phone calls ended.

These two notable groups of kids and the teen rebellion all took place from December 1999 through August 2000. During that same period of time, Molly had been promised another newborn baby, had waited for months for the baby to be born, had prepared and even picked out a name, and had finally come to the conclusion that the baby had never existed. It was a situation that had no logical explanation; there just was no baby after all. It had definitely been a year of riding an emotional roller coaster. She still loved the ministry that God had given her and still felt she was at the center of God's will for her life, but at the same time, she felt like she had been through the hardest year of her ministry. God knew that too and, in his special way of intimately knowing what each of his children need, sent Molly a special gift at the end of that same difficult year. It was a life-changing gift in the form of a little boy named Dito.

[A LESSON TO LEARN: God will guide each of us down many different paths and avenues. Sometimes, we may clearly see His hand, and other times, we won't understand what He is trying to accomplish. Yet we can lean on Romans 8:28, which says, "And we know that all things work together for good to them that love God, to them who are the called according to his purpose." Sometimes, it might take years before we understand the whys. Maybe God is allowing a difficult time as a means of ministering to others later. Or sometimes, things that seem so unbearable will later be just sweet, laughable memories. Whatever the case may be, God knows best, and he will always be there for his children.]

Chapter 8

Betsy

Molly had been without a vehicle for the first four years that she was in Costa Rica. Even after Biffy, Buffy, and Boodles arrived, they did not have a vehicle and were traveling everywhere on the public bus system. Yet within a month of their arrival, the Heflins, who had given them their first little house, offered them a twenty-year-old VW van that they fondly named Betsy.

After four years of not driving, Molly was slightly anxious the first time she sat behind Betsy's steering wheel. Several other things added to her anxiety. The Costa Rican streets were full of potholes that needed to be dodged, and she only knew the bus routes. More cars were being driven than there were roads to drive down, making San Jose bumper-to-bumper traffic, and Costa Rican drivers often did unethical things like stopping in the middle of the street to chitchat with someone in the car next to them or turning right from the far left-hand lane, and so on. When Molly expressed these concerns to Polly, she very politely told her to shut up and drive.

When their first test drive took them down a street loaded with holes, Polly gave Molly an exasperated look as the car jostled back and forth and bumped up and down from hole to hole. Molly apologized that it was impossible to HIT every hole, meaning that it was impossible to MISS every hole. Ironically, what came out of her mouth in her confusion was a much more accurate statement; there were undoubtedly too many holes to hit them all. Eager to get off that particular street, Molly turned the corner only to find that she was traveling the wrong way down a one-way road. She also noted that all the other drivers must not have been too happy about it as they would not stop honking their horns. In her frustration, Molly said she didn't know how to drive in Costa Rica and that they might as well take the van back. Polly blurted out that there was no way that was happening and to just keep driving straight ahead. They eventually made it home, where Molly collapsed on the couch, happy to be alive. It wasn't long before Molly grew accustomed to the roads, potholes, the fun little dodging game they provided, and all of Betsy's little quirks.

Betsy had her own personality. If she were in a peppy mood, she would start right up. If she was feeling lazy, all the kids would have to get out and push so Molly could jump-start her. She was a teaser also. Whenever Molly would turn left, Betsy would tease the people or other cars on the street corners by honking very loudly at them. It happened with every single left-hand turn. Many of them didn't take too kindly to the teasing and would yell unkind things back at her. If someone in the front passenger seat were trying to roll the window up, she would tease them by letting the window get within inches of the top and then drop right down out of sight, time after time.

Being old, Betsy was quite persnickety and was constantly breaking down. The Heflins had a favorite mechanic for her who knew her medical history. Any breakdown along the road consisted of walking to a pay phone, calling Brother Heflin, who, in turn, would call the mechanic, and waiting on the roadside until he arrived. Molly began paying attention and saw that he was always tinkering and banging on the same side back behind the motor. When she asked him, he showed her some cables that he said would sometimes come loose from bumping down the road. Molly put a hammer in the glove compartment, and the next time the van broke down, she got her hammer out, banged for a while, and got back in the van. It started right up, and Boodles yelled with glee that Mommy was a mechanic. That handy hammer saved them many a search for a pay phone and long waits for the mechanic.

Betsy also had a problem with flat tires. Molly didn't purposely search out the nails in the road, but Betsy seemed to be drawn to them like a magnet. Molly had never in her life heard of a car having as many flat tires as Betsy did. Molly and Polly became experts at changing tires. It seemed like hardly a month would go by that they didn't get to practice their newfound tire-changing skills.

There was one flat tire incident that would never be forgotten. They were still living in the old house and hardly ever got a chance to get away. However, a group of missionary ladies began having a once-a-month missionary breakfast and invited them to join the group. By getting their neighbor to watch the kids on those mornings, they began attending and enjoying the short little time of fellowship and a buffet breakfast at a nice hotel in San Jose.

On one particular month, they weren't even a mile down the road from the house when Betsy decided to get a flat tire. Fortunately, they had a spare and scurried to change the tire so as not to miss their once-a-month special day. Unfortunately, to their dismay, after changing the tire, they watched the spare tire flatten out like a pancake at the buffet breakfast as they lowered the vehicle. However, at that precise minute, a man they knew from church came by and, seeing their predicament, flagged down a taxi and loaded up the first tire to take it somewhere and patch it up.

While waiting for him to return, they considered forgetting the breakfast getaway as they were certainly going to be late. But finding a babysitter was no small feat, and getting a morning away from the kids was, for Molly, only a once-a-month occurrence she wasn't going to surrender without putting up a fight. So, they waited, and fortunately, when he came back, he stayed long enough to do the second tire change for them. After putting the flat spare in the back of the car, he turned the key a little too hard and twisted it almost to a breaking point. There was no way they were going to be able to get the key into the ignition without it breaking entirely off. The man felt so bad that he flagged down another taxi to take the key to a locksmith. Unfortunately, as was often the case when making a copy of a key, the new key did not work.

Their Good Samaritan was not going to surrender without putting up a fight either, and before they knew it, he had flagged down a third taxi and was off in a flash. When he returned, he had the locksmith with him, toolbox and all. He filed the key and tried it, then filed some more and tried it again. With each new fortunate and unfortunate situation, Molly and Polly laughed louder. They had come too far to turn back now. Finally, the key worked. They waved goodbye to the Good Samaritan and his new friend the locksmith and sped off to the breakfast, laughing the whole way.

By the time they arrived, there were only ten minutes left before the buffet would close, so Molly and Polly hurried to the line, scooping onto their plates the last spoonfuls of the precious morsels that their taste buds had so looked forward to having. A few of their favorites were no longer available, but they were just glad to have made it on time to eat. The other ladies had long finished eating but, of course, had not finished chatting. They expressed that they had been worried about them and enjoyed listening to their morning adventure.

As time went on, it seemed like every possible breakdown that a car could have, Betsy had. They replaced this and that, and still, she would trudge along as best as possible. Between the breakdowns and the flat tires, they never knew when they left the house if and when they would arrive at their final destination.

One day, as everyone was heading out to the car, Molly saw Coodles heading back into the house. When she asked him where he was going, he replied that he was going to get a book in case Betsy broke down along the way. When he returned to the van, he was carrying the "M" encyclopedia, which was one of the thickest volumes. Oh, how well he knew Betsy! After that, each time they left the house, it was a different volume but always one of the thickest ones.

When the group from the States came to help with the construction, Polly wanted them to taste Costa Rica's fresh pineapple, so she hopped in Betsy for a quick trip up to the Cartago open market. It was only a ten-minute trip into town, and Betsy certainly could handle that without some major upset. Yet, as time passed and Polly did not return, Molly began to wonder. Then, the phone rang. Polly said that Molly would never believe what had happened to Betsy. Molly told Polly to go ahead and give her the news because she would believe anything from Betsy. Polly told Molly that the motor fell out in the middle of the street. Molly told Polly that she couldn't believe it. Polly told Molly that it was true.

An hour later, when the tow truck finally pulled up with Betsy, they heard the whole story. Polly was stopped at a light on one of the busiest downtown Cartago streets. When she tried to shift into first gear because the light had changed, she heard a huge clunk, and the car stalled. As she tried in vain to start the car again, she noticed people on the street pointing toward the back of the van with shocked looks. Finally, she got out to see what all the commotion was. There lay Betsy's motor in the middle of the street. By this time, the cars behind her were impatiently honking. One grumpy old man was hollering at Polly to get that piece of junk out of the street. Polly asked him how he suggested she do that. Molly was glad she had missed that particular breakdown because frustrated people frustrated her. Polly, on the other hand, could hold her own in frustrating situations. She waved people around the van until the tow truck could come tie the motor into place with an old rope and haul poor, tired, and extremely offended Betsy home.

Each of the American visitors had his own solution to fixing the problem. Every answer to the problem sounded extremely complicated and expensive. Yet, they all agreed on one thing: the repair would take days if not weeks. But since Betsy belonged to Brother Heflin, the first thing they did was to call him. He had Betsy towed to her faithful mechanic, and to everyone's surprise, the mechanic brought her back the following morning all fixed up. The bar across the bottom that supported the motor simply rusted out and broke. The mechanic just welded in new support rods, and the problem was solved. It may be important to note that the pineapple was great, the best their guests had ever tasted. Mission accomplished, Betsy!

Betsy had the privilege of being towed many other times. On the craziest of them all, Betsy was actually in perfect health and running fine. Molly and Polly were driving through downtown Cartago with the first four kids, Biffy, Buffy, Boodles, and Coodles. Molly had been looking for a file cabinet and noticed one in the window of an office supply. Looking for a parking spot and walking back to the store with four kids in tow sounded complicated, so Polly suggested she just pull over long enough for Polly to run in and price the file cabinet. That sounded great, and she pulled over to the curb and left the motor running.

No sooner had Polly disappeared into the store than two police officers pulled in front of the van in a tow truck. Suddenly, Molly remembered the latest news about which everyone was talking. So many people were parking illegally that a section of the police force was driving around in tow trucks to carry off the offenders. The kind police officer walked to the van and motioned for Molly to roll down the window. He immediately recognized Molly as a foreigner and began speaking very slowly and loudly. He pointed to his badge and said, "PO–LICE–MAN." Since he was treating Molly as though she may not know Spanish, she carnally got the idea of using his presupposition to her advantage. Molly also began speaking Spanish very slowly and with a strong English accent, "OH, VE-RY, VE-RY GOOD." He then explained slowly, loudly, and with lots of hand gestures that she was not allowed to be parked there. Molly wondered what was taking Polly so long; surely Polly could get her out of this mess. But there was no Polly to be found, and Molly knew she was on her own.

"OH, HERE NO, VE-RY WELL, NOT PARKED, CAR RUN-NING, GO-ING NOW, GOOD-BYE."

She started to put the van in gear but the officer shook his head very emphatically, then whistled to his buddy and motioned him to back up the tow truck. About that time, Polly finally came back and, shocked to hear Molly's dramatic presentation of struggling to speak and understand Spanish, caught on to what was taking place and jumped right into the conversation.

Even Polly, the great negotiator could not sway the police officer from his determination. The zealous police officer was not going to give up his new power of hauling off violators as though they were a first-place trophy. Polly asked where they were supposed to pick up their vehicle, how were they supposed to get there, and what about the poor children. He told her they could all just sit tight in the van and proceeded to attach a chain to the front of their vehicle. Polly asked if they could just follow the tow truck to the police station. Apparently, that would take all the fun out of it for the officers because he said that was absolutely not possible. They raised up the van with Molly sitting in the driver seat, Polly in the passenger seat, and three frightened children hanging on tight in the back seats. Meanwhile, the fourth child, happy-go-lucky Boodles, who thought this was the coolest thing and acted as though they were in a parade, smiled out the window, waving to the onlookers. Up and down the streets they went toward the police station. Molly felt they seemed determined to hit as many streets as possible as if they were showing off their prized catch from a fishing trip, warning all others to beware.

Molly was totally embarrassed, and Polly laughed the whole way. Once at the police station, they were lowered down, paid their fine, and were free to drive off immediately. Such unnecessary nonsense thought Molly, and all because of a filing cabinet. Polly wouldn't let Molly forget her deceptive attempt to worm her way out of being towed. Molly really didn't need to be reminded of the incident; the stares they got while being towed through the crowded streets were not something she could ever forget. Molly did, however, remind her that it was Polly's idea for Molly to park and wait that got them into trouble in the first place. Then Polly, who had already lost the battle with the police officer and wasn't going to lose to Molly, reminded her that Molly was the one who wanted to price the filing cabinet, and there the conversation ended, that is, temporarily, for Polly never stopped sharing Molly's part in the escapade with anyone who would listen.

Betsy really couldn't be blamed for all her health problems. She was, after all, twenty years old when she came into the home, and in VW years, that's already pushing old age. Then she gave them ten more years of faithful service, six of which she had to climb the steep mountain pass into Cartago at least five or six times a week with a van load of people. It was before the time of seatbelt laws and car seat regulations, and even city buses were overcrowded with people standing in the aisle all the time without any consequences. Poor Betsy was not just handling normal loads in her old age, but she was also handling far more people than intended. She was an eight-passenger van, and the family grew to more than eight in a very short amount of time. Oftentimes, they were taking extra neighbors to church with them. Once, on a special Sunday, they had twenty-four passengers in the van. Bless poor little Betsy's metal heart, as so much was expected from her.

As time went on, the next thing to wear out on poor Betsy was the big sliding passenger door. It kept trying to escape as if it were embarrassed by the rest of the family. At first, it would fall completely off every once in a while. Soon, it was falling off every time someone tried to open it. They had it looked at and supposedly fixed it, but it just kept coming off. So, naturally, Mechanic Molly simply learned how to get it back on. It was a tad bit tricky, as everything had to be lined up perfectly and could only be done with good lighting.

On several occasions, the door fell off after evening church services. Molly would try to get it back on, but in the dark, it was too difficult. Finally, tired and wanting to get home, she would stick the whole door into the front row of the van. They would put the smallest kids safely against the opposite side windows and the biggest ones on the first row to hold onto the door. Then they would drive home with a gaping hole on the side of their van. Once again, Boodles would happily wave to people out the window, but Biffy would crunch down as low as she could in the van and gripe the whole way about the embarrassing situation. On such occasions, the thought would occur to Molly on the drive home of keeping a flashlight in the glove compartment, but on arriving home, she would forget. She would never think of it again until, of course, the door fell off again after an evening service.

It finally got to the point that no one was allowed to open the side door at all. There was a small passage area between the two front seats, so everyone would get in the front door of the van and scoot to the back. Occasionally, someone new would ask for a ride home from church. As their hand would come close to the sliding door, they would suddenly jump back in shock at hearing a vanload of kids and adults holler "NO." Then, whoever was sitting in the front passenger seat would get out, allowing the still-shaking newcomer to get in and pass to the back.

Another of Betsy's problems was that most of her window clamps didn't work, making it very easy for anyone to break into the van. They tried not to leave important things in the car and couldn't even imagine anyone bothering to steal Betsy. One day, though, they had a quick errand to run in Cartago with the whole gang in tow. Apparently, a petty thief passed by, noticing a window that was slightly opened, and saw it as an opportunity to look for hidden treasures inside. Reaching in the small opening, he unlocked the forbidden sliding door and jerked the handle downward, hoping to get in and out as quickly as possible. Little did he expect the door to fall off in his hands. As he frantically struggled to get the door back on, Molly, Polly, and almost a dozen kids came around the corner, catching him. As Molly stood, giving him a puzzled look, he feebly tried to explain that the door had fallen off. Molly told him that it only happened when someone opened it and that he really didn't need to be opening doors that didn't belong to him. Eleven little kids in a line climbed into the van, all giving the guilty man ugly looks as they passed him. Molly grabbed the door out of his hands, stuck it back on, and they drove off while he still stood there, staring in shock.

Another thief didn't have much better luck because God's watchful eye protected Molly from what would have been a tragedy for her. She had a handful of old reel-to-reel home movies from her childhood. Those movies were precious to her, and she wished to give her children the same gift. So, back when the family was only seven children large, she saved up money and bought a used VHS camera. Cell phones didn't exist, and video cameras were just coming out, so even a used one was extremely expensive and meant a big sacrifice to buy. They picked it up on the way to the mid-week church service. Those early cameras were so big that the carrying case was the size of a briefcase. Molly didn't want to leave her new toy in the car but was too embarrassed to walk into church with something so big. She decided to hide it under the driver's seat and carefully slid the camera out of sight.

After church, she was chatting with friends when a couple of the kids came running in, yelling that the sliding door of the van was opened (this was before the door had begun falling off), and they had been robbed. Terror-stricken Molly ran to the van, opened the front door, and thrust her hand under the seat. There was the huge camera still in its place. Molly sighed a massive sigh of relief. Immediately, they began checking to see if anything was missing, if anything had been taken. The only thing gone was baby Kiffy's "diaper bag." It really wasn't a diaper bag at all; it was a purse. There were so many other important things that baby Kiffy needed when she arrived that Molly picked one of her old purses to serve as a bag for Kiffy instead of buying one. The thief had peered in the window, seen the purse, imagined it full of valuables, grabbed it, and ran without closing the door behind him. He had run off with an old purse, two cloth diapers, baby plastic pants, and a used baby dress while leaving behind a camera worth hundreds of dollars. Molly chuckled to herself on the drive home imagining the thief's face when he opened the purse.

Betsy did, however, experience one robbery during her life with them. Since Polly had a driver's license by this time, she wanted to take Betsy to a slumber party in San Jose that her friends at Bible seminary were having. It started too late to go on the bus, and Polly wanted to get home quickly the next morning, so Betsy seemed like the perfect solution. After all, Betsy sat in front of their house in Cartago all the time with no problem, so they couldn't imagine there being one in San Jose. When she arrived, however, the party hostess warned her that the neighborhood was not very safe, and it was risky to leave the van parked out on the street. Unfortunately, there was no other option, so Polly just said she would keep an eye on it.

The girls laughed and giggled and ate and watched movies into the wee hours of the morning. Polly would look out the window at intervals, but she couldn't imagine anyone trying anything with a house full of wide-awake people inside making so much noise. Every time she glanced out, there was Betsy, sleeping peacefully against the curb. In the morning when she was sneaking out to leave early, she saw it. Betsy was indeed sleeping peacefully, lifted up on cinder blocks, with all four tires gone. Calling Brother Heflin to explain that situation was one of the hardest things Polly ever did. But Brother Heflin was such a good missionary and so understanding. He bought brand new tires and sent the mechanic out to put them on Betsy. Molly hoped that with new tires, they wouldn't get as many flats, but it didn't seem to help.

Once, the Lord saved them from what would truly have been a tragedy, and the whole ordeal began with one miserable cockroach. To fit thirteen kids in their eight-passenger van, Molly would seat the girls in the front sections with little ones on their laps and the bigger boys in the back, where one would normally put their groceries and over where the VW motors were located. Molly tried her hardest to always make sure that back door was locked to prevent accidents. Yet between looking for last-minute lost shoes and changing last-minute dirty diapers, there were times when they rushed out without locking the boy's back door. The boys would always tell her it was unnecessary because they couldn't get out that door when it was latched shut, whether it was locked with the key or not. Molly liked to take the extra precaution, but she started to believe them and was less cautious. Anyway, back to the cockroach. Molly was innocently driving down the road when Mr. Cockroach made his appearance on the ceiling of the van. Out of the blue, Molly heard thirteen children screaming and pushing as they tried to look for places to get away from the unwanted cockroach in the small, overly crowded van.

Since most of the girls were yelling for someone to kill it, Floodles decided that he would be said hero. From his spot on top of the motor in the back section, he pushed himself backward to kick his foot all the way to the ceiling and, in one slick move, was able to squash the cockroach against the ceiling, taking it out of its confused misery. Meanwhile Molly, still driving, was trying to calm the screaming children. It wasn't working, though, and in fact, the screams were actually quite a bit louder. She glanced in her rearview mirror to try and figure out what the increased commotion was and saw the rear door opened upward and Joodles running in the street behind the van. Apparently, when Floodles pushed back, he did so with such force that he pounded Joodles into the latched back door that supposedly couldn't open, and low and behold, it did open. Joodles fell in a sitting position on the pavement and immediately sprung up and started running. Traffic was slow enough on the busy street for the taxi behind them to easily come to a full stop, but he was not very happy. Molly pulled over to let Joodles climb back in the van. The taxi driver passed them up, yelling at the top of his lungs. Molly asked the kids what he said, but they only told her that she didn't want to know. Molly felt horrible for being such an irresponsible mother but thanked the Lord that at least Joodles's heavenly Father had protected him.

Naturally, they had thoughts of someday getting a bigger and newer vehicle, but they knew it was financially impossible. Nevertheless, poor Betsy seemed to be breaking down more and more.

One Mother's Day, the kids asked Molly if she needed to run any errands. The kids were always so obvious when they were trying to be sneaky that Molly was sure they were planning something and just wanted her out of the house, so she took off to run errands by herself. That was Betsy's least cooperative day of all. She did alright in the morning, but in the afternoon, right when Molly was excited to get home to her "surprise," Betsy started acting up. Nothing could convince her to be a good girl and take Molly home. Molly tried her hammer trick, but that apparently was not the problem, and she soon found herself in a dirty, greasy garage waiting for the mechanic to work his magic. Molly couldn't remember what Betsy's problem was that day, but she remembered that it was taking longer than usual, and the longer she sat in that grease trap, the more upset she became. Of all days, why did this have to happen on Mother's Day? The kids had even told her what time to come home, and she was more than two hours overdue. All she could think of were her disappointed children, waiting and waiting, not knowing why Mommy didn't come home.

Molly finally made it home and got her surprise. The kids were very forgiving; they knew Betsy very well. Later that evening, Molly called a family meeting. Betsy had gone too far this time; it was the last straw. They desperately needed to begin seriously praying for a newer, bigger vehicle. Molly asked that it be included in every prayer, whether they were praying as a family before a meal or praying in private. She ended the short meeting with the first prayer for a new vehicle.

Less than a week after that meeting, and without having shared their desire with others, Molly received a phone call from her sending church in the States. They wanted to do something nice for the home and had voted as a church to send $15,000 for a new vehicle. Molly couldn't believe her ears. Once again, the big question was, why hadn't they started praying earlier? A few days later, the church called a second time. The deacons had talked it over and felt that $15,000 wasn't enough; they would be sending $20,000.

With the money, they purchased a thirty-passenger Toyota Coaster minibus. Costa Rican laws placed lots of demands and upgrades on public vehicles that were older than ten years. As a result, it was common for private owners of small public service buses, mostly tourism vehicles, to just sell them when they were ten years old and buy new ones. The bus was in excellent condition, and although it was ten years old, that was twenty years younger than Betsy. The cost of the new vehicle was, wait for it, exactly $20,000, thank you, Lord. It came at a good time because just a few weeks later, they got child number fourteen and child number fifteen.

They hung on to Betsy for several more years, using her as a second vehicle for short errands. Years afterward, they were finally able to buy a newer fifteen-passenger van, and Betsy was sold to a neighbor for $200. Molly wished later that she had kept some little part of Betsy as a memory like she had done with the doors of the old house. But Betsy was in pretty bad shape by then, really needed all her remaining parts, and there was absolutely nothing left of her that was worth keeping. Bless her little heart; she had earned her retirement. It is quite notable that regardless of all her little quirks, she was the only vehicle they ever owned that was given a name. She was truly loved.

Chapter 9

Dito

Losing a baby who had been promised to her for months hit Molly very hard. She thought back to how they had prayed for a baby girl, and within months, God had given them Kiffy. Then, they had prayed for a baby boy, and once again, within months, God had answered their prayers with one-day-old Doodles. Now the same little Doodles was six years old and was asking Molly for a baby brother. Ever since Gliddles and Gladdles had left, he had been the only boy among the little ones and was beginning to feel suffocated by his four little sisters. One day, he even told Molly that the two of them could just sneak off together without telling anyone, buy a little brother, and surprise the whole family. Molly told him it was best to just pray, and they began to do so. They prayed longer than before, and yet it seemed God was saying no.

Finally, there was a lady who wanted to give her unborn son to Molly. They waited for months for the child to be born. Molly never met the mother, but since everything was being done through a faithful member of the church, she simply trusted that it was all on the up-and-up. They said the baby would be born in March, and he wasn't. Then they said they didn't know the due date because she was poor and not under a doctor's care, but for sure, April would be the month. Nevertheless, April came and went and there was still no baby. This was to be the longest pregnancy in the history of mankind.

Molly had already set up the baby crib, bought a few little baby items, and was praying by the side of the crib every night. Now she was beginning to doubt there was a baby but found it impossible to believe this Christian brother, who seemed to be growing spiritually, could be inventing the situation. Next, she was told that the baby had been born with a liver problem and had been transferred from a rural hospital to the Children's Hospital in San Jose. Molly asked a nurse she knew who worked there to check on the baby, but she found no baby and no record of a transfer from that rural community within those days.

Molly knew that she had been fooled. It was a huge disappointment. While waiting for the baby, the same church member had borrowed money from Molly. Molly waited for him to pay her back about as long as she had waited for the baby's birth, but he never did, and several months later he left the church. As it turned out, she was not the only church member he owed money to when he left.

While pondering the fact that it seemed God did not want to give them another baby, the Lord laid on her heart the idea of asking the government for a child with a specific "special need." Since she already had fifteen children in the home, she thought about what type of special needs would be within her ability to help. She concluded that helping a blind child would probably not be too difficult. This idea might have come from the fact that she had a blind cousin and rather knew what to expect.

While in the social services office for a different reason, out of pure curiosity, she asked the social worker if she knew whether or not there were any blind children who needed a home. The lady told her that she thought there was one but knew nothing about the child's age and didn't even know if it was a girl or a boy. She said she could call and ask and disappeared into a back office. While she was gone, Molly began to pray that the child be a boy, five years old or younger, to be a little companion for Doodles. When she came back, she said there was indeed a blind child, a little four-year-old boy. Molly's heart leapt for joy. A meeting was arranged with the director of the adoption division of child services.

Molly spent the next two weeks walking on air and telling everyone how God had answered her specific prayer. By this time, Molly was almost forty-two years old, and like her aunt, her hair was graying prematurely. The silly thought occurred to her that the director would think Molly was too old to handle such a young special needs child. She had never wanted to dye her hair, though friends had been trying to talk her into it for years, and now she was rushing to the hairdresser for a new look, a whole head of beautiful brown hair and no gray. Molly didn't want to take any chances of losing her little boy.

After what seemed like an eternity, the day finally arrived for the meeting. While waiting, her curiosity got the best of her once again, and she asked the receptionist what the possibilities were that the director would give her the child. The secretary replied in no uncertain terms that if she wanted the child, he was hers. Nobody else would ever take him; everyone wanted a perfect child. The words rang out in her ears and pierced her heart. It was her first encounter with the reality that there were no prerequisites for taking in a special needs child; they were more than eager to get rid of them.

Soon afterward, Molly was called into the office. The director opened a big book full of children eligible for adoption and started to read, "Oh yes, Eduardito, blind, epileptic, brain-damaged, non-verbal, unable to crawl or walk . . ." Molly felt her heart pierced through for the second time in less than a half hour. Her little boy was so much more than she had bargained for. The director went right on talking as though she was trying to make a sale. Molly had come in planning to convince her that she would be a good mother, and suddenly, the tables were turned, and she felt she was being backed into a corner to make an immediate decision on this child. She told the lady that she had not known that the child had so many problems and that with fifteen other children, she felt he might be too much for her. She kicked up her sales pitch with how cute he was, how perfect he would be for their home, how few and well-controlled his seizures were, and then sprinted off to bring her a picture of the jewel of a child. When she brought the picture back, Molly's heart melted just a tad. He was indeed the cutest little thing in the world. She agreed to visit the child but made it very clear that she was not promising anything.

As she got in the car to drive home, she was extremely depressed. She began to pray, and though God did not speak to her in an audible voice, she understood perfectly the conversation.

"Oh Father God, my little boy, my little boy. This is not the little boy I wanted," she prayed.

Then God asked, "He isn't? I believe he is exactly what you asked for. Didn't you say boy, didn't you say five years or younger, and didn't you say blind? When did you ask that he have no other problems or that he be intelligent?"

Molly knew that God was right and called a family meeting when she got home. She explained his various problems and how much of Mommy's time and their time he would need. She also told them what the receptionist had said about nobody else ever wanting him and his being stuck in a government home his whole life. Those who remembered the government homes begged Molly not to leave him there. They took a secret vote, and Dito won with thirteen yeas and only two nays.

Molly took Doodles with her for the first meeting. Her attitude had been changing, and she was eager to meet him. Molly and Doodles fell in love with Eduardito within minutes. He was such a precious little boy, an absolute treasure. Doodles wanted to take him home that very day, but they would be visiting him once a week for a month before he would be allowed to go home with them. He was cute, happy, and oh-so good-spirited. He wasn't much more than a baby, for though he was four years old, his size was that of a small two-year-old. Molly videotaped him so the rest of the clan could see him, and they, too, fell in love.

The month seemed to pass so slowly. The long wait made Molly nervous because people kept asking her if she was sure that she knew what she was doing. One day, she confided to Grandma that she was not sure how much Eduardito would be able to learn. Her mother, with the wisdom of a good grandma, said that even if he couldn't learn much, at least they would all be able to love on him.

During those visits, Molly learned a little about Eduardito's history. He was the result of a relationship of incest between two siblings. When he was born, ironically on Mother's Day, his mother had given him to a neighbor, who, in turn, realizing that he was not normal, had turned him over to the government. At only two months of age, he had his first epileptic seizure. Not only did the ladies who cared for the children have no idea what to do, but they also had no access to a vehicle in which to take the baby to the hospital. They chose to just wait for the seizure to end, but it wasn't ending. Finally, they called for a taxi, but by the time it arrived and they got the baby to the hospital, he had been convulsing for two hours. Testing showed that having waited so long to get him medical attention had caused additional brain damage, especially on the left side of the brain, where the seizure had started. The left side of the brain controlled the right side of his body, leaving him with limited movement in his right arm and right leg.

Molly also had to visit him at his special needs school. The social workers said that he needed to continue in school because he had advanced since he had been there. Molly didn't see them doing anything with him that she couldn't do at home. For the first fifteen minutes, they sat in a circle hitting tambourines while listening to music. Then Dito played with a bowl of clothespins for a while and fell asleep at the table, making Molly wish she could take a nap too. She was happy to see that her little Eduardito was the best-behaved child in the class, even though he was also furthest behind in development. All the other children could see and play and do things he couldn't do, but they all also spent the morning screaming and crying and throwing themselves on the floor. Eduardito just remained calm in the middle of all the chaos going on around him. That encouraged Molly since he would soon belong to a very busy and often very loud family. Eduardito did, indeed, prove himself true to his calm character through the years, regardless of loud parties, Vacation Bible Schools, or just daily living in the children's home.

Finally, the exciting day of bringing Eduardito home came, and he immediately became the center of attention. Everyone in the family loved him, and everyone wanted to baby him. In hopes that he would recognize who he was and maybe one day be able to say his own name, Molly shortened his long name of Eduardito to just plain Dito, and the name quickly stuck. He soon became their greatest joy, uniting the family every day with the new and funny things he would do. Molly began hearing almost daily, "Mommy, come see what Dito is doing." By the time Molly got there, she would find seven or eight kids around him happy or laughing. He became a companion to Grandma, who had been accustomed to sitting in the living room all day reading. She would sit watching him playing on his little mat for hours and talk to him in English as though he understood every word.

Dito was the happiest child Molly had ever seen. Should he, on some rare occasion, begin to cry, Molly knew that he was in pain and needed to go to the doctor. He came into Molly's life at exactly the right time. Her Great Physician, the Lord, knew just what she needed to heal her aching soul when He lovingly brought Dito into her life. He became one of the greatest joys of her ministry. He loved to cuddle up like a little teddy bear and seemed to fit perfectly into Molly's arms. Every night, she would sit in her rocking chair, hold him in her lap, turn on her lullaby tape, and sing to him. He would curl up in her arms and stay very still, never squirming like the other kids. He absolutely loved music and didn't seem to mind that Molly wasn't a very talented singer. Sometimes, he would even join in the song with sweet little high-pitched noises of his own. Molly was sure he thought he was really singing.

The name Eduardito means "Guardian of Happiness," and Molly felt that the name fit him perfectly. He was her calm in the midst of the storm. As she rocked him, she would often begin crying but with tears of joy because she knew that little Dito would never rise up as a rebellious teen and tell her that he didn't want her to be his mother. It had been a very hard year, and Dito was her breath of fresh air. God had even given him a ministry, and he was ever so good at being a faithful guard of happiness.

The little guardian of her happiness also provided her with a relaxing experience any time he and she could escape by themselves to the grocery store. In the early days, she had loved to go with the whole gang to the grocery store just to see the looks on the other shoppers' faces at all the little people calling her Mommy and asking for this or that. Often, she would catch people counting the children crowded around Molly's cart. As the family had grown, the novelty of shopping with twelve or more kids had worn off.

Shopping with Dito was totally different. He just sat there in the front of the cart, moving his head from side to side, making happy cooing noises and smiling. He would never start pushing and shoving, never get lost in the store, never snuck extra items into the cart, and never even asked Molly for this or that. If the aisle was empty, Molly would go faster and sway the cart from side to side. Dito would laugh and laugh. Molly imagined that he thought he was on a ride at the amusement park. There was not a shopper who saw him who didn't have a smile for him and a smile for Molly. What a delight he was, bringing so many smiles to so many people. Dito had Molly walking on air.

The family soon learned all of Dito's favorite toys and his favorite games to play. His all-time preferred way of playing with toys was pretty amazing and was shown to Molly by the ladies who cared for him in the government home. They laid him flat on his back in his crib, surrounded by all his toys. He would spin around on his back, feeling for his toys with his feet. When he found one, he would grab it with his feet and carry it to his hands, examine it with both hands and feet, and if he found that it was not his favorite toy, he would then lay it down and continue looking for another toy with his feet. When he finally found his favorite toy, he would balance it on his left foot, leaving his right foot close by for added support, and begin to spin the toy around and around in circles with his hands. The game reminded Molly of the pictures she had seen in storybooks of bears at circuses lying on their backs and playing with big balls using all fours. Little Dito could play this game for hours at a time. He was so talented at the pastime he himself had invented. Molly purchased a good-sized mat to put down in the living room so he could play his game out where all the people were instead of by himself in his crib back in his and Molly's room.

Occasionally, the toy would fall, sometimes even bumping Dito in the head. He didn't seem to care, must have known that bumps were just part of life, and would pick up the toy again and continue to play. Only if his favorite toy fell somewhere out of his grasp would he begin to play with another toy. But he would only play with it for five or ten minutes and then set it aside and choose another toy, play with it, and set it aside, and so on and so forth.

At first, Molly wanted Dito to learn to play with other things, but seeing that nothing else brought the same joy, she would rush to pick up the favorite toy and change it out for whatever else he happened to be turning around on his feet at the time. Since the left side of his body was quite a bit more useful than the right side, it made perfect sense that he would choose to use both his feet and his hands to play. His coordination and ability to have invented this cute game made Molly think that there really was a degree of intelligence trapped inside this little body who was unable to verbally communicate with the world around him.

Eventually, the inevitable happened, and Dito's precious favorite toy was broken beyond repair. Molly had already been duct-taping chipped edges for some time, but the toy was now even beyond the help of duct tape, and Molly was frantically scouring toy stores for its twin. It was a hard plastic toddler toy piano, black with about eight colorful keys. Each key played a different song, and with Dito's twirling, the song was constantly changing whenever the piano had batteries in it. Dito loved music but played with it just as enthusiastically, whether it had music or not. The top half of the piano formed into a handle for carrying, which also made it easy for Dito to grab hold on for twirling. A look-alike could not be found anywhere. Molly bought several other toys with lights and music and approximately the same size as his favorite.

They finally found a chubby white, yellow, and red plastic toy guitar that he seemed to enjoy just as much, with the neck of the guitar also making twirling easier. Molly went out and bought several more when they saw how much he liked it. In fact, during the next fifteen or so years, they would purchase probably more than a dozen of the same toy. Molly could not be in a toy store without looking for one.

When sitting on the couch, Dito's favorite hand toys were two toddler-size Lego-type building blocks. Molly would put them in a plastic container next to him, along with many other small toys. He would pull the toys out one by one, feel them with his hands, and throw them to the floor until he found one of the building blocks. When he found one, he would set it in his lap and continue pulling toys out of the box, looking for another one. There was only one size he liked, the size with eight dots on the top, and both blocks had to be exactly the same. When he found the second plastic block, he was no longer interested in the box of toys and oftentimes pushed the whole container off the couch onto the floor. Then, he would begin to twirl the two blocks in his hands for a while, snap them together, twirl some more, pull them apart, then more twirling and snapping and twirling and pulling apart and on and on.

Dito's only other favorite toys were any shaped squeaky doggy toys. He loved the high-pitched sounds he was able to get from them whenever he would squeeze, and like with his other favorites, he could entertain himself for hours playing with them. Molly did not particularly care for the shrill sound that would go on and on but learned to live with it on his account. Sometimes, Molly would be in a supermarket with Dito and a half dozen other kids. As they passed the doggy toys, the kids would beg Mommy for a new toy for Dito. They would stop and place a toy in Dito's hands. If he threw it down, they would put it back and try another one until he was happy with the sound and the squeeze of a toy and kept it in his hand. Molly giggled inwardly at the strange looks this little practice got from other shoppers passing by them.

Aside from his favorite toys, Dito had three other favorite games. The first was bouncing on Mommy's bed. When Molly would lay him flat on his back in the center of the bed, he would begin to pound his legs together on the mattress so hard that it would lift him into the air. Once he was bouncing all the way into the air, he would begin to laugh and continue bouncing and bouncing and laughing and laughing. The second was swinging in a special kiddy chair they added to the swing set in the backyard. Once again, he would just swing and laugh and laugh. His third favorite was water, either in a bathtub or swimming pool. He would sit happily, slapping the water with his hands and laughing as the water splashed up into his face.

Dito was, without a doubt, the happiest child Molly had ever seen. His laughter was contagious, and he possessed a special power to unite the family in laughter. Everyone loved him, was ready and willing to care for him, wanted to hug him or tickle him, and looked for ways to make him laugh. In fact, they soon realized that Dito laughed every time he would hear someone sneeze. Kids would purposely get close to him and fake a sneeze to see if he would laugh. Sometimes he would, but usually, he was pretty good at recognizing sneezes, would realize it was a trick, and would remain silent with a contemplative look on his face. His hearing was so good that Molly could actually be in another room of their big house, sneeze, and suddenly hear Dito laughing in the living room. They all began laughing every time Dito sneezed and learned that, for some reason, he did not find his own sneezes funny but would stay very serious as though he believed that he didn't deserve to be the brunt of everyone else's laughter. Such a silly boy!

About a month after Dito arrived, Molly and the kids were performing an annual Christmas play in one of the local churches. After the service, a lady in the congregation approached Molly and asked if Dito had come out of the government home in Cedros. When Molly answered that he had, she said she had thought she recognized him. This nice Christian lady had worked for a short period of time at that home when he was a baby. She told Molly that knowing he had many issues, she used to rock him at night and pray that God would do the impossible and give him a home where he would be loved. She was thrilled that he had answered her prayer. It amazed Molly to learn how God had been working behind the scenes to answer the prayers of one godly woman.

Molly wanted to get Dito involved in therapies immediately. She was excited because his old home left her with a schedule of one free physical therapy a month for several months through the social medicine system. She was eager to see how they worked with him so they could imitate the therapy at home. The instructions said to bring a towel and an extra change of clothes. Molly was thrilled; it sounded like the therapy would be in a swimming pool, and she knew how much he loved the water. Unfortunately, not only was it not in a pool, but the reason for the towel broke Molly's heart. The therapist was very rough with her baby, pulling and twisting his arms and legs this way and that. Her happy baby boy cried and screamed for an hour.

At first, Molly took the position of "no pain, no gain" with the session. Yet as the minutes passed by, her heart sunk deeper and deeper. Was all this really necessary? She could not justify upsetting him so greatly. The towel was there solely to clean up the messes of his tears constantly flowing as well as the messes of other bodily fluids flowing from his nose and mouth that accompany deep distress. Molly almost wished she had brought another towel for herself. The only idea she left with was how not to work with Dito and purposed to never take him back.

Molly began looking for private therapists and settled on two very nice ladies, one for physical therapy and one for vocational therapy. Each therapist worked with Dito once a week. Sometimes, there were some grunts and groans, but no more tears. Each one gave Molly a list of things to work with him each day. They started by trying to teach him to crawl and walk by himself. He had not started to crawl yet but soon learned. He could actually already stand by himself for five or ten minutes but would not take a step unless someone was holding his hand. To teach him, they got a small medical walker. Dito would grab either side with his hands, and by tying a belt to the front, the children would pull the walker around the room, and Dito would follow the walker step by step. Each child would walk Dito around the room ten times every day. Finally, after almost seven months of working with him, Dito took his first steps on his own with no help at the age of five years and two weeks. He was surrounded by a big circle of children and adults all jumping and shouting for joy, cheering him on.

Once Dito could walk and crawl, he taught himself a new game. He would crawl off his mat to a wall, always the same wall, pull himself to a standing position using the doorposts, then walk sideways around the room, leaning against the wall with both hands for support. Every few steps, he would stop and swing his head from side to side as though trying to look around. He would walk through the doorway of two connecting rooms, make his way into the second room, then close that door and start beating on the door like he was trying to get out. Molly would come to his rescue, through the adjoining room, open the door, lay him back down on his mat, and the same game would start over; crawling to the wall, into one door, around to the other, closing the door, and beating against it to get out.

At the time Dito came into their lives, Molly had always been the only teacher in their home school. She was an educator at heart and enjoyed the less rigid homeschool form of teaching and learning. She would teach for one or two hours with all the kids together and Dito lying next to her on his little mat. Then, she would send the kids off to complete their individual assignments, leaving her with time for Dito or other things. Even though the kids were not being constantly watched, they had to stay at their desks, and their goals would be checked and graded in the afternoon. She was also reading about and implementing other homeschool ideas and adding new materials. One such idea was to use the older children to teach the younger. Each older child was responsible for one younger sibling.

On Monday, Molly would pass out to her student teachers the material they were responsible for teaching to their particular pupil for that week. They would divide into their teacher-pupil groups for about forty minutes after their morning recess time. On Friday, they would all gather together in the living room. Each teacher-student pair would stand in front of the whole group and do an oral presentation of the things their student had learned that week. Molly loved the idea. It freed her up for forty more minutes Monday through Thursday, taught the older kids responsibility and leadership qualities, and gave each younger child some one-on-one time with a "teacher" who was helping them on their specific level.

Molly felt confident in the materials she had chosen and the quality of education her children were receiving. Nevertheless, since their growing home was now like an open book, others who did not understand the homeschool concept felt like the kids were not getting a good education if they weren't all sitting quietly in a formal classroom, being carefully scrutinized by a qualified teacher for at least six hours a day. Brother Neff encouraged Molly to step out of the school and find a new teacher for their education because she clearly had too many things on her plate.

At first, Molly felt not only hurt but also disappointed. She couldn't imagine not being her children's teacher. Fortunately, when they made their need known, the Lord soon sent them a sharp young lady eager to dedicate a few years of service to the mission field. After her,

God was faithful to provide teachers through the years, some from the States and some Costa Ricans. Molly quickly saw the wisdom in the change. She was still the school's administrator, still in charge of choosing the curriculum, but was now free to work on school projects, teaching a few classes such as Bible, helping children with individual learning problems, preparing kids for government testing, and dedicating time to Dito's therapy. What she didn't have to do was be with the kids all morning and early afternoon and grade loads of papers.

Eventually, God provided a permanent teacher for the school. Lolly, who had worked with the kindergarten children in Cartago, had moved to a house very close to the home and needed work. She served faithfully for many years, patiently working through the ups and downs of each of her students.

After reading lots of books and researching therapies, Molly came up with a plan of things to work on with Dito. They made a small round table with the center cut out for Dito to sit in, surrounded by therapy articles. Sitting in his chair, he worked on tasks such as putting pennies in a piggy bank, stacking rings on a pole, rolling a car, putting shapes in a box, building a tower of blocks, picking up a ball, pulling clothespins off a can, playing a small keyboard, ringing a bell, and so on. In addition, Molly prepared a ten-phase therapy from ideas in a special education book. Each phase contained five to fifteen commands that he needed to master. Once four commands in a phase were mastered with 80 percent accuracy, he could begin with commands from the next phase. His very first assignment was to touch his nose on command. Between the new teacher, the older children, and Molly all spending a minimum of thirty minutes with Dito a day, he was getting between three to four hours of therapy a day.

They began by first asking him to touch his nose. If he did not do it within a few seconds, which, of course, he didn't at first, the therapist would take his finger, touch his nose with it, and praise him for a job well done. Nevertheless, the task was only recorded as correct if he touched his nose on his own, in which case he would receive a tiny snack such as a cookie bite.

On Dito's first day of therapy, he was told to touch his nose 704 times and received a 2 percent accuracy grade. They would spend several minutes on the "touch nose," then play some with the stacking, pushing, and pulling toys, and then return to the "touch nose" command. By day eleven, little Dito had been told to touch his nose 5099 times and was up to a 74 percent accuracy. Though he was not supposed to continue to the next command until reaching 80 percent accuracy, he was wearing out his teachers faster than they were wearing him out, and Molly thought it best to start the second command, "wave hi," to conserve the sanity of her helpers. Having less success with "wave hi" than they had with "touch nose," they continued forward to "clap hands" and "put on hat."

In the end, it turned out that Dito was basically a one-command boy, never making it to even a 50 percent accuracy with any of his other commands. The other eleven commands in phase one were never even tackled, nor were phases two through ten ever touched. Only his nose was touched. Dito had failed miserably in his specialized kindergarten class that Molly had so carefully put together. He also failed Potty Training 101 even after vigorously working on the course for about ten years. He did, however, master several of the other tasks, especially the rings on the pole, the pennies in the bank, picking up the ball, and pulling off the clothespins. He also got really good at picking up his little snacks with his fingers and carrying them to his mouth. They tried to teach him to feed himself with a spoon, and although he was able to get the spoon to his mouth, as soon as he took the bite, he would fling the spoon across the room. No matter how many times they tried to show him to return it to the plate to get another spoonful, whenever he was left on his own, everyone was ducking flying spoons.

They learned very quickly that Dito also had a special talent for taking off his shoes and socks. They would put them on him for his many walks, but as soon as he was back on his mat, shoes and socks were off. Of course, since he had more coordination in his left foot than in his right hand, it made sense that he didn't want anything on his feet. Molly even tried to keep at least the socks on with Velcro, but to no avail. She eventually gave up and let him be her barefoot boy. That was not much of a problem if they were at home, but anytime they went anywhere with Dito in his stroller, they were constantly stopping him from taking off his shoes or backtracking to find where he had dropped them. It wasn't too difficult in a supermarket but became very complicated when rushing through an airport with fifteen kids who were each already in charge of keeping up with one carry-on and one personal item.

On the family's first outing to the amusement park with Dito, they discovered his favorite rides there, and they were not the little kiddy rides or merry-go-round. Dito loved fast circles, velocity, and the feeling of falling. Thus said, his favorites were roller coasters, the giant seashells that spun around in endless circles, and the junior tower that would take a person some twenty feet in the air and drop them down, time after time. But there were no rides that compared to his all-time favorite. It was called the Octopus. Molly would sit with little Dito in a cart at the tip of one of the octopus's tentacles. Then they would begin revolving around the octopus's body at a fast speed while each tentacle rose and dropped and rose and dropped, also very fast, and each individual cart twirled around endlessly, you guessed it, at the speed of light or close to it. It was a triple-action ride.

Molly could remember a time when this type of ride thrilled her, but that had been a long time ago. While Dito laughed and laughed uncontrollably with delight, Molly spent the whole ride clinging on to him for dear life and wishing it would end. Dito could ride it several times without tiring, but Molly could only handle it once and then would look for some other unsuspecting volunteer to accompany him.

The fright of the octopus was nothing compared to the chair lift experience that Molly had with Dito at the Arizona State Fair. The swinging chair hung from a cable some thirty or forty feet above the fairgrounds and carried its passengers across the fair from one corner diagonally to the opposite corner. When Molly was invited to a mission conference in Arizona, she had arranged for Holly, their substitute cook and housekeeper, to go with her and help with Dito, whom Molly was not willing to leave behind in Costa Rica. As an added blessing to the trip, they were able to spend some time with her brother, who lived in Arizona and had invited them to the fair. Each seat in the chair lift held two people, but since Holly was nervous about being so high in the air with Dito, Molly told her that she would go with Dito, and Holly could go with her brother. What could be easier? Dito was used to sitting, and they would get a fantastic view of the entire fairgrounds from way up there.

Getting on and off of the chair seemed easy enough. She and Dito just had to stand in position until the chair came up behind them. Then they would sit down, and off they would go. Molly saw that on the return trip, getting off would be equally as simple. They would simply stand up, and a conveyor belt would carry them in one direction and the chair in the other. They could do this, no problem.

There were a few things, however, that Molly did not calculate into the equation. The first was the fact that she herself was afraid of heights and always got nervous in situations that involved them. The second was that Dito loved his freedom and hated things like seatbelts and bars that threatened that freedom. Although the seats had no seatbelts, which would have actually been better, there was a metal bar that extended across the front, obviously to prevent them from falling off the chair. Molly placed Dito's hand on the bar so he would have a place to hold on and soon realized that he felt the bar was infringing on his freedom and wanted it immediately removed. He began to push against it, grunting in a complaining way. She didn't know how tightly that bar was locked in. But in her mind's eye, she imagined it flying open and the two of them sitting there practically dangling between heaven and earth with nothing to stop them from plummeting forty or fifty feet into the deep-fried pickle stand.

Molly scooted closer to Dito and put one arm behind him and one in front, like a side hug, trying to calm him down. As she did this, her brain, which had not done any calculating before getting on the ride, began calculating at high speeds. In a split second, it told her that there was a good foot of space between the seat and the bar, plenty of room for a ten-year-old child to slip right through should that child suddenly have an uncontrollable seizure. Molly's spirit immediately began to pray, knowing well that God had not been included in her brain's calculations. But her brain would not stop calculating and next told Molly that she would not have the strength to hold on to said ten-year-old for the diagonal length of the fair from corner to corner should he slip off the seat. Her spirit weakened, and in fright, she pleaded with the Lord to get her out of this mess. She felt her hands become sweaty and her heart beating harder. Yet, her silly brain would not stop its thinking. It then calculated that the drop would be from too far up to land favorably on her feet with Dito in her arms without a parachute. There was so much sudden calculating for the carefree mind that had just minutes before been admiring all the cool sights at the State Fair.

Molly would have liked to think back on that experience and remember how calm she had remained and how she had consoled herself in the fact that she knew that God was in control—He certainly was—but fear took the place of faith, and that was not the memory she later had of the situation. In desperation, she glanced behind her to see how far they had come. She calculated that they were not quite halfway across the fair. She knew it was a there and back round trip, but maybe she could flag down the operator and get him to let her off at the corner before the return trip. Then with her feet on solid ground, she would gladly run across the entire fair to fetch Dito's stroller and bring it back to him. Yes, that's what she would do, get off at the corner, and she was almost halfway there. They had this; it would just be a few more minutes. She busied her mind with hanging on for three or four minutes. She was holding Dito's hands so he wouldn't keep pushing on the bar. They were playing their little hand-squeeze game, and he seemed to have calmed down slightly.

Then, for no apparent reason, all the chairs on the line came to a slow stop. A stop had not been calculated in her three to four-minute "you can do this" wait. The chairs had not stopped before. Molly glanced at Holly in the chair behind them, who hollered back, questioning whether or not this was normal. Molly shook her head. Could the ride have possibly broken down with her and Dito suspended precisely in the center? Molly tried to give a reassuring look to Holly in the seat some fifteen to twenty feet behind her. But the whole incident was just too incredible, and they both started giggling out of pure fright since there was not much more that could be done. Yet just as quickly, Molly decided that getting hysterical was probably not the best plan, and if she kept looking at Holly, that was most likely what would happen. She turned away from Holly and resumed praying and making promises to God if He would only get them safely back to solid ground.

In the middle of her prayers, Molly's silly mind began its crazy calculations again. If the ride was broken down, it might be hours before they could get it fixed. What were they to do? How would maintenance get them down? How patient would Dito be if they were trapped for hours? In reality, it was only maybe four minutes later that the ride resumed, but it seemed more like ten or fifteen minutes. As it turned out, they had stopped it to help an elderly lady off the ride. All that worrying for nothing.

When the ride resumed, Molly breathed a sigh of relief. It would not be long now. Yet when they got to the opposite side where Molly was planning to get off, she realized that it was nothing more than a turnaround point. No friendly little man was standing there to help people off. There was a man in a control box, but he seemed to be engrossed in whatever his job was, and Molly could not even get his attention. She considered hollering out to him, even though it would go against her personality, but by that time, she and Dito were already at the return curve. It was a sad Molly who watched as the seat did the U-turn and started the long trek back. Her prayer for the trip back was simply that there be no more stops. The stop in mid-air had been a killer. Oh, the bliss when they finally arrived and Molly felt her feet touch the ground as they stepped off and she held tight to Dito, walking him to his stroller. She truly wanted to go down on her knees and kiss the ground, but fortunately, thought better of it. Instead, she just kept repeating, "Thank you, Lord; thank you, Lord; thank you, Lord . . ."

[A LESSON TO LEARN: There is a little lesson to be learned even in this silly event. Oh, how quickly we run to God when we find ourselves in some "emergency" situation. Had it not been for the experience on the ride, Molly would have gone to the fair, had the greatest time all day long, and never given a thought to God or had any little chat with Him. The Bible says, "Pray without ceasing" (1 Thessalonians 5:17). Yet, because she desperately needed the Lord, she had the longest prayer meeting she had all week there, suspended in the air. May we make the Lord our all-day, everyday friend, thanking Him and praising His name in each detail of our lives, in the good times as well as the difficult times. He deserves to be more than our 911 operator.]

In the area of language, Dito learned to recognize only a few words, such as "take this," "no, no," "Dito," and of course, "touch nose." The only word he ever learned to say is the uh-huh sound a person says meaning yes, so the whole family would joke around about what a positive fellow he was. Everyone would get into long uh-huh conversations with him. He would say uh-huh, and anyone within earshot of him would answer back uh-huh. Grandma, who spent the most time in the living room sitting with him, could carry on the uh-huh conversation for a half an hour or more.

One time, Molly was in the kitchen when she heard the familiar uh-huh. She responded in a loud voice with an uh-huh so that he would know that she was close at hand. Once again, she heard the familiar sound, and she continued answering. After continuing the conversation for a good fifteen minutes, Molly went to the living room to praise him for a good conversation and give him a little kiss. Molly found Dito sound asleep on his mat and Giffy in the rocking chair next to him, rocking away and smiling. Molly realized she had just spent fifteen minutes in an uh-huh conversation with bilingual Giffy.

Another favorite trick the kids had was to ask Dito carefully planted questions to tease each other such as, "Am I pretty?" "Uh-huh," he would answer. "Is so and so ugly?" "Uh-huh," came the reply. "Am I your best friend?" "Uh-huh." "Is so and so dumb?" "Uh-huh."

Between the poor nourishment in the government facility and being on a high dose of epilepsy medicine, Dito's defenses were very low when he came into the home. The first year with Molly, he had to be put on antibiotics five times. Molly began researching nourishment and soon came up with a new diet and a list of supplements for him. She even found one supplement that she believed helped with his epilepsy. After the first year, Dito rarely got sick except for his epilepsy.

Dito's epilepsy was extremely severe. At first, he was on one medicine and would have only two or three seizure days a month. As he grew, the seizures increased, and his doctor put him on a second medicine. When that didn't seem to help, the doctor's first suggestion was brain surgery to remove all the damaged areas of his brain. They could not guarantee Molly anything. He could possibly lose the few little talents he did have. The doctor felt that since he didn't do much anyway, it didn't matter if he could no longer play his little games. Molly was also told that there was no guarantee that surgery would work, as he still may have seizures.

Molly would not even consider putting her baby through that. The doctor's next suggestion was a much stronger medicine. She said they did not like to use it on typical children because it affected their learning, but once again, Dito was practically incapable of learning, so it would be fine for him. They were still very involved in Dito's daily therapies, and it hurt Molly to hear the doctor talk in such a cruel manner, but she insisted it would help his epilepsy, and Molly agreed to try it. Dito did indeed go for three months without a seizure on the new medicine, but at the same time, he became a totally different child. He was so tired he could not do more than a few minutes of therapy without falling asleep at his small table. He became an angry little boy Molly didn't recognize. He was so mad all the time that he was scratching and grumbling at everyone who came near to him, especially those trying to do therapy with him. He also totally stopped his little game of crawling to the wall, standing, and following it around to close the door. Their joyful child was gone.

Molly returned to the doctor and told her that she preferred to have a happy boy with a few seizure days a month than a mean seizure-free child. The doctor, who was so pleased with his progress, did not take that well. Indeed, she did not even believe that what Molly was saying about his behavior was true. She told Molly that she was a rebellious patient, and threw both her and Dito out of her office, telling Molly not to ever come back. Molly was so in love with little Dito that what shocked her most was a doctor who never wanted to see this precious patient again. How could anyone not care about sweet, innocent Dito? Yet she didn't, and Molly was forced to look for another doctor.

Dito ended up having four other doctors through the years. Every new medicine they tried on him would work for about two years, become ineffective, and need to be changed. After a few years off a med, he could usually return to it. Thus, the medicine rotation went on and on and on. By the time he reached puberty, he was up to three medicines at a time and having seizures three or four days a week. He would often have a seizure as soon as they got him up to walk, and they would have to lay him back down. Therapies became fewer and shorter, and Molly decided to let him live his own happy life, playing with his favorite toys on his mat and sitting up and rocking backward and forward whenever he felt like it. They would do a little therapy occasionally and sit him up on the couch for a while with his box full of toys.

Dito's blindness was not caused by damage to the eyes but rather to the optic nerve. The doctors said that his eyes could see, but there was no way to measure how much sight his brain could register. Sometimes, if a toy were held in front of him and he was instructed to take it, he would seem to glance and then reach straight for the toy. At other times, it seemed that he would just move his arms around as if trying to find the toy. White objects seemed to be easier for him to see.

Dito's hearing was perfect, and he absolutely loved music. He was always happy listening to music and would hum along in his own little way. Whenever all the kids were practicing specials, Dito would begin to make loud happy noises. It thrilled him to "sing along." Whenever the kids would stop singing, he would stop too.

Dito brought so much happiness into their home and bound everyone together in such a wonderful way that Molly began thinking that every family ought to have a special needs child. Each new little thing he did brought joy, and he was so lighthearted and easygoing that he gladly cooperated in his therapies and the little dress-up games the girls played with him as though he were their own personal, real-life baby doll. They would dress him in this or that, with all different hats on, sit him in a laundry basket, attach a jump rope, and pull him all through the house. He would sit contentedly in his little limousine, cuddling a stuffed animal and making cute, happy oohing and aahing sounds.

One day, at one of his many therapies, they announced that they would be having a group support session for all the mothers while they waited for their children to finish their therapies. The therapist in charge of the parental group encouraged them to open up about their feelings. Molly expected each one to begin sharing their children's advancements and victories. To her surprise, one by one, they began expressing their problems, disappointments, and how difficult it was to cope with the child's limitations. Molly couldn't believe what she was hearing. Being able to serve Dito was a great blessing to her whole family, not at all a heavy burden to be endured.

One lady whose daughter had suffered brain damage at age two had actually thrown away all of her daughter's baby pictures from before the damage because it was too painful to look at the pictures. Molly was in shock. She had a house full of children she longed to have baby pictures of but had none. How could someone attempt to eradicate a portion of their child's life and memory?

Molly was not one to speak out in group meetings, but it got to a point that she couldn't remain quiet. She knew that each child was different and that each family's struggles and burdens were different, but most of these children were more advanced than Dito. She told them how she had chosen Dito specifically because he had special needs, what a joy he was to have in their family, and what happiness he brought them all with each and every new little thing he learned. Remembering that he had recently failed kindergarten, she added Grandma's words as though they were her own words, saying that even if he couldn't learn much, at least they could all love on him. She was hoping that once she shared something joyful, others would join in on happy moments, but they all just stared at her for a few seconds and continued sharing their complaints.

[A LESSON TO LEARN: The lessons that Dito taught to everyone in the home and even to others outside the home were numerous. They were lessons such as compassion, sacrifice, love, patience, kindness, gentleness, and genuine servitude. Many of the lessons he taught them, time and time again, as his students were often slow learners. He also managed to individualize the lessons for what one person learned from Dito was totally different from what another learned. They were surprised at how much more of a blessing he was to them than they were to him.]

[ANOTHER LESSON TO LEARN: There are terrible tragedies in life, but God is able to give grace and bring good out of difficult situations if we let Him. The mothers who only saw the tragedy in their child's condition seemed resentful, as though they believed God had not treated them fairly and they deserved better. Had God felt the same way as these mothers, He would have rejected all of us, for we are all flawed, none of us measure up, and the awful tragedy of our ugly sinful condition before a holy God far outweighs any physical tragedy. But God did not choose to love us because of our beauty, talents, or strengths. He chose to love us in our weak and helpless condition. In fact, God did not choose us despite our faults and weaknesses, but rather, He chose us because of them! Have you come to understand this kind of love, seen your own sinful condition, and realized that Christ is your only hope?]

[YET ANOTHER LESSON TO LEARN: Dito lived in a carefree world, totally relying on those who served him. It was amazing to think how there was a refrigerator of food and a pantry full of snacks just steps away from his mat, and yet he was totally oblivious to them; he didn't even know such things existed. On a few occasions through the years, the teenage girl responsible for feeding Dito his supper would forget it was her night to feed him. Then, around 9:00 p.m., those cleaning the kitchen would find his cold food sitting on the stove, waiting to be heated. They would holler out that Dito hadn't eaten, and the responsible party would gasp and jump up from their nightly video to warm his food and feed him. He would just be waiting patiently. He knew nothing of the delicious chicken and vegetable meal prepared for him and wasn't going to get up and heat it himself. If you were to put a 1,000-dollar bill in his hand, he would have crumpled it up and thrown it down. He had no idea of the fun things he could buy with it.

Likewise, God has a world of blessings and riches waiting for us. Do we even know they are there, or do we live in our own carefree world, totally missing them? Are we twirling our cheap little toy guitars for hours on end, unaware of such greater treasures within our grasp that God has waiting for us? Consider the priceless treasure of God's Holy Word. "For the word of God is quick, and powerful, and sharper than any two-edged sword, piercing even to the dividing asunder of soul and spirit, and of the joints and marrow, and is a discerner of the thoughts and intents of the heart" (Heb. 4:12). God's Word lights our way, "Thy word is a lamp unto my feet, and a light unto my path," (Ps. 119:105) and feeds our hungry souls, "Man shall not live by bread alone, but by every word that proceedeth out of the mouth of God," (Matt. 4:4). "As newborn babes, desire the sincere milk of the word, that ye may grow thereby," (1 Pet. 2:2). "How sweet are thy words unto my taste! yea, sweeter than honey to my mouth!" (Ps. 119:103). God gave us His Word to show us His love and point us to His dear Son Jesus Christ, our Savior, who Himself said, "Search the scriptures; for in them ye think ye have eternal life: and they are they which testify of me" (John 5:39). The Bible can be read from cover to cover 100 times, and on the 101st time, new insights will open up, truths never seen before because it is the living Word of God. Never neglect the Word of God.

Think about what a treasure there is in the privilege of prayer. The Almighty Creator of the universe welcomes us to talk to him personally at any time in any place. That is not something to be taken lightly. Grab hold of that blessing that is always a whisper away.

Ponder the riches that serving the Lord is both through blessings in this life and treasures in heaven, "Lay not up for yourselves treasures upon earth, where moth and rust doth corrupt, and where thieves break through and steal: But lay up for yourselves treasures in heaven, where neither moth nor rust doth corrupt, and where thieves do not break through nor steal: For where your treasure is, there will your heart be also" (Matt. 6:19–21). Take hold of God's treasures.

While Dito didn't have the physical or mental capacity to appreciate the comforts and pleasures all around him, we do have the capacity to accept God's spiritual treasures that are right in front of us for the taking. Let us not miss out.]

Chapter 10

The Next Generation

Neddles, Niddles, Noodles, Naffy, Niffy, Nuffy

A little over a year after Dito became part of the family, Molly accepted the largest group they ever had, six siblings. One of Molly's very good friends was the director of another children's home. Their home was different in that they took in temporary children who were not yet declared abandoned, usually keeping them for a maximum of two years. During that time, they worked with the parents, presenting them with the gospel and trying to help them resolve family conflicts. The idea was to return the children to a more stable family. That was not always achieved. Sometimes, parents did not respond, and the director needed to find a home for the children, or the government would step in, and that was usually not a good thing.

Molly's friend was especially concerned about this family because no one would ever take in six siblings together, meaning that they were doomed to be separated. The little ones would be adopted out, and the older ones would probably remain in the system until they were eighteen years old. Once again, Molly had a hard time saying no, and they were soon welcoming them into the home. There were three boys and three girls. The boys were Neddles, age thirteen, Niddles, age nine, and tiny Noodles, age two. The girls were Naffy, age eleven, Niffy, age eight, and cute little Nuffy, age five.

With each new child who came into the home, there was always an adjustment period for everyone. Needless to say, accepting six new children at one time multiplied all the adjustments by six. They were their own family, and for a prolonged period of time, it seemed like the home had two families in a competition of "ours against yours." And even though the competition was fourteen against six, it really seemed like the six were winning more often than not. They came in like a whirlwind, putting the home in a state of total confusion. They had come from a home with a completely different set of rules, and Molly had to constantly correct them and explain over and over again what was and what was not appropriate in their new home. In addition, any little problem that started up against one of the new kids was met by five other new kids defending their sibling. Molly's heart went out to the children who had lived with her ever since they had been little tikes and were constantly being told to scoot over and make room for more. She felt that this time, she had asked them to scoot just a little too far. In a single day, the family had grown from fourteen children to twenty, and Molly could now see that the difference between the two numbers was huge.

Yet another change was that the noise levels skyrocketed throughout the house. Although Molly had always looked for a balance between indoor and outdoor activities, she now let them have unlimited outdoor time to cut down on the noise inside. This was probably not the best idea, as Molly soon found out. The siblings had come from a very large organization that had eight houses with ten kids and house parents in each house. They were used to running wild on a large piece of property among eighty kids all looking for trouble. With so many kids and so many hiding places, looking for a boyfriend or girlfriend was common, as was hiding behind buildings when finding one. Soon, Neddles had his eye on Biffy, and Niddles was trying to make up his mind between Miffy or Muffy. Eventually, many months later, the dust cloud began to settle, and the group of six slowly merged into the family.

The siblings were the last six of twelve or thirteen children from the same mother but with several different fathers. Just among these six, they represented four different biological fathers. There had been complications with the birth of the youngest child, which caused the baby to have to be born by Caesarean. Soon afterward, the mother suffered a serious infection from the surgery. With no one to care for her younger children, she turned six of them over to social services temporarily before returning to the hospital to treat the infection. Since all the older children were long gone, she left only her fourteen-year-old daughter at home to take care of the house while she was away.

Once in the government system, social workers began questioning the children individually. The oldest boy, Neddles, who was only eleven at the time, said that he did not want to return to his mother and that anywhere would be better than being with her. On further questioning, he said that his mother was renting his older brother to an adult man who was abusing him and several other boys who lived in his house. Neddles was sure that he would be the next in line to be rented out. His mother had already taken him to the man's house to meet him a couple of times. On his testimony, the kids were taken away permanently, and papers were begun to declare them abandoned.

The mother did absolutely nothing to get her children back. Although, at first, she was allowed to visit, she never showed up for any visitation days. Soon, she was refused visits. The older sister, however, was faithful to visit, so her visitation privileges were extended when they were translated to Molly's home. This meant that once every two months, Molly would take them to the social service office to see their sister. By this time, she was sixteen years old and working as a waitress to support her mother. She would tell the children that their mother loved them very much and then pulled out bags of gifts and snacks that she claimed the mother had sent. Molly knew that the sister had really purchased the things since she clearly said the mother was not even working. At the end of the visit, all would send their love to their kind mother.

Little five-year-old Nuffy would ask the sister to tell her mother that she loved her very, very, very much and to thank her for the gifts. Since Niffy had not seen her mother since age three, Molly doubted she even remembered her. It pained Molly greatly that her children were being deceived at every visit. Yet since they were such a close-knit family, Molly felt it would be counterproductive to contradict the sister, especially while she herself was still fighting for them to bond with everyone else in the home.

The same sister who was so kind to most of the group was awkwardly ugly toward Neddles. She blamed him for all her siblings being taken away from her because he complained and let him know how she felt in no uncertain terms. As a result, the other siblings began thinking of him as the bad guy and destroyer of their happiness. Neddles tried so hard to be the protective older brother and hero, but to no avail. Besides being the traitor, he had a slight speech impediment, was struggling in school, and was always bragging. All these things aided in driving his siblings away from him and made him the brunt of all their jokes.

Neddles seemed not to care. He knew that what he had said was true and was happy to be in a new permanent home, as well as eager to make Molly happy. The truth is, she had never seen anyone so eager to please and such a hard worker. Anything that needed to be done, Neddles had done that before, knew exactly how to do it, and was off doing it in no time. No jobs were done halfheartedly. If he was going to clean the kitchen, he started by pulling every pot and pan out of every cupboard, and every fork and spoon out of every drawer, and piling them all on the tables in the dining room area. Then he brought in a bucket of water and lots of suds, which he began slopping here and there. The whole process scared Molly the first time she saw it, but he assured her he knew what he was doing, and she decided to not even watch. Hours later, he called her into the cleanest kitchen she had ever seen.

There indeed seemed to be no job that Neddles would not tackle. He attacked the ceilings with the same vigor as the kitchen, then the fans, and then the bathrooms. His biggest problem was that his mouth seemed to work every bit as hard as his hands, and soon, everyone was tired of hearing him talk about himself and all he had done and could do.

The next child, from oldest to youngest, was Naffy. She was quite the opposite of Neddles. Naffy almost never talked, she was extremely shy and could hardly even read a poem out loud in their private homeschool. She kept her own things neat but did not volunteer for extra jobs. Other than oral presentations, she did very well in school. She had been like a mother to little Niffy and Noodles since they were babes, and they came to her constantly for their every need. In fact, she was very attached to any baby and always had one in her arms at church. Noodles was especially attached to her and would look for her every time he needed a mother figure. Being so young, Noodles slept in a bed in Molly's room, but it was Naffy who had to come tuck him into bed at night and give him a kiss. Molly tried to build a bond with him in several different ways, but he didn't need her. He had Naffy, and that was enough.

Naffy also had the talent and patience to fix all the girls' hair, except for Niffy, who did not want her hair "fixed." The artistic creations that she could produce on top of each girl's head were quite remarkable. However, the price of beauty that had to be paid by each of her young clients was hours of having their heads jerked this way and their hair tugged that way.

After the family had been in the home for a little over two years, Brother Neff asked Molly to make a trip to the States for the Lighthouse Children's Home annual camp meeting. At the time, there was no way Molly could take all the children, but she would always take Dito with her when she traveled, not trusting his care to anyone else. Since Giffy had never been on a trip to the States and was always talking about going, Molly decided to take her to help out with Dito. On further consideration, knowing Giffy's limitations, she decided to also take Naffy. She was very mature, having had to play the role of mother from a very young age, and Molly was counting on her to help with both Dito and Giffy.

The foursome traveled all day Saturday, and by Sunday morning, Naffy was feeling so bad she could not even go to church with them but stayed by herself in the dormitory where they were being housed. Instead of getting better, she began feeling worse, and by Monday morning, they were off to the doctor only to find that Naffy had appendicitis and needed to be hospitalized. What timing! These were the only two weeks in the year that she would be out of Costa Rica, where all children, by law, had their medical bills covered. But obviously, this could not wait, and though the problem seemed too big for Molly to handle, it wasn't too big for God.

The operation was quick and simple, but she would need to remain in the hospital for several days. She was so shy and so unsure of her English that she asked Molly if Giffy could stay the night with her, and they got permission for Giffy to do so. Thus, Molly lost both her Dito helpers the first week and had to tend to all his needs in between their visits back and forth to the hospital. Though Naffy was out of the hospital quickly, she was rather sore for most of the trip and never much of a help, which was the reason Molly had brought her along. That was a minor problem, however, in comparison to the problem of how they were going to pay the hospital bill. Yet, as was already mentioned, it was not too big a problem for God, and the silver lining of the whole experience was the remarkable way He took care of everything. A very good friend who had served in their homeschool for several years was now a social worker with specific connections to the very hospital where they had taken Naffy, go figure. She filled out the paperwork for them, and they were accepted into a program that took care of the entire hospital bill. In addition, the doctor decided not to charge them for the operation, so they owed absolutely nothing, praise God. He had been one step ahead of them the whole time.

Their second week in the States was the famous Lighthouse Children's Home Camp Meeting they had traveled to attend. Brother Neff asked Giffy, who loved to talk, to give a testimony the first night, and she did remarkably well all on her own. When he told Molly he would like Naffy to give a testimony the following evening, Molly tried to talk him out of it by explaining how very shy she was. He was quite determined, though, and said that Molly could stand right next to her and translate. As they walked to the platform, Naffy kept whispering to Molly that she couldn't do it, and Molly kept replying that she had to do it.

Soon Naffy was standing in front of the microphone staring into a large group of scary-looking people. After she had been staring for an awkwardly long period of time, Molly told her to say something, anything. She said, "Hola," and Molly translated, "Hi." This was followed by a second long period of staring, with Molly whispering for her to tell the nice people who she was, Naffy saying her name, and Molly translating, "I'm Naffy." As the silence of the third awkward stare grew longer, Molly wished she could crawl under a rock. She whispered to Naffy to say something else. Naffy asked what she should say, and Molly told her to thank the people for all they had done. Naffy said, "Gracias," Molly translated, "Thank you," and the two of them exited the platform, walking briskly. Brother Neff never asked Naffy to give a testimony again.

Niddles was a loud, happy, nine-year-old fellow with a very outgoing personality. Since he loved joking around and being the center of attention, he made friends easily. He was also a good athlete and loved playing soccer. He was an intelligent boy who would have gotten great grades in school had he not loved goofing off so much and being such a clown in classes. He was only a little over a year older than Doodles, and for the first time in years, Doodles had a friend close to his own age.

Niffy also loved to joke around but mostly with people she knew well. She was not loud and didn't want to be the center of attention. She just liked doing silly off-the-wall things. She was very athletic, and Niddles always wanted her on his team when they played soccer in the gym. When the family finally began spreading their wings and making friends within the home, she teamed up with Muffy, and they became inseparable friends. This was not a good idea. Muffy had become known for being cruel, and Niffy had several issues of her own. The two together spent their days looking for mischief and always finding it. Niffy, like Naffy, had to have her appendix removed, but fortunately, she was in Costa Rica at the time.

Little five-year-old Nuffy lived in the shadow of the older kids. Though everyone protected two-year-old Noodles, they must have felt that Nuffy could handle things on her own because nobody babied her, and indeed, they mostly ignored her. But ironically, to Noodles, Nuffy was very important, right next to Naffy in importance. Noodles spent most of his day following Nuffy around or calling out to her. The two were very close playmates. As she grew, they found her to be a good student and fast learner who did well in all her school subjects. She was never athletic like Niffy but liked to play house and with dolls. Reading became another of her favorite pastimes. You could almost always find her with a book in her hand in either English or Spanish.

Yet, Nuffy had another side to her. Though she was so fast at understanding book knowledge, she lacked common sense. Everyone would scratch their head in amazement at how a girl who did so well in school could ask such silly questions or do such silly things, but she did. Molly wondered if her silliness was her way of grabbing back the attention of which her siblings had robbed her.

As Nuffy grew and began to help in the kitchen, she became known for burning everything. The family joked that she had even burned water—an obvious impossibility—when, on several occasions, hot empty pans were found on hot burners. She was also notorious for being the last one on the bus whenever they went somewhere. After

Molly honked for her to hurry several times, Nuffy would run out the front door with her shoes, makeup bag, and several other items in hand. Then, no sooner would she sit down than she would remember something else, dash off the bus, and run back toward the house for another armload of things. She was even known for jumping in the shower at the exact moment she heard the call for everyone to get on the bus, then rushing out after they had been waiting for about ten minutes, with her wet hair flapping in the breeze.

Then there was cute, innocent-looking Noodles, who, to put it mildly, turned out to be a not-so-innocent handful. Though his siblings protected him from the other children in the home, they themselves had very little patience with his annoying ways. Noodles would cry over anything and everything. His favorite time to cry was when Molly called the children to line up for a meal. Since he loved to eat, there was really no logical explanation for the crying to start up right at the moment that they were trying to pray and begin serving the food. Molly decided that the little fellow could clearly see that this was the best time to get everyone's attention all at once, and oh, how he loved attention.

In his craving for attention, Noodles would always make it a point to do just the opposite of what was asked of them. If they were walking somewhere, and Molly said that she would lead the way, in a sneaky sort of way, he was suddenly way out in front of the group. If she switched it up and said she wanted everyone in front of her and no one lagging behind, soon they were looking for Noodles and finding him a quarter of a mile behind them.

Once when he was about six years old, Grandma and Grandpa Heflin took them all out for pizza. When it was time to go, Noodles ran into the bathroom precisely as everyone was told to go get into the car. He was only being his attention-getting self, for he had already made a trip to the bathroom, except that nobody noticed he was not with them. Nor did they miss him on the entire half-hour drive home. Finally, maybe after being home for twenty minutes or so, someone finally realized he wasn't with them. Molly immediately called the restaurant, confirmed he was there, and rushed back feeling oh so guilty and thinking that he must have been in tears by that time. They found him sitting at a table smiling as he ate his second bowl of ice cream. Molly's guilty feeling suddenly disappeared, and she spent most of the drive back home bawling him out.

As a small child, he had the problem of breaking all his toys. He wouldn't break them eventually; he would break them the same day he would get them. Once, he got a nice, battery-operated car with doors that opened. Molly went all the way through the little speech about taking care of it, but when he ran off to enjoy his new toy, she mumbled to the older kids around her that it probably wouldn't last much more than two days. Twenty minutes later, Niddles brought Noodles and the car back with the door torn off. She reprimanded him and reminded him that he was to take care of it. He shook his head, "Yes," and ran off with the car for a second time. Less than thirty minutes later, Niddles brought Noodles' car back, packed full of mud. Molly gave up.

Things did not get any easier as he grew older. No matter what instructions Molly was giving to the group, upon finishing her explanation, Noodles would raise his hand and give his "why don't we" instruction for his "better" way of doing it. He was also the neediest child Molly had. Every day he needed something. He needed soap, shampoo, deodorant, new sneakers, dress shoes, a new toothbrush, toothpaste, white socks, black socks, blue polka dot socks, a flashlight—it was always something. If he got in trouble at school, his explanation of what had happened would get so complicated that it would send Molly into a tizzy. He wasn't a very honest child but was very good at making one think he was by putting just enough truth in his stories to make them believable. Then, upon talking to someone else, there was suddenly a whole new side to the story.

Once, at the age of sixteen, after Molly had been listening to his stories for some fourteen years, he was trying to convince her of a real whopper of a story. He was getting very frustrated because it was fairly obvious that she wasn't buying his story. With an urgency in his voice, he blurted out, "For the first time in my life, I'm telling you the truth, and you don't want to believe me."

"Well, well, now I wonder why that would be," replied Molly.

Regardless of his annoying characteristics, Noodles had several redeeming qualities. He was outgoing and friendly with all visitors. He was a very intelligent child and had no academic problems whatsoever in school. In fact, he was reading before the age of five, after only three or four weeks of kindergarten. Molly had several who read before five but couldn't remember any learning in so short a time unless it had been Coodles. Unfortunately, books and learning didn't hold the same importance to Noodles as they had to Coodles since learning to him was no more than something that had to be done.

Around the house, Noodles was a hard worker, always completing his own chores as well as other extra jobs. If Molly had some job that she was sure nobody would want, she would ask Noodles, and he was willing do to it, whether it was a paying job or not. Just like all his other brothers and sisters, all his personal things were neat and in order. For such a big family that had come from tragically dysfunctional parents, it was awesome how each one kept their personal belongings impeccable and in perfect order.

Poodles

It was almost another four years before any new permanent children came into the home. Those were years when many of the first generations were growing up and moving on with their lives. Several oodles and iffies were no longer with them, and the group of twenty that they had when the six siblings had come along had already dwindled down to a mere thirteen children. By this time, after sixteen years of ministry, Molly liked the number thirteen very much, but any time the home went down to a mere fourteen kids, Brother Neff would get nervous and start asking how they could get more. This particular time, he had been talking about new little ones for a while, and everyone's ears and eyes were open for children who needed a permanent home.

At the same time, Dito's vocational therapist had become good friends with Molly and talked to her often about another job she held teaching a kindergarten class of about ten children who all had cerebral palsy. She invited Molly to visit her class and witness firsthand how she worked with the children. Molly gladly accepted the invitation and soon joined in with the children and teacher as they sat in a circle on the floor. One of the little boys made his way over to Molly, sat in her lap, and stayed with her for the entire class. He was a thin little fellow with weak, uncooperative limbs but a bright and happy personality. He obviously came from a Christian family because he began to quote verse after verse of Scripture his mother had taught him. Immediately, the gears in Molly's head started to turn and her heart to skip beats. *Slow down Molly, slow down.* But it was too late, the idea was already there of helping a child who could not run and play with the other children but did have a mind to learn and understand God's Holy Word.

Shortly afterward, Molly made an appointment with the same director of adoption who had given her Dito. She had only one question when she entered the office. She asked if there was a small child with cerebral palsy who needed a permanent home. The director had a surprised look on her face, picked up a pile of eight to ten file folders sitting on the corner of her desk, and began thumbing through them. She pulled the file she was searching for out and placed it on the top of the stack, explaining that it had just come in a few days earlier. She opened the file to reveal the picture of a darling little five-year-old boy named Poodles with big brown eyes and blondish hair. There was no doubt in Molly's mind that God had sent that file to her desk at just the right time.

Poodles's mother was a fifteen-year-old teen with a drug addiction when he was born. He was born prematurely, weighing less than two pounds. The father was nowhere to be found, and the young mother gave the baby to the grandmother. The alcoholic grandmother had many issues of her own and was no more fit to care for the child than was the mother. At only eleven months old, the police found the baby left in a basket in a local bar. The family never adhered to the requisites of recovering the child from social services, and he was declared abandoned. At the age of five, he was still waiting for a forever family, but nobody wanted the thin, fragile boy who could not walk. It appeared that his future was very bleak.

In the orphanage, he was placed in a playpen so the other children would not harm him and spent most of his time sitting there, watching TV. No one worked with him, no one tried to help him, and he was completely ignored. Finally, a therapist was sent to the orphanage, and it was discovered that Poodles could learn. Slowly, he learned to stand, walk with a walker, and to repeat words.

Plans were made, papers were written up, and visits were scheduled. On the first of those visits, Molly stood at the front door, watching Poodles scurrying up the driveway between two social workers who were holding tight to his hands. He was moving as fast as his thin, crooked legs and braces would carry him, with a smile extending from ear to ear. His huge smile and excitement brought tears to Molly's eyes. He had been told that he was going to have a family, and he was thrilled with everything they showed him. Considering the life he had lived, this had to be the happiest day he had known. The other children fell in love with him immediately, as did Molly. After each visit, it was so difficult to say goodbye and send him back to the government home. He had to make visits to his new home for a month before he was allowed to stay.

Finally, the day came for them to pick Poodles up and bring him home permanently. Molly loaded all the kids into the big bus so everyone could participate in the homecoming. All were happy, and Poodles finally had a real home. From the very start, he was a happy, positive boy. He tried not to let his physical problems slow him down too much. There were so many things to do in his new home, and he wanted to play with every toy, look through every book, and even have his turn to bang on the piano. Yet though he tried his hardest at everything, he did have several limitations. His paralysis was mostly in his legs, although his hands were slightly affected.

Since he had been left to himself most of his life, his vocabulary was spotty. He could say simple phrases like what his name was, how old he was, or what an object was, but he was unable to communicate more complicated concepts. Yet he wanted to be a part of his new family so desperately that he took to repeating everything that Molly asked of the children. Molly would say, "Everyone line up for dinner," and Poodles, "Everyone line up for dinner." She would ask, "Whose turn is it to pray?" and he would parrot, "Whose turn is it to pray?" Molly thought having a little echo was the cutest little thing, but it frustrated the other children. Several kids came to Molly in private and asked her to make him stop repeating everything. Molly knew he just wanted to talk but didn't know what to say. Just to see how well he could communicate on his own, Molly told him the story of Noah's ark and then asked him to tell her the story he had just heard. He just stared at her; he didn't even know how to start. It was a couple of months before he could finally tell a story and engage in simple conversations.

Poodles could use his little walker to get around but preferred by far to crawl. His knees were very hard and calloused from crawling, and the children called them "camel knees." He would sometimes bark as he crawled and said he wanted to be a dog when he grew up. In addition, in the government home, they had not even attempted to potty train him, which, of course, became Molly's first goal. In less than two months, he was no longer having accidents during the day and only wore diapers at night.

The other first thing on the agenda was doctor visits. Molly disregarded all his social medicine appointments and looked for private doctors. They made appointments with a neurologist, pediatrician, orthopedic doctor, dentist, and optometrist. He also immediately began having therapy with Dito's physical therapist and his vocational therapist. Molly learned so much from the doctors about everything he needed and how they should work with him. He got new braces for his legs, new glasses, new Canadian crutches, and lots of little things that would be useful in his therapies. They made a special piece of furniture for him that was supposed to help straighten his knees, which were normally bent at almost a ninety-degree angle. It looked rather like a step ladder with a cushion to lean against on one side and a little table at the top. He was to stand strapped against the cushion, legs completely straight, for thirty minutes, twice during the day.

This was the perfect time for the older kids to take turns working with him on his numbers, colors, vowel sounds, and Bible verses. Molly didn't know how many verses he would be able to learn, but she started out with five visualized cards, with a picture on one side and a verse on the other. In a week's time, he could already quote all five verses by just looking at the picture that corresponded to the verse. Molly had a difficult time trying to make up enough verse cards on the computer to keep up with him. In five short months, Poodles knew fifty verses of Scripture word perfect, as did all the kids who were working with him. Poodles advanced so quickly in every area that it was obvious that all he had lacked to advance was a loving family and people who would work with him.

At evening devotions, when Molly would sit in her rocking chair, Poodles would crawl up to the chair and look up with great big eyes, wanting to be picked up. Molly would hold him in her lap during the devotion, and he would sit very, very still. At the end of devotions, he would look up to her face, touch her silvering hair with his feeble little hand, and say just two words, "Pretty Mommy." Molly really wasn't very pretty, but Poodles was so happy to finally have a Mommy who he knew loved him after years of not being able to call anyone his Mommy. Molly would touch his hair back and say, "Cute Poodles," and he was indeed very cute.

Raddles, Riddles, Raffy, Reffy, and Riffy

Poodles had only been with them for a little over two months when a new family of five came into the home. Molly had felt so overwhelmed when she had received the family of six siblings that she told herself she would never do that again, and now, counting Poodles, once again, they had six new ones in a short period of time. Nevertheless, somehow, the transition did not seem quite as earth-shattering as the first group of six had seemed, except for one little fellow. The family of five siblings came from the same temporary home as the family of six. The father or fathers were absent from their lives, and the government had already placed them in one of their homes previously for neglect and later returned them to the mother. When the two boys, Raddles and Riddles got to be more than she could handle, she sent them to live in the Christian temporary home where Molly's friend was the director. The mother kept the girls a little while longer, and then one day, left them, telling her oldest daughter, who was nine years old at the time, that she was going to Nicaragua and would come back later. The neighbors, learning that the girls were alone, contacted the government, and they, too, were sent to the same home as the boys. Like the group of six, they had been in the home for quite a while with no visits from the mother, and finding a home for all five would be difficult. Since they had been praying and looking for new kids, and, having room for a larger group, Molly felt that the Lord would have her accept a large family once again, taking their number back up, this time to nineteen.

All three girls were fairly calm and obedient, rarely causing any problems. They also did well in their studies. Raffy, the oldest, was eleven years old when they came into the home. She turned out to be the best artist out of all the generations, effortlessly drawing beautiful pictures. Though she was almost five years younger than the older girls, by the time she was in her late teens, she had become close friends with Kiffy, Fluffy, and Naffy.

Reffy was seven years old when she came into the home and was a tad bit quieter than the other two girls. As she grew, her interests included photography and playing the guitar. While she had never been very athletic before, in her early teens, what she wanted more than anything for Christmas was a skateboard. Molly had never seen her happier than when she was carrying around the nice skateboard she got that year. Yet, as with many things that kids think they can't live without, the skateboard phase lasted less than a year, during which time young Reffy was probably seen more often proudly carrying her board around with a smile on her face than she was riding it.

Sweet-tooth Riffy was only five years old when she arrived. She was affectionately nicknamed Dora the Explorer for her similar appearance to the cartoon character with her short dark hair, bangs, and big dark eyes. She was a happy little girl who avoided fighting and any other form of trouble. She soon became a good companion for Poodles as they played, laughed, and worked on simple kindergarten materials together all morning long while the others were at school. When she first came, she didn't care much for normal healthy food but was always quick to get anything sweet into her mouth. Once, when some of the bigger kids were going to walk down to the mini market to get some snacks for Molly's birthday, Riffy asked Molly for some money to go with them. She said she knew exactly what she wanted to get Mommy for her birthday, a chocolate-covered strawberry. Apparently, Riffy had seen them before and had always thought they looked delicious. Molly smiled at Riffy's enthusiasm to buy her a gift, however minimal it might be. When the girls returned, Molly's mouth was already watering at the thought of her chocolate-covered strawberry, but Riffy had nothing in her hands. Confused at seeing ice creams and chocolates for Mommy in everyone else's hands, Molly asked Riffy where her chocolate-covered strawberry was. Two very round, partly scared, and partly sad eyes looked up at Molly as Riffy confessed that she had eaten it on the walk home. Bless her little heart; it not only looked delicious but was irresistible as well.

Years later, Molly was not a bit surprised when, as a teen, Riffy asked to take some dessert baking and cake decorating classes. Soon, all the younger kids were placing their orders for their birthday desserts. Her talents weren't limited to only the kitchen, though. She had a nice singing voice, played the viola and the guitar, and even dabbled in oil painting.

The two boys in the family, Raddles and Riddles, were nine-year-old fraternal twins who could not have been more opposite of each other had they tried. Raddles was a fairly good student with a talent for drawing cartoon characters. Riddles struggled through school. When he wasn't daydreaming, he spent most of his class time gazing out the second-floor school window at nearby construction projects, wishing he could be down there working instead of reading and writing at his desk. Riddles was different from his brother in the area of artistic abilities as well in that he could not even sketch a decent stick figure.

But the biggest difference between the two boys was their disposition. Those who had worked with Raddles in his previous home had said he was somewhat of a discipline problem, but Molly soon realized that was an understatement. Though he could have done well in school, he was full of anger and rage. On the other hand, Riddles was a happy child who found joy all around him.

There had been discipline problems with many children down through the years, but Raddles's anger was explosive and often resulted in damage to furnishings or, even worse, to other people. Molly and many other authorities, in the home and outside the home, worked with him for years in counseling, prayer, positive reinforcement, discipline, and anything else they could think of doing. Pastors in Bible conferences had even gathered around him to pray on more than one occasion. He would have his good days, and everyone would be encouraged, but then there would be another explosion.

Sometimes they would find themselves in a vicious circle. The older kids were unwilling to put up with the tantrums of the new nine-year-old and would bully him and try to take things into their own hands. But the strong-willed child, instead of yielding, would fight back harder, even though he was quite a bit smaller than the teens, which, of course, only upset them more.

By the time Raddles was thirteen years old, he became very difficult to control. He had given numerous children nose bleeds, broken a head or two open, attacked Noodles in the face with a nail clipper, causing him to need four stitches, and been the cause of many other bumps and bruises. He had even hurt Poodles, who was not only a special needs child but was four years younger than Raddles. In his anger, he had thrown him to the ground, chipping one of his front teeth. He had also, in a scuffle, cut a missionary's head open who was helping a teacher get him out from under a table. Some days, teachers refused to allow him in the classroom, and Molly had to tutor him in the house.

Other problems Raddles had were making weapons, stealing, constant bad language, taking little kids up on roofs, turning over furniture, and damaging cars and buildings, and the list kept getting longer. Molly had even taken him to social services, where he had also received counseling and been told that he would have to leave the home if he kept hurting the other very small children in the home. By this time, there were several new very small children in the home whom everyone felt were in danger.

Finally, shortly before his fourteenth birthday, after an incident with a three-year-old, the board of directors asked Molly to turn Raddles over to social services for the safety of the other children. The original plan was for him to be allowed to have visits with his siblings, but the constant struggles that social services had with him never allowed for setting up visits. Raddles ended up living in a cycle of street living, jail, rehabilitation centers, and back on the streets. All of his siblings, Polly, and Molly have tried to help him in countless ways and continue to pray that he will allow Christ to work in his life to break the cycle.

Riddles was so different from Raddles that Molly honestly asked herself if they could possibly be the offspring of two different fathers. He was not only a happy child but was also obedient and hardworking, willing to help on any project. He was friendly and kind. He became Dito's best friend. No one loved Dito as Riddles did. He knew all of Dito's ticklish spots and would have him laughing uncontrollably. Molly would ask Riddles how he got him to laugh so loud. He would show her, and Molly would try to do the exact same thing in the exact same place, only to watch Dito lie there with a blank expression on his face as if he were telling Molly that some folks just don't know how to tell a joke. Riddles liked to put Dito in his wheelchair and take him out into the sun. He would run him up and down the driveway or in fast circles in the gym, once again making him laugh.

The one personality trait about happy-go-lucky Riddles that rather bugged Molly was his love of scaring people. He was the kid who always hid behind doors and jumped out with a loud yell to laugh at the scared look on his innocent victim's face.

Once, the boys were working on digging a big hole for a new septic tank. After working all afternoon, some of the boys asked Molly to come see how deep the hole was getting. She had nothing to do with the project, but they kept insisting she see the hole. They seemed so excited about the job they had done that she decided to go take a look and be an encouragement for them. By the time they neared the hole, they seemed to be nudging her forward, and feeling suspicious, she warned the boys not to push her into the hole. They insisted they only wanted her to see it. She had barely looked in and commented on how deep it was when Riddles, who was buried in the dirt at the bottom of the hole, sat up with some kind of loud roar and accomplished his goal of scaring her half to death. She jumped so high that it was a miracle she didn't lose her balance, fall into the hole, and land right on top of him. Fortunately, they had probably thought of that ahead of time because she seemed to have a boy on either side of her holding her arms. Everyone was laughing loudly, except, of course, for Molly. Embarrassed at having walked right into their little trap, she commented on how dangerous that had been and how it wouldn't have been so funny if she would have had a heart attack, then turned around and exited the scene.

As Riddles grew older, for the most part, he outgrew the need to scare people but never outgrew the joy of playing practical jokes on them. His slapstick sense of humor drove Molly up a wall in a good sort of way. She did not share that particular sense of humor.

Nevertheless, the best thing about Riddles was his sensitivity to spiritual things. Though he had struggled through school and hating reading the whole time, after graduation, to everyone's surprise, he decided to go to Bible college. Three years later, he had suddenly developed a love for reading and an appreciation for studying, go figure. He later went on to marry a wonderful Christian woman and went into full-time Christian service.

[A LESSON TO LEARN: Raddles and Riddles started life on the same day, faced the same struggles, and by God's providence, found themselves in a Christian home at age nine. There they heard the same gospel story of Christ's great love and forgiveness, learned the same Bible verses, and had the same opportunities to respond. One humbled his heart before God while the other hardened his heart, and the direction that each life took was a clear consequence of each one's choice. God reveals truth to us but always leaves to us the choice of how we respond. Have you humbled your heart and accepted God's dear Son as your Savior or hardened your heart to his Word? "For with the heart man believeth unto righteousness . . ." (Rom. 10:10a). The choice is yours.]

A Little Bit More about Poodles

This chapter cannot end without making mention of a tragic Poodles story that took place eight months after his arrival at the home. The problem actually started from an incident Molly had with Miffy and Muffy, who, by this time, were sixteen and fourteen years old. They each had their ups and downs through the years, but both seemed to be going through a particularly rebellious stage now that they were well into their teen years. The newest problem Molly was having with them was that they were sneaking out the front gate to talk with a group of boys who hung out in the street, usually playing soccer. The house rule was that nobody was allowed off the property without permission. Since their neighborhood was not very safe, Molly was especially protective of her girls. Fortunately, there were plenty of other kids who kept Molly informed when they slipped out the gate, and she would call them back in.

This particular day, Molly was told that Miffy and Muffy had gone on down the street to the neighborhood mini-market type store. Molly took several other kids with her and marched down the street to get them. She didn't make a scene, just simply told them that they didn't have permission to go to the store and needed to go back home. But knowing teenagers, that was probably enough to embarrass them in front of their friends. As soon as they were home, Miffy started yelling that she wanted to be taken back to a government home. She said that she knew Molly wanted to be her mother, but she wasn't, and she didn't want her to be. Years before, similar words had devastated Molly, but now she had heard them too many times to be hurt again. She imagined they would settle down, and everything would be back to normal in the morning.

Molly awoke to find the girls already packing their things. It was unbelievable. Nobody had ever wanted to be returned to a government home. Those who had threatened to leave before all hoped that relatives would receive them. But, unbeknown to Molly, they already had the idea that they would just tell the social worker they wanted to live with their biological mother and would be sent there immediately. Nevertheless, things did not quite work out that way. Little did they know it would be many months before they would make it to their mother's house, and once there, they would stay less than two months before they would be off looking for a new place to live.

The girls could not be convinced to stay, and Molly finally took them to the government office and dropped them off. They had come to Molly ten years earlier with only a backpack full of belongings. She dropped them off with four bulging garden-sized trash bags stuffed to the brim with their things. From the look on the social worker's face, no child had ever been dropped off with so many possessions. The social workers and psychologists immediately interviewed the girls as to why they didn't want to stay at the Lighthouse Home. This, of course, was done after Molly had left, but she would soon learn what they had said.

Had the interview been done in the Cartago office that Molly had always worked with and by the social workers she knew so well, it probably would not have amounted to much, and she would have had an opportunity to speak as well. Unfortunately, within the last year or two, they had opened a new office in Tres Rios, and Molly had been informed that they would be handling all their cases since they now lived in Tres Rios. She had not had many dealings with the new office and was not acquainted with the people who worked there. Nevertheless, they were about to become acquainted. Days after the girls left, four ladies showed up on Molly's doorstep unannounced, asking to talk with her. The group consisted of a social worker, psychologist, lawyer, and the director of the new Tres Rios office.

The first thing the director said when they sat down was that they wanted to make some changes to Molly's home and needed to know if she was willing to make those changes. It was a trick question, and Molly knew it. If she answered no, she would be in big trouble, and if she answered yes, she was giving them permission to do whatever they would like. In retrospect, she should have answered their question with another question, asking what kind of changes they would like to make. Yet feeling pressured, Molly's answer must have sounded defensive to them, even though she tried to say it in the calmest voice she could muster up in such an outnumbered, unexpected situation. She told them that she would make any changes that did not interfere with her religious convictions. It sounded like such a safe answer to her, but they wrote in their report that she was rebellious to change.

The girls had complained about the dress code, being homeschooled, not being able to leave the property by themselves whenever they wanted, not being allowed to stay out late, and having to go to church. Molly explained that she tried her hardest to provide a home environment and that all families had their rules. The rules were made with the best interest of the children in mind; they were there to protect them. During the conversation, she referred to the kids as "her children" and was corrected by the director, saying, "Our children." Molly questioned, "Your children? I signed papers to become their legal guardian, I house them, feed them, teach them, clothe them, know each one of them personally, including their likes and dislikes, and receive no money from you, and they are yours and not mine?"

"Yes, that is correct," was her simple answer.

The girls had also complained about being spanked on certain occasions. Actually, spanking was only one of many forms of discipline and had been approved by the government office in Cartago when they had started the home. When they asked Molly about the use of a paddle, she told them that after explaining to the child why they were being disciplined, they leaned over the bed and received two or three swats. No child had ever been physically damaged or scarred by the swats. Immediately after the discipline, Molly prayed with the child, hugged him or her, and assured the child of Molly's love. She didn't find out until later how they had interpreted her explanation.

After finishing their interview with Molly and confiscating her paddle, they asked her for a private room where the psychologist could interview each child individually. Molly provided her with a room, and the children were called in one by one. Each interview was only five or ten minutes long, and they found no child who was unhappy or who had any complaints about the house rules. As she called each child for their turn to answer questions, she realized that the ladies were not only unaware of their names but unaware of how many children she even had, oh, but they called them "their children."

When she called Poodles for his interview, they must have thought he couldn't speak because they said they did not need to interview him, but speaking about Poodles, there was one other thing that needed to be discussed. Apparently, the paperwork on Poodles that Molly had signed had not been the legal guardianship of Poodles. She had only been given a six-month protective custody, and the six months had already expired. Maybe the office that had previously handled his case had done this as a trial period to see if Molly was really willing to commit to caring for Poodles before giving her legal guardianship. She felt it was easy to resolve and told them she was ready and willing to sign the guardian papers. To her surprise, she was told that the issue had already been discussed, and they were not sure that Molly's home was the best place for Poodles. Molly brought to their attention the great advances Poodles had made and called him to meet the ladies.

When he came out, she began showing them everything he had learned in the past eight months. They just sat there with blank looks on their faces. Evidently, they were not impressed. Though they tried not to show any emotion, it was only too obvious all the ways Poodles had advanced. It was undeniable that Poodles was being well cared for and was a happy child. Yet, they continued the interrogation. They asked Molly if she had taken him to all the doctor's appointments he had scheduled when he came into her home. She answered that she had chosen rather to take him to private doctors. Certainly, they couldn't argue with that. Anyone who could afford a private doctor always preferred that route over an appointment at the social medicine clinics. Sure enough, they did not comment. No clear conclusions seemed to be reached, and since they had not specifically told her to change anything, Molly felt that the entire interview had gone very well and they had been satisfied with her answers. She was wrong.

The following week, the psychologist returned, announcing that she wanted to see their school classroom and have a second interview with each child. The interviews were longer, and there were clear conclusions at the end of them. Although each child seemed to be learning at their appropriate age level, she was troubled that none of them knew in what grade they were studying. They were educated in a one-room schoolhouse where everyone was working in different booklets according to their abilities. They all knew what booklet of each subject they were doing, but they had never memorized that booklets 1001 to 1012 were first grade and 1013 to 1024 were second grade and so forth. They also knew how well they were doing according to whether they were on the same level as other students their age. But the lady could not get past the fact that they could not tell her their grade level. It seemed more important than how well they were reading or what math skills they had mastered. The conclusion was that the children would have to be put in the public school as soon as possible to establish their grade level. Molly could not believe her ears. It sounded ridiculous; indeed, it was ridiculous.

Molly told her that they did have grade levels and that she could tell her the exact grade level of each child. Absurdly, it was not enough for the teacher and administrator to know their grade levels nor to tell the children their grade level; it could only be confirmed in a public school. But would an already overcrowded public school even accept her children right now at the end of the first trimester? The psychologist had no suggestions on how it might be done, but it was undoubtedly imperative that it be done, that it must be done, and that it must be done immediately. She would expect Molly to turn in public school report cards at the end of the next trimester. And with that tidbit of information, she was out the door.

Molly was stunned at first, but the more she considered it, the sillier it seemed. The psychologist had just completed two separate interviews with each child in the home, and the only thing she could find as an area in which to criticize their home from what the children had told her, was that they didn't know their grade in school. That didn't seem so bad. They could deal with this.

After giving it some thought, she remembered that the large Christian children's home that had given them two groups of siblings had their own government-approved school. Certainly, her friend would accept Molly's kids in her school for a while, at least until things calmed down. She kind of owed Molly a favor for opening her home to eleven of her kids. Besides, all of her elementary students who needed to know their grade level had been from that ministry in the first place. Molly was right; she was happy to help out. Although they did not charge anything for them to attend the school, it still meant a big extra expense. The school was over an hour's drive away, and with other children remaining at home who needed to be cared for, they had to hire a driver who would take them and pick them up each day. Then there was all the extra gas and the wear and tear on the van every week. But all in all, it still seemed better than putting them in a local public school where they weren't known.

The government only cared about the children in grades one through six. The kindergarten children could stay home; after all, they knew they were in kindergarten. The government didn't stress any schooling beyond the sixth grade either. Elementary school was mandatory, but they literally did not even care if the children continued studying after that. This meant everyone from seventh grade up could also continue learning at home. There were only six children who had to wake up early and travel long distances to and from school. They placed each child in the grade that corresponded to the booklets they had been doing at their homeschool. None of them had a bit of trouble keeping up. It was not long, though, until Molly felt their behavior going downhill. Though it was a Christian school, all the students came from troubled families, which was why they were in that home in the first place. Molly had to deal with the bad habits they had come to her with all over again. She desperately wanted her kids back home. As soon as the trimester ended, she turned in their report cards to the government and secretly began homeschooling them again.

Meanwhile, Molly was very much mistaken to have thought that her answers had satisfied the social service workers. When the psychologist left after the second interview, she thought getting the kids' report cards would be the last of it, but it was only the tip of the iceberg. On Friday afternoon of that same week, at 3:30 p.m., a messenger from the Tres Rios office showed up at her door with a letter. It said that Poodles was being removed from her home and that she needed to have him ready to be picked up, with all his belongings, on Monday afternoon.

Molly's heart ached terribly. This could not be happening. What were they doing? They knew Poodles was better off with her than he would be in a government home. She glanced at her watch; their office closed in thirty minutes, and she had to go fight this. She grabbed her keys and was off. She rushed in and asked to talk to the lawyer who had sent the letter. When she came out, Molly begged her, with tears in her eyes, to reconsider her decision to take Poodles out of their home. She recapped all the advances he had made. She reminded the lawyer that she had seen firsthand how happy he was and that he was being cared for very well. She told her there was no way a government home could give him all he had with Molly and that his chances of ever being placed in another loving home were next to impossible. She knew this lady had to recognize that what Molly was saying was true. She asked the lady to give her a chance, give her time. She was willing to make changes. She said that before Poodles had come into her home, he had to make visits for a whole month so it would not be a traumatic experience for him. She asked how it was possible that now there was no problem with putting him through the trauma of jerking him out in one day and taking him to a government home he had never been in with people he didn't know. (His last government home was in a different city, hours away, but she knew he was being taken to Cartago.) His previous government home had also insisted that the Lighthouse Home construct the piece of furniture Poodles needed to stand in twice a day before he could move to the home. Did the home in Cartago have all the furniture Poodles needed ready and waiting? Molly was grasping at straws, trying to think of anything she could to make her case.

As she continued pleading, she began to notice something. The lawyer just kept shaking her head, but she also, like Molly, had tears in her eyes. She was not arguing with Molly or defending her decision. Indeed, Molly saw that it had not been her decision at all. She had been forced to write the letter. When she spoke, she only said there was nothing she could do; it had already been decided. She finally whispered to Molly that if she did not like the decision, she could write up an appeal, she had seventy-two hours from the time Poodles left to turn in a written appeal.

On Monday afternoon, all of Poodles's things were packed and ready. The psychologist came right on time to pick him up. Molly asked her to sit for a minute so she could explain a few things about Poodles. She had typed up several pages of tidbits of information about Poodles for them and was now going through the various lists. There was the list of his favorite foods and how he liked them prepared, the list of what he didn't like to eat, the list of a few healthy supplements and when each should be taken, the list of therapy exercises, when, how, and how often they were to be done, the list of his favorite toys and things to do, the list of kindergarten tasks that he did each day, the proper way to put his braces on, the proper way for him to sit, the wrong way for him to sit, which was the way he liked to sit but was not allowed to, and so on.

The minutes turned into almost an hour of explanations. But the psychologist never interrupted her and never acted impatient. She was serious, not in an angry sort of way but rather in a sad sort of way. Though she never had tears in her eyes like the lawyer, Molly got the idea that she was not very excited about having to take this little boy out of a home where he was obviously loved and drop him off at a government facility. The last thing Molly turned over to the psychologist was a photo album full of happy pictures of Poodles with all his family members, so he wouldn't forget them. At the back of the album were the pictures and words of all fifty Bible verses he had learned so he could practice.

When the explanations were finally finished, Molly called all the children together, took little Poodles into her arms, and prayed that God would take care of him and help her find the means of getting him back. It was a very sad day, one of the hardest days of their lives. Everyone was crying as they watched him get into the car. Molly wasn't sure how much Poodles understood about what was happening. He was the only one smiling as he waved goodbye through the window. He must not have understood. Most likely, he thought he was just going for a ride and would be back shortly. The following morning, five-year-old Riffy came up to Molly and told her not to worry because she knew exactly where she was going to hide if those people came back to take her away. How sad, thought Molly, that this tiny little girl was so worried she was planning her escape from the people who were supposed to be protecting her. When Molly asked her where it was, she told her it was behind the church next door. Molly just gave her a hug and told her she thought that would be the perfect place, but hopefully, they wouldn't come for her.

Although it was difficult to let Poodles go, Molly knew deep down that God was in control and that she must trust that He alone knew why He was permitting this trial. She began writing up her appeal immediately and going from office to office to find out exactly what she should do. She felt that in a matter of days, the situation would be straightened out, and Poodles would be given back. Yet as the days turned into weeks, she was no closer to getting him back. It seemed that it was Molly's turn to learn the lesson that sometimes God says, "Wait," and that even, "No" is an answer. What a difficult lesson to learn. And the hardest part of waiting was not knowing.

If she could only have been sure that she would get Poodles back and that it was just a matter of waiting a while, everything would have been easier for her. She would ask herself how it could possibly NOT be God's will. She would answer her own question by thinking that God's ways are far above ours, and He indeed might have a different plan for Poodles. Oh, how she longed to hold Poodles in her arms and sing to him. She would kneel by his bed every night and pray for him. But God was silent. On how many occasions did Molly turn everything over to God, trying to thank him for the problem and see God's purpose for it and all the good He would bring about through it, but then soon afterward start worrying again? Yes, time after time, she would give it all to God, and time after time, she would take it all away from Him and place it back on her own shoulders.

Many times, Molly wished she were handling the situation better, but she couldn't stop thinking of poor little Poodles separated from the only family he had ever known and for no good reason. It was clear to her now that this was no more than a power move. They were simply trying to flex their muscles to let Molly know who was in charge. Those ladies were using an innocent, special needs child as a pawn in a chess game to put Molly in checkmate. Well, they might have had her in check, she wasn't in checkmate yet, and she was going to fight.

If there was any real question about her integrity, Molly thought, why were seventeen other children left under her care? They had said it was for Poodle's own protection. Why didn't the others need to be protected? After another trip or two to the Tres Rios office, and Molly was pretty sure it was the director and one social worker who were the real culprits. They wanted nothing to do with her and wouldn't even give her an appointment. Then Molly learned that the government lawyer and psychologist who had come to her home in the group of ladies had quit their jobs. Molly wondered if it hadn't been because they, too, were seeing the injustice the other two ladies were committing and wanted nothing to do with a job like that.

To add insult to injury, Molly was not even given permission to have visiting privileges, even though they were aware that it was her desire to do whatever was necessary to get Poodles back. Molly felt like a criminal, indeed. Mothers guilty of severe neglect or abuse were still allowed to visit their children, but Molly wasn't. On top of that, her appeal was not going well either. First, she was told to turn it into the wrong office, and it got lost in the system. One by one, she tried three different lawyers, all of whom promised her the world and never did anything. In desperation, Molly went to her old office in Cartago. Maybe they could help her. She knew for a fact that Poodles was in a home in Cartago, and maybe since they knew Molly well, they would let her visit Poodles. They told her that having visits was a long process of paperwork and that if they started on that, it could delay her appeal.

She did find at that office, however, a lady willing to help. The worker met with her and explained how and where to present her appeal and what things would help her case. Days later, she returned a second time to the office in Cartago. Although she knew she couldn't visit Poodles, she stopped at KFC to buy him some chicken, his favorite meal. She hoped someone would have compassion and drop it off where he was being housed, telling him that his mother had sent it. When she got there, everyone in the office seemed to be ignoring her. She would try to ask questions, and it was as if she was invisible. They would all just walk away. Finally, a social worker walked by and whispered to her in passing to fight it and not give up. As quickly as she said it, she was gone.

After a while, the secretary, a lady Molly had known as far back as when she had taken newborn Doodles into the office to start paperwork on him, signaled her with her hand to come near. The secretary looked this way and that, as though she were in a spy movie, then moved with Molly into a corner of the room. She explained that the lady who had talked to her in the previous visit had been fired, apparently for helping Molly. How the director in Tres Rios could have so much power over another office, or indeed, how anyone even knew that the lady had assisted her was beyond Molly's comprehension. As it turned out, it was supposedly because she had overstepped her boundaries. One office was not allowed to give aid in decisions of another office's cases. No wonder everyone was afraid to talk to her; their job was on the line.

She also told her that the office in Tres Rios had asked for the files of all of Molly's children. She said they had turned over to them all the files accept Dito's file, which they were hiding. Evidently, removing Dito from the home was their next chess move. Everyone in the Cartago office was mad at the Tres Rios office. They felt they had gone crazy. Molly thought so too.

Molly was about to ask if someone could take the chicken to Poodles when the front door opened and a lady pushed a stroller through the door. Sitting in the stroller was Molly's very own dear Poodles. The caregiver who was pushing him had just brought him back from a doctor's appointment and had stopped by the office to talk to a social worker about an unrelated matter. Poodles hollered, "Mommy," and Molly hollered back, "Poodles." It was a God-planned, God-given meeting. What were the chances of both of them being there at the same time? But Molly's heavenly Father knew how she longed to see Him and how much it would mean to her.

They had been apart for two weeks, but it had seemed like an eternity. Molly ran to him and picked him up. Though she wasn't allowed to see him, nobody did anything to stop her. Everyone in the office, moved with compassion, silently watched on with tenderness in their eyes. Even the lady who had wheeled him in left him with Molly and disappeared to her meeting in some back office. Molly held him in her lap and sang to him as he clung to her. Then she walked with him, showed him pictures of his brothers and sisters, went through all his verses, talked to him, and hugged him tightly. Poodles ate all his chicken, enjoying every bite. They had almost an hour of time together. It was a beautiful time for both of them, but for Molly, it went by too fast. When it ended and they were wheeling Poodles out, this time he was not waving and smiling. This time it was a very sad face that looked back at Molly.

Frustrated that the lawyers were doing nothing and exhausted at trying to figure things out by herself, Molly remembered a good Christian lawyer lady they had consulted with before on other legal matters and made an appointment with her. As soon as she had explained the situation, the lawyer called in another lawyer friend from the office across the hall. This lady had already fought and won several legal battles with the child welfare office. She was a real go-getter who was eager to help out the minute she heard Molly's case. The two of them started to work immediately.

First, they went to the Tres Rios office and, as lawyers, were able to access and read the case against Molly. After reading the documents, Molly's lawyer friend told her that had she not already known Molly, she would have thought she was a horrible person from all the things it said about her. She was written up as an aggressive lady who could not possibly care for a special needs child. They accused her of confusing the children under her care because she was throwing them on tables, beating them with a board, and then telling them that was love. They also accused Molly of putting Poodles's life at risk because she had not taken him to any of his socialized medicine appointments. They had twisted and changed everything that Molly had said. The lawyers also read the appeal that Molly had written by herself and saw that the entire format was incorrect. Though it was well past the deadline for her appeal, they were somehow able to get an extension and began putting together an appeal in the correct way.

They had her give them all the receipts from the doctor's appointments she had taken Poodles to as well as receipts from his new braces, crutches, glasses, his tricycle, and all other therapy materials they had purchased. In addition, she turned in progress reports from both of his private therapists, letters confirming future doctor appointments and therapy sessions as proof that his health needs were being met, and the names of people who worked or had lived in the home and were willing to give testimonies of Molly's character and good relationship with her children. They also told her that it would help for her to take an anger management course because it would show a desire to change her "aggressive behavior."

Molly once again contacted her friend at the large children's home who worked with seriously dysfunctional families. She signed her up for a course designed especially for aggressive parents entitled "Disciplining Without Hitting," and even agreed to attend with Molly. She told Molly ahead of time that she would hear several things that went against her beliefs and biblical principles but that it was important not to make comments or disagree, just sit quietly with her mouth closed. Some of their comments and suggestions were so off the wall that Molly's eyes would grow big, and a light little questioning sound would begin ascending from her vocal cords. On these occasions, a nudge in her ribs from her friend would send the sound right back down her throat.

One of their wildest pieces of advice was in answer to a lady's question of what to do when a preteen child begins to yell loudly in one's face spouting out dirty words. The answer was to very calmly pull out a sizable amount of money and give it to them. You then tell them that they should go down to the store, buy an ice cream or whatever they wanted, and come back when they are feeling better. Molly's eyes must have been extra big that time as she turned and looked at her friend because the nudge in the ribs was a good deal harder, almost painful. When they left, Molly told her that her surprised look was from her imagining fifteen other kids yelling in her face the following day and then holding out their hands for their money if she were ever to follow that advice.

Time continued to go by slowly, and Molly continued to wait for some kind of resolution. Two or three weeks after the God-planned surprise visit in the Cartago office, Molly received a phone call. Any time the phone would ring, her heart would skip a beat, hoping it was someone with good news. This time, it was another Christian friend she had met years earlier in some kind of mandatory training session that everyone who had government children had to attend. She had been sitting right next to Molly and, being quite a talkative woman, was constantly raising her hand to put in her two cents' worth. From the comments she was making, it became fairly obvious very quickly that she and Molly were family, sharing the same heavenly Father. Molly turned and asked her if she were a Christian, and when she had answered yes, a friendship immediately formed. She and her husband had been housing government children for more years than Molly. She was calling simply because she said another friend of hers, who cared for children in a government home, had told her she was caring for a child who had been taken away from her "gringa" friend. She was curious to know what was going on and if she could help in any way.

In the conversation, Molly learned that she sometimes went to the center where Poodles was to visit with her friend. She consented to going and getting firsthand information on all that was happening in his life. Though it had only been a couple of weeks since she had seen Poodles, every day that went by seemed more like months.

Molly would probably have been better off had her friend never called her back with the report on Poodles's situation. She said that Poodles spent most of his time locked in a room by himself. This was done to protect him, as the home he was in had a lot of big street kids who were mistreating little Poodles. They said he always talked about his home, cried for his Mommy, and would wake up as many as five times in the night, crying. Hearing this was especially painful because they all remembered him as such a happy boy. It brought back memories of him crawling on the floor, playing with cars, riding his tricycle, and laughing with his brothers and sisters. What should have been happy memories only seemed to cause more pain. Yet the good that came from it was that through the same friend, they were able to send Poodles little notes from all the kids along with a Bible coloring book and crayons. Molly hoped that maybe, somehow, that gesture would let him know they were still thinking about him, working on getting him home.

Had Poodles been an older child who could understand that Mommy was doing all she could, it would have been easier for Molly to wait. But she was constantly battling negative thoughts and questions. Did Poodles think that she had abandoned him? Would he forget them? What if they were never able to get him back? She also worried more about him because she knew he hadn't come to a saving knowledge of Jesus Christ. He had learned many Bible verses by memory, but he was not yet able to understand what they all meant. He did not realize he was a sinner and that his sin separated him from God. He still needed to learn that Jesus Christ had died on the cross to pay the punishment in full for his sins and the sins of the whole world. Upon understanding that, he would need to see that there was nothing he himself could do to earn heaven; he needed a Savior. Then he would need to put his faith and trust in the finished work of Christ alone. Believing in Christ and accepting him as his Savior was the only way that he would be able to go to heaven.

[A LESSON TO LEARN: The situation was often discouraging, yet Molly found much comfort in several passages of Scripture and in friends. She was happy that God had surrounded her with good friends to confirm to her the truths of God, which she knew. God was still in control; God's hand was on the entire situation. She must wait on the Lord. She found passages in the Bible about waiting on the Lord and also passages revealing, as she felt, that the problem stemmed from a direct attack on her Christian principles. That was nothing new. Throughout history, Christians have been persecuted in far worse ways than most of us are now, but God sees, knows, loves, and hears His children and will work what is best for each of them.

Some of the Scriptures that meant the most to her were as follows

Psalm 27:11–14: "Teach me thy way, O Lord, and lead me in a plain path, because of mine enemies. Deliver me not over unto the will of mine enemies: for false witnesses are risen up against me, and such as breathe out cruelty. I had fainted, unless I had believed to see the goodness of the Lord in the land of the living. Wait on the Lord: be of good courage, and he shall strengthen thine heart: wait, I say, on the Lord."

Isaiah 40:29–31: "He giveth power to the faint; and to them that have no might he increaseth strength. Even the youths shall faint and be weary, and the young men shall utterly fall: But they that wait upon the Lord shall renew their strength; they shall mount up with wings as eagles; they shall run, and not be weary; and they shall walk, and not faint."

Isaiah 49:23b, 25b: "And thou shalt know that I am the Lord: for they shall not be ashamed that wait for me. . . . for I will contend with him that contendeth with thee, and I will save thy children."

Psalm 34:20–22: "He keepeth all his bones: not one of them is broken. Evil shall slay the wicked: and they that hate the righteous shall be desolate. The Lord redeemeth the soul of his servants: and none of them that trust in him shall be desolate."]

    Molly was excited the day her lawyers called and told her they had turned in the new appeal with all the documentation, receipts, letters, and proofs that they had accumulated, and it had been accepted. She was so sure that now it would be only a matter of days. Ever since he had been taken away, each day, from 8:00 a.m. on, she would be waiting for a phone call, would run to the phone when it rang, and would breathe a disappointed sigh when she found it was not the call for which she was waiting. Now she was running to the phone even more anxiously. During the day, she would keep a close eye on the clock, waiting, and waiting. After 4:00 p.m., when she knew all government offices had closed, the little balloon of hope hidden in her heart would deflate as she realized she would have to wait sixteen hours before the office would open up again, and her hope balloon would inflate itself anew.

Friday mornings were especially frightening. On those days, Molly had only eight hours in which to receive a call, and then the offices would close for the weekend, and she would be forced to wait sixty-four full hours before she could even begin hoping for a call. Weekends were also difficult because she knew how much Poodles loved to go to Sunday school. She was tortured by the thought of all his brothers and sisters enjoying Sunday school while he sat alone in a locked room, wondering what was happening.

Finally, Molly received a call from her lawyers. They had found a friend who worked in the main office of the president of children's welfare. She confirmed that their file was on the desk of the president of the department, but it had more than twenty other files on top of it, and they had to be read in the order they had been received. There was no way of telling how long each case he was considering would take.

After waiting for an answer for three and a half months, they got their verdict. The president of the children's welfare department ruled that Poodles was by far better off in Molly's home than in any government home in the country, and the Tres Rios office had seventy-two hours to return the child to Miss Molly. In their little game of chess with Molly, the Tres Rios office was now in check. They were forced to return Poodles but weren't going to do it without moving one more pawn to irritate Molly. After having done nothing for him for all that time, now they enrolled Poodles in a special needs school a half-hour drive away. He would need to attend every day. Of course, by this time, that was the least of Molly's concerns; she just wanted her boy back.

As soon as Poodles saw Molly, he hollered out her name instead of calling her Mommy, reached his arms up, and gave her a big, long hug. That hug was very important as they were watching carefully for Poodles's first reaction to seeing Molly. After a brief conversation between them and Molly's lawyers and a few questions addressed to Poodles, in which he continued to refer to his mother as Miss Molly, they were ready to go. As they stood to leave, Molly let out a little gasp when she saw how crooked Poodles' legs were, but the lawyer silenced her with one look and motioned her to hurry out the door. When they got him home, he got on his tricycle and was immediately driving all around, laughing and playing with his brothers and sisters as though nothing had ever happened. But most importantly, Miss Molly became Mommy again.

Poodles had several setbacks from the months he was gone, but Molly trusted that God would give them back the same little boy they had in time. He could only remember about a fourth of the verses he knew and had forgotten many of the letters and vowel sounds he had learned at kindergarten. He had absolutely no strength in his thin little legs, as he had never been worked with nor had a single therapy the whole time. His legs were even more crooked than when he had originally come into the home, and he was totally unable to straighten them. He was also unable to stand alone or walk with his Canadian crutches. Molly doubted that they had even been putting his braces on him.

As previously mentioned, many of the kids were rough street kids, and Poodles had learned several dirty words from them and how to talk back to authority. He was fully potty-trained when they had taken him from Molly, and they gave him back in diapers. They would have to start over from scratch with him, but he was home, praise the Lord.

When Molly took him to his new school on Monday morning, the teacher was very surprised to see him. She could not understand why they had even enrolled him there. It was a school for children with severe disabilities. Everyone in his class was in a wheelchair, non-verbal, and almost unable to move. The teacher had her hands full with physical therapies and trying to reach into each child's world and find a way for them to communicate. She asked Molly to please bring him only three times a week and to bring things with her that he could work on as she had no materials for his level of learning. Molly was delighted. Not only did he not have to come every day, but on the days he did come, Molly was his teacher, bringing all his work from home. She wasn't sure what the social workers' purpose of enrolling was, but it turned out to be a special time of re-bonding for Molly and Poodles. At the end of the month, there was only a month left in the school year, the teacher gave him a grade of 100 percent in every area, and made a note saying that he was too advanced for the school and could not return.

Months later, Molly was at the courthouse, picking up some legal documents when she happened upon two of the social workers who had fought her so hard. They greeted her and sat down next to her to wait for their turn to be called to the inner offices. Molly was super surprised at how friendly they were being. For some time, Molly had been concerned about what would happen when they found out the kids were being homeschooled again. She decided it would be better for her to confess than for them to find out by themselves. She thought this would be the best time since they seemed to be in extra friendly good moods. She braced herself and broke the news to them. To her delight, they told her that was fine, and there was nothing to worry about now that they knew their grade levels.

Molly returned home completely perplexed at their change in attitude. Why on earth were they so extra friendly? She would soon find out the answer to that question. A few weeks later, she needed to go to the Tres Rios office. When she walked in, if she hadn't known better, she would have thought she had walked into the wrong office. She didn't know a single person working there. The entire office staff, including the director, social workers, psychologists, secretary, and even the chauffeur, had been fired for bad decisions they had been making. Molly was sure that their Poodles's decision was included in that. When Molly introduced herself to the new staff, their eyes lit up, and they immediately attended to her needs, as though she were a queen. No wonder the other ladies had been so friendly. They knew they were being investigated, and their jobs were on the line. They had no desire to stir Molly up again. After all, she had good lawyers.

She realized that God had made her somewhat of a legend in the children's welfare offices, someone with whom no one wanted to mess. She also realized that God, in his time, had answered her prayers far beyond what she had expected. Apparently, God, too, knew how to play chess, and Molly's one thought was, checkmate. She never again had a problem with social services.

Four years later, on their way home from church, Poodles expressed a desire to accept Christ as his Savior. As Molly talked to him, she knew that now he realized he was lost and needed a Savior. He understood that Christ had suffered and died on the cross, taking the sin of the world upon himself to pay the punishment and satisfy the justice of a holy God. That day, in simple faith, Poodles trusted in Christ as his Savior.

Chapter 11

Jerry Cornsnapple

Like most young ladies, Molly had thought about marriage since her teen years, although she felt she could also be happy remaining single. Unfortunately, she seemed to constantly run into a slight complication in the area of men. From the time Molly was a teenager until the Children's Home was started, every time a guy acted like he was madly in love with her, which there were only four or five of them, he did not check all the boxes of what she wanted in a man, and every man she thought did check all the boxes, and she would have been interested in, probably another seven or eight guys, had no interest in her.

There really weren't that many boxes that needed to be checked off. She looked for someone who was humble, hardworking, showed a genuine love for the Lord, felt a definite call into full-time Christian ministry, and cared about missions. Though she dared not make being handsome one of her check boxes, as she herself was a far cry away from being a beauty queen, there was a box called "not overly ugly" and another one about having a socially acceptable personality as opposed to being awkward or a jerk.

All that being said, Molly knew when they started the children's home that she was stepping into a dangerous zone of limiting her possibilities of marriage even further. With such a houseful of kids, she would need not only to have a husband with similar spiritual goals but also someone who was sympathetic to the ministry to which she was certain God had called her. Notwithstanding, the call to work with children in need of a home had such a powerful pull on her heart that not much else mattered. So, she contented herself in her ministry and stayed quite occupied as a single mother. Molly's aunt had never married and had lived an active life as a school teacher and traveling the world in her summer vacation. Later in life, she had also been a substitute mother to seven little girls in a children's home. All that actually sounded like a very appealing and fulfilling life.

While accepting that she might remain single, deep down, Molly held on to a little ray of hope that maybe God would someday bring that special man into her life. Thus began what seemed like a never-ending cycle. Her children, their quirks, and life constantly moving between laughter and tragedies kept her active, happy, and satisfied until an eligible bachelor would show up out of the blue. Then, she would begin pulling the petals off the "he loves me, he loves me not" mental flower for months until the last petal would declare loudly that he did not love her. This was followed by the realization that the guy was not all she thought he was, that he didn't really check all the boxes, that she would have been miserable as his wife, and that she could only thank God that He had saved her from ruining her life. Immediately, she would launch into some new project to work on, which inevitably led to problems to solve and life situations at which to laugh. At this point, she would acknowledge that she was quite content with God's goodness and the wonderful, exciting life he had given her to lead. She would then remain happy for months or even years until, out of the blue, someone showed up, and the cycle would start over.

When the children's home was around fifteen years old, and Molly had gone through the flower petal cycle some six or seven times, God brought Jerry Cornsnapple into her life. The home had been invited to sing at a mission conference of one of their local supporting churches. They arrived to find that a blind evangelist from the United States had also been invited. By the end of the service, Molly was pretty impressed by the guest speaker. He dynamically played the piano and sang in a powerful, perfectly tuned voice. His sermon was equally dynamic and all about Christ. Molly also just happened to notice that he appeared to be very close in age to herself and had no ring on his finger. She spoke to him after the service about her blind son, Dito, but after that brief encounter, it would be some time before she would see him again.

A good two or three years later, Molly answered a phone call from the pastor of their church. He had invited the blind evangelist for a revival meeting. Since he only spoke English, he wanted to know if he could stay in the children's home, where everyone knew English. Molly's mind flew back to the mission's conference, and she readily told the pastor that they would be glad to host him. The revival meeting was a huge success, the greatest in the history of their church. The pastor offered a study Bible to the person who brought the most visitors. Many members worked hard, and there were about 230 first-time visitors during the five-day meeting. Even more wonderful was that sixty-two people gave their hearts to the Lord, accepting Christ as their Savior.

Jerry Cornsnapple slept in one of the boys' rooms that week. At the time, the kids did not have access to any electronics. The boys were fascinated to hear his laptop talking to him and watched him reading his electronic Braille note tablet with his fingers. He chalked up a few points with them by letting them sneak in a few children's videos on his laptop. They thought that was cool, much neater than just watching a video on TV.

In the afternoons, over coffee, there were several conversations about the Scriptures. Molly, and even Polly on the days she was there, would ask questions about perplexing passages, and they were both amazed at Jerry's knowledge of the Scriptures. Having spent so many years preaching and relying on his memory had turned him into a living concordance. For any verse that was mentioned or asked about, he could say the exact book, chapter, and usually the verse where it could be found in the Bible.

Throughout the week, Molly noticed that all Jerry's sermons were centered completely around Christ. Christ was explained, and his cross was exalted in every possible way. Each night, he made the gospel come alive in a marvelous new way that not only spoke to the unsaved but fascinated the saved and led them to love Christ and his redemptive work so much more.

Molly couldn't help but make a mental note of the fact that Jerry checked all the boxes for a potential spouse, even the "not too bad looking" box. Though it was certainly not time to go flower picking and petal pulling in the "he loves me, he loves me not" garden of life, she did start plucking petals in the "he might be interested, he might not be interested" section of the garden. After all, they had shared several long, interesting conversations that week.

At the end of the week, Molly gave Jerry a music CD the home had made for one of their trips to visit supporting churches in the States. As she handed it to him, she mentioned in a subtle manner that all her contact information was on the back of the case. They had talked so much she felt like they did share a friendship, and maybe he would try to contact her. A few months later, she plucked off the last petal, coming to grips with the realization that "he might not be interested."

Life went on, and Molly got a phone call about a sixteen-year-old blind boy who needed a home. They had heard about him when Dito had come to live with them, but Molly felt they could only take Dito at the time. Now they learned that he still did not have a home, and Molly agreed to pursue the possibilities of taking in the teen. They mentioned he needed to learn Braille, and the teaching heart in Molly began researching the Braille alphabet and methods of teaching it. She threw herself wholeheartedly into the task. Once she had learned the alphabet, she purchased a Braille slate and stylist and prepared several verse cards for him to begin reading and studying. Like with other kids, he would need to visit them for a month or so before a decision was made.

Since the blind child was older, he was allowed to stay the entire weekend. Molly realized the first weekend that he was not learning Braille not because people had not tried to teach him but because he had no interest in learning. He knew what it was and how it functioned but did not want to spend any time at all trying to read it. In fact, his only interest seemed to be the radio and the set of headphones he brought with him. Some of the boys took him out for walks and tried to get him interested in other things, but to no avail. As soon as he could, he was back inside with his radio, listening to music and soccer games. On Sunday morning, they almost had to pry him away from the radio and drag him to church. Molly felt he was just shy or insecure in his unfamiliar surroundings and that he would do better as he began to feel more at home. Nevertheless, the following weekends were worse than the first as he complained about everything, including the food and having to go to church on Sunday. It seemed that he just preferred to live in his own little world. They tried everything they could to reach out to him but found it difficult to help someone who didn't want to be helped.

On the fourth Friday afternoon, when Molly showed up at his government home to pick him up, the caretaker in charge said that he refused to come out of his room and did not want to spend that weekend with them. Apparently, there was an important soccer game scheduled for Sunday morning that he just had to hear. Molly knew then that it was not going to work out. He was not a little boy who could be trained, he was a sixteen-year-old teen who was clearly already making his own decisions. They had worked with him for an entire month and had not made any progress. She felt that even the children had done their best to try and make him feel at home. Molly called the social worker and told her she did not feel he was right for their home since he didn't even care to spend a weekend with them. Maybe all the effort she had put into learning Braille would pay off with another child somewhere down the road. Of course, she was thinking of a younger child, not a forty-nine-year-old child, but then one never knows when and where a newly learned skill will come in handy.

Many months later, and a little over a year after Molly had last spoken to Jerry, she received a phone call on a Saturday afternoon from the pastor of a church in a province on the opposite side of San Jose. He needed a translator that very night and wanted to know if any of Molly's boys were available. The gears in Molly's mind started moving, and her immediate response was negative. The only boy at the time who was both old enough and understood enough English to translate was Goodles, and he might not be interested; he really hadn't done much translating. On top of that, it was such a last-minute thing, and the next morning was Sunday, and she hadn't finished getting everything together for her class, and then there was the distance and getting everyone dressed and ready, and coming back late, and so on. She very graciously explained that she didn't think they would be able to help. The pastor then asked if she knew of anyone else who could help as they had a blind evangelist speaking, and their regular translator couldn't make it that night. Molly's ears perked up at the words "blind evangelist," and her entire tone and story changed. Suddenly, she was telling the pastor that if they were in that big of a predicament, she was sure she could talk Goodles into translating, and he could count on them; they wouldn't let him down.

No sooner had she hung up the phone than she was rushing dinner and calling all the kids in from outdoors to bathe and put on dress clothes. Needless to say, she then had to answer a lot of when and why questions several times over. This was followed by more rushing about, and finally, out the door they went.

Before the message, Jerry thanked Molly publicly for helping them out at the last minute. He then went on to explain that the previous year, he had the privilege of staying in the children's home for a week. He praised their hospitality and said what a blessing Molly and her children had been. The message, as usual, was a powerful,

Christ-centered sermon. After the service, he seemed so happy to be back and said that he would be in Costa Rica for a whole month this time. Molly wondered if she would get another chance to see him during the month. One could only hope.

On Monday, Molly received a phone call from the missionary who was responsible for Jerry's meetings in Costa Rica and arranging his schedule. He explained that Jerry would be preaching in the San Jose area on several different occasions during the month and asked if he could stay with them during those times. Years later, Molly learned that the call had stemmed from a matchmaking plot that the missionary and his grown daughter had come up with.

By the next Saturday, Molly was heading to the bus stop in a dangerous area of San Jose to look for Jerry. The host missionary, whose work was an hour outside of San Jose, had put Jerry and his suitcase on a public bus and called Molly to let her know what time the bus was due to arrive. It was an area that received buses from all directions. First, Molly was held up in traffic. Then, she arrived at the general area to see dozens of buses parked all the way around the city block. She jumped out and started running around the block, looking for a bus from Palmares.

Rounding the second corner, Molly saw Jerry crossing the street, led by the bus driver who didn't know what else to do with him when he didn't get off the bus, and neither of them could understand the other. Molly started hollering his name and running toward them. A relieved look spread across both of their faces. She saw that this man truly did walk by faith, not by sight. This was not his first time to step on public transportation in simple faith, not knowing exactly where he was going or how he would communicate.

Molly soon learned more about his big heart for missions. He had made eight or nine trips to the Philippines, one to Australia, probably fifteen or more to Honduras, and this was his seventh mission trip to Costa Rica. On some of the trips, he had traveled with pastor friends, but on many of them, he had been traveling alone. As more and more opportunities opened up in foreign countries, he had told the Lord that wherever a door would open to share the message of Christ, he was willing to go.

On this particular month of revival meetings, Jerry stayed in the home a couple of different times. By the time Molly took him to a different bus stop for a meeting outside the San Jose area, she felt like their friendship had grown. She couldn't help but ask herself, though, if it were just more of her own wishful thinking. On the other hand, she mused, maybe those months of studying Braille weren't in vain. She was certainly too old to continue playing her mental petal-picking games. If he was interested, great, but if not, she needed to get past it like all the other times and get back to the point of realizing how happy and blessed she was in the ministry God had given her. She determined to write him a letter in Braille. It would not be a gut-spilling letter, just an appreciation letter that should either scare him off or arouse a curiosity or interest.

Molly's short little note ended up being about three pages long, but that wasn't too bad considering that a Braille Bible consists of eighteen huge volumes. She would give it to him at family camp where he would be preaching toward the end of his month of meetings. They had attended the camp several times in the past, but this year, Molly had told the kids they wouldn't be going back because caring for Dito and all the little ones was too difficult at camp. It was a decision the kids kept reminding Molly about when she told them to pack their bags because they were heading for family camp. That there had been a change of plans was all Molly would answer them, but certainly, the older ones had to have their suspicions by now.

Molly's family was assigned to sleep in the nursery, just as in previous years. It allowed them some cribs for the little ones, easy access to the bathrooms, and a little bit of privacy. The camp went from Thursday to Sunday of Easter weekend. That meant there were very few days to make her move, and fearing she might chicken out, on the first day, she ventured out on a little hike to the visitor apartments section of the camp. She took a few kids with her to use the old "taking a little family hike and just happened to be passing by" excuse. It was a poor excuse at best for few people carry three-page Braille letters with them on friendly little hikes. The main door to the apartments was open, and Jerry and a family friend who was like a second mother to him were drinking coffee. They all greeted each other, she handed him the letter with a brief explanation, and Molly and her kids quickly exited to continue their family hike.

It was a letter in which she thanked him for his faithful service to the Lord and his love for missions. She expressed how she appreciated his willingness to serve the Lord despite his limitations and how much his command of the Scriptures and his Christ-centered messages meant to her. The last paragraph was the clencher. It was something that stuck out in Jerry's mind, and he would remember and tell people about for years to come, to Molly's embarrassment. She wrote that a little over a year ago, the Lord had brought a very special person into her life, but then he left, and she didn't hear from him again. She followed by writing that now that person was back, and she was hoping that he did not disappear this time. The letter ended by simply asking if he ever wanted to get in touch with her, and then included her contact email and phone number. Jerry later referred to that day as the day the blind man's eyes were opened.

The following day, with Dito napping and all the kids involved in various games, Molly ventured out on a second hike toward the visitor apartments. Her curiosity was killing her; she wanted to see his reaction to the letter. As before, the door was open, and the same two people were once again enjoying coffee. Nevertheless, it seemed to Molly that his second mother friend was greeting her with more enthusiasm. Jerry himself also seemed upbeat and happy. She noted that he was definitely not trying to avoid conversation with her. In fact, they invited her in to sit and chat a while. As to the letter, he only remarked that he was surprised that she could write such an extensive letter in Braille. After about a forty-minute visit, Molly left encouraged but not yet convinced.

By the end of the family camp, Jerry had only about three or four more days left to his stay in Costa Rica. It was suggested that it would be easier if he were to travel back to San Jose on Molly's bus, and she would take him to the airport. Of course, she jumped right on that idea, and he agreed. The conversations in those last days were longer and extended out into new areas of likes, dislikes, interests, and so on. When she dropped him off at the airport, he promised he was not going to disappear this time and asked if he could phone her the next day.

Jerry did phone the next day and the next and the next. In fact, the phone calls soon turned into two phone calls a day, morning and evening. There was never a day without a phone call. Sometimes, if he had a preaching engagement, the phone calls were short and late at night. Other times, they were an hour long. Molly was finally able to stop pulling petals off flowers. It was obvious that they were both very interested, and things seemed to be getting more serious.

In late July, Jerry told her he was very busy the next day and would not be able to call her in the morning but would be talking to her in the evening around 9:00 p.m. When 9:00 p.m. and then 10 p.m. came and went without a call, Molly began to worry. After another hour of anxiously waiting and pondering this explanation or that, Jerry surprised her by walking in the front door. Apparently, some close friends had surprised him at church the night before by offering him their frequent flyer miles to go visit his girlfriend. He had gone straight home, purchased a ticket, and contacted Polly to pick him up at the airport. It was a pleasant surprise for both of them.

He only stayed for a short five-day visit but insisted on taking her to a nice restaurant before he left. On Thursday evening, Polly, Buffy (who was home from Bible college at the time), Jerry, and Molly drove up the mountain to a fancy restaurant that overlooked the city lights of San Jose. While the ladies stood outside next to the short stone wall enjoying the view, Molly didn't even notice when the other two ladies walked off. She turned around from the view to find Jerry going down on his knees with a tiny box in his hand. Polly and Buffy stood at a distance, filming everything. Molly was caught completely off guard; she had not suspected anything but quickly answered yes to his question.

Over a wonderful meal, Molly heard about the missing pieces of the puzzle. She had not suspected anything because the trip had been as much of a surprise to him as to her. How could he buy a ring if he didn't even know he was going to Costa Rica until Sunday night? As it turned out, the reason his friends had offered him their miles was because they had gone with him some time earlier to buy the ring and were getting impatient for him to pop the question.

Though the next six months were full of activities, they still seemed to go by so slow. In late August, Molly made a trip to Florida to meet Jerry's family. During her two-week stay, she was even able to accompany them to one of his meetings. At the end of the two weeks, he flew back to Costa Rica with her for two more weeks, during which they did a tad bit of wedding planning. While there, they celebrated his fiftieth birthday. When he left, she knew she wouldn't see him again until mid-January, a week before the wedding.

Sloodles

Amid the planning and preparations, thirteen-year-old Sloodles came into the home. Poor Jerry was still trying to wrap his mind around becoming a dad to eighteen children, and before the wedding even took place, number nineteen showed up. Little did they know it, but within a year and a half of marriage, they would have eight more new ones, and in a little over three years, they would hit their all-time high of twenty-eight kids, teens, and young adults. Boy was he in for the ride of his life.

Getting back to Sloodles, he had been living with a family who was not his own and had been referred to the child welfare department for showing up at school with lacerations on his arms. When interviewed, he confessed that some man living in the home had done it, and he was immediately removed from the home and offered to Molly. It was always more difficult to take in teens, but he seemed to adjust quickly and do fairly well most of the time.

Unfortunately, the people he had been taken away from lived nearby and soon found out where he was. After he had been in the home for a little over a year, they showed up at the front gate. It was New Year's Eve, and they were bringing him a plate of food from their family cookout. It was totally uncalled for as the Lighthouse was having their own cookout. It was a New Year's tradition in Costa Rica; everyone did it. They stood there for about fifteen minutes as he ate the plate of food, apologizing and telling him how much they missed him.

Sloodles changed after that visit. Every holiday, he would mope around with a sad look on his face, separate himself from everyone else, and refuse to be happy. Sometimes, even on birthday party nights, he would sit alone on the ping pong table in the corridor with a "poor me" look on his face. Of course, he would position himself right in front of the large kitchen window, either to make sure all the happy people inside knew he was miserable or to try and make them miserable as well. It did no good to go outside and coax him to come in and participate. They had tried that several times, but he refused to have fun. Whenever the special event was over, he would return to his good old self.

Sloodles stayed in the home for four years until one day, in anger, he packed his bags and went down the road to the house he had been at formerly. Molly didn't even call social services. Years earlier, she had contacted them about another seventeen-year-old who had left, and they had just told her to let him go.

Jerry Continued

Since the time Jerry and Molly had announced their engagement, Brother Neff was extremely supportive and helpful. The church of a very close pastor friend of his gave a large offering to turn Molly's end of the house into a larger space that would include a good-sized master bedroom, a small living room, and a tiny kitchenette area. Other friends of his came down to work on the renovation. It was completed several months before the wedding.

Jerry and Molly were married on January 19, 2008, twelve days before Molly's forty-ninth birthday and almost nineteen years after the home had started. Her three brothers came from the States for the wedding, and it was the first and last time since Molly's teen years that her mother, "Grandma" to the kids, had all four of her own children together in one place. Every child in the home played a part in the wedding. Molly also had a niece and an uncle, her father's brother, there to share the special event. It was a perfect wedding with no unexpected delays or mishaps.

Jerry planned a wonderful seven-day Costa Rica honeymoon. First, they spent two nights in the mountains close to the place where they got engaged. From there, they went to an all-inclusive hotel on the beach for three nights and ended the week with a two-night stay in a fancy resort with thermal pools in the northern part of Costa Rica. Molly marveled at how he could research and reserve three so different, yet also special places. The view was best in the first place. In that high mountain site, they had a jacuzzi in their room that overlooked all the night lights of the entire San Jose valley. The food was best at the beachfront hotel. There, if you didn't like what was offered on the all-you-could-eat buffet at each meal, there were snack bars opened from early morning to late night, where one could choose from a variety of fast foods. The most marvelously relaxing experience was in their last place, with its multitude of hot springs, each with a sign of the exact temperature of every individual pool. Molly had never been so pampered in all her life.

Once back at the home, Molly began the process of resuming the motherhood responsibilities of nineteen children while adjusting to the added responsibility of married life. Meanwhile, Jerry began the process of being a dad. Things were not always easy, though, and the transition did not always go smoothly. All the children had been in agreement with Mom getting married; in fact, they had been so friendly to Jerry on his visits. Now, however, they were realizing that they not only had to share their mother's attention with someone very dear to her, but also that he had somehow jumped all the way up to the top of the totem pole in one day. It was most difficult for the older ones who had been with Molly for most of their lives and were used to only having a mother to accept having a father.

It was equally as difficult for Jerry, who wanted to take his position of authority but, being much more authoritative than Molly, was feeling like an unwanted intruder any time he got resistance from the kids in daily conflicts. But God, who had always helped them through each new addition to the family, bonded hearts. In time, Jerry was able to settle in and began getting more involved in the daily activities of the home.

His first project was taking over in the area of electronics. Because of his blindness, he had been working with and learning computers, equipment, the internet, and so on for almost twenty years. They provided great tools for his Bible study and preaching. This turned out to be a great asset to the home. Molly thought that if a computer didn't work, you threw it away and bought another one. Jerry believed in installing his screen reader, finding out why it didn't work, and fixing it. Immediately, he began working, starting with the router, and improving the network in the home. Soon, the home had Wi-Fi networks in all of the buildings. He also started updating Molly's desktop computer, which she was on the verge of tossing because it refused to cooperate. Updating was a new vocabulary word for her.

She didn't even know what it was, much less that it needed to be done. Jerry found that she only had about 200 Windows updates that hadn't been installed in what Jerry called her "dinosaur computer." Molly corrected him by explaining that it couldn't be too much more than ten years old and certainly wasn't a dinosaur. Jerry was surprised to learn that none of the staff knew very much about technology. He definitely had his work cut out for him as staff members began bringing him their computers after hearing Molly brag about how much better hers was working.

Jerry also brought the children into the twenty-first century. Hearing Molly complain about how the children were constantly leaving their DVD videos in disarray and getting them all scratched up, he bought an external hard drive and ripped them onto it. My, my, who even knew that such a thing as an external hard drive existed? While doing that little job, he added loads of new videos to their collection. Then, he encouraged Molly to get a flat-screen TV, something else she didn't realize everyone but them already had. One day, he told Molly he would like to get the kids a surround sound system for their TV. She, of course, had no idea what he was talking about but told him to go for it.

Although Jerry did not have much financial support, he was one of the most generous people Molly had ever met. He wouldn't think twice before buying this or that for the kids or doing something nice for them. Once, in his early years, the teenage girl in charge of dinner one evening wanted to make hot dogs. They were allowed to use anything in the pantry for an evening meal but only had a small sum of money each night to buy anything lacking at the local store. Since there were never hot dogs in the pantry refrigerator, she went and bought them. The allotted money allowed for each child to have half a hot dog but a whole bun. That was dinner. It left such an impression on Jerry that he shared the story in a meeting in the States a few months later. A friend of his came up after the service and told him that he would be sending money each month for the hot dog fund.

Other friends joined in, and it soon became the special activities fund, a small monthly offering that allowed Jerry to provide for the kids many cookouts, pizzas, hams, and many other special meals through the years that were normally outside their budget.

In addition to everything else, Jerry helped tremendously with the music ministry of the home. Since Molly had never advanced enough to feel comfortable playing the piano in public, they had always relied on soundtracks for their specials. These were difficult and costly for Molly to get ahold of, limiting them to singing the same handful of songs over and over again. Now, they had their own piano player, complete with loads of new songs.

Although most of his ministry was now to serve Costa Rican churches, playing the piano and preaching, Jerry continued his evangelism ministry as well. Two or three times a year, he would travel back to the States for meetings. If he was only going to be there for two weeks of meetings, Molly could accompany him on occasions. Other times, he would travel by himself and be gone anywhere from three to six weeks. For years, he and Molly continued with his once-a-year trip to Honduras for a special week of meetings. On another occasion, Brother and Mrs. Neff, Polly and her husband, and Jerry and Molly were all invited for a week of meetings in the Dominican Republic. He also made a couple of trips to Panama, and once, he was even privileged to preach in Japan when he and Molly made a ten-day trip to visit some dear missionary friends.

It was soon very obvious that Jerry was not only very capable of taking care of his own needs, but he was also remarkably helpful in finding lost objects. One day, Polly walked in the office and told Molly that she had lost the cap to the marker she was carrying in her hand and couldn't imagine where it was. Immediately, Jerry piped up and told her to look on the floor next to the filing cabinet. She looked down, and there it was. He had heard something fall to the floor some half an hour earlier. On another occasion, Molly and a couple of the older children had been searching frantically for a very important notebook.

Finally, Jerry said he could help and asked Molly what it looked like. Skeptically, she told him it was a normal, one hundred-page, spiral notebook. As she exited the room to continue her search elsewhere, she chuckled to herself at the impossibility of him finding something they had not been able to find after having been looking for quite some time. Her chuckle was cut short when, less than a minute later, he held up the missing notebook and asked if it was the one. Molly, happy that he had found it while upset that he had done it so quickly and effortlessly, asked him where he had found it. She was even more upset when he pointed to a stack of papers she had already thumbed through twice. That wasn't the only instance; it actually happened quite often. They lost count of how many times he found keys and other items for which the whole family had been searching.

The entire household found it to be so true that those who had lost one of their five senses naturally depended more on the other four senses, making them sharper. Jerry was often everyone else's sense of hearing, smelling, feeling, and tasting. They could be riding in the bus, and he would announce that it sounded like this or that needed attention or was about to go out. Sometime later, when the sound or feeling got obvious enough to have it checked out at the mechanic's shop, the problem was exactly what he had said it would be. If the lights in the house were to suddenly go out, which was not uncommon in Costa Rica, while scared children ran in circles, screaming, he would be the first one to provide them with some form of light while mumbling under his breath how remarkably handicapped all sighted people were.

All the kids had nightly chores to do, and Jerry accidentally became the number one chore inspector. At morning devotions, he would sit at what looked like a clean table to everyone else and say that the tables had not been cleaned well the night before. Stunned, they would glance around, trying to understand what he was talking about, and sure enough, he would be scraping a few crumbs into the palm of his hand or scratching a tiny dab of dried jelly with his fingernail. He was the one to step on the candy wrapper everyone else had been stepping over and declare that whoever did the floors the night before had not done a good job. His nose was also very sensitive to trash that needed to be taken out or things that had not been cleaned, as was his taste to food that had too much or too little of this or that.

Jerry learned to recognize each child not only by the sound of their voice but by their smell, either their natural smell or the cologne or perfume they tended to use. Even the sound or scuffing of their shoes or their stride or pouncing when they walked would give them away. In his early weeks in the home, kids would come right up to him and start waving their hands in front of his eyes, thinking he didn't know they were there. That game ended rather quickly when he began asking every time what they wanted. Even sneaking around was more difficult for them as Jerry would tell Molly that he heard kids outside or in an office at times when they weren't supposed to be there, often even giving the exact names of the offenders.

Jerry was a God-sent addition to their home, and nobody recognized and appreciated it more than Molly, probably because she benefitted more than anyone. He took joy in providing Molly with special things she had never had before. Molly took joy in feeling spoiled and receiving for her birthday something other than a chocolate bar and yogurt that she had given the kids money to go to the store and buy. The first of her special gifts was a Kindle tablet from which, to her surprise, she could read hundreds of books. She loved to read and now she could carry all her books with her in her purse. On other occasions and holidays, he treated her to a big fancy desk chair and a nicer cell phone.

The reclining love seat that lifted her tired legs, and on which Jerry had insisted, was another luxury perfect for their new date night. After they were married, Brother Neff was the one who insisted they have a night off each week. In years past, there had been three or four other times that Brother Neff had made Molly get away for three days to rest. Molly enjoyed those times but always felt so behind with the educational ideas that were constantly cramming themselves into her head that she would end up taking her work with her and spending the whole time "catching up." Thus, for the first couple of months, Molly would push back in her lovely new recliner on date night with a lap full of notebooks and papers to take advantage of the fact that the kids could not interrupt her. Jerry encouraged her to put the papers away and relax. They began listening to audiobooks, especially by Molly's favorite author, Charles Dickens. They also watched old shows on TV and went to the mall to eat. It didn't take long to begin looking forward to this new addition to the weekly schedule.

Soon, notebooks and paperwork on Jerry and Molly's night off no longer crossed her mind. In fact, years later, she arranged things so as to have most of the day off and not just the evening and really looked forward to that day each week. More years passed, and they were knocking off the trip to the mall to eat and ordering food to be delivered to the house. The kids told them that their date night was boring. They agreed fully and expressed how wonderful being bored was. They had learned the blessing that ordinary, boring, nothing-special days could be.

What she most enjoyed, though, was that Jerry was such a good listener. Though, in addition to the kids, she was constantly communicating with close friends who labored with her in the home, there was something special about having a soul mate with whom she could share all her thoughts, frustrations, and problems, but most of all, her heart. Jerry often had a better understanding of life's situations than she did, as his was untainted by feminine emotions. He often shared a new perspective on things that she had never considered. There was nothing that she felt she couldn't share with him. He was always willing to listen and usually sympathetic to her feelings. When there were disagreements, they were able to work them out quickly.

In addition to everything else, marrying Jerry changed Molly's way of teaching as well. Soon, she wouldn't teach a Sunday school class without sharing it with Jerry first. He always had something to add that had not come to Molly, either a thought, a type of Christ, or an entire outline. His insight was so amazing that she encouraged him to write a children's devotional book together with her in which the kids would do the illustrations. Jerry chose types of Christ in the Old Testament as the theme, which, of course, was so typically him. It turned out to be a bigger project than they had bargained on, but they did finally finish and publish the book.

Chapter 12

And the Family Continues to Grow

Woodles

Almost two months after the big wedding, eight-year-old Woodles came into the home. He had been living with an aunt who was struggling to care for him, physically and financially. There was no possibility of him returning to his parents. The boy's mother had abandoned the family long ago, and the father, who had a serious drinking problem, was living a very unstable life with a woman who had been mistreating Woodles. When the aunt heard about the home through the pastor of her small Baptist church in a rural area of Costa Rica, she was eager to learn more. A few weeks later, after several phone calls, she made the long trip on the bus to San Jose to see the home and leave her nephew there.

Woodles was a very shy but obedient little fellow who rarely caused any discipline problems. Because of his difficult past, he had never been to school, and although he had the intelligence to catch up, he lacked motivation. Studying was at the very bottom of his priority list, and thus, he struggled through school, just getting by. He was such a happy-go-lucky child that he paid little attention to anything.

A month or two after Woodles's arrival, the home had a mission trip planned in a remote town in the southern part of the country. Each child was responsible for preparing their own backpack. Molly went over the list several times of what they needed to pack. Afterward, she asked each child if they were sure they had everything. They had done this many times before without a problem. The youngest kids had someone to pack for them, but from about seven years old and up, one was in charge of their own packing. They arrived at their destination to find that they needed to go shopping because Woodles had not packed any underwear, pants, or his belt. Indeed, the only dress shirt he had for the three-day meeting was several sizes too big and was missing all its buttons. That was the year they moved the age of self-packing up to twelve years old. When they arrived home, they discovered that Woodles had left his brand-new beautiful Bible down south in the boonies.

Molly hoped Woodles would become more responsible as he grew older, but that didn't happen. Even as a young adult, every time he came back to visit, he would leave something forgotten, his phone, keys, some important paper, or even a whole backpack. The kids would bring Molly the forgotten item twenty minutes after Woodles had gone, and she would call and tell him not to worry about it. Sometimes he hadn't even missed it yet.

One Thanksgiving, Woodles arrived early, excited about the once-a-year huge meal. Having arrived so early, they sent him and two others to pick up a few things they needed for the meal. Woodles returned holding a box with eleven donuts in it and one more in his mouth. Molly asked him why on earth he was filling up on donuts when they would be eating a big meal in half an hour, after which there was a whole table dedicated to pies and desserts. He insisted that he could handle both; he wasn't going to miss out on a delicious Thanksgiving meal. By the time the meal was served, Woodles was on his third or fourth donut and was no longer hungry. So, he prepared a big plate of food and stuck it in the refrigerator for later. Although he stayed all afternoon and into the evening, he never did get hungry and determined that he would take his meal with him for a late-night snack. Of course, he went off and left it in the fridge. Molly watched from day to day as the plate of food got older and older, waiting for its owner to come back and claim it. After about a week, it didn't look near as delicious as it had on that first day, and Molly finally tossed it. He never ate so much as a bite of the big meal everyone waits for all year long.

Another funny Woodles story was when they were visiting a church outside the San Jose area. Molly made zip-lock snack bags for each kid to eat in the car so she wouldn't have to worry about looking for a cheap enough place to feed the whole gang. Each bag contained a fruit, cookies, juice box, chips, and just a hot dog without the bun. When Raddles opened his bag in the dark car, it slipped out of his hands and hit the floor. The hot dog fell out of the bag and rolled forward in the van a whole row, where Woodles somehow found it, wiped it off, and popped it into his mouth before Raddles knew it was missing. While still enjoying his treasure, he got down on the floor to search for more. Raddles had retrieved the bag by this time, but Woodles spotted the cookies that had also fallen out of the bag. With a swoop of his hand, he reached out and grabbed them up, opened them, and started eating as though they were his. Soon came the calls from the back row, "Where's my hot dog? Where are my cookies?" Several kids helped search but to no avail. They had mysteriously disappeared.

It was more than fifteen years later that the case was finally solved and laid to rest in one of those family reunions where everyone started sharing stories from the good old days. The confession evoked loud laughs from everyone. Luckily for Woodles, Raddles was not present at that reunion. But then, of course, had he been present, Woodles would have stayed as quiet as he had on the day of the runaway hot dog.

Although shy Woodles felt right at home within weeks after his arrival, it was quite a while before he began opening up about his past. When he finally did begin sharing, his story was worse than those of the wicked stepmothers in the fairytales. He had, indeed, spent much time with a stepmother who had two children of her own, both younger than Woodles, and hated Woodles because his father naturally preferred his own son to her children.

Woodles's father's house was one of many on a large ranch that had been passed down for generations. Though it was true they had plenty of land, they had small houses, and the individual families of the inheritance lived in poverty and dirty conditions. Woodles told of his stepmother locking him in an outhouse any time his father left and leaving him there all day until he returned. She would purposely mix dirt in his rice at mealtime. If there was juice or some special treat, it was all for her own children and never shared with Woodles. Once, she put a menthol rub intended for sore muscles in his eyes. On another occasion, she put a blindfold on him, tied his hands together, and dragged him a long distance through several farms, then ran off and left him. When he got the blindfold off, he had no idea where he was, not recognizing anything around him. Fortunately, there was a little back road nearby. When a car finally came down the road, they picked him up, took him to town, and asked around until someone recognized who he was, knew where he lived, and got him back home.

Though Woodles never attended school, once, he was with his father, the school gardener at the time, on a special school day that included a raffle. Out of pity, the teachers allowed the poor little boy to participate, and he won a big yellow toy tractor. It was the first toy he had ever owned. He played with it all day and laid it next to him that night while he slept. The next morning, the tractor was gone. He looked for it all day long but never found it. He learned many years later that his stepmother had torn it apart and thrown it away.

Meanwhile, Woodles's grandfather saw these injustices and kept getting involved, which stirred up many family ruckuses. Finally, he told the father that if he didn't find another place for Woodles to live, he would call social services and have him removed. And thus began Woodles's months of house hopping. He would spend a couple of weeks with this aunt or that uncle until they said they couldn't keep him permanently, and off he went to another relative. It seemed that nobody wanted the cute little curly-haired boy but God. The child's almighty Creator, who had been collecting his tears and listening to his cries, worked out all the details and carried him to a loving home far away, where he could learn about God.

As a teen, Woodles was still so shy that every year when it was time for youth camp, he begged to stay home. Large groups of teens made him nervous, and he had no interest in making new friends. Molly would make him go anyway; it was one of those decisions that the kids weren't allowed to make for themselves. She knew from experience how life-changing camps could be. Yes, Woodles was a good kid, but he would never be a leader; he just didn't have it in him. But God, once again, saw something in Woodles that everyone else had missed. By the time he was eighteen years old, he was not only looking forward to youth camps, but he was also the leader of one of the teams, loudly cheering on the members of his team. When he left the home at age twenty, he became very involved in a good church. A few years later, he quit his job to start Bible college and begin working on staff at the same church.

[A LESSON TO LEARN: Woodles's story reminded Molly of the time that Samuel anointed David to be king of Israel. Nobody else expected David to be the one God had chosen. All of his brothers were bigger, older, and stronger, but, one by one, they were refused by God (1 Sam. 16:7), "But the Lord said unto Samuel, Look not on his countenance, or on the height of his stature; because I have refused him: for the Lord seeth not as man seeth; for man looketh on the outward appearance, but the Lord looketh on the heart."

As the Lord looks at your heart, what does He see? First, He needs to see a heart that has trusted in his Son Jesus Christ for salvation. Then, and only then, He needs to see a tender, loving heart that He can mold for a special purpose, something that He has waiting for you as soon as you say, "I'm willing, Lord. Use me."]

Fliddles

Four months after Woodles, sixteen-year-old Fliddles came into their lives. The government called Molly with a special case. Fliddles was being transferred from one home to another. Erroneously after signing the release form from one home on Friday afternoon, they found he couldn't be admitted to the other until Monday morning. They only needed a place for him to spend a weekend. Though Molly knew from experience that older teen boys did not work out well, she accepted him on the basis that it was only one weekend, and she felt she could help with that. When the teen got out of the car, a strange feeling came over Molly that she had seen him before. She could not place him, nor could she stop staring as her mind scrutinized why this boy looked so familiar. Within minutes, it hit her that he bore a distinct resemblance to her very own Floodles who had been with her since he was five years old and was now twenty-two. As the social worker handed her the paperwork to sign, her eyes quickly scanned the page for the boy's full name. There it was, Floodles's and Fluffy's same last name. Here was a brother who they had never seen in their lives and didn't even know existed coming into the home seventeen years after they had arrived.

After getting Fliddles settled in his room, Molly sat him down and told him the good news. His eyes grew big with wonder as he heard about Floodles and Fluffy. Then, she took him out to find his brother and sister. First, they found Fluffy, who was playing in the gym. Molly called her over and calmly told her that she would like her to meet her younger brother Fliddles. Fluffy, who was not known as an emotional person, could not stop crying as she greeted her sibling. Floodles was equally glad to meet his brother and immediately stepped into his role of the older brother. Molly watched from the window. The boys were walking around and around the gym as Floodles began telling Fliddles the most important thing he wanted him to know, that Jesus loved him and died on the cross to pay for his sins. It was just like Floodles to talk to him about God before anything else. Molly marveled at how many of Fliddles's gestures were just like Floodles's, even the stride of his walk, though they had never grown up together.

On Monday morning, Molly talked to the social worker. She felt, given the situation, that it would not be right to divide the siblings any longer and asked permission for him to stay. Of course, they were happy to leave Fliddles with his other family members, and he remained in the home for five or six years. Floodles and Fluffy soon learned they had many other brothers and sisters, spread out everywhere and, being now young adults, were able to find them all as well as their mother and father. Yet, it was always clear in both of their hearts and minds that Molly was their mother and the Lighthouse their home.

Taddles and Toodles

Only a week after Fliddles came, the home received two new sisters, ages nine and twelve. Then, the following week, Taddles, age seven, and tiny two-year-old Toodles came into the home. Once again, they had grown by five children in a short period of time. It was thought that the sisters would be a permanent addition, but after only about eight months, they were transferred to a smaller Christian home, which all felt would be a better fit for them.

Taddles and Toodles remained in the home for years. They were the youngest of a group of at least five siblings who had been removed from their home for neglect. They were a rough group of kids from a rough drug-dealing family. The siblings were not happy about being removed from their home and were wreaking havoc and making life impossible for the ladies in charge of the government home. After several months of wrestling against the system, in one final organized attack, they teamed together to destroy the building in which they were housed. They turned over furniture, broke out all the windows, destroyed the telephone, marked up the walls, and so on. The damage was such that they were forced to close the building and transfer all the children to other homes. The guilty group of siblings was completely divided by sending each one to a different home. The two youngest were kept together and offered to Molly. The two-year-old had actually been in a home for smaller children, but seven-year-old Taddles had helped his siblings destroy the building. When they were going to be divided, they had yelled that they would each escape from any home where they were placed.

Taddles did have his happy moments of playing nicely and especially liked to build things with Legos. He was as cute as a button, and Molly could see the older boys really trying to help him feel at home. Everyone knew his life had been difficult. At seven years old, Taddles told stories about having worked many jobs to buy groceries for his mother. Together with his siblings, they had worked hauling blocks and sand at construction sites, watched and washed cars on the street, delivered drugs to clients, and heaven knows what else.

Knowing where Taddles had come from, it was always so nice when one could see a smile on his face, yet more often than not, his anger would get the best of him. He was an angry child from an angry family. He would habitually overturn his school desk when he was told he had wrong answers or rip up the book and toss it across the room. Any form of discipline was difficult at best. As he grew, his anger seemed to get worse rather than better.

The idea Taddles's siblings had given him of escaping stuck in his mind. Every time he was mad, he would tell Molly that he knew where his mother lived and how to get there. The neighborhood he was from was a dangerous area a few miles from the home. He would storm out the front gate and sit on the curb at the corner. Knowing that any kind of confrontation out on the street would not be right, Molly would send one of the older boys out to calm him down and bring him back. His defiance of authority also grew. He thought nothing of yelling terrible things in the face of teachers and other authorities.

Taddles was especially cruel to his little brother, who was a full five years younger than him. Maybe he chose him to pick on because the other boys were all much older and bigger, and he was the only one he could safely beat up. Whatever the reason, hurting Toodles became a daily occurrence. Molly was constantly telling him that he needed to be the one protecting tiny Toodles, not hurting him.

One Saturday morning, Molly intervened for the umpteenth time to stop a battle between the brothers. Once again, he stormed out the front gate, and once again, Molly looked for one of the boys to go get him. Riddles went out but came back to inform Molly that he wasn't on his usual corner. Molly sent all the older boys out to look for him. At the same time, she got in the car, and with Riddles, they began scanning the neighborhood street after street. They even followed the road that he had always said led to his mother for several miles, but they never found him.

By this time, Taddles had been in the home for almost four years and was eleven years old. Molly was beside herself with worry. She filed a missing persons report with the police, and when he didn't show up all day long, she spent most of the night worrying how he would survive in the street. When there was no word of him on Sunday, Molly was in the social service office first thing Monday morning. The social worker listened to her story for about two minutes and then very calmly gave her an appointment for Friday. Molly couldn't believe her calm, but then she had no way of knowing that, by this time, all his other siblings had already escaped from multiple government homes. The social worker was practically waiting for Molly to come in with this news. On Friday morning, she was told that he had indeed made it back to his mother, and they had found him there.

Life was never easy for Taddles after he left. The social worker kept Molly informed occasionally on his whereabouts. He was with his mother until they caught him dealing drugs on the street. From there, social services moved him to live with his grandmother. Apparently, that didn't go well either because they soon had him sitting in their office, begging to be returned to Mommy Molly. By that time, he was close to thirteen years old. Molly knew that not only was he more streetwise, but that if she had struggled to control him at age eleven, it would be more difficult at age thirteen.

Molly's greatest fear, though, was for Toodles. She was sure that if she were to accept Taddles back, the next time he ran away, he would take Toodles with him. In fact, for a long time, she feared that he would come back for Toodles, coax him out of the gate, and be gone with him in a flash. Maybe he would tell his family where he was, and they would come and kidnap him. Molly recalled once seeing their angry mother yelling at a government worker that she would get all her children back, no matter what she had to do. Molly couldn't even imagine her little boy who had been protected from such a life for over four years, who indeed had no memory of his former life, being returned to a life of neglect and heartache. It became a constant concern to Molly.

Toodles was so tiny when he came into the home that Molly couldn't believe he was already two years old; he looked like a one-year-old. He was Molly's little chipmunk baby with the chubbiest little cheeks she had ever seen in her whole life. It had been a long time since they had such a tiny person, and everyone went crazy over the chubby-cheeked little fellow. Everyone wanted to carry him, play with him, and spoil him. Kiffy and Doodles, the two who had themselves been babies in the home, especially went overboard carry Toodles around, playing and caring for him.

Toodles was non-verbal when he came but had invented his own language, which was a combination of noises to represent some words and sign language to represent other words. Between the two, he could get across almost anything he wanted to communicate. If he wanted peanut butter on a piece of bread, he would put his index finger in his mouth and pop it back out quickly as though he was licking his finger clean. If he wanted a car to play with, he would hold an imaginary car in his hand and move it around an imaginary track while making the rumbling sound of a car engine. If someone hit him, he would point to the offender, hit himself wherever he had been hit, and then rub the spot with a sad look on his face. Some of his charade sentences were so elaborate they were quite impressive. Slowly, he learned words but he was close to four years old before he began talking in complete sentences. He would pronounce each word clearly but individually, leaving small gaps between words that made him sound like a robot.

As a child, Toodles liked to tease and joke around with teens and young adults. One day, a young lady came who needed to do some community service hours as part of her university classes. Molly asked her to take the three little ones out to the garden and play with them. Without telling her, Toodles decided that hide-n-seek would be a neat game to play. After only a couple of minutes in the garden with the children, as soon as her back was turned, Toodles had disappeared. He certainly was a sneaky one, and not even the other two children had seen him go. She looked for a minute or so, calling out his name but quickly panicked when there was no answer. Molly was taken aback when she entered the house out of breath and worried to tell Molly she had lost her child in less than ten minutes. Knowing that he couldn't be far away, Molly calmed her down and went out to find him. When he wouldn't answer Molly's call either, she called several of the other kids to join in the search, and they began to scour the property. As time passed, and Toodles still didn't show up, everyone was called on to help search. They could not imagine where he could have gone.

Molly, now rather frantic herself, went up to the gate to determine whether or not he could have snuck through the bars and gone out onto the street like his brother had always done. On her way to the gate, something caught her eye. There was a drainage pipe that had been put in to catch the rainwater coming off the street. The pipe had about a twelve-inch diameter, just big enough for a small five-year-old child, and was completely uncovered. Molly had no idea there was an uncovered pipe, but there it was right in front of her. Her head started spinning as questions poured into her mind. Could he have crawled in there? Could he have just kept crawling in further? Could he be stuck in there somewhere? They stuck a flashlight into the pipe and hollered his name, but there was no indication that he was in there.

Though the pipe was still in the back of her mind, Brother Neff made her aware that his having slipped through the bars was even more probable. He kindly offered to get in his car and search around the neighborhood while Molly stayed at the home, continuing the search on the property. Molly thought that was a great idea. Nevertheless, three minutes later, Brother Neff came and asked Molly for the keys to the van as he couldn't find his car keys. Molly gave him the keys and stood at the doorway, watching as he pulled the van out of the carport. Once the van pulled out, Molly had a clear view of Brother Neff's car parked on the other side of the van, the very car he had wanted to take. She also had a very clear view of the tiny little figure hidden under the car. She leaned her head closer to the ground and confirmed that little Toodles had been found. Molly called him to come out and hugged him tightly. She asked him why he was not answering to his name. He explained that at first, he was just playing a game with the lady, but when everyone got involved and started hollering his name, he figured he was in big trouble and was afraid to come out.

Of course, they all realized how God had protected him. They didn't even want to think about what might have happened if Brother Neff had taken his own car. Yet, thinking of it was all Molly could do, and the "what ifs" remained in her mind for days. The very next day, the maintenance man was sent out to put a permanent drain cover on the pipe in question. Molly never heard where God had hidden the car keys, but that was one time that she was very glad that the keys were not where they were supposed to be.

Though Toodles was slow to begin talking, by the time he started school, he was perfectly at his grade level and never had a problem in school. Indeed, he seemed to enjoy learning. He was one of the few boys in the home who actually liked reading and was always looking for a new book to read. Another big interest he had was constructing things like Legos and models. In fact, some of the other boys who didn't care much about Legos would ask him to put theirs together for them. If he got some kind of model or Legos for his birthday, he would be off to his room and wouldn't be seen again until he had finished it. He was also very interested in history, armies and wars, Star Wars movies, and video games.

Fortunately, none of Molly's fears of his family coming for Toodles came to pass. Years later, Taddles showed up at their gate three or four times, but by then, he was old enough to realize that Toodles was in the best place he could be and needed to stay there. On one of his appearances at the gate, they learned that Taddles never was sent back to school after leaving the home. He ended up with only about a fourth-grade education, which made it difficult for him to get an honest job. Deep down, Molly always felt that Taddles's escape had hurt and affected little Toodles more than he showed. Although his anger was not as drastic as his other family members, Toodles always struggled with anger problems and even with the idea that escaping was the answer to all his problems.

Piffy and Puffy

After Taddles and Toodles, there was an eight-month rest before the next set of siblings, Piffy, age sixteen, and Puffy, age fourteen, came into the home. It was another one of those situations where the government asked Molly to take them in for a week or two until other arrangements could be made. At the end of the couple of weeks, the government called to inform Molly that they were having a hard time placing them in another home. Although Molly did not like to receive kids this old, remarkably, she had not had a bit of a problem with them; they seemed at home, were making friends, and the others were accepting them well. Molly agreed to keep the girls.

Piffy and Puffy's mother had disappeared from their lives many years ago. They had been living with the grandmother, who was very old and sickly. Both her legs had been amputated due to diabetes. The girls stayed with the elderly lady, helping to care for her until she died. The grandmother had other grown children, but none of them were willing to take in the children of their sibling, the prodigal, trouble-making daughter, when their mother died. In fact, one of their aunts had not even agreed with all the attention the grandmother had showered on her granddaughters. As soon after the funeral as possible, the aunt packed up their things and dropped them off at the social services office.

The older of the sisters, Piffy, was very timid and difficult to get to know, usually keeping to herself. Molly never saw a rebellious attitude in her; she was just a serious person. Once in a while, she would participate in conversations with a group of teens at the dining room table, and Molly would see her smiling. Most of the time, though, she would just work quietly on her schoolwork and home responsibilities and living in her own world. She was friendly to Molly but never really wanted to open up to her. She stayed in the home for two and a half years and left while she was still only eighteen years old.

The younger sister, Puffy, was quite the opposite of Piffy. She was bubbly, talkative, and loved getting involved in all kinds of activities. She worked on the bus route at times, taught Sunday school, and participated in teen activities. Puffy stayed in the home after high school and after turning eighteen to go to Bible college, where she did very well. She didn't leave the home until after she had graduated from Bible school.

Triddles

Several months after the two new sisters came, six-month-old baby Triddles came into the home. God had finally given Molly the baby boy she had prayed for a good ten or eleven years earlier. The same social worker who had brought Fliddles, Taddles, Toodles, Piffy, and Puffy always thought of Molly when she needed a fast place for a child. Molly was surprised when she called and offered her a baby since the social worker knew that Molly had asked for permanent children. They had never offered her a baby before; babies were the perfect candidates for adoptions. Molly asked her if it would be a permanent placement. She made Molly believe that it would be, telling her that the mother had been passing the baby around from relative to relative and apparently did not want the child. It was true, in his short little life he had lived a time with each aunt and uncle. His latest house had been with the twin brother of his mother. He would not last long there as his uncle's wife had no interest in taking in the baby. Fed up with his irresponsible twin sister, the uncle himself dropped the baby off at the social services office.

From the minute the baby arrived, Molly's heart melted as she saw two huge dark eyes staring at her from a chubby round face. He had a big smile and, according to the social worker, had been sitting in his carrier seat all day long, quiet and happily smiling at everyone who passed by him. Since little Toodles had a doctor's appointment scheduled that same afternoon, as soon as the social worker left, Molly took Triddles along to let the doctor check him out. When the doctor removed his diaper for the examination, both the doctor and Molly gasped. Triddles had the worst case of diaper rash the doctor had ever seen, with bright red open sores. When his blood work came back, although he was chubby, he had anemia. He had been fed on a diet of sugar water, a common practice among needy people in the absence of the mother to feed the baby.

Shortly after Triddles's arrival, the ladies of the church decided to throw him a baby shower. Molly held him in her lap as she opened each gift. She would hold up each piece of clothing to show Triddles and clap. Triddles would smile big and clap too, evoking oohs, aahs, and loud laughter from all the ladies. There wasn't a single gift that did not receive his applause. By the end of the party, he had won the heart of every lady in the church.

On Sunday mornings, as Molly sat holding Triddles, a lady would tap her on the back and motion for Molly to let her hold the baby. Molly would pass him back. Then, a lady in the next row back would motion for a turn to hold the baby. By the end of the service, Triddles could end up anywhere. If Molly were sitting three-fourths back in the lefthand section of the church, Triddles could be passed through the center section and end up at the front of the righthand section.

Molly was so happy to finally have a baby again. They enjoyed all the new little things he was learning, such as his first solid foods, holding his own bottle, and crawling. But then came the unexpected phone call. The mother had shown up at the social services office and was requesting a visit with her baby. Though Molly was crushed, she had no choice but to take him to the visit.

As she sat waiting in the office with Triddles in her lap, a strange thing happened. The minute the door opened and the mother walked in, Triddles started crying. He had not seen his mother for four months, but he remembered her and feared her. The mother walked in with her own mother, a sister, and two other children, a brother and sister of Triddles. They were all led into a conference room with a long table. The mother tried several times to hold Triddles, but each time, he would begin to scream. Finally, the new social worker, for it was not the same lady who had given Triddles to Molly, asked Molly to hold him so they could continue the meeting. That helped calm things a little, but it was, nevertheless, still difficult to resume talking. Though Triddles's older sister, an eight-year-old girl, sat very still, his five-year-old brother kept jumping on top of the conference table and pouncing around. He seemed to be completely unaffected by the reprimands of his mother, grandmother, and even the social worker. After much coaxing and many threats, the child would crawl off the table for a few seconds and jump right back on top. Finally opting to talk above the noise of his crazy dance performance, the social worker gave the mother a list of requirements to have her child returned. Molly left the meeting stunned; she could possibly lose her baby. Tears rolled down her cheeks the entire drive back home. What would she do without her baby? What would become of her baby?

After that initial meeting, Molly had to continue taking Triddles for visits once a week. It was always the same. Triddles would sit on Molly's lap, and the mother would watch him from four or five feet away. Any time she began getting too close, he would start crying. Another social worker at a nearby desk would look at Molly with raised eyebrows and shake her head in sadness every time it happened. But when Molly tried to point out the phenomenon to Triddles's social worker, she only made excuses. She said he was afraid because he had forgotten her and saw her as a stranger. Molly argued that he was afraid because he had NOT forgotten her. She explained that at church, he would readily go to anyone who held their hands out to him, whether they were a stranger or not. The social worker said his mother deserved an opportunity to recuperate her child and that he would get used to her.

One month later, they broke the news to Molly, Triddles was definitely going to be returned to his birth mother. Molly was devastated. Though she had tried to prepare herself for this, she couldn't even imagine life without him now. Worse than that, it pained her to think of him growing up in an environment where he was not going to learn about God and His gift to the world of Jesus Christ, who took the payment for their sins through his death on the cross. She felt it was an anguish too difficult to bear and cried over the decision for many days.

At some point during her crying and praying, she came up with an alternate plan. She would make friends with Triddles's mother. First, since Triddles had accumulated many possessions in his time at the Lighthouse, she would offer to haul his things to her house. She knew the mother did not have a car and would arrive on a bus, making it impossible for her to carry both Triddles and his things back to her house. That would allow Molly to see where he was living in hopes of visiting him later. Second, she would invite the mother and her children over for Sunday dinner. That would allow the mother to see that he had not been in a government orphanage but in a family setting where he was well cared for and loved. Third, she would explain to her that she, just like his mother, loved him and wished to continue having a part in his life. She would offer to babysit him any time the mother needed her to do so. Knowing that she had been accustomed to passing him from home to home, she was sure she would take the bait.

Of course, Molly was not planning to let the social worker in on her plan and, thus, was running a little bit of a risk. Nevertheless, Molly felt so sure that the social worker was making a huge mistake that she was willing to take the risk. If only Molly and the mother were friends, she reasoned; there were no laws against friends visiting one another. The desire to fight for Triddles was so strong because she saw him as a helpless baby who had no choice in the matter. Though it was true that other children had left her home, many of them she had known were temporary, others had been returned to relatives who had stepped up to assume responsibility for them and the children were in agreement to go, and still, others were teens who were making their own decision to return to their families. Triddles didn't fit into any of those categories, and Molly felt compelled to at least make an effort to fight for him.

It was while they were waiting in reception to talk to the social worker that Molly offered to drive her home. Looking around at the bags full of Triddles's things, she readily agreed. When they got to the house, Molly was dumbfounded. Apparently, the mother had basically been living on the street. One of the requirements for her to get her son back was to have a house. Since her mother, Triddles's grandmother, was already caring for the other two children, she had no room nor desire to house Triddles and his mother. Consequently, she had asked her alcoholic father, who had been divorced from his wife years ago, if they could live with him. He was happy to have them. As he welcomed Molly into his home, the strong smell of liquor on his breath almost knocked her over. Since the mother spent most of her time in the street, Molly knew that this was the man who would be caring for Triddles.

And the Family Continues to Grow

The rickety old house was set behind a squeaky, almost fallen gate and a yard full of garbage. It consisted of a total of four very small rooms. Each room had one piece of furniture. The living room had an old sofa, the two bedrooms each had a bed, one twin-sized and one double, and the kitchen had an old-fashioned school desk with a microwave on top. Molly held up a carton of milk she had brought for Triddles as she looked around for a refrigerator. Triddles mother took it from her and, explaining that she would keep it in the neighbor's fridge, was out the door. When Molly asked her for a phone number to call and inquire about Triddles, she learned that it would also have to be the neighbor's number. Molly's only consolation as she laid little Triddles on the bed was that he had fallen asleep, and she would be able to sneak out without hearing his cries or looking into his sad eyes. It wasn't much consolation, for she spent the entire drive home imagining his shock when he woke up to find himself in a new place and without all the people he had grown to love.

Molly forced herself to stay away for the first month, allowing him to grow accustomed to his new situation. The timing worked out perfectly. His first birthday was in a month, and Molly called for permission to bring him a little cake and a gift. She took Raffy with her since she had always enjoyed helping with Triddles and also took Toodles, who was the closest in age to Triddles. The two of them had spent lots of time together while the others were at school. When they arrived, they found Triddles at the opened door, clinging to a makeshift baby gate and crying loudly. Molly picked him up and began to console him. Gradually, he settled down but remained very serious. The grandfather said he was waiting for his mother, that every time she left, he would cry until she came back, refusing to let the grandfather pick him up. That was a surprising change for Molly. His fear of his grandfather had outpowered his fear of his mother; she was now his guardian angel. According to the grandfather, she left quite often and stayed gone for hours.

Since there was no place to put the cake, the grandfather put the microwave on the floor and brought the school desk to the living room for the cake. They gave Triddles his gift, which he didn't want to open. Finally, Toodles opened it for him, a bright big red firetruck. Neither the cake nor the gift brought a smile to his face. Raffy, who was determined to get a smile from him, picked him up and began swinging him around and doing everything she could think of to make him laugh. Finally, they began getting small smiles, but nothing like the happy baby they had remembered. They had been there for almost an hour before the mother finally came home. When the visit came to an end, Molly was happy that they had been able to visit but saddened that Triddles did not look at all happy.

Around this same time, Jerry and Molly had been aware that they needed to make an overdue trip to the States with a group of the children. Molly had typically taken children to the States to visit supporting churches and look for new sponsors every four or five years. It had already been five years, but with a baby that Molly was sure the government would not allow out of the country and other new children whose abandonment papers were not finished, it had not been possible. Now with baby Triddles gone, Molly felt it would be the best time for a trip. Keeping busy would help her leave Triddles in God's hands, stop dwelling on the pain, and go forward. Since this would be the first time they would not be taking the whole group of minors, they would make it only a two-month trip instead of the usual three months. She was most concerned for four-year-old Toodles. She sent him to stay with some close missionary friends along with one of the older girls so he wouldn't feel lonely. That would leave only two young boys and four teens and young adults in the home. She got special permission, not an easy task, for three of the teens whose papers were not completed to leave the country and left for the States with a group of eleven kids.

Right before she left, she invited Triddles's family over for Sunday dinner. The mother accepted the invitation, probably more out of curiosity than anything else. They had a lovely meal, and then Molly implemented the next phase of her plan by telling his mother she would be willing to watch Triddles whenever she needed a babysitter. She carefully explained that she would be gone for two months but to count on her after that time. When they returned from the States, the older girls who had stayed in Costa Rica told Molly that Triddles mother had called numerous times, wanting to talk to Molly.

Molly immediately called the neighbor's number to talk to her. She said she had lots of errands to run and asked if Molly could pick up Triddles on Monday morning and watch him for the day. Molly was walking on air. She would have Triddles for a full day. Triddles was walking by then, not on air but on the ground, and everyone enjoyed seeing all the new things he could do. On Monday night, the mother called to say that she had not finished her errands and if Triddles could spend the night and another day with Molly. On Tuesday night, she received the same phone call. To make a long story short, it was a month before the mother returned to take Triddles for a weekend, promising to bring him back on Monday morning. After only being gone for four months, God was already working to give Triddles back to Molly. She had been correct in her hypothesis that the mother was not really very interested in caring for her own child.

After that, Triddles's mother said she would take him for the weekend every other week. With time, that turned into a weekend once a month, and with more time, that turned into a weekend every two months. At first, Triddles would put on his little backpack, wave goodbye to everyone, and happily go down the hill and out the front gate with the mother. Deep down, it hurt Molly that he seemed to enjoy these little outings, but it was, after all, a chance to go somewhere and do something that no one else was doing. As he grew, he began feeling more uncomfortable with his weekend retreats. Once, the mother picked him up on Friday afternoon and, on Saturday morning, called to ask Molly to come and get him. He had cried all night long, had not let her sleep at all, and refused to eat. From that time on, the visits did not include spending the night. Molly was to drop him off in the morning and pick him up in late afternoon. Eventually, she was to drop him off and wait for a call to pick him up. The call usually came some three hours later since he refused to eat lunch at their house.

Once, when Triddles was around five years old, Molly was driving him to her house when she saw the mother in a park. She stopped the car, pointed to his mother, and told Triddles to get out. He said he didn't want to, but Molly insisted that she was waiting for him, and he needed to get out. He got out and stood looking at Molly with a sad face. Molly ignored him and drove off. When she went back to pick him up, he just kept asking her all the way home why she had dumped him out of the car. Soon after that, the visits ended altogether.

Eventually, one of the social workers with whom Molly had a good rapport found out that Triddles was back with Molly. She advised her to take the mother to a lawyer for a document giving Jerry and Molly legal guardianship so the government would not take him away. By this time, Triddles was about seven years old, and the mother had two other smaller boys, giving her a total of five children, each one with a different father. Her hands were full with the two little ones, and she had no interest in Triddles. As she sat playing with the red-headed one-year-old baby in her lap, the lawyer turned around and asked her if she would consider giving Triddles to Jerry and Molly in adoption. The question surprised everyone as they had not even been talking about an adoption. The mother answered that it was all the same to her as long as they didn't tell the grandfather who had said that a child wasn't a dog that you just give away. Molly cringed when she said that. It sounded so cruel, and Triddles was sitting right there; however, he seemed unaffected by the comment.

This was a milestone for Molly, who had tried to adopt Doodles and Kiffy when they were small. Both had come into the home as babies from sources other than the government and had no families, but Molly had been refused, never getting through the government red tape. She had been able to adopt four adult children at their own request and two other adult children jointly with Jerry, but never a minor. Strangely enough, this time, they would see that the paperwork would go through, although it would take years. They felt as if God had just handed them this child.

Just as with so many of the kids, Triddles had his own little idiosyncrasies that made him a distinct individual. From the time he was only two years old, everyone had figured out that he would be very athletic. Molly would watch the tiny little figure running around in the gym, passing a soccer ball from one foot to the other, and then kicking it straight in for a goal. She marveled at how a little person who had only been walking for a year and a half could be so coordinated. At age eight, he discovered baseball and traded in his soccer ball for a bat, glove, and tennis balls as a safe replacement for baseballs. For months, the gym was transformed into a baseball diamond. One group from the States that had come several other times and knew that soccer was about the only sport played in Costa Rica brought a whole suitcase of soccer balls, only to find that baseball was trending at the Lighthouse. Unfortunately, there were only two baseball gloves, an old one that had been around forever and the one Triddles had gotten for Christmas.

When his birthday rolled around a few months later, Triddles told Molly that what he most wanted for his birthday was for the other children to have baseball gloves so they could play better. Touched by his petition, Molly purchased four more gloves, two black ones for the boys and two pink ones for the girls. Eventually, the kids got bored of baseball, partly because most things get old, sooner or later, and partly because over-competitive Triddles got angry any time his team wasn't winning to the point that few kids wanted to play with him. Most of them returned to soccer; after all, they had a suitcase full of them. Triddles wanted to move on to other sports and tried his hardest to get others interested. He dabbled in volleyball, American football, tennis, pickleball, and watching hockey. Ultimately, he settled on basketball. He would practice shooting for hours each day and, whenever possible, watch games or highlights in the evenings.

Even though Triddles was so very athletic, there was a time in his childhood when he also seemed to be the clumsiest child. If someone was going to stumble and their entire plate of food scattered across the floor, it was going to be Triddles. If a mug was to be dropped and broken, it had fallen out of Triddles's hand. If milk was spilled, it was Triddles's milk. If Triddles himself were to fall and hurt himself, it could not be a simple scraped knee; it had to be big and major.

Once, Molly dashed out in the car for just a couple of minutes and returned to find that her little four-year-old had been lying on a skateboard, riding it downhill when he had suddenly been thrown from the board and had skidded across the pavement face first. When Molly came home, some of the older girls frantically and in a totally uncalm manner told Molly to remain calm and not get excited. Baffled by their instructions to her that they themselves were unable to follow, Molly walked through the door, searching for the something that was obviously going to produce the opposite effect of calmness. There was Triddles looking at her wide-eyed, his forehead, nose, and cheeks all scraped up and bloody. Oh, how she hurt for him, but he was a brave little boy and wasn't even crying.

On another occasion, he fell backward and, trying to stop his fall with his hand, sliced his thumb on a two-inch-high tin planter, an accident that required several stitches. On still another occasion, he had a permanent lateral incisor tooth knocked straight out of his mouth when someone hit the opposite end of a PVC pipe he was looking down.

Another Triddles oddity in Molly's eyes was her little athlete's attention to his personal appearance and the orderliness of his things. She had never seen the combination of athlete and orderly in any of her other boys. From the time he started attending school, he went with his hair combed just right, his belt on, and his shirt tail tucked in perfectly, and remaining tucked in perfectly during and after recess. None of the other boys even wore belts; all of them left their shirt tails hanging out, and most of them went to school with their hair looking just as it looked when they got out of bed in the morning. Speaking of beds, from the time he was five or six years old, his bed was made army-style, just waiting to have a coin bounced off it. When he started taking a turn cleaning the kitchen, the cook couldn't stop praising him for the way he left the kitchen impeccable, better than the older kids.

Two particular days were especially stressful for Molly as far as Triddles was concerned. The first was Sunday morning. Triddles would choose his Sunday clothes on Saturday night, but when morning came, he had changed his mind. In those days, the boy's clothes were locked in a separate room because another boy, Noodles, was changing his clothes four or five times a day or wearing three or four shirts at the same time. As Molly opened the door so each boy could get their clothes, Triddles would already be bringing back his clothes from the night before to choose something else. Once everyone had their clothes, Molly would lock the door. Five minutes later, without failure, a sad little Triddles would be looking up at her, needing the door opened again because that shirt or those pants weren't quite right. She would open the door again, he would choose a third time, and Molly would praise his choice as just right and close the door. Twenty minutes later, about the time Molly was feeling that the Sunday morning drama was over, Triddles would show up in tears. He would beg and plead to trade off some particular piece of clothing that he insisted clearly did not match or did not fit quite right. Only once they were in the bus and out the front gate, far from the dreaded locked door, could Molly truly let out a sigh of relief.

The other stressful day was haircut day. For hours before the lady barber arrived, Triddles would explain to Molly what she needed to tell her about his hair. Though the poor lady had been cutting his hair for years, there was always some kind of special instruction he needed to give her. It needed to be rounded here or squared there, or she should use clipper settings 2 and 3 on the sides, settings 3 and 4 on the back, or maybe taper up settings 1, 2, 3, 4, and 5 and use scissors on the top. The explanations were endless, but the final results usually brought tears because she had not done it like he had said; she just didn't know how to cut hair.

Ziffy

One month after baby Triddles was returned by his mother, little two-year-old Ziffy came into the home. She had already spent a few weeks in another Christian home that happened to be overcrowded with toddlers at the time. The directors called Molly in hopes that since they were a larger home, they would be able to take her. The smallest girls at the time were ages nine and eleven, so they would certainly have room for one small girl.

Ziffy's neighbors had called social services because they heard her crying in the house for hours and hours every day. When they had knocked on the door, nobody answered, but the baby girl continued crying. When the government investigated, they found there was also a smaller baby boy living in the home as well. Apparently, the mother would go out every day, possibly to house-cleaning jobs, take the baby boy with her, and leave little Ziffy alone in the house, strapped tightly into a stroller all day long. Though the mother cleaned other people's houses, hers was quite dirty, as was poor little Ziffy herself. Her hair had been chalked full of lice. The problem was so extreme that the directors at the previous home had been forced to shave off all her hair. Molly spent the first couple of months taping little pink bows in her hair but would still have people telling her what a cute little "boy" she had or asking her what "his" name was. Hence, they purchased elastic bands with oversized bows on them and remedied the problem until her hair was long enough to make two little ponytails that stuck straight up in the air on either side of the top of her head.

Ziffy was still so young, having just barely turned two, that Molly felt it was best for her to sleep close by in the adjoining room to Jerry and Molly, where Triddles had his crib. They positioned another crib next to Triddles and settled down for the night. By this time, Triddles was really good at sleeping the whole night through. Ziffy was almost eight months older than Triddles; certainly, she was sleeping the whole night through as well. With each little one in their own crib and tiny eyelids weighing heavy, Molly turned out the lights for a peaceful night's sleep. Some two hours later, her eyes flew open at the sound of Ziffy's screams.

Molly was in a pickle. She thought it would be best to let her cry herself back to sleep rather than teaching her that she would be picked up immediately at the slightest cry. On the other hand, her cry was anything but slight, and Molly was sure she was going to wake Triddles. Dreading two crying babies, she went against her instincts, grabbed Ziffy up, and hurried into a separate room. There she began trying to "reason with" (haha) a confused two-year-old outside her familiar environment. For an hour, she tried everything she had ever read, heard, used, or thought of to calm her new baby and lull her back to sleep. Finally, walking on tiptoe, she carried a sleeping Ziffy back to her crib and laid her down as softly as possible. Then, sneaking back to her own bed, pulling up the covers, and letting out a silent sigh, she closed her eyes. If she had needed to count sheep to fall asleep again, she wouldn't have even reached ten woolly critters before Triddles's crying began. By the time she made it to his crib, wide-eyed Ziffy was rolling over, standing up, and drawing in air for another screaming session.

When nights two and three didn't go any better than Ziffy's first night, Molly graduated Ziffy up to suddenly being a big girl. They packed the crib away and escorted Ziffy to the opposite end of the house, putting her in a big girl's bed in the big girls' room. She supplied the teen girls with a nightlight, thinking that might help, and her best wishes as they embarked on a new phase of their home economics motherhood course. They soon found that the nightlight was absolutely no help at all and that Ziffy's lungs were strong enough for a three-hour middle-of-the-night cry. Plan C was resorting to leaving the bathroom light on so as to sleep in a semi-lighted room. That practice would come in handy if any of them ever got a night job where they needed to learn to sleep during the day. Most importantly, though, it actually did calm Ziffy enough for everyone to get a full night's sleep. In the long run, Molly was glad she had moved Ziffy in with the big girls as it was close to a year before they could turn off the bathroom light and go back to the nightlight. She did feel a tad bit bad for putting the teens through that, but she got over it; after all, she was still having to deal with Triddles. It was a poor excuse because, as previously stated, he was already sleeping the whole night through.

During the day, Triddles and Ziffy soon grew to be good friends. Ziffy would sit him down on the back step, put her arm around him, and talk gibberish for long periods of time. Very little of what Ziffy said was understandable, and Molly wondered how Triddles was ever going to learn to talk. Even how she pronounced Triddles's name was far from any resemblance to the true pronunciation. The older girls laughed when they finally figured out who Ziffy was talking about and laughed even louder when they explained the strange nickname to Molly. But the pronunciation stuck, and Triddles's name was exchanged for a permanent nickname.

During the day, the teen girls really enjoyed having a little sister to dress up and baby. Ziffy was so hungry for human contact that she would extend her arms to everyone, wanting to be picked up and carried. And everyone enjoyed hauling her here and there. Once her hair grew out, Naffy loved trying out all her new hairdos on the unsuspecting little guinea pig, oops, that would be princess, the unsuspecting little princess.

They soon realized that Ziffy had a stubborn streak in her. When she was called, she would stand firm, staring down whoever called her. They could call several times, but the staring would continue until they took steps toward her. At that point, her feet would break free from whatever strange power was gluing them to the floor, and she would hurry toward them. Fortunately, Molly was not alone in her effort to train Ziffy. God had also blessed the toddler with three older no-nonsense sisters who helped keep her in line.

When Ziffy was eight years old, she was included in a group of kids who traveled to the States. As the days turned into weeks, it seemed like they were constantly having problem after problem with Ziffy and her stubbornness. Molly had never known Ziffy to be so disobedient. She seemed determined to make life impossible for the young violin teacher, Jolly, who traveled with them and whom Molly had asked to oversee the girls. Almost every day she would come to Molly with a new problem she was having with Ziffy. Molly would deal with each problem, but the next day, it would be something else. Molly was beside herself; she had never had so much trouble out of Ziffy.

Well into the trip, Jolly came bursting into the room with a "you're not going to believe this one" look on her face and pointing to the direction she wanted Molly to hurry toward as fast as possible. They were in the mission's house of a faithful supporting church. Molly walked into the front bedroom to find Ziffy jumping on the bed as high as she could and grabbing the chain of the fan far above the bed. Molly imagined the fan being pulled right off the ceiling on the downside of the jump, but that was probably an exaggeration. Ziffy knew her little game was over the minute their eyes locked. She stopped as quickly as inertia would allow. Molly asked her why on earth she was doing these things and being so bad. Ziffy answered that she was taking advantage of the fact that Fluffy didn't come on the trip. She had to misbehave while she had the chance. Fluffy, who was an adult by that time and Molly's right hand in the home, ran a tight ship on the girl's end of the house and wouldn't let Ziffy get away with anything. That explained it all.

The other problem they had with Ziffy on that same trip was that she was constantly leaving her sweater in churches. Each time they got to a new location, Ziffy would announce that she didn't have her sweater, and they would look for a thrift store to buy her another one. They must have gone through more than a half-dozen sweaters during the three-month trip.

Although Ziffy loved to tease people and got a good laugh from practical jokes played on them, at other times, she was a complainer and a tad bit negative. One day, a social worker called, telling Molly she wanted to interview Ziffy and Toodles. Molly wasn't sure what the interview was about but used the drive to the office to prepare Ziffy. She told her to be sure and tell the social worker that she had been a good girl and was very happy. Obediently, she walked in the front door, pulled herself up at the counter, and told the receptionist that she was a good girl and very happy. Molly whispered to her that she wasn't the right lady and asked her to sit down. At length, each of the two children was called in individually and interviewed.

After talking to each child, the social worker called Molly in for a conversation. Apparently, the interview was to determine whether or not to turn their papers over to the adoption department, and obviously, Ziffy had forgotten everything she was supposed to say. The social worker said that Ziffy showed no bonding with Jerry and Molly or anyone else in the home; she had complained about everyone. When she was asked if she would like to be adopted and have a new mommy and daddy, she jumped on the idea. She said she would love to have a different family and that all her big sisters were mean to her anyway. Molly, who knew Ziffy well, felt that she saw the whole interview as an opportunity to be a tattletale and get everyone else in trouble, exactly why Molly had tried to prepare her.

On the other hand, the social worker said that Toodles had indeed bonded because he answered that he already had a mommy and daddy, that he wanted to live with them forever, and that he didn't need to be adopted. She then explained that Ziffy's paperwork would be passed to adoptions, and Molly would sign as her legal guardian. It all sounded quite confusing, but Molly didn't worry about her paperwork being sent to the adoption office, knowing that it was very rare for a child over five, and Ziffy was seven at the time, to be chosen for an adoption. Additionally, she said that Toodles's paperwork would not go to the adoption office. He would remain under the guardianship of social services, thus giving Molly the option to adopt him.

What was confusing to Molly was that in her thinking, if she was signing guardianship for a child, that solidified their place in the family, but that was not true. She decided to take advantage of this meeting to clear up her misunderstandings. Within minutes, for the first time, she understood why she had never been able to complete a child adoption. Evidently, any time she signed guardianship papers, though there was even a note added to their birth certificate identifying her as their guardian, at the same time, her signature disqualified her from ever adopting that child. Somehow, they said that particular law was to protect minors from child trafficking, although Molly couldn't understand how. Nevertheless, she was allowed to raise them their entire childhood but not adopt them unless it was done when they became adults. Normally, every child who came into the home needed to be handled in this way. But this was the social worker who had given her Toodles some seven years earlier, knew what a mess his birth family was, and was filled with compassion when he so clearly stated that he already had parents and wanted to stay with them forever. The office had gotten way behind on the paperwork, and Molly had never signed to be his guardian. Now he would remain under social services guardianship, giving Jerry and Molly an opportunity to adopt him.

Molly left the social worker's office, still pondering what she had just heard and noticed the lawyer was sitting alone in her own office. She stepped in, repeated what she had just been told, and asked what her next step should be. She even mentioned that they had recently started paperwork on Triddles. The lawyer told her that although all adoptions eventually went through social services, as a government lawyer, she could not start the process. She told her to use the same lawyer who was doing Triddles's adoption but to ask her to send all the papers to their office in Tres Rios. If the lawyer sent everything to the San Jose branch, where Molly was not known, she would probably be turned down. This lawyer at the local office, however, promised she would approve any adoption that came to her desk with Molly's name on it. Molly left the office very excited. She thought back to all the years that she had worried about Toodles being stolen from them, and now it seemed that God was opening the door for a second child adoption.

As for Ziffy, she continued in the home, never going into an outside adoption, and was always just as well-adjusted and bonded as all the other children. The social worker had truly read her wrong in that one thirty-minute interview. Molly had known it was so from the moment they had spoken about Ziffy. By her teen years, most of her stubbornness was a thing of the past, and she actually grew to have a very compassionate heart, especially for elderly people. She was always asking her teacher, Lolly, how her special needs sister and elderly parents were doing, sending them notes and telling her she was praying for them. She was also very generous, willing to give away a blouse to her teacher if she commented that she really liked it. In addition, she became a favorite among the adults at church, joking around and making friends with them, carrying their plates to them at church dinners, and so on. Although she had her share of normal teenage trauma and problems, there was never any doubt that she loved Jerry and Molly as her parents and that they loved her as their daughter.

A Few More Coming and Going

Only four months after Ziffy arrived, three new siblings came into the home, girls ages six and eight and a boy ten years old. They were supposed to be a permanent addition to the home but ended up being another temporary group. Although the government had said they had no family, from somewhere out of the blue, a long-lost aunt showed up, asking for the children. The government approved her to accept the children, and they left a little over a year after they had come.

That same year, several other temporary kids showed up. And so it was that in a little more than three short years of married life, Jerry and Molly went from parenting nineteen to parenting twenty-eight. Included in that number were eleven children who were twelve years old and younger and seventeen teens and young adults. Life was just a tad too busy; the group was much too big to maintain a family atmosphere, and frustration levels were high. Fortunately, between temporary children leaving and others going into adulthood and moving on, in less than half a year, the numbers began going back down. Sometime later, when they were once again below twenty kids, Molly began feeling a sense of relief and hoped they would never again have more than twenty children in the home.

[A LESSON TO LEARN: Over the years, Molly began to realize many of the things that she had feared never came to pass. Oh, that we could keep in mind that God knows the future, loves us immensely, can do all things, and will do what is best for each of us. Instead of worrying, let us pray, refusing to guess at our own future. Rather, may we place it in His hands time and again, trusting in His direction and wisdom regarding our lives, even when our finite minds can't understand His plan. Proverbs 3:5–6 says, "Trust in the Lord with all thine heart; and lean not unto thine own understanding. In all thy ways acknowledge him, and he shall direct thy paths."]

Chapter 13

Staying Busy

Projects

Having been educated as a teacher, Molly's mind was exploding with "exciting" ideas that she wanted to try out on the precious little jewels that the Lord had loaned to her. Of course, the precious little jewels were not near as excited about all of Molly's neat ideas, especially since a large part of them had to do with education. Nevertheless, Molly was sure that in the long run, they would appreciate all the projects.

First and foremost, there were the memorization projects. They memorized endless poems, the names of all the Costa Rican presidents in order, countries and their capital cities, dates of all the Costa Rican holidays, the periodic table of elements, the Morse code, the seven ancient Wonders of the World, the seven Natural Wonders of the World, the books of the Bible forward and backward, the plagues of Egypt, the kings of Israel and Judah in order, and so on.

Naturally, the most important part of memorization was Bible verses. Molly picked what she thought were the fifty most important verses, decided to stick with those, and started teaching them. But every time she heard a sermon, read a devotion, or prepared a Sunday school lesson, she was always finding more equally as-important verses. And so the important verse list grew and grew. As the children in the first generation got older, Molly felt that there were some longer passages and complete chapters that needed to be added to the list and, finally, even whole books of the Bible. Eventually, the list got so long that Molly offered one hundred dollars to anyone who quoted 1,000 verses by memory in groups of five verses at a time. Unbelievably, five or six teens did reach the goal. The verses were illustrated on the computer, laminated, divided into folders, hung on doors and walls, and gone over in the morning, in school, before meals, and at devotions. They were printed on letter-size paper, half sheets, file card size, and I.D.-sized cards. Through the years, verse booklets were made in many different formats, some in black and white and others in color.

Molly was great at thinking up projects and working tirelessly to prepare her elaborate ideas on the computer. Unfortunately, she was not so great on the follow-through. With the first few verse booklets, the child would simply get a sticker next to every verse they memorized. Then came the great idea of a new booklet. It was a very time-consuming project in which the verse was illustrated in black and white, but separate color illustrations were made and laminated to be put over the black and white ones with a glue gun when the child learned the verse. It sounded like a great idea in theory, but Molly forgot to calculate how many children she had, how quickly they would be saying the verses, how many illustrations would have to be glued in their booklets, and how many would have to be constantly re-glued into the booklets when they fell out. Soon, kids were forever asking Molly when she was going to glue in all the illustrations of all the verses they had learned. They used the booklets for a couple of months and decided to move on to a different type of booklet. All that was left of that project was a shoebox stuffed full of little laminated pictures representing hours and hours of work that never got glued into the booklets.

As the years passed, Molly also ended up with a collection of devotional booklets she had prepared for the children. Some were based on various topics, some on the verses they had been memorizing, and some on chapters or books of the Bible. A handwritten family copy of the Bible is another project. Each child, from the youngest to the oldest, was assigned verses, chapters, or books of the Bible to copy in their best handwriting. It turned out to be a bigger project than they thought. It has been started and stopped for many generations, but they haven't given up yet. To this day, they are still working on the family Bible.

One time, Molly came up with an elaborate Christian character game she thought she could use both on family night and in Sunday school. She worked on it for weeks, but when it was finally completed and tried out on the kids, it was too complicated, took too long, and the kids were bored halfway through the game. Yet her silly brain couldn't just bury the game as a failed project. She thought of a way to make it less complicated and not so long. After several more weeks of preparing things on the computer, the new, improved edition came out. It was definitely a smidge better, but the family probably never even played it more than just a dozen times, usually when they had visitors.

Lots of Molly's project ideas involved computer illustrations and laminating. Most of them were also quite complicated. If she wanted to give them something spiritual and homemade for one of their Christmas presents, she couldn't just make a bookmarker for each kid. Instead, she had to make a keyring of fifty miniature laminated verse cards. But wait, if fifty verse cards would be neat, how neat would it be to make three key rings of fifty verse cards for each kid? They could each have a key ring of important verses, a key ring of Psalms and Proverbs, and a key ring of the names of Christ and salvation facts. Then, she would get her teacher, Lolly, involved in helping her with the project. Poor Lolly dreaded hearing the words "Christmas project" and even more so when the ideas wouldn't come into Molly's head until two weeks before Christmas. So what exactly would have been so bad about a simple bookmarker? Even Molly herself would tire of her projects smack dab in the middle of preparing them. She would tell Jerry that this was absolutely her last major project. She really and truly wanted to quit thinking up new ideas, but then there would be a need at school or an idea would come to her from something the pastor said in a sermon. Suddenly, she'd be making a huge cross with Velcro pictures that illustrated the different names of Christ and, soon after, a smaller cross for each child.

Not all projects were related to computer-made visual aids. One Christmas, they bought Bibles, put salvation tracts in them, and wrapped them up as Christmas gifts to hand out to their neighbors. A couple of times, they did treasure hunts and had to follow the clues to find the treasure. During one epoch, they would gather every afternoon, spread out in the living room, and have forty-five minutes of reading time with soft music playing in the background. There was also a season when they were gathering in the afternoon to listen to German tapes as a third language. Some kids learned a few more common phrases than others, but nobody ever mastered the language. Another time, they would meet in the afternoon to listen to audiobooks on tapes they had rented from the library. Needless to say, the children were not always as excited about new projects as Molly.

One of the most cringed-upon new projects was the morning walk idea. Having at least one time for family devotions was a daily occurrence. For years, that time was in the evening, but somewhere along the way, Molly decided that the first thing in the morning would be better. Since the children seemed awfully sleepy in the morning, Molly decided they would take a walk around the neighborhood to wake everyone up. The boys always wanted to take the German Shepherd dog that they had been given. Certainly, he could have been an excellent dog had he ever been trained, but Molly was not a dog trainer; she had her hands full trying to train children. Though he was several years old, the dog thought he was a friendly little puppy and was constantly jumping up on the little ones and knocking them over. On their walks, though the bigger boys thought they were training him, he was in control the whole time, dragging the boys wherever he wanted to go. Sometimes they would manage to get him, more or less, settled down and walking by their side, holler out for Mommy to see how well he was doing, and suddenly, he would see something he wanted to investigate closer up and bolt off at high speed, hauling his young "trainer" behind him. The boys who were taking turns "walking" the dog were always wide awake by the time they returned to the house for devotions. They only walked a little over a kilometer and, toward the end of the journey, stopped at the local store for fresh fruit and bread for breakfast.

Speaking of fresh fruit, the healthier diet project was another frowned-upon idea. Molly had read so many things about health regarding Dito that she felt she owed it to her children to protect them from unhealthy food choices. The project started out with rather strict measures, carrot juice and green juices every day, fresh fruits, and organic foods with an emphasis on live enzymes. She began going to an organic open market with a different couple of kids early every Saturday morning before the rest of the kids were awake. Although the healthy diet plan only lasted a handful of months as she let up slowly with their continual complaining, she did continue going to the organic market for two or three years. Basically, juicing and organic eating quickly became too expensive, and there was not a single child who was not resisting the idea. Molly consoled herself by thinking that between Costa Rica's great variety of fresh fruits and their lack of as much processed food, her kids had a healthier diet than the majority of kids in the United States. As for the supply of powdered green juice she had purchased, it became one of the better choices for punishing disobedient children.

Cooking was not exactly Molly's favorite thing to do, but every once in a while, she would find a recipe or just think up a new meal to try. These became known as Mommy's experiments. Some experiments came out better than others, but in a general sense, experiments weren't a favorite either. If a child came into the kitchen asking about dinner and the word experiment was the answer, they usually left the kitchen groaning. Coodles was especially sensitive to experiments and would leave groaning louder than others and commenting about Mommy and her experiments. With time, Molly learned what things worked better than others, and in later generations, the word *experiment* was no longer frowned upon but was actually welcomed.

One of the wildest projects was selling eggs. It was something they had done in Molly's youth group to earn money for summer trips. Molly tweaked the idea, made identification badges for each child, and hit the streets. It was at a time when they were saving money for a trip to the States. Molly wanted the children to feel like they had worked and had a part in making the trip possible. She divided the children into four groups, with each group having big kids and little ones. Then she bought a dozen eggs and put three eggs in each of the four baskets. They were instructed to go up to a house and ask the people if they would either buy one egg for any donation of money to help out the Children's Home or donate another egg. The original idea was to get an egg from one house and sell it to the neighbor, then get another egg from the next house, and so on. Molly gave them the choice of buying or donating. Since the houses in Costa Rica are so close together, they could cover a block in ten minutes. Molly would drive around, picking up the different groups and delivering them to their next block. Within about three hours, they would be heading home with all kinds of donations, clothes, food, toys, and so on, at least four dozen eggs, and the equivalent of a little over one hundred dollars.

For maybe two months, they went out once or twice a week. By that time, Molly was every bit as tired of the project as they were, if not more tired. The trip was going to be so expensive that what they were earning was just a drop in the bucket, and it was still so far in the future that the kids weren't seeing the fruit of their labor. Molly decided to take them out just one more time and promised that the money would be used to buy pizza. It was in the days when pizza was a rare treat and was well appreciated by everyone.

A few years later, Molly tried another work ethics project. Using the parable of the talents as her pattern, she gave each teenage child the equivalent of twenty dollars. They had one month to turn the twenty dollars into forty dollars. If they could do it, she would double their money, giving them a total of eighty dollars. Some of them bought and sold donuts, some baked brownies, still others drew pictures and sold them at church, and one even made miniature cars and trucks from paper to sell. All but one teen reached the forty-dollar goal and doubled their money.

Another project went into effect every January and February, which were Costa Rica's summer months. They were filled with Vacation Bible Schools and camps. The same sweet lady who had inspired Molly to become a ventriloquist at a young age in a children's camp had also headed up Vacation Bible Schools at Molly's childhood church. Molly couldn't forget the impact her ministry had on her to serve the Lord and desired to impact children in the same way. The lady had not only been a ventriloquist, but she had also been a dynamic teacher and had included a hilarious little old grandmother act in all her camp and VBS programs. Molly longed to imitate her style of teaching and jumped at every opportunity to lead a VBS. She, like her mentor, had a little old grandma act, ventriloquism, gospel illusions that Brother Neff had taught her, puppet skits, and she tried to prepare exciting lessons to lead children to Christ. Every year, of course, Molly took all the children with her, not only to learn more about Christ but in the hope that they, too, would be impacted to serve the Lord.

Many, many years later, Molly was surprised to read in an old newsletter that one summer, in two months, she had led six Vacation Bible Schools and three children's camps. She knew that it had been a dream come true for her at the time, but she couldn't figure out where she had gotten the energy to do such a thing on top of all the daily challenges of a house full of kids.

As the kids grew into teens, two or three different times during trips to the States, Brother Neff took them and Molly to Christian children's ministry week-long conferences. There they attended classes on a multitude of children's ministry ideas, from ballooning to clowning to puppets to visual aids to methods of teaching to gospel illusions and illustrations to craft ideas, and so on. Molly was thrilled that her teens had the opportunity to participate in the conferences. They went back to Costa Rica and became involved in the children's ministries of their church, another dream come true for Molly at the time. Sadly, as adults, many forgot their zeal to spread the gospel. Still, Molly praises God for those who have continued to serve the Lord; they have made every sacrifice worthwhile.

One recurrent event that was more just a family time thing than a project was the good old sock fight night. They would pull out all the socks in the house, roll them up into tight little balls, and divide them evenly between the girls and the boys. Next, using a long couch, they would divide the big living/dining area in half. Each team could arrange the rest of the furniture on their side as blockades. At the count of three, they would begin firing socks back and forth, each team staying on their side of the room. The fighting would go on for two or three minutes. They could throw socks at the other team members but not in their faces. The idea was to get rid of all your socks before the call to stop. Sometimes, teams would hoard up socks to try and calculate stopping time and toss them to the other side at the last minute. Every now and again that plan would work, but often, they would calculate too soon, and the other team would have time to gather up the socks and throw them back. Other times, they would misjudge the timing and be stuck with all the hoarded socks. The rule was simple: when Molly hollered at them to stop, they had to immediately drop everything and stick their hands in the air. Any flying socks after the word *stop* were returned to the thrower's side. Socks were collected and counted, the side with fewer socks was the winner. They would play several rounds, changing sides after each round. It was a once-in-a-long-while activity that was fun, different, and broke up the monotony of daily living.

Dramas

The annual Christmas drama tradition was one project from which nobody could escape. It was another one of those little old things that Molly saw and couldn't get her brain to leave alone. While at Bible college, she was able to attend a few live theater performances, and they fascinated her. How neat would it be for the family to prepare annual Christmas plays? Thus, the never-ending tradition began.

The first drama was with the first seven children, three of them being very small. Still, it was an easy year as they only presented the drama in about four churches. It was in a family setting where Molly and the four older children were trying to decide on a Christmas card. As each person suggested a card, they would freeze in position, thinking about it, and Polly would bring the three little ones out and place them on a small, framed table to form the Christmas card. The little ones dressed as angels for one card, shepherds for another, kings for a third, and finally, in a manger scene. Poor Polly had to get them off the table, herd them backstage, change their costumes, and have them back out on the table by the time the family's conversation had gotten to the next card. At the time, Floodles had just turned seven, Fluffy was four, and tiny little Kiffy was only two years old. Being the smallest, she stood front and center on the table, where she could be seen clearly. The other two took their places farther back on the table and on either end.

The children had no problem with the arrangement until one particular church. Kiffy took her spot and proudly spread her little angel wings high above her head. However, Fluffy felt that the smallest angel was crowding her out and needed to scoot closer to the front of the table. The short angelic argument they had did not go well as angel Kiffy, being sure she was in the right spot, was determined not to budge. She ignored Fluffy's instructions to move forward, turned toward the audience, and spread her wings a little higher. Fluffy, refusing to be ignored and every bit as determined to move Kiffy as

Kiffy was to not be moved, pushed her from behind in an effort to force her into the correct spot. The two-year-old miniature angel teetered and tottered back and forth and back and forth, very close to the edge of the table for several seconds while time stood still and onlookers all gasped. Besides being much too far away to be of any help, Molly's feet seemed frozen to the platform, and Polly was out of sight backstage. A few people in the front row stood to rush for her, but Kiffy regained her balance alone, avoiding disaster. Bless her tiny little heart as she continued in character, with her arms held up in the angel position while tears streamed down her pouting face. At the end of the scene, Polly grabbed her up, carried her off stage, and to everyone's surprise, brought her back to the table three minutes later, dressed as a little sheep and smiling big. The miracle-working power of a piece of candy popped into a two-year-old's mouth is quite amazing.

As the family grew, the Christmas drama would become a little more elaborate. For many years, the goal was always bigger and better, with more kids, more songs, more props, and more church presentations. So much work went into each play. The children were not professional actors, but some of them loved the attention and were great actors. Many others didn't care for the attention, and Molly struggled to get their cooperation. She couldn't just have a country-wide audition to replace those who weren't interested in acting. They would usually start learning their lines as early as October. After that, since the group was far too big for each person to have a microphone, there were weeks of repeating their lines loudly, clearly, slowly, and with expression. Next, memorizing and practicing songs were added. Meanwhile, props, backgrounds, and costumes had to be prepared.

As the years passed, they even added a video they would project up on a screen during certain parts of the play, usually during the songs. Adding video meant purchasing a green screen and endless filming and picture-taking. When all that was ready, Molly would go to Coodles's house, who was now married and had a family, and work with him all night to put the pictures and video clips together, adding music and special effects. He was so talented at creating videos and could do anything Molly wanted. She tried paying attention to learn how to do it herself, but he was too fast and too talented for her to catch everything.

Molly loved Christmas drama time. It wasn't unusual for her to be standing on stage in the middle of a play and come up with an idea for the next year's play. It was also not uncommon for her to have several ideas for the following year jotted down by the end of January. Although the kids complained about having to spend so much time practicing, Molly felt like they enjoyed it as well. In September, the children were already asking if the play was ready, if they could read it, or how many lines they had that year. It really seemed like they were excited to get started on it. They soon had friends in all the different churches whom they couldn't wait to see again.

Preparing the dramas was only half of the work, for, naturally, after the preparations came the performances. It grew to the point that they were doing sixteen performances a year. Molly thought that was great. She felt that with all the work that went into the preparation, the more people they could reach with the message of the real meaning of Christmas and the gospel, the better.

With each play, they had to pack everything up using endless checklists, carefully fit it into the bus, and drive to the church through Christmas traffic. Timing was essential, with needing to get there in plenty of time to set everything up. Then they had to do the play, break down the set after the service, pack things up again according to the checklists, haul it back out to the bus, drive home, and carry everything back into the house so it could be set up the following day for more practice. A few churches would give each child a gift, so the gifts, torn boxes, and crunched-up wrapping paper also had to be unloaded. Other churches would hand out bags of candy, apples, and grapes to everyone. Others would give them groceries and used clothing that needed to be taken inside the house.

Often, it was quite late by this time as some churches would have donuts or a meal for them and even take them out for pizza after an evening service. Most churches would give them a love offering, which was the only way Molly was able to provide a nice Christmas for so many children. Shopping for that nice Christmas had to be squeezed in between the presentations. Needless to say, December was always busier than usual.

While the scenes were being presented on stage, oftentimes, there was much more drama backstage than out front. Whenever Molly wasn't stopping a fight or calming a situation backstage, she couldn't help but laugh and shake her head at all that was going on behind the scenes. She often felt like the audience might enjoy the backstage drama more than the actual drama. She definitely learned a lot about the manipulating tactics of children. She saw it often, children who could turn on and off their tears in a matter of seconds.

One particular example remained like a recording in Molly's mind. Somewhere around the age of five or six years old, little Triddles became one of her best actors. He obeyed all the acting rules they had practiced, speaking up loudly, clearly, slowly, and with lots of expression. It was very important to him to perform his part perfectly and, as a result, was getting big acting parts with lots of lines. Yet at that same age, Triddles was often a whiner and complainer whenever things weren't exactly what he wanted them to be. Maybe he was complaining about itching from the fake mustache glued under his nose to make him look like a man, or maybe it was some other part of his costume that was uncomfortable. Molly couldn't quite recall the main issue, but he was very upset, and right in front of her, he stomped his little feet and cried real tears in his objection to whatever it was. Molly was frantically trying to calm him down as he was supposed to be out on stage in just a few seconds. Just then, Triddles heard his cue, and without missing a beat, he wiped his eyes and was out on stage quoting his lines happily and with full expression. That little rascal was a better actor than she had realized.

The Christmas play was obviously their biggest Christmas tradition. In fact, it left little room for much else. Yet it was important, and it gave the children lots of memories that they would talk about for years. The only other Christmas memories were a few things that they included in their hectic schedule. There was a day for decorating the house and a few gingerbread house-decorating contests through the years, sometimes judged individually and sometimes judged girls against the boys. Then, of course, Christmas Eve could never be complete without homemade Christmas cookies, usually made by Kiffy in the early years and Riffy in the later years, hot chocolate, and everyone sitting down together to watch *The Muppet Christmas Carol.*

In the later generation, Molly's phone would ding during the movie with pictures of the older kids sitting in their homes watching the same movie, many with their own children. Christmas morning was for reading the Christmas story together, opening gifts, and sharing Christmas stockings and a nice meal with as many of the grown children who could make it back for the day. There was also the tradition of going out to a nice ice cream parlor after all the dramas were done as a reward for their hard work.

Some of their favorite dramas were good enough to just be rewritten a tad and used again two or three times. Most years, though, Jerry and Molly would sit down in August and start putting on paper the ideas they had been thinking about for months. Since Jerry turned out to be good at making any play more meaningful, it was easiest for them to think the whole thing through in English first and then translate it into Spanish. Once translated, Lolly would read it through to make grammatical corrections, and Polly would read it through to add a few jokes.

Christmas play number twenty-two was one of those years that Molly came up with an idea in January. It was a brainstorm of an idea, a play of all plays, that would outdo them all. In fact, Molly reasoned that maybe it would be best to just do this same play every year. It could become a tradition in itself. After all, people sang the same Christmas carols every year, and their families watched the same Christmas movie every year and always laughed and enjoyed it. Doing the same play would save time. They could use the same props and backdrops, the same costumes, the same songs, and study the same lines every year. They could even work on perfecting it more each year. It would be great.

The setting was to be a mansion in which a deceased grandmother had left hidden clues to a secret treasure that her surviving relatives were fighting to find first. The clues were based on the seven "I AMS" of Christ in the gospel of John. Each clue was found in a different room of the mansion. At the entrance, they found the "I am the door" clue. Other clues included the Bread of Life in the kitchen, the True Vine in the dining room, the Light of the World in the library lamp, the Resurrection in the bedroom, the Good Shepherd in the garden, and the Way, the Truth, and the Life in the car in the garage. The play consisted of seven scenes as each clue was found.

In between scenes, all the children had to go backstage, make slight changes to their wardrobe by putting on scarves, hats, and coats, and then rush out to the opposite side of the stage to become carolers. They would sing a song as the video rolled of the relatives searching for clues in fancy mansion rooms that had been photoshopped into the homemade movies. At the end of the song, they would rush backstage, take off the caroler garb, and pop out for another live scene.

The filming, editing, mansion backgrounds, and special effects, though overly time-consuming and nowhere near professional-looking, all came out better than ever before and better than expected. The children all learned their lines well. The play itself had a good balance between humorous moments and thoughtful scriptural truths. It also had a powerful gospel message at the end when it was discovered that Granny, who had really not died yet, wanted to share her greatest treasure of Christ with her lost relatives.

They felt strongly that they had reached their goal of preparing their best Christmas play ever, but as they began taking it to the churches, many unforeseen circumstances weighed heavy on Molly, physically and emotionally, and her enthusiasm began to sizzle out. First, some churches were quite small, leaving less than a yard width of space for their backstage area, where each member of the family was constantly rushing in and out at the same time. Added to the chaos was the normal pinching, shoving, and arguing of siblings and kids losing props and pieces of their wardrobe from not putting them in the individually marked boxes that each of them had. Really, thought Molly, seven scenes, and all with wardrobe changes. What on earth was she thinking? Secondly, the play was longer than usual. Most of the plays they had done weren't any longer than thirty minutes, and this one was over fifty minutes, with no place nor chance for any of them to sit down and catch their breath. Every second was move, move, move, go, go, go. That was hardest on the youngest ones, ages five, six, seven, and eight.

Next, there were the bells to keep track of. The teens had some bell specials, and most of them held a bell in each hand, which, of course, were to be set back down in the famous individual boxes, but often, in the rush, they got left in the wrong place. Notwithstanding, the bell specials went well and added to the beauty of the play. They also had to keep track of four little toy accordions. If only the accordion special of the four little ones had gone over half as well as the bells. Their Christmas carol special was barely recognizable, even though they had practiced for hours on end.

The biggest bubble burster, though, was that Noodles did not cooperate. Indeed, he seemed determined to do everything in the world to complicate matters. When he was supposed to be here, he was there or, worse, nowhere to be found. When he was where he was supposed to be, he was pushing someone or arguing with his teacher Lolly, who was also backstage helping to maintain order. At other times, he forgot to wear part of his costume or entered scenes late. Once, he totally disappeared right in the middle of the performance. That was quite the feat in such a small area where there was pretty much no place to disappear. Oh, but there was a place. The video they had made was played on a screen that sat on top of a small table covered with a sheet. The table was from their kindergarten class and happened to be the same table Kiffy had almost fallen off many years earlier. It measured three and a half feet long and slightly over two feet tall, much too small a space for an oversized fourteen-year-old, but that is where they found him.

As Noodles got out from under the table, he hit the flimsy legs of the table, which began wobbling and, in turn, wobbled the screen on top of it. Molly imagined all of their scenery suddenly falling, but they managed to steady everything. According to Noodles, he was just trying to stay out of everyone's way. Molly made it very clear that it was not to be his private hideaway, but he still repeated the stunt at two or three more churches.

By the end of December, Molly was completely wiped out. Absolutely no ideas had come to her about next year's drama, and she didn't even want to hear the words *Christmas play*. She was worn out enough to make herself sick and spent almost a week in her recliner with a bad case of some kind of flu or virus. She thought her usual drama and excitement would return once she got her strength back, but that didn't happen. Oh, there was no doubt in her mind that it was the best play they had ever performed, but she had reached the goal she had set out to reach, and her brain, like a pendulum, swung in the opposite direction, believing that from now on, simple was best. She not only did not ever want to make a tradition out of this "greatest" drama, but she refused to let her mind even think about dramas. Sad to say, she would never again feel the same thrill about Christmas drama time. Maybe the passing of time had something to do with the decision. They had already performed twenty-two years' worth of dramas, and Molly was almost fifty-five that year.

No ideas came until August rolled around, and Molly was forced to sit down and think. When Jerry and Molly finally put their minds together and thought of something they both liked, most of the work was in the preparation and very little in the presentation. It was about a family sitting in their living room, discussing the places they were visiting through a time machine their grandmother had gifted them for Christmas. The time machine took them to types of Christ in the Old Testament. All of the time machine scenes had been filmed ahead of time, and the family just sat in their living room watching the video. It had no backstage or costume changing and no alternate dramas going on behind the scenes. Jerry and Molly just sat in make-shift easy chairs in the living room setting the entire play long. The children sat on the floor around them.

Once in a while, a child would stand and move around or step into the time machine, but most of the play was simple family conversation and the video. Molly sat smiling as she watched Noodles. There was no backstage, and he was under the constant watch of the attentive audience with no opportunity to drive Molly crazy. All was calm. Naturally, there were a few people who mentioned that the play was a little slow, and they missed all the activity of previous years. Molly just smiled. She felt that it was perfect and knew that they could not possibly understand.

The most wonderful thing about that year's play was that God, who was always so attentive to Molly's needs, sent three sweet, musically talented sisters from the States to help with the drama. They specifically came for the month of December to help with the music of the Christmas play. They were hard-working girls with good attitudes and joyful spirits, ready to help in any way, and they were a breath of fresh air for Molly, completely taking over the music preparation. Two of the sisters came back the following year on a short-term mission trip. One of them, Jolly, became the music teacher, giving classes in violin, viola, and piano. Molly had a dedicated music teacher helping with the Christmas play for four more years.

Even with the added help, from that point on, they continued to look for ways to keep the Christmas play as simple as possible. Her new motto was less is more; she just didn't have the energy she had before. By the time Molly was sixty years old, after having prepared twenty-eight years' worth of plays, she was ready to end the Christmas play tradition; she felt it had run its course. That was when she found out that the annual Christmas play was not only a project from which no child could escape, but she could not escape either. When they tried to explain to the local churches that they wanted to go in a different direction, start new traditions, and make Christmas a special family time with less pressure, many insisted they come to their church regardless, even if it were just to sing a few specials. By this time, they had already been putting into practice the philosophy of less is more for several years, but even in that, there was so much preparation involved, more than anyone could possibly understand. In the end, Molly was outvoted, and it was settled that they would do a small presentation of about twenty minutes but only in the churches that faithfully supported the home. That cut them back down to only about nine presentations a year. All the focus on a spectacular production was finally replaced by a simple desire to exalt Christ alone.

[A LESSON TO LEARN: May our service for the Lord always be just that, service for the Lord. Yes, we should give him our best, and yes, we should strive for excellence, but only to bring honor and glory to his name and only to point others to Christ. How many times does our service for Christ scream to others, "Look at me; look what I can do" rather than, "Look to him"? That is exactly what Satan desires. He wants us to be so caught up in ourselves that people see us instead of Christ.]

Prayer: Father, may all that we do point others to your dear Son, Jesus Christ, that he may truly receive the glory.

Chapter 14

Staying Busy – Part 2

Trips

Trips to the States were the biggest and most complicated of all their projects. Not only did the trip itself have to be planned, but there were also so many hoops to jump through to get the children out of Costa Rica and into the States. Molly first had to get letters of permission from social services for each child Those letters came with a one-month time limit for the children to exit the country. During that time, she had to call and make appointments to apply for the children's passports, go back and pick up the passports, get an appointment for a VISA in the U.S. Embassy, leave time for troubleshooting, buy tickets, and pack. Any of the separate offices could deny any of the children at any point. In fact, through the years, each office had, at some time, denied some or all of the children, which resulted in more paperwork in more offices.

From their early beginnings in 1990 through 2018, they made seven trips to the States with groups of children, plus several more with just one or two children. In length, four of the trips involved three months of traveling, two trips were only two months long, and the last trip was only three weeks long. It was made to attend Fluffy's wedding, but they took advantage of it to be in new churches for several weeks.

Trip of 1990

The easiest trip was the first one when the home was less than a year old and there were only four children. Maybe government offices weren't quite as picky in those years as all the passports and VISA procedures went off without a hitch. The hardest part of that trip was saving up for six plane tickets at a time when finances were so scarce. To achieve that, no luxury items were allowed, not so much as a roll of paper towels. For months on end, they ate rice, beans, and cabbage salad, with very little else. Molly encouraged everyone by telling them that when they got to her parents' house, there would be plenty to eat, and it wouldn't be rice, beans, or cabbage.

On their first night in the States, Molly's father quietly pulled her into the kitchen next to the pantry. He pulled out a huge bag of rice and told Molly not to worry about food. Molly's mother had told him how much rice Costa Ricans ate, so he went out and bought plenty in hopes that they would feel at home. Molly smiled and thanked him, but inwardly, she groaned. The following day, being so pleased with his own thoughtfulness, Molly's father also wanted Polly to know that he had purchased the rice. Polly was still learning English at the time and did not quite understand the point he was making. Like he had told Molly, he was explaining that she need not worry because he had purchased plenty of rice. She thought he was explaining that in the States, they weren't accustomed to eating much rice. Apparently, she was speaking better than she was understanding because Molly's father had no problem understanding Polly when she told him not to worry about them. After all, they were sick and tired of rice and didn't want any at all. Molly's father turned and walked away with a sad look on his face.

Another interesting event on their first trip to the States was when Molly decided to take them all across the Mexican border for a weekend mission trip. Anyone could easily pass the Mexican border without a passport because they needed tourism. But some twenty or so miles into the interior, there was a point where documents were checked. It was at that point that the Mexican immigration officer pointed out to Molly that the U.S. visas clearly stated that it was good for only a one-time entry into the States. Unable to believe what she was hearing, Molly took the passports and immediately opened one to the visa page. Very clearly in big letters, it said ONE-TIME ENTRY. Molly imagined Polly and the kids being stuck in Mexico, possibly even having to fly back to Costa Rica from Mexico. They were traveling with several missionary families in a Greyhound bus converted into a mobile home. The other missionaries encouraged Molly to enjoy the trip and not worry, so she tried her best to do just that.

At the border crossing on the return trip, they sat all the Costa Ricans in the back section and all the American missionaries in front. As Molly held her breath, the U.S. immigration officer stepped on the bus, looked around, stepped back off, and waved them to cross the bridge. Usually, they required each person to say out loud that they were a United States citizen. This officer didn't ask any of them to state their citizenship, thank you, Lord.

During the rest of the trip, they were able to visit churches in Texas, New Mexico, Arizona, and California, picking up a little more support and lots of material donations to take back with them. Molly never would have imagined such generosity. Each child received so much nice clothing that they ended up leaving all the clothes they had brought with them to take back better clothing that had been given to them. And that was how it was with every trip they ever made. They would take only a backpack of old clothes with them and bring it back stuffed with nicer clothing. They had so much "stuff" that Molly bought about ten of those old pressboard trunks. The trunk itself was a tad heavy, but in those days, each checked bag could weigh seventy pounds. Their little group was certainly a sight for sore eyes as some friends helped them haul everything into the airport. They didn't expect problems with the bags as they were to be checked through all the way to Costa Rica. Unfortunately, the airline had a problem, a plane was delayed, and they were put up for the night in a hotel in Dallas, Texas. The airlines didn't make them take the baggage to the hotel but rather just blocked it off in a section of the airport.

The following day, they needed to retrieve the luggage and get it to the check-in counter. Molly was glad to see men with huge carts willing to help people with their bags. But, bless Molly's innocent little heart, she had no idea what all those nice little cart-pulling men expected for tips. In her mind, though he was hauling twelve pieces of luggage, he loaded it, pulled it about one hundred yards, and unloaded it all in about ten minutes. Calculating the hourly wages back in those days, she felt two dollars was more than generous. Apparently, Molly was oblivious to some kind of basic rules on tip-giving because the man was not at all happy with her generosity. First, he stood staring at the tip in his hand with a look of unbelief and then started complaining in a very loud voice about what a cheapskate Molly was. She quickly retrieved the two dollars and replaced it with a five-dollar bill, hoping to prove to him and all who had heard his loud complaints that she was indeed not a cheapskate. To her surprise, he looked at the five dollars and continued his raving, pointing, and hollering about how many bags he had transported on his cart. Now Molly understood they were paid by the bag and not by the hour. Certainly, ten dollars would appease him. He was still not too happy but finally turned and walked off, mumbling loudly. They all turned at once, and, smiling at the staring crowd, went on their way. Molly couldn't help but think how happy any Costa Rican would have been with her two-dollar tip.

Trip of 1994

Though a trip to the States was a lot of extra work and expense, they found that between special offerings, new sponsors and prayer warriors, and other donations, they were very helpful and more than paid for themselves. Therefore, after the first trip, they would try to make a trip every four to seven years. By the time they made their

Staying Busy – Part 2

second trip, they had nine children, the youngest being nine months old and the oldest having just turned thirteen years old.

Once again, there was only a short window of time to get all the paperwork done, but Molly felt things were looking good. The kids would get their passports on Monday and didn't have their visa appointments until the following week on Tuesday. But when Molly went to pick up the new passports, she was informed that they would not be issuing a passport to little nine-month-old Doodles as they weren't convinced that he was Costa Rican. Molly was dumbfounded. She pointed out that she had clearly presented them with a Costa Rican birth certificate for the baby. The head honcho of immigration came out, a short little lady with a bulldog-looking face, and pointed out to Molly that the birth certificate had the words "unknown" on the lines for the mother and the father. She said that for all she knew, he could have German parents. Molly told her that he didn't look German; he looked Costa Rican. The grumpy lady didn't appreciate the comment. She told Molly to go back to the social service office that had given her the letter of permission for the child to leave the country and ask them to rewrite the letter, specifying that the child was Costa Rican. This began the five-day rat race to prove Doodles's citizenship.

Social services told Molly that it was obvious he was Costa Rican. Yet, when she asked them to put that in the letter, they refused. They said it was their job to give exit permission, but it was not their job to declare citizenship; that was immigration's job. Molly went back to tell the immigration lady what they had said, but she only referred Molly to some other government office that might be able to help her. That office sent her to another office, and that office to another. Molly spent Monday, Tuesday, Wednesday, Thursday, and Friday going from one end of San Jose to the other, looking for answers. Everyone seemed to agree that Doodles was a Costa Rican, but it was nobody's job to say so.

On Friday morning, Molly was standing in some kind of registrar's office of some eight or more workers, each one with a computer in front of them. The man at the front desk looked Doodles up, and it very clearly stated on the computer screen that he was Costa Rican. Molly asked if he could print that page for her, but their computers weren't connected to any printers. Since this was before the days of cell phones, she asked if anyone had a camera so she could take a picture of the screen. No one did, and of course, it was no one's job to write a letter stating that, according to the computer, he was Costa Rican.

Finally, a man at the last desk piped up and said that according to the Constitution, the child was Costa Rican. When Molly asked him for an explanation, he pulled out a small booklet titled *The Political Constitution of the Republic of Costa Rica* and read Article 13, paragraph 4, which declares any infant found in Costa Rica, of unknown parents, to be a Costa Rican by birth. The man then told Molly that it was Doodles's constitutional right to have a Costa Rican passport and that she could purchase the same little booklet at any bookstore.

Molly thanked him, rushed out of the office, found a bookstore, and purchased her own copy. Returning to immigration for the umpteenth time that week, she plopped the booklet on the secretary's desk, opened to the page on citizenship, and said she was demanding her child's constitutional right. The secretary read the paragraph, took the booklet to the grumpy little boss lady, and returned five minutes later, stating that they had decided to issue Doodles a passport and that she could pick it up on Monday. Molly couldn't understand how the head of immigration did not even know the four simple rules that constituted Costa Rican citizenship by birth. Nevertheless, she thanked her kindly and left. On Monday, she picked up the passport, on Tuesday, she was at the American Embassy, and the following week, they were boarding a plane for the States. Once on the plane, she felt relieved but didn't really breathe easily until they were out of the airport in the States and loaded in the Lighthouse van.

On that trip, they traveled with Larry and Paula Neff for three months. Years later, Molly couldn't really even remember where they had gone and what churches they had visited. She did remember, however, another airport incident, in which, this time, their plane arrived late, causing them to miss their next flight. She remembered being told that their airline didn't have any more flights for many hours but that the computer showed that another airline had a flight shortly, and if they hurried, they could get on that one. The lady pointed to the end of the long L-shaped ticket counter section of the airport to where the other airline was located. Turning around and hollering for everyone to gather their things and run for it, Molly herself led the way, pushing Doodles's stroller. Polly and eight little obedient children all grabbed their carry-ons and started running after Molly, giggling as they ran. Unfortunately, that airline did not have eleven empty seats, and they pointed Molly to another airline close to where they had just come from. Since they had just spent over three hours sitting on an airplane, the bigger kids were more than happy to stretch their legs with a nice run, so Molly pointed the other direction, and they all took off, laughing this time. Of course, four-year-old Kiffy and six-year-old Fluffy had the disadvantage and became discouraged as they lagged behind while struggling to maneuver the wheels on their little carry-ons.

When most of the group made it to the next ticket counter, you guessed it, they pointed Molly to an airline right next to the one they had just come from. It would have made a great but unbelievable scene in a movie, yet this was real life. This time, as the big kids turned and ran the other direction, they almost plowed down the two little ones who were only about halfway to the latest destination.

By now, the whole group was laughing very loudly, and Molly had no time to look around, but she wondered if any traveler was waiting for his flight who sat watching and enjoying their funny little back-and-forth drama. And if in the small world we live in, he had also been in the airport when Molly had so much problem figuring out the tip, he would for sure have labeled them by now "the crazy lady and the kids." They finally got tickets and were running off one more time, this time to catch a plane that was supposed to leave in just a couple of minutes.

There were several other things that found a permanent spot in Molly's memory about the trip. She remembered young Kiffy needing to stop very often for bathroom breaks. Brother Neff was used to traveling with teens who did not need quite so many stops. One day, they had already had so many stops, and Brother Neff seemed so frustrated that on the next stop, Molly made sure everyone got out of the van and went to the bathroom, whether they felt they had to or not. Meanwhile, Polly bought some delicious-looking watermelon in the convenience store. It was indeed deliciously sweet, so much so that she couldn't stop eating it. After a longer-than-usual rest stop, they were back on the road with the hopes of driving several hours before the next stop. Yet, about twenty minutes down the road, Polly was surprised at how fast two big containers of watermelon could go through one's system. Fearful to say anything, she sat as still as possible for what seemed like an eternity. To her relief, Kiffy piped up a few minutes later, calling out for a bathroom break. When questioned how that could even be possible, she explained that the last stop was for number one, and now she needed a stop for number two. Polly was more than happy to speak up on Kiffy's behalf, stressing that she was only four years old, and everyone needed to have patience with her. Of course, as soon as they stopped, Polly volunteered to make the sacrifice of taking her to the bathroom, grabbed Kiffy by the hand, and hurried to the bathroom just in time for both of them. From then on, Polly refrained herself from eating watermelon on travel days.

Molly also remembered that baby Doodles very quickly learned to recognize the big white van and hate it. That tiny fellow knew that once he was strapped into that car seat, it was going to be a long, hot day of sitting still at an age when he had just learned to crawl and was loving the freedom of getting around. As soon as they opened the door to get in, he would start crying. Even getting back in the van after stops would send him into crying fits that would make all the other kids bustle around, looking for just which toy would calm him down this time.

Staying Busy – Part 2

When they weren't traveling, they were staying in the Lighthouse Children's Home in Mississippi, and Doodles had the idea that he needed to make up for lost time. All the kids would sit in the living room area of the huge building to watch a video, and Doodles would immediately take off, crawling as fast as his little arms and legs would take him. They nicknamed him Fire Ant because he was so small, moved so fast, and was often wearing his bright red jumper. His goal was to get to the opposite end where the stairs were. Oh, how he wanted to know what was at the top of those stairs and explore the second floor. Oftentimes, Fire Ant would be halfway up the stairs before someone would miss him, holler, "Fire Ant," and scamper to the opposite end of the room to rescue him. They would bring him back, set him down, and off he went again. Though all the rescuers tired of the game, it seemed like Fire Ant never did.

Another memory was Kiffy, Fluffy, and Floodles running in one day, screaming at the top of their lungs. There was a little playground outside that probably didn't get used often since the girls in the Mississippi home were older teens. But naturally, Molly's little ones were very excited about going out to the playground. What nobody knew was that there was a beehive under the kiddy slide. As soon as the three little ones began to climb the ladder, the frightened bees burst forth to protect their hive by attacking the intruders. It pained Molly to see all three of them crying in agony together. Floodles and Fluffy each had two bee stings, and poor little Kiffy had five bee stings, all on her back. Fortunately, none of them showed any type of allergic reaction and recovered normally.

Another tragic memory was Biffy falling off of a top bunk in the middle of the night. The loud thump woke Molly up, but since no one started to cry, she supposed someone had jumped out of bed to go to the bathroom. After listening to the water run for several minutes, Molly decided to check and make sure everything was okay. She found Biffy in the bathroom rinsing her mouth out with water. She had bitten her tongue when she fell but was such a brave girl that she was taking care of it by herself. Molly looked at it but couldn't see much as it was still bleeding. Biffy said she was fine, and, assuming that biting one's tongue was not exactly life-threatening, Molly went back to bed. But when she checked Biffy out in the morning, she was surprised to see one side of her tongue sliced all the way through. They rushed her to the doctor and found that there was still time to stitch the tongue back together. It was Molly's first experience to watch one of her children being stitched. She thought it would be an interesting experience. Maybe it would have been easier to handle had it been a knee or an elbow, but a tongue? From the very first stitch, Molly felt queasy, and then the room started going around in circles. Fortunately, whether because she was swaying back and forth or just that medical people are keenly aware of those things, the doctor picked up quickly on her apprehension and asked her if she would like to sit down. Molly was more than happy to take a seat and a deep breath. She glanced over a time or two from her safe chair that was planted solidly on the floor, but mostly just gave the capable doctor a mental thumbs up to carry on the necessary procedure.

Molly's belief that nursing was not the right profession for her was pretty much confirmed that day. Nevertheless, through years of colds, the flu, fevers, broken bones, asthma attacks, allergies, bruises, cuts, bites, burns, stitches, seizures, appendicitis attacks, emergency visits, hospital stays, and messes to clean up, she felt that substitute mothering often came very close to imitating the nursing profession. It is worth mentioning that there were at least a dozen more emergencies requiring stitches in which she did not need to sit down, although she could never get through any of them without a frown on her face, several suppressed groans and grunts, and a deep hurt in her heart for the patient.

There was also a very embarrassing memory connected to their second trip. Their visit to the States coincided with the annual camp meeting in Mississippi, where pastors and church members come from many different states to enjoy preaching and fellowship. Brother

Neff was so happy to show off the members of the newest Lighthouse home located in Costa Rica. He had fallen in love with a Costa Rican dish called "gallo pinto," which was really no more than rice mixed with beans and a few condiments. He came up with the bright idea of announcing that they would be enjoying an authentic Costa Rican dish for one of the evening meals. Being one of his favorite foods, in each service, he praised the delicious dish that everyone was going to have the privilege of tasting. He absolutely couldn't say enough about the marvelous gallo pinto. Naturally, he asked Molly and Polly to be in charge of the meal and pointed them to the rice and beans. The ladies looked at each other with a "that's easy enough" look and told Brother Neff that it would be no problem.

Regrettably, there were several factors the ladies had not thought of at the moment that they had answered Brother Neff so confidently, the first of those factors being that neither of them was a very good cook. Other factors included never having had the privilege of cooking for 250 people, not knowing how to cook rice in a regular pot as opposed to a rice maker, whether cooking it in one big pot or several smaller pots was better, how long it would take to cook that amount of rice, and so on. To make a long story short, they probably didn't start cooking early enough and probably put too much rice in too big of a pot. The rice was not cooking.

Supper was supposed to be served at 6:00 p.m., and it was not cooked yet at 5:45. It was not cooked at 6:00 either and was still raw at 6:15. Then to make matters worse, Molly got a phone call from Costa Rica in the midst of the tragic meal preparation. It was from her mother, who had chosen to stay in Costa Rica babysitting their little dog rather than traveling around the country. She had felt that something was not quite right and had gone to the doctor. He told her she had a large tumor on her liver that needed to be removed. Molly asked if she wanted them to return, but her mother said that Lolly was helping her with everything and that Molly was not to worry. Yeah right. How was Molly not going to worry? The phone call was interrupted by cries for help from the kitchen. (For those interested, days later, the doctor removed a benign tumor bigger than a baseball from her mother's liver, and she recovered quickly and beautifully.)

Getting back to the meal, they tried a few desperate last-minute measures like transferring half of the rice to a separate pot and stirring the rice a little, but it was much too late for those measures to change anything. It was as if those stubborn little grains of rice were determined to remain hard, refusing to soften. At 6:30, Brother Neff told them to throw in the beans and serve the food. They tried to explain that the rice was still raw and hard, but he didn't care. He pointed out that the services started at 7:00, and they had been waiting for half an hour for the food, they'd have to eat it as it was. So, they served the crunchy gallo pinto while Molly and Polly hid in the kitchen, hoping that Brother Neff would not mention the cooks' names. When the dining hall emptied, much quicker than usual, they came out of their hiding place in the kitchen and began clearing the table by throwing practically untouched plates of gallo pinto in the trash can one by one. Their only comfort was that in the service that followed, Brother Neff didn't ask for a show of hands from all those who had enjoyed the Costa Rican meal. Molly mentally added a professional cook to the list of professions she was not cut out to execute.

Of all the memories of that particular trip, none was better than the night that Coodles accepted Christ as his Savior. The day after the tragic camp meeting meal, Coodles came to Molly right at bedtime and asked to talk. At the time, the whole Costa Rican group was sleeping together in bunk beds in the first-floor dormitory of the Mississippi home. Molly got the rest of the kids in bed, turned out the main light, and took Coodles into the large bathroom where they could have some privacy. They only talked for a short period of time. Molly asked a few questions and realized that it was obvious that Coodles understood and was sincere in his decision. There together, sitting on the floor in front of the shower stalls, Coodles told Molly that he knew he was a sinner and that Christ had taken the punishment for his sins through his death on the cross. In a simple act of faith, ten-year-old Coodles placed his trust in Jesus Christ. Thank the Lord that after all is said and done, camp meetings are not about "gallo pinto" but about preaching the good news of salvation. And above all else, thank the Lord that our salvation is not based on the feeble efforts of weak little humans who sometimes can't even get a simple meal right but on the work of the perfect, all-powerful, holy Son of God, who, through conquering death, offers us eternal life in heaven.

The last memory of that trip involved God once again providing what they needed when they needed it. It was a Sunday morning, and they were traveling from Mississippi to New Orleans. They would be in two churches in New Orleans and fly out from there on Monday morning. They had left early, in plenty of time to get to the Sunday morning service, but the van was giving them problems. A staff member from the home in Mississippi was driving them and had turned around several times, telling Molly that the van seemed to be losing energy. As they were puttering along, Molly began encouraging the driver to get off every time they were coming up on an exit. Yet, each time, he would tell her that he felt the van could go a little farther. Molly was afraid of getting stuck on the interstate, far from civilization, with a car full of little people. In her fear, she kept pointing out exit after exit and wondering why he was refusing to exit and look for help.

Soon, the van was crawling along very slowly, and finally, to Molly's relief, he exited and looked for a pay phone. Thumbing through a phone book, he called several churches of like faith, but they all said they couldn't help; there was no one who could come to their rescue, or they were too far away. Finally, they found a church that was only some ten minutes away and was willing to help. The church brought a van and a mechanic to them, left the mechanic, and loaded the whole gang up to take them to the church service. At the end of the service, the pastor came to greet them. He explained that they had just had a big banquet the night before and had so much spaghetti and other leftovers that they had been wondering what they were going to do with all of it. They led the group to the fellowship hall and not only provided them with a full meal but also packed up snacks for them to take with them. By the time they finished eating, the mechanic had repaired the van and refused any kind of payment. Molly couldn't stop thinking of God's provision as they continued on their way. No wonder God had not encouraged the driver to exit earlier; He knew exactly where the food and mechanic were and worked everything out to perfection.

Trip of 1998

The next group was even larger, consisting of sixteen kids and a couple of extra helpers who stayed only the first month or less. The group was so big that they were divided between two vans. Once again, Molly couldn't remember everywhere and maybe not every state they were in but remembered being in churches in Georgia, Tennessee, Indiana, and then going back southward to Mississippi, Arkansas, Texas, and New Mexico. Once again, it was quite a lot of traveling requiring a good deal of flexibility. Molly never knew from place to place whether they would be sleeping on carpet, cots, beds, or air mattresses. For the most part, they stayed in churches. Usually, the churches would have different members bring in food for them. When they traveled, fast-food chains with dollar menus were their favorites. Some churches had washers and dryers, and at other times, they spent their afternoons sitting in a hot Laundromat. Clothes pretty much had to be washed every three or four days. And thus, they traveled for three months in a nomadic lifestyle like a modern-day band of gypsies.

One of the first stops was a week in Knoxville, Tennessee, for a homeschool conference. They were sleeping on cots in the second-floor classrooms of a Christian school that was out for the summer. The boys stayed in one room with Brother Neff and the girls and ladies in another. The director of the school explained to them that the school was located on a rather shady side of town and that it would be best not to be out late at night.

The school had a motion-sensitive alarm system that automatically turned on at 10:00 p.m. They had exactly two minutes to deactivate the alarm system as soon as it started beeping. If the code was not imputed within those two minutes, the sensors turned on, and any movement in the hallways would set off the alarm. Each night, Brother Neff would wait in the office to punch in the passcode at 10:00 p.m. on the dot. He had Molly with him the first night so she would also know how to do it in case he wasn't there sometime. Molly quickly learned the four-number passcode and saw how simple it was to disarm.

Several nights later, Brother Neff asked Molly if she could disarm the alarm because he wanted to go to bed early. With everyone else in bed, Molly and Polly sat in the office talking and waiting for 10:00 p.m. When the alarm beeped, Molly stood and very calmly punched in the code that she remembered. To her surprise, the alarm continued to beep and blink red rather than showing the green disarmed light. She must have gotten the numbers in the wrong order. Quickly, she tried a different combination of the same numbers; she was very sure of the numbers. When that combination did not disarm the system, Molly panicked, knowing that the clock was ticking off its two-minute time limit. She quickly began trying other combinations one after another. She was punching them in so fast she couldn't even remember which ones she had already tried. The fact is, four numbers can be combined in twenty-four different ways.

Polly ran upstairs to see if Brother Neff was already asleep and found him fast asleep and snoring. When she returned, she heard Molly yelling to her from the office not to step into the hallway as the alarm was now fully activated. The alarm system only covered the hallways, not the front foyer, classrooms, or offices. From the foyer, Polly hollered back to Molly to come out of the office and try to crawl slowly down the hall, keeping close to the wall. Obediently, Molly started a very slow, inch-by-inch crawl, pressed tight against the wall. Halfway to the foyer, a sensor spotted her, and the alarm began to blast loudly. Both ladies jumped and felt their hearts thumping rapidly. Molly told Polly to go back upstairs and calm the children. They had been told that the alarm alerted the police department of a break-in. Molly was expecting the police to arrive at any minute. Not knowing what else to do, she opened the front door and stood in front of the school in the night air in her bathrobe with both hands stretched straight up in the air in surrender.

After standing there for several minutes, waiting for the police, she began to question what she was doing. This was the neighborhood where they weren't supposed to go out at night, and she was standing there with the front door wide open in the position of surrender. She went back in, closed the door, and peeked out every now and again, looking for the flashing police lights. Polly returned from upstairs with the news that everyone was sleeping right through the loud siren alarm. Though it seemed like an eternity, within ten minutes, the phone began to ring. Molly ran back to the office. It was the school principal. He had received a phone call that the alarm was sounding. He told Molly the correct code, she punched it in, and the alarm stopped immediately. She had been under the impression that once the alarm was activated, it was too late to punch in the code, but that was not the case. Sure enough, Molly had the right numbers in the wrong order. What a scary night! Worn out, they climbed the stairs, giggling over one more silly predicament they had gotten themselves into. As she lay down, Molly was ever so relieved to have the whole ordeal ended. Never before had a little cot felt so comfortable, and she was soon fast asleep.

On that same trip to the States, Molly was very excited when Brother Neff suggested visiting her home church in El Paso, Texas. They had been supporting Molly since she had left for the mission field and, at one time, had even taken a work group to Costa Rica. The group had visited in the early years of the Tres Rios home. They had put in ceiling fans and built the cabinets in the kitchen and the bunk beds in the rooms. In fact, the group had asked them to purchase the hardest wood available for the bunk beds. Polly was told that would be almond wood and purchased enough for eight bunk beds. As it turns out, maybe the very hardest wood wasn't totally necessary as it burnt out several of the electric saws the group had brought down for the job. The head carpenter did not look like a very happy camper, but eventually, all eight bunk beds were finished, some of the work being done with axes, and would undoubtedly last until the rapture and beyond.

As with any group that came down, Molly had planned all the home's favorite recipes for the visitors, even though they were a little more expensive than their normal mealtime menu. Molly remembered this group of workers to be such big eaters and so used to snacking between meals that they spent the first day complaining that they were hungry. Finally, they piled in the van and went shopping on their own. They came back with loads of snacks and junk food that they wanted added to the menu. Molly did so, and from there on out, no one could have possibly complained about being hungry.

Now they were in the church in El Paso and would be singing specials and giving testimonies in several Sunday school classes as well as in the morning service. When they entered the young married couple's class, the teacher who was introducing them was one of the men who had gone on the mission trip and also happened to be the one who had insisted on the shopping trip years earlier. As he introduced the group, Molly realized that he had a totally different memory of the meal on that first day of their trip. Maybe he was only trying to encourage the students in his class to get involved in missions and help those who were less fortunate than themselves, but Molly felt he could have chosen his words a tad better. His first words might have been to have a part in the Lighthouse ministries, but his very next statement was that he had been there and knew exactly the poverty in which they lived. Molly's ears perked up, and her eyes opened wider, as did those of her older children. Then, this dear Christian brother, God bless his soul, said that the food they had eaten on their first day was so bad it was literally like eating out of a garbage can. He continued that the kitchen pantry was so empty that they immediately had to go out and spend hundreds of dollars on food, but they were just happy they could be a blessing to the children. If her best meal had tasted like garbage to him, she wondered what he would have thought of the gallo pinto in Mississippi.

About that time, the whole Costa Rica gang would have loved to look for a rock to crawl under, but there was no time to sulk in the embarrassment of the moment because, just then, he called them up for the songs and testimonies. In the end, they had a good day, and everyone seemed to enjoy their presentation despite the introduction they had been given.

They stayed in El Paso for several days before moving on to New Mexico. Molly's mother still owned the house in El Paso where Molly had grown up. She had left a single young man in charge of renting out the individual rooms. Since all of them were Christian young men and members of the church there, they very graciously agreed to spend a few days in other places and let Molly and the kids have the house while they were in El Paso. Being able to stay with her kids in her childhood home meant so much to Molly. Though the first four kids had stayed there years earlier, this was different. They were probably too small to remember very much from that trip, and now there were twelve other kids who had never seen where Mommy had lived.

The feeling of nostalgia took control of Molly's emotions. She wanted them to see her house, her room, and the walk-in closet across from her room that she had cleaned out and made into her secret headquarters when she played detective as a child. She longed to point out the window in her room that she would jump out of to escape from the bad guys and the big tree in the front yard from which she and her brother would spy on the entire neighborhood through their binoculars and jot down their findings. She showed them the elementary school she attended, the streets she walked down to go to and from school, and the park where her brother played Little League baseball. She explained how that same park would flood at least once a year when El Paso got its little bit of annual rain, how the flood water would form a little lake, and how the kids would come from all around to play in the water and catch tadpoles. She also showed them her high school and marveled that with all the new renovations, the only thing that was still recognizable was the corner on the other side of the street where her father would pick them up after school each day.

Molly knew that all those things were not really that important to her kids, but each memory was immensely important to Molly. She was glad she had taken the time to make such a big deal over every detail as the house was sold several years later, and there would be no going back to it. Without a house there, and since all of her brothers had moved to other states and her husband's family lived in Florida, there might never be a reason to return. El Paso would remain only a fond memory.

Soon, the trip had come to an end, and they were packing to go home. It was still in the days when all airlines were friendly and allowed each passenger two free seventy-pound bags, a carry-on, and a personal item. As usual, each child had only brought a backpack of clothes to the States with them, but they had all been collecting things since the moment they had arrived. Meanwhile, Molly had been collecting suitcases, asking in every church for donations of old suitcases they no longer needed and had quite a collection. She also purchased several more trunks for bigger things they planned on taking back. By the time they finished packing, they had fifty-six suitcases and carry-ons, plus all the backpacks and personal items. They put a piece of duct tape with a number on each one and assigned a certain number to each older child. Everyone only had to make sure they had their five pieces of luggage, and Molly kept track of the total number counting by fives, from the oldest to the youngest child.

When the nice attendant behind the counter saw the sixteen children standing there, many in charge of suitcases but all of them weighted down with backpacks and carry-ons, she told Molly to put everything through the checked baggage. Molly protested that she couldn't pay the extra baggage fee but was told there would be no charge. Sixteen kids let out a huge sigh of relief as they took their backpacks off and passed them through the counter. That would certainly make traveling easier.

Nevertheless, once again, delayed flights did not make traveling easier. Their first flight was late, leaving them only minutes to get to their next gate. After checking the gate number on the board, Molly pointed the older kids in the right direction and instructed them to run ahead and let them know a large group was on their way. Once again, they found themselves racing through an airport. By the time they arrived at the gate, the passengers had already boarded the plane, and they were just about to close the doors. Without thinking, the attendant checked their tickets and hurried them through the entrance and onto the plane.

As they walked down the aisles, looking for seats, it soon became apparent that there were not going to be enough seats for all of them. Molly spoke to a flight attendant, who went to the front of the plane and began whispering to another flight attendant. Lo and behold, they had given nine of their seats to standby passengers, thinking that Molly's group was not going to make the flight. Each of those standby passengers sat comfortably in their seats, seatbelts already buckled, happy that they were lucky enough to board and would soon make it to their destinations and eagerly awaiting families. Now Molly and eight children were left standing in the aisles as the flight attendants went to each standby passenger and broke the news to them that they needed to collect their belongings and exit the plane. If Molly had been a cat, and looks could kill, she would have lost all nine of her lives in that five-minute period of time. Surprise, surprise, not one of them was happy about having to leave. Molly felt so bad for them that she tried her hardest to keep a straight face while inside, she was jumping for joy that they had made their flight.

Once all the standbys had exited, she immediately hurried down the aisle, barking out instructions of who should sit where and which of her children should change with which other child. Obviously, they had arrived too late to ask to be seated close to each other and were spread out from the very front to the very back. Of course, the situation was already embarrassing enough that she wasn't about to ask strangers to change seats. She did, however, want a big child as close as possible to each small child. In those friendly airline days, they got a meal on long flights, and her little ones would need a family member nearby to help them. Therefore, so-and-so needed to be closer to so-and-so, and someone needed to change with this kid to be closer to that kid over there, and what's his name should change with what's his face, and whoever sat here needed to help whoever sat there. Children scurried to their feet, making the necessary changes.

Then suddenly, without being asked, a man stood and changed seats with an older child, allowing them to sit next to a younger one. Other passengers saw his goodwill and followed suit, standing and making necessary seat changes. Who was that nice man, who, with one act of kindness, helped get everyone settled in a good place? In Molly's mind, he had to be the same imaginary man who had lived through the tip incident and the fifty-yard dash times-three incident with them. She knew that he called her the "crazy lady and the kids" but imagined him wanting to help out because, by this time, he was beginning to feel like family.

Once Molly had made a final head count and knew that everyone was in a good place, she sat down, let out a sigh of relief, and enjoyed the flight home, complete with a meal, choosing the chicken instead of the beef.

Trip of 2005

The next trip was the biggest ever, with twenty-one people traveling all together. However, it was unique in that they had a home base.

They stayed in the dorms of a church's Bible college that was out for the summer. Staying in one spot had many advantages and made the three-month trip much easier. It certainly eliminated a lot of constant packing and unpacking as well as most of the long traveling days. It also allowed them to have somewhat of a stable life and get more schoolwork done. Since Costa Rica's school year was from late February to November, they would always take their work with them but usually got less than half of it done. Now that they were not traveling much, having them busy with schoolwork kept them out of trouble during the day. Even though they did take several days for outings, such as amusement parks, museums, zoos, and other things, they still got more schooling done than on any other trip. They also had the blessing of a kitchen to cook in and washers and dryers in the dorm rooms. Oh, the luxuries they enjoyed through the kindness of those loving Christian brethren who thoughtfully put up with them for three months.

There were enough supporting churches in Indiana to keep them busy the entire trip. On Sundays, they would travel a few hours, be in one church Sunday morning, travel a bit more to be in a church for the evening service, and head back to the dorms at night. On Wednesday nights, they would choose churches that were closer to their home base. During their time in the States, they did make a one-week trip to Texas with a stop in Arkansas. That adventure was mainly to attend the wedding of a young lady who had taught in their school for several years.

Though this trip was easier, Molly soon found out that even staying put had a few disadvantages. The biggest disadvantage was that Molly's teens had plenty of time to grow close to the church teens. They were good teens, but teens will be teens, and Molly desperately wanted to avoid teens thinking they were falling in love at such young ages and under such temporary circumstances. The "gringo" gang of teens knew that the Costa Rican gang had school in the morning, but by mid-afternoon, they were arriving in full force to "hang out" in the gym.

Thus began the rumors that she likes him, and he likes her, and thus began the added job of chaperoning teens. It became more of a job than Molly wanted as most of them seemed to have nothing else to do with their lives; they were on summer vacation and would have stayed until midnight if Molly had let them. Molly did have other things to do. There was Dito to care for, clothes to wash, meals to prepare, papers to grade, clean-up chores to assign, and the constant dragging of different kids away from their friends and all the fun in the gym to do their assigned chores.

The Bible college consisted of a big gym area with hallways on either side. The girls' dorm room was on one side, and the boys on the other. Molly decided that the best way to handle it was to send her own kids to the dorm room at 9:00 p.m. in hopes that the others would then leave. Even that plan posed a problem. Knowing that the boys' and girls' dorms were separated by a huge gym, Molly had brought their maintenance man on the trip to be in charge of the boys. Although Molly would take all the girls in and told him to do the same with the boys, he was apparently somewhat of a pushover, and the boys talked him into extra time every night. So, while Molly was under the impression that all her children were tucked safely in bed, the boys were sneaking off to Wendy's and walking up to the drive-through to order since the restaurant area was already closed. That only worked a couple of times, though, before the manager told them they needed a car for the drive-through.

Fortunately, teens love to brag about getting away with things, and after about a week, the boys started sharing their evening escapade stories with the girls. That very night, the girls shocked Molly by playing the "that's not fair; the boys get to stay up" card. Molly put the girls to bed and went out to see what was going on. Sure enough, the boys were quietly hanging around in the gym with their friends, but the maintenance man was nowhere to be seen. Molly found him sound asleep in the boys' dorm while six-year-old Noodles was jumping from bed to bed. His idea was to give the older boys a little extra time while he put Noodles to bed, but it seemed that Noodles was putting him to bed. Like with every trip, by the end of the three months, Molly was ready to go home.

By the end of the trip, as was always the case, there were lots of things to pack up and haul back to Costa Rica. In addition, this group being made up of mostly older children, Molly found that teen girls could collect clothes, shoes, and other "junk" faster than little ones. Each had taken only their usual backpack to the States, but Molly allowed them a backpack, carry-on, and a seventy-pound suitcase on the return trip. Everyone's second checked bag was to be used for things for the home. Even with that allotment, they were having trouble fitting everything into their suitcases. Kiffy had gone to the States eager to spend all the money she had received for a Latin girl's special fifteenth birthday called her "quinceañera." Having found endless good deals in thrift stores, she was loaded down with good-quality clothes and shoes. Molly finally designated one of the extra suitcases to overflow clothes and one to only shoes. By pulling out all their shoes and putting them in the shoe suitcase, they were left with more room for their other things since shoes were bulky and took up so much room. By the time everything was packed, they discovered they had three too many suitcases. It was then that they remembered that a group from nearby was going to take a mission trip to Costa Rica within the next couple of months.

Sadly, it was not until they were back in Costa Rica, patiently waiting for the extra suitcases, that they received the news that the group had canceled their trip. The news hit the girls the hardest, as the shoe suitcase was among the ones left behind, and shoes were very important to them. Kiffy felt it worse than anyone since probably half the shoe suitcase was full of all her birthday shoes. At first, they hung onto the hope that some other group would come down soon. Yet, as the months went by, the hope of ever seeing their little treasures diminished. Over a year later, Molly encouraged a family that was coming down to go and ask for the suitcases. They were long gone, and nobody seemed to know whose feet the precious shoes ended up adorning. Hopefully, they were a blessing to someone who truly needed a blessing, just as the many full suitcases they did bring back were to them. They certainly had no reason to complain.

Trip of 2010

There were no more trips to the States until after Jerry and Molly were married. Since Jerry planned the itinerary and had his own circle of contacts, they were able to visit lots of new churches in different areas than those they had visited previously. Molly had always worked hard to get permissions for the entire group of children, but she knew that there would be no way to take everyone this time. Several of the new kids' cases were very delicate, and their parents were fighting with the government to get them back. There was no way social services would allow them to leave the country, but at the same time, they really needed to make a trip to the States.

There were eleven children whose papers were in order and would be able to leave the country, plus Jerry, Molly, and another young lady, Volly, who was serving in the home as a short-term missionary. Jerry's home church loaned them a fifteen-passenger van, and they pulled his utility trailer behind for all the "stuff" they knew they would be collecting. Molly thought it would be an easier trip because they would be traveling for only two months instead of three. Nevertheless, a few other factors would make it a difficult trip, the biggest being that both special needs boys, Dito and Poodles, would be traveling with them. Dito's special gluten-free, lactose-free, chicken and vegetable diet required lots of planning as well as carrying along his small rice maker for cooking his food separately. He was a teenager by then, fourteen years old, and every time he needed a diaper change, it usually called for a full change of clothes because of so much leakage. That meant more dirty clothes and more hot Laundromat visits. They would not have nice dormitory beds but would be mostly sleeping on church floors and constantly packing and unpacking. Their route would take them from Florida to Georgia, Alabama, Tennessee, North and South Carolina, and back through Georgia to Florida.

They borrowed some air mattresses and bought a few more in an effort to make life a little easier. At their first stop, Molly was very appreciative that the bigger boys looked for the nicest air mattress for their aging mother, one that was a little wider and thicker and just looked better. Weren't they such sweet children? She settled in for a good night's sleep but found that in less than an hour, her nice air mattress had lost all of its air, and she was sleeping flat on the ground. Everyone else seemed to be sound asleep, so she slept as well as possible on the floor. Since many of the mattresses were borrowed, she expected to find out in the morning that other mattresses had also deflated in the night. Lo and behold, hers had been the only one. That morning, while they were still inflated, she chose a different one for the rest of the trip and had no more mattress problems from then on out.

On that trip, the children were spoiled not only with clothes and shoes but also with special outings. Everywhere they went, the people wanted to take them places. They went to more museums, zoos, parks, pools, and amusement parks than on any other trip. The children probably had the idea that kids in the States spent their summers visiting one attraction after another. The truth of the matter was that Molly's kids visited more places in two months than many kids in the States would visit in their entire childhood.

One particular amusement park was most memorable. The majority of its attractions were geared more toward teens, being basically every kind of roller coaster imaginable. Molly's kids all got divided up among the folks who had invited them, leaving Jerry and Molly caring only for Dito. It was a very, very, very hot day, 112 degrees Fahrenheit to be exact, much too hot to be outside for hours.

Jerry and Molly found only one little snack bar that had air conditioning. They ordered something small and busied themselves eating ever so slowly to make it last as long as possible. There were signs indicating that only paying customers were allowed, so they knew they couldn't camp out there all day long. When they had occupied their little corner of the establishment for an awkwardly long period of time, they finally mustered up enough courage to exit the building and face the scorching heat once again. Dito was not his usual happy self but was slumped all the way forward in his cloth stroller, resting his head on his knees. Even he was aware of the fact that it was too hot for enjoyment.

For some time, they wandered from place to place, up and down sloping hills (all amusement parks seemed to be built on hilly ground), looking for little patches of shade. Finally, someone from their group passed by and pointed them toward a log-type water ride that they said was an easy ride with a few ups and downs, small splashes of water, and hardly anyone in line waiting. It did look like it would be easy enough to get Dito into the log boat, certainly looked refreshing, and she knew Dito loved up-and-down rides. They left his stroller at the door and walked Dito up the four or five steps at the entrance. Once inside, they saw that though there wasn't a line for the ride, there was a long trail of swerves, then steps up and steps down, and over bridges and more steps down and more steps up and more zig-zags until Dito was worn out from walking and was trying to sit down. Molly was equally worn out, encouraging him to keep going, holding him steady so he wouldn't fall, and, at the same time, trying to guide Jerry around curves and up and down stairs.

By the time they sat down in the boat, Molly was wishing hopelessly that it was a twenty-minute ride so she could recuperate. Of course, everyone knows that rides are at best five minutes long, and it was over long before Molly could catch her breath. She had a habit of talking to Dito even though she knew he didn't understand and told him she hoped he had enjoyed the ride because it was his first and last for the day. That was probably fine with Dito. The effort in that heat to get on a ride wasn't worth it.

They had gotten a little wet refreshment from the ride but had dried off within minutes in the hot sun. So, they trudged forward, walking here and there, checking their watches regularly, and counting down the minutes until closing time when their "fun" day at the park would come to an end. Finally, a maintenance man, seeing Dito slumped over, told her she should take him down to the splash area for children. They had long dried off, and that sounded fantastic. They took off in the direction he had pointed and soon found themselves in a big area with huge plastic flowers misting out water, spitting frogs, and splash pads that periodically squirted water up in the air here and there. Little children in swimsuits ran in circles among the little fountains of water while moms sat on nearby benches watching them. At the moment, it looked like the next best thing to heaven, and Molly led her little group to the very center of the area.

As the cool mist brushed across her face, she told Jerry that she just wanted to stand there for a second, basking in the ecstasy of the moment. No sooner had the words come out of her mouth than a huge burst of water fell down from somewhere high above, soaking all three of them from head to toe. It was quite a bit more water than they had planned. The little children continued running in and out of the sprinklers, untouched by the drenching waters. Molly glanced upward with her perfectly curled hair-sprayed bangs now straight and plastered to her forehead and immediately saw the culprit. She had positioned them right under a huge tub of water that filled up and tipped over every so often. Jerry and Dito were just as stunned as Molly. Dito sat straight up for the first time all day, moved his head to the right and to the left, and laid back down on his lap. All the mothers sitting on the benches giggled at them, and Molly just smiled back, acting as though it had all been part of her plan.

Molly's curiosity got the best of her, and she moved their dripping wet bodies over to benches to sit and time how often the tub would fill up and tip over. She found that it tipped over every fifteen minutes. Leave it to Molly to stand them directly in the line of fire at exactly the right second. In Molly's book, that particular theme park officially became the least amusing amusement park of them all.

Due to the way the schedule was set, they stayed in one nice-sized church twice, once toward the beginning of their journey and again after making the full circle of other churches. The church had sent several groups to Costa Rica and was excited about hosting them in the States. They had a teen center complete with a ping pong table, a pool table, and even an air hockey table. The church had filled the snack bar area with sodas, chips, and sweets. As they walked in, the pastor pointed to the full shelves and told them to help themselves because it was all for them. The kids' eyes got wide with excitement while Molly's got wide with worry. In a conscientious mother manner, she immediately set down rules as to how many snacks were allowed and at what times. There were so many things they had never seen or tasted she was sure that otherwise, they would make themselves sick trying to taste everything. Even so, between the snacks, the games, and the places they took the kids, it soon became their favorite church. When they left, they were excited to know that they would be returning toward the end of the trip.

It was a very long two months. Molly felt like the summer was hotter than usual. Many of the churches were small and didn't have as nice a setup as the big church. Once, they even had to drive into town to shower at the YMCA. Yet, all the churches were happy to have them and went out of their way to feed and provide for them during their stay, as well as spoiling them with special activities and sightseeing adventures. Mostly, it was just the heat, long days in the car, the Laundromat, and the inconvenience of packing, moving, and unpacking that was wearing on everyone.

Finally, they were finishing up and heading back to the children's favorite spot. Molly was so thrilled to have Volly along. She was always happy and upbeat, glad to help with anything, and actually enjoyed driving, which made traveling days easier on Molly. They already knew they had a long, hot day ahead of them, but suddenly, it became longer and hotter when they blew a tire. Something was definitely not right; they had just dealt with this same problem only weeks earlier. After a previous flat tire, they had purchased some used tires that were in excellent condition, and now they were already worn out. They changed the tire a second time but knew they would have to take the van to be checked, and that check was wearing on Molly's mind the whole last half of the day. It wasn't until several days later that they were able to have it checked. Not being a mechanic, Molly only remembered certain words like wheel bearings, front-end alignment, and $560.

Getting back to their travels, the added delay on a hot day was extra wearing on the nerves, but finally, they had arrived at their destination. Molly's first job when arriving anywhere was getting Dito settled in and comfortable. Upon completing that job and going out to see how the unpacking of the trailer was coming along, she found that the trailer hadn't even been opened. She entered the teen center to find everyone already eating snacks, drinking Cokes, and playing pool and air hockey. They all knew the drill—they had been doing it for two months—and there was no excuse for them to run off without unloading first. Molly reminded them of their responsibilities in an irritated "what on earth is going on" type of voice. Sure, it had been a long, hot trip, but the teens spent most of their car travel time taking naps. She ordered them to leave their snacks and games and get outside immediately to do their work first. As she turned to lead the group out to the van, one of the boys who had already been giving Molly problems during the trip made a comment that became the straw that broke the camel's back. His comment was that it was very easy for Molly to tell them to unload the van when she didn't do anything.

That was probably not the best thing for said teenager to remark after a hot day on the road. It only took ten seconds for Molly to remember all the headaches from paperwork to get the kids to the States, all the meals, the diapers, the Laundromat, the planning, the problem-solving, and the watching and caring for the group that had fallen on her shoulders. The next ten seconds were dedicated to thinking of all the nice places the kids had gone, the restaurants they had eaten at, the snacks, the donuts, which, by the way, they had eaten so many donuts they were tossing boxes of them in dumpsters because no one could stand to even look at another donut, and the list went on and on. Molly felt her ears growing even hotter than they had been all day long. She jumped in the trailer, said something about forgetting it because she could do it herself, and started throwing suitcases out. At first, everyone was stunned and just stood there, staring. Then Doodles, now a teen, spoke up and asked his mom to settle down and let them do it. But Molly's momentum was in gear now. She was wound up like a wind-up toy, and her arms just kept grabbing and tossing and grabbing and tossing until nothing was left in the trailer except boxes of donated books that they never unloaded.

Just as all wind-up toys wind down, Molly was out of energy by the time she finished, left all the bags on the pavement, and went into "check" on Dito. She knew he was fine, but she also knew that being with him was the safest place to be; he was a calming force. Molly felt absolutely terrible about having lost her temper in such a drastic manner, but fortunately, none of the suitcases were any the worse for it. The kids finished bringing everything in and came to check on her. They were all noticeably worried and told her they thought she was going to have a heart attack. Upon careful consideration, she realized they were right; it was a possibility. It had not been her finest moment. She had risked hurting her own health, could have even hurt someone else, and all over nothing more than an unthoughtful comment, how silly.

[A LESSON TO LEARN: Of course, that was neither the only nor the last time Molly got upset, but that was, without a doubt, the most disturbing. It was an eye-opening experience of how easy it is to lose one's self-control, the danger of being led by our emotions, the weakness of sinful man, and the importance of allowing God's Holy Spirit to rule in our lives and give us His grace to face every situation He allows to come our way.]

Trip of 2017

Some seven years later, they really felt it was time for one more big fundraising trip to the States. Just like the "greatest Christmas drama" of all Christmas dramas, Molly felt that this was going to be the "trip" to top all trips. Above all, they would be blessed to have their music teacher Jolly traveling with them this time, the same teacher who had been helping with the dramas in recent years. Molly had met her in one of the mission trip groups that had come to visit. She had asked her if she would ever consider a year-or-so-long mission trip to teach violin. Fast-forwarding several years, she had come and taught Molly and several of the children to play instruments, including piano, violin, and viola. They had all worked very hard and had six or seven beautifully arranged hymns polished and ready to perform. Molly was on cloud nine. It was a dream come true. Now they would not only have Jerry playing the piano, but he would also be accompanied by six violins, two violas, and a guitar on some songs.

Jolly had worked very hard preparing the specials and very hard on the singing parts as well. They had never before had such a well-prepared program. They even had professional-looking booklets made up, highlighting each child and explaining their ministry.

Once again, Jerry got on the phone and put together an itinerary that would take them on a three-month circular journey. They were to begin again in Florida and travel up through Alabama, Tennessee, Kentucky, Illinois, over to Indiana, Ohio, West Virginia, Virginia, North and South Carolina, Georgia, and back to Florida.

Molly knew it wasn't going to be easy, but she hoped a few factors would make it easier than the last trip. First, Holly agreed to care for Dito in Costa Rica so he would not have to make the trip and suffer through hot travels. Poodles, who also had problems traveling, would only be going for the first two weeks while they were still in Florida. He had a few doctors' appointments for new braces, but then he would be traveling back with Kiffy and Lolly, who were going along for a couple of weeks of vacation. Second, there were, once again, several children who could not travel because their papers weren't ready. In fact, they were a group of only eleven people this time, eight Lighthouse children, Jerry, Molly, and Jolly. What could be easier than eight children and a teacher in charge of the presentations? Molly was truly looking forward to the trip and getting more excited by the day. She felt sure it would be the most wonderful trip ever.

There are verses in Scripture that tell us not to boast about the future, and God soon reminded Molly in some very powerful ways that he was in charge of tomorrow, not her. That said, though God certainly blessed greatly during the three-month trip, it was not without its trials, several of them easily resolved, while one of them being the biggest tragedy they had ever faced.

The United States Embassy caused the first problem after Jerry had finished the itinerary, personally speaking to dozens of pastors, and had purchased all the plane tickets. The visa appointment had always been one of the easiest of the multiple steps of getting the kids to the States. With written invitations from churches in the States and the full permission from social services for the children to leave Costa Rica, agents were more than willing to grant visas to a children's home to visit supporting churches. On this occasion, though, Molly was slightly suspicious when the agent asked her to have a seat for a moment while he reviewed the case. Still, she sat down, confident that he would soon see that she had previously taken five groups of children and several individual children on short trips to the States and that they had always returned before their visas had expired.

After about a fifteen-minute wait, the agent called her to the window to inform her that all eight visa petitions had been refused because he did not feel he had sufficient evidence to prove that Molly would return the children to Costa Rica. Molly could not believe her ears. This could not be happening! She had brought all the normal paperwork. What more did he want? What more had he expected? She briefly mentioned the evidence that she had been running the home for twenty-eight years and had taken several groups already; those trips and children were in their system. She also mentioned that she would be in serious trouble with the Costa Rican authorities if she didn't return government children. In addition, she had turned into him a whole list of churches complete with pastors' names, addresses, and phone numbers that he could call for references. None of that seemed to matter. Nor did it matter to him that at $160 a piece for the visa appointments, his refusal was costing them over $1,200, not to mention the plane tickets they had purchased. There was really no logical reason for him to refuse them, other than being able to do anything he felt like doing. He was kind enough not to put any restrictions on how long they would have to wait to reapply, should they be lucky enough to get an appointment before their flight left in two weeks.

Eight very sad kids walked out of the embassy that day, but Molly had too much work ahead of her to mope around. Someone recommended a travel agency right across the street from the embassy as a place that could get a quick emergency appointment for them. They stopped in on their way out and left them all the information on each child to try and get new visa appointments. That very day, they paid for and secured new appointments that were normally a two-month wait for the following week. That, in itself, was a miracle. Molly went home and began to collect anything and everything that they thought might show proof that the children planned to return to Costa Rica. They called and scheduled for after their return date both dentist appointments that they needed to keep and doctor check-up appointments for each kid. They made up official-looking school registration documents showing they were enrolled in Lighthouse Christian Academy of Costa Rica through December, not mentioning that was actually their own home school. Then they scheduled a piano/violin recital with all the children on the program that was again for a date after

Staying Busy – Part 2

their return. They also had several pastors from the churches they did dramas in write letters of invitation for the children to return in December and perform as they had done for over twenty years. They got statements showing they had bank accounts, and Molly got copies of old resident cards proving she had lived in Costa Rica since 1985. They prepared the papers that showed that the Lighthouse Children's Home was an established foundation and recognized as such by the Costa Rican government. Lastly, they found two pastors in the States who were personal friends of senators whom they asked to contact the Costa Rican Embassy on their behalf. Molly could not imagine anything else they could possibly take to make their case.

They had one advantage going into their second interview. It was prohibited for the same agent to interview them a second time. Their new agent was an older man with a totally different demeanor. His first question was why they had been refused earlier. Molly explained briefly and, setting her large manila folder of documents on the counter, told him she had brought every evidence possible regarding their eminent return. From what Molly could tell, he didn't even glance down at the folder. All he did was ask for Woodles and Riffy, the two eighteen-year-olds who would be traveling with them, to step forward. It was always more difficult for teens eighteen and over to get visas as they were the ones most likely to remain in the States. Both of their passports showed that they had already visited and returned from the States; that was a plus. He asked about their schooling, and neither of them had finished high school yet, another plus. He only briefly asked Riffy about what instrument she played but then turned toward Woodles. Molly's heart skipped a beat. Woodles was a shy, quiet kind of teen in those days, and she wondered if he would be able to think fast enough to give good answers. There were only two questions. What instrument he played was the first question, and the answer was the violin. Then came the million-dollar question. He asked Woodles which song was his favorite song to play. Without batting an eye, Woodles answered, "Amazing Grace." The agent raised his eyebrows while his eyes grew wide with surprise. In one short, wise answer, Woodles had validated who they were.

Immediately, the agent told Molly that he had decided to give her the visas. As he signed and stamped papers on his side of the window, Molly picked up the thick envelope that he had never even opened and, with a quiet smile, pointed her children out the door. The silence continued as they walked through the embassy courtyard and out the front gate. As soon as the gate closed behind them, the jumping, cheering, shouting, and whistling began. They were going to the States, and though they would indeed get there, the trials of the trip were not over yet.

The visas were approved on a Tuesday, exactly one week from the date they were to fly. The passports with the visas in them were to be mailed and picked up at the post office on Friday. They were glad when they got to the post office and found the passports were right on time since their take-off date was so close. Each child had to be present to pick up their own passport. There was no problem with Riffy and Woodles's passports, as they were eighteen or older. But the postmaster declared that the minor children were to have at least one parent present to retrieve their passports. This was, once again, a problem they had never previously had. Molly showed them the papers that named her as their legal guardian, but they insisted that was not the same as a parent, and they had been instructed to turn over passports only to the parents. Molly explained that having been declared in abandonment, it would actually be illegal for them to give the passports to the parents who had lost their parental rights. She could not understand how they could have permission from both social services and immigration to take the children out of the country, but the postmaster was not going to allow it. That was clearly not his decision, and she had shown him all the proper paperwork. He said he would need a letter from the child welfare office addressed directly to the postmaster allowing him to deliver the passports. Molly left the post office and hurried to social services, but as my readers probably already guessed, they said it was not their responsibility to tell the postmaster what to do. She returned to the post office, and after more begging and explaining, he agreed to call the director of the main office. He called several times but never received an answer.

Finally, 4:00 p.m. rolled around, and the main office was closed until Monday. He told her it would probably be best to go directly there first thing on Monday morning. So, they had come in to pick up their passports quickly, spent all afternoon in the office, and were leaving without the passports. With a thousand other things on her list, this was the last thing Molly needed, but it couldn't be helped. On Monday morning, they arrived at the main office first thing in the morning in dress clothes and with instruments in their hands. As it turned out, the director was a Christian man, listened as they played several hymns, and called the postmaster, requesting that he give them their passports. They went back to the post office and picked them up, with less than twenty-four hours left until takeoff.

Snoodles

There would be six minors staying behind in Costa Rica, five permanent children whose story will be shared later, and a new nine-year-old boy by the name of Snoodles. Molly had been reluctant to accept a child right before leaving on a three-month trip to the States, but the social workers were experts at convincing her of emergency situations, and naturally, this was another one. Snoodles had come into the home only six weeks before the trip.

He was a talkative, slightly husky, cute fellow with lots of stories to tell. His mother had become a Christian and was taking him to church when she fell ill and died of cancer rather suddenly. Snoodles was sent to live with his father, whose wife and children were quite surprised when Snoodles showed up on their doorstep with his suitcase in hand. They had never known that Snoodles even existed, and thus, he was not very well accepted into the family. Since the father was a trucker and seldom at home, there were constant arguments about who would care for Snoodles.

After a few months of house jumping from one relative to another, Snoodles ended up being dropped off at the Children's Hospital by heaven only knows which relative. When during his month or so stay in the hospital, nobody ever came to visit, his case was turned over to social services, who then placed him in the Lighthouse Home. Upon arrival, they provided Molly with a paper, listing the things he had been treated for in the hospital. Most of them were medical terms that Molly probably wouldn't have understood in English, much less in Spanish. He came with only two medicines, an inhaler for his asthma and a cream for a severe skin condition that they said had greatly improved in the hospital but still looked serious to Molly. Within days, Molly noticed a cough that would get better for several days and then get bad again, but it was probably part of his asthma problem as they had not given her any other instructions or medicines for it. As the weeks went by, it seemed that Snoodles was often sick. Molly commented to Jerry that she had never seen such a sickly child. If it wasn't one thing it was another.

Notably, Snoodles was much more interested in spiritual things than most new arrivals. Maybe having so recently lost his mother kept him thinking. Molly didn't believe in pushing children to make a decision for Christ the minute they walked in the door. She first wanted them to come to an understanding that they were lost sinners in need of a Savior and learn who Christ is and what he had done for them. Accepting Christ as their Savior needed to be their decision. Yet, it was within only a day or two that Snoodles got into a long conversation about spiritual things with Riddles, and that very day, he gave his heart to Christ. Molly felt sure he had understood. He enjoyed talking about Jesus and, at every prayer meeting, would raise his hand and request the church to pray that his lost family members would accept Christ as their Savior.

There is always an adjustment period with new kids, but sadly, Snoodles's seemed to be dragging on longer than others. Some kids are a tad different and have a harder time making friends, and he was one of them. Molly never saw any of the other kids hurt him in any way, but they were quick to tease and criticize him. Kids can easily find fault in others, and Snoodles seemed to have a way of giving them ammunition to do so. He was constantly talking about his father and that when he came for him, Snoodles was going to travel with him in his truck and not have to go to school. It was common for the children to want to think well of their father and believe that they would come for them, but maybe it was Snoodles's constant vocalizing of his fantasies that turned the others off to him.

Another thing the children didn't like was that Snoodles was lazy in school. Many of them also had problems with laziness; that didn't seem to bother them, but they couldn't stand it in him, saying that he was worse. The teacher also confirmed that he did very little in school. He would complain all morning long about not doing his schoolwork because he was not feeling well and couldn't concentrate but then be well enough, as the other children kept pointing out to Molly, to ride a bike all afternoon.

Since Snoodles's health was so up and down, it was difficult to determine when he was just being lazy and when he really felt bad. One lady who was helping in the home was sympathetic to him. She made him Jello when he said he wasn't feeling good and often checked his temperature. Of course, this didn't help him make any points with the others. The kids complained to Molly that he would talk normally until that helper came in and asked how he was, at which point he would get a sad look on his face and tell her he wasn't feeling very well. They claimed he was only doing it to get Jello and juice boxes from her.

Then one day, Molly saw it for herself. Several kids were in the kitchen with Molly, talking and laughing, and Snoodles joined in and looked perfectly fine. When the helper came in, he immediately got a sad look on his face. The others all turned and looked at Molly to see if she had noticed. The helper touched his forehead and told Molly he had a fever. Snoodles needed Molly to be sympathetic, but she went over to him, felt his forehead, and very nonchalantly told the helper that he didn't seem very hot to her and thought he would be fine. Though Molly was a stickler about letting fever fight sicknesses and limiting the use of over-the-counter drugs until absolutely necessary, it was still her duty to be more compassionate and show more concern. This was one of the many times that she totally blew the opportunity.

Finally, Molly saw what she considered the first breakthrough day of Snoodles bonding with the family. They had their annual field trip to the amusement park when Snoodles had been with them for about a month. He was neither lazy nor sick on that day and eagerly rode all the rides. He seemed to really enjoy the day, and Molly felt like the others were beginning to accept him. A few days later, after a common conversation among several children and Snoodles around Molly's kitchen table in which everyone was laughing and having a great time, Molly told Jerry that she thought the kids were being more friendly to Snoodles, and he was finally feeling like family.

Before leaving for the States, knowing that they would be gone for some time, Molly wanted to do something special for the group that would not be able to go on the trip. On the Saturday night before the trip, they took only that group of six up to the mall for a meal, ice cream, and a little time with Mom and Dad. It was another good day for Snoodles. He was feeling good, ate all his hamburger, and spent the evening laughing and joking around with the others. Molly was happy to see him doing better with the others; what a relief.

Unfortunately, by Sunday afternoon, Snoodles had another relapse in his health. This time, there was no doubt that he had a fever, and his cough had returned once again. Molly gave him something for the fever and made sure he was getting his asthma medicine at the right times. After having had several good days, she was sad to see him getting sick again right before she left. Yet, he was so up and down that she hoped he would feel better by the next day.

Staying Busy – Part 2

Of course, the following day was the Monday morning they all hit the ground running. While Molly and Lolly were busy trying to get the passports, Polly was helping with several other last-minute errands that Molly had been unable to do because of the fight with the post office. The other lady helper was left to watch the remaining kids. Snoodles seemed to be the same, neither better nor worse, but they had seen this pattern in him several times in the last six weeks. Molly made a mental note to have Polly make a doctor's appointment for him as soon as their plane took off and the dust from their early morning departure had settled.

That night, or rather in the early morning, when Molly made her nightly journey to the bathroom, she could hear that Snoodles's cough was getting worse. It seemed that he couldn't stop coughing; it had never been that bad. She grabbed his asthma inhaler and headed to his room in hopes that opening his air passages might help. As she walked into his room, he was vomiting in the trash can. Molly shone her flashlight in the can and was shocked to see that whatever it was, it was a dark brownish-red color. This was not good. It was 3:00 a.m., and she was supposed to wake the travelers at 4:00 a.m. She ran to wake Polly and asked her to take Snoodles and Fluffy to the hospital immediately. By this time, Fluffy was a young adult, and when Polly needed to return to wake the remaining children, Fluffy would be able to stay at the hospital with Snoodles. Molly didn't even take time to dress Snoodles but just got him up and started walking him out to the car in his pajamas. Halfway there, he turned around and said he needed his shoes. Molly told him to get in the car, and she would get them. He continued without her, and as soon as she got the shoes and tossed them in, they were off. Molly breathed a sigh of relief to know that Snoodles would soon receive medical attention. With that last unfinished detail completed, they were finally off to the airport with no more delays.

Even though the plane left fairly early, they had two different layovers and wouldn't make it to Orlando until the evening. The first layover was in Panama. While waiting for their next plane, Molly was shocked to hear her name over the intercom, asking her to call Polly. Though the Wi-Fi connection was terrible, she was able to get through. Polly was asking them all to pray. Snoodles had a serious infection and was on a strong antibiotic. If he didn't begin to respond positively, there was a risk that he could suffer some sort of brain damage. They prayed for young Snoodles, and Molly felt sure that the medicine would start having a positive effect soon.

When they finally got to Orlando, they still had a two-hour drive to their final destination. Not wanting to make things any later, Jerry suggested getting fried chicken from a Publix grocery store and just eating fast in the parking lot. Molly could think of nothing faster or cheaper than that. They had not even finished eating when Molly got another phone call. It was from Brother Neff, and he asked Molly what she was going to do about the Snoodles situation. Molly told him that Polly was on top of the situation and asked if he had heard anything new about his condition. Brother Neff told her that Snoodles was dead, and he felt she needed to return to Costa Rica immediately. In shock, Molly hung up, and in one of those conversations with God in which one has no idea what to say, she called out, "OH FATHER GOD, NO, NO, GOD, NO, NO, NO, OH LORD, WHY? WHY? WHY GOD? NO, NO, NO."

After talking to Polly, she learned that Snoodles had contracted an aggressive form of meningitis and had passed away in the early afternoon. Fortunately, it was not the contagious form, or they would have all had to have been quarantined. Polly was beside herself with grief and told Molly that she wouldn't ask her to return for any other reason, but she couldn't handle this one alone. Their first stop was Jerry and Molly's house in Spring Hill, where Jerry's parents were living. They waited until they arrived there before telling the children the news. It was a sad arrival to the States, and lots of tears were shed by everyone. Woodles was greatly affected and asked to talk. As he cried, he spoke of how heartbroken he was that they had all treated Snoodles so poorly. Molly remembered the indifference she had shown in the kitchen that day when he said he felt bad, and her own lack of compassion cut into her soul.

Kiffy would not let Molly travel back alone, and that evening, Jerry purchased two tickets to Costa Rica for the next day. Early in the morning, she left the group of children she had worked so hard to get into the States under the care of Lolly and Jolly and headed back. It was a difficult trip, but Molly was grateful to have a kind daughter by her side for moral support.

Having booked the tickets at the last minute, they had to take anything they could get. What they got was from Orlando to Houston, then a long layover and a late night trip sitting on the last row of the plane, two center seats, one on each side of the aisle. That flight seemed longer than usual due to an extended period of strong air turbulence and accented by grief, the darkness of night, and being separated from Kiffy on the flight.

Snoodles's body was turned over to the family, and Polly and Molly were not invited to the funeral. In fact, amid their mourning, there were rumors that the family would be filing a lawsuit, either against Molly or against social services. How convenient after never having cared for the little boy who had been praying for them. On Thursday, social services interviewed Molly and Polly. With pictures of Snoodles smiling, first at the amusement park and then again at the mall only three days before his death, negligence on their part was out-ruled. Just the same, Molly paid a visit to their family physician, searching for answers. Given the information that Molly had, the doctor felt that there had been nothing more than either she or the hospital could have done for Snoodles. Molly, with a heavy feeling of guilt, asked if things could have been different if she had brought him in a day earlier. He explained that either he or any other doctor would have put him on the wrong kind of antibiotic, and it wouldn't have helped him at all. He also felt there was a possibility of him having had some previous head injury that made him more susceptible to that particular type of meningitis.

On Friday, the police department arrived to inspect the house and the condition in which they were living. The visit was very short. They had expected to find that he was living in a confined, dirty place and were overwhelmed to walk, instead, into such a spacious, nice house. They complimented Molly on her labor and left. Between the interview with social services and the police visit, nothing more was ever said about a lawsuit.

On Saturday, there was nothing left to tend to, and Molly and Kiffy returned to the States so as not to miss the Sunday services. It had been a very rough week, and Molly was still feeling quite melancholy and would be feeling so for several weeks to come. Try as she would to make sense of it all, she just couldn't.

[A LESSON TO LEARN: The fact that sometimes there are no answers was a hard pill for Molly to swallow. Yet most of us have had to swallow that very pill more than once in our lives, many under much more difficult circumstances. Our finite minds want to understand everything that our great infinite God is doing, and it just can't be done. It's not wrong to try to understand, for certainly God has lessons He wants us to learn through our trials. Nevertheless, sometimes we will never fully understand the hows, whys, and timing of the things that God allows into our lives. At those times, understanding is not nearly as important as just trusting that He is still lovingly in control. There were many things Molly never understood, but she was forced to focus on what she did understand. She understood that God knew, God loved, and God was always good. Letting go and keeping our eyes on Him alone, His Word, and His promises are more than enough; it has to be.

Psalm 73:21–28 says,

> Thus my heart was grieved, and I was pricked in my reins. So foolish was I, and ignorant: I was as a beast

before thee. Nevertheless I am continually with thee: thou hast holden me by my right hand. Thou shalt guide me with thy counsel, and afterward receive me to glory. Whom have I in heaven but thee? and there is none upon earth that I desire beside thee. My flesh and my heart faileth: but God is the strength of my heart, and my portion for ever. For, lo, they that are far from thee shall perish: thou hast destroyed all them that go a whoring from thee. But it is good for me to draw near to God: I have put my trust in the Lord God, that I may declare all thy works.]

[A SECOND LESSON TO LEARN: Molly was comforted to know that Snoodles was not only in the arms of his Savior but also united with this mother, the only family member who had truly shown love for him. Naturally, through it all, her greatest comfort was that God had noted this quirky little boy with a tender heart for the things of the Lord. He knew his life would be short and had mercifully brought him into their home just in time for him to give his life to the Lord. The fact of the matter is that all of us are a bit quirky in some way or another. So, when God looks past your quirkiness and sees into your heart, does He see a heart that is tender to the things of the Lord? Or does He see a heart that is too busy taking care of itself and what it loves to have time for God? Oh, if only a self-centered heart like that could only understand that it is more than just living in their own quirkiness or maybe making a little time for God. May that heart, recognizing its own sinful condition and desperate need of a Savior, humble itself before it is too late, for as we have seen, no one has the surety of life tomorrow.

Jeremiah 29:13 says, "And ye shall seek me, and find me, when ye shall search for me with all your heart."]

Most of the remainder of the trip was easier than other trips they had taken. Since there were fewer children, accommodating them was easier. In four or five different places, they were happy to have been invited to stay in the homes of friends who had visited Costa Rica through the years on mission trips. Of course, being in homes set Molly on edge with thoughts of something getting broken or kids getting too loud, doing or saying the wrong thing, and so on. Just the same, sleeping in beds rather than on air mattresses in church nurseries was worth the worry, especially since, to some extent, staying in churches produced the same set of worries.

The trip did have one more bump in the road, which all started on the third week of their travels. They had made it all the way to Bolingbrook, Illinois, when ten-year-old Thuddles, a child yet to be introduced in a later chapter, started feeling sick. On a Friday, he was complaining of pain in his leg. By the following day, he also had a headache and a high fever. Molly was a nervous wreck. What if they had been wrong about the meningitis not being contagious? How many more were going to get sick? When he seemed no better by Saturday evening, Molly was very much on edge and unwilling to take any risks. They took him to a local clinic. She felt obligated to explain their recent tragedy, but after checking him out, they felt sure he did have an infection, though it was definitely not meningitis. They did, however, want him transferred to a hospital for more testing. Already feeling relieved by their findings, Molly would have preferred that they simply give him an antibiotic and send him home, as they would have done in Costa Rica. But Thuddles was in their system now and wouldn't be getting out until they said so. Therefore, off to the hospital in an ambulance they went.

Molly was not a happy camper. She felt physically and emotionally drained and thought she couldn't take any more. She spent the entire week in the hospital feeling sorry for herself. Thuddles, on the other hand, was loving the attention. He was already an attention-getting type of kid and thought it was great to have everyone making a big to-do over him. Every nurse who came in, no matter how many times she entered during the day, received from Thuddles, over and over again, a big, "Good morning," "Good afternoon," or "Good evening" and "How are you doing today?" Next, someone got the bright idea of bringing Thuddles his violin, so now he felt he needed to serenade doctors, nurses, and visitors alike.

Meanwhile, Molly just wanted out. She didn't want to be patient, happy, or look on the bright side. She just wanted to continue with all the others the plans they had made. There were a few positives. She was grateful that it was becoming obvious that Thuddles illness wasn't serious. She could also think of two other boys who would have themselves been complaining the whole time had they ended up in the hospital. She supposed happiness from Thuddles was easier to listen to than complaining. She was already doing a great job on the complaining side; she certainly didn't need any help there.

She felt it was safe to push for a rapid discharge from the hospital and showed signs of impatience every time she was denied. Thuddles had been feeling great since his second day in the hospital. He had no pain, no fever, and was taking no medication except the antibiotic. It was obviously working. Yet the doctor wanted an exact diagnosis of what kind of infection he had, couldn't discharge him until he had it, and kept ordering test after test in search of it. Molly cringed every time he ordered another test, knowing this little "five-star hotel," as Thuddles seemed to think of it, was not going to be cheap. She tried to explain to him that they could not afford all the testing and extra hospital days, but he just kept on ordering tests. One day, the doctor ordered an MRI of his leg. The very name sounded expensive. The following day, he ordered a second MRI a little lower on the same leg. Molly asked why they hadn't done the whole leg all at once on the first day. The doctor said he had the same question; that's what he thought they were going to do. So grew her frustration from day to day.

Finally, after a week in the hospital, they were getting out. She asked the doctor what the results were of his exact diagnosis needed to leave the hospital. He told her they never got one, but the boy was clearly getting better. That had been her exact same comment four days earlier. However, as an added precaution, he would continue the antibiotic for two more weeks through a pick line in his arm. Molly had never heard of a pick line. It sounded scary and certainly wasn't common practice in Costa Rica. Once it was explained, it seemed easy enough, though she would have preferred just giving him pills. Nevertheless, the important thing was that he was getting out, and they could move on to Indiana, or could they?

With the doctor's very next breath, he said a nurse would be assigned to make a house visit twice a week to check on his progress, to take a blood sample after a week, and eventually to remove the pick line. Molly realized that the rest of the gang would be moving on, but she would be staying behind until Thuddles's treatment was finished. Her frustration skyrocketed again. She was already embarrassed by all the ways their host had been put out by the situation and all the help they had already given them. They were staying with their music teacher's family. Molly had been leaving the kids there every day while she was at the hospital, the parents had been transporting her back and forth to the hospital several days when their van was needed for other group activities, and her mother had kindly taken several turns with Thuddles in the hospital to give Molly a break. In fact, so far, Molly had only missed one church presentation because the teacher's mother had stayed in the hospital for the other two. How could she possibly impose on the sweet family for two more weeks? She asked the doctor about a nurse in Indiana taking over the home care, but he had no connections there and was not willing to take the risk.

They finally came up with a plan. They would all go together to Indiana for the weekend. Then on Monday, Riddles, now grown and driving, would bring Molly and Thuddles the four-hour drive back to Illinois and drop them off to be there for the checkups and blood work during the week. The following weekend, he would come back for them, and they would do the same thing. This way, although she felt she would still be imposing on Jolly's family, at least they would only miss two Wednesday night services instead of six services. But before the second weekend, the blood work had come back perfect, and the doctor finally permitted them to go on and finish the treatment in Indiana. They were free to go.

So, who did they meet up with in Indiana? The same social worker who had filed papers when Naffy had been hospitalized years earlier. Once again, she helped them out, and once again, their hospital debt was canceled. They did have to pay about $2,500 for the first clinic, the ambulance, and a few other things, but God had once again taken care of the large hospital expense.

[LESSONS TO LEARN: Oh, the many lessons we can learn when God squeezes us in ways we do not want to be squeezed. Maybe the Lord wanted Molly to learn to give thanks in all things. If that was the case, she failed that test most miserably. Maybe she was to meditate on Romans 8:28, "And we know that all things work together for good to them that love God, to them who are the called according to his purpose." That meditation did not happen. Though she never would have admitted it, there was definitely a bit of a pride problem in her with which the Lord needed to deal. Yes, she had been through several struggles. And yes, it's easy to lose heart when it seems like problems are flowing in one after another. But all of that should have been more reason to keep her focus on the Lord. Her only focus was on herself, and that is pride. SHE had dreamed of this trip, SHE had been so excited about it, and SHE had worked so hard to make it a reality, but SHE was the one missing church services and family outings while everyone else was enjoying them. SHE, SHE, SHE. Yet, when God had stepped in and kept her from going on several different activities and three different church services, He was, in essence, telling her that He could handle things all the same without her. Wow, that hurt, but it wasn't about her anyway; it was all about Christ being glorified. How foolish she had become to think that she deserved front and center stage at every church and in every presentation. Yet, her little "it's not fair" pity party was the proof that it was a lesson she still had to learn.]

Prayer: Oh Father God, have mercy on us when, in the name of serving you, we forget to give Christ the preeminence. Colossians 1:18b–19 says, "That in all things he might have the preeminence. For it pleased the Father that in him should all fulness dwell." May it always be clear to us in this world of "believe in yourself," "you can do it," and "you're the greatest," brainwashing that we remember we must believe in Christ, can do all things through Christ, and that Christ is the Great One, not us, Hebrews 1:3 says, "Who being the brightness of his glory, and the express image of his person, and upholding all things by the word of his power, when he had by himself purged our sins, sat down on the right hand of the Majesty on high."

Molly probably never learned any of those lessons their whole trip long. She was too busy doing and constantly moving forward to stop and consider. Thankfully, she later began understanding a little better. Oh, God would undoubtedly have to bring many refresher courses back into her life, but hopefully, someday she would have gained the wisdom to leave Christ on the throne and think to add the words, "Lord willing," to all of her future plans. The most important thing to remember here is that if you are going through something, God knows you need it.

Regardless of the setbacks, God blessed their trip with new supporters, new prayer partners, new friends, several special outings, less heat than the trip before, and no problems with the van Jerry had purchased for the trip. They were even able to sell the van at the end of the trip for $700 more than they had paid for it. In addition, one of the biggest blessings of the trip was being able to take the children to the Creation Museum and the Ark Encounter, a beautiful experience. God poured down on them far more blessings than any of them deserved. Thanks be to God for His unfailing love and mercy.

Chapter 15

A Little More About Dito

Dito had two tragic accidents in his lifetime. The first one was when he was only five years old. Molly needed to drive some of the older kids to their government tests and, on her way out the door, instructed the young lady who was going to watch the kids to sit Dito on his potty chair. What Molly failed to remember on her rush out the door was to turn off her curling iron. The helper also failed to notice it and sat Dito down with the curling iron right above him on the sink. Since he was used to sitting there still by himself for long periods of time, she went off to do something else. He found the cord and pulled the curling iron down onto his foot. Instead of bouncing to the floor, it just lay there on his bare foot. He began to scream, and Joodles heard him and ran to help.

When Molly returned half an hour later, she was heartbroken to see what had happened. The doctor said it was a second-degree burn. They went through several very difficult weeks of putting on creams and changing bandages before he was completely healed. Since he didn't like the bandages any more than he liked his shoes and socks, he was always trying to rip them off and had to be watched constantly.

The second accident happened when Dito was twelve years old. It was right at the time he was beginning to have daily seizures. Dito had just finished his morning bath. The teen whose chore it was to bathe and dress him stood him next to his bed with his hands on the rails for just a second while he got his diaper and clothes ready. It had been a common thing for years to leave Dito standing up, holding on to something. But this morning, in that split second of time, a bad seizure jolted his body backward, and his head hit full force against the cement-tiled floor. The teen quickly picked him up, saw that he appeared fine, and laid him in his bed to finish dressing him. At that time, it was also common for Dito to remain completely exhausted or knocked out after a seizure, so no one thought it strange that he had to be carried out to his mat.

What was totally strange, though, was when he began to whimper five minutes later. Polly, who had just arrived because it was her day to run errands, was the first to notice him. Molly was at the dining room table starting the school's opening sessions out of earshot from Dito's complaining. Polly walked in the front door and immediately asked why Dito was crying. It was so uncommon for Dito to cry that it was always considered a red flag. The teen instantly explained the seizure and said he had checked Dito out and hadn't thought he was hurt. By this time, he was crying louder, and they swept him up and put him in the van, his head resting in Molly's lap as Polly drove them to the Children's Hospital.

Upon arriving at the hospital, Molly was still not sure whether he was reacting to a recent medicine change or whether it was his fall. She explained both possible explanations as quickly as possible, and within minutes, they had determined that he was bleeding internally from the fall. In those days, there was only one brain surgeon in Costa Rica who operated on children, and he happened to be at the hospital prepping for surgery at that very minute. While they wheeled his un-operated patient out of the operating room and wheeled Dito in, he spoke briefly to Molly. His brain was swelling rapidly. They would have to remove part of his skullcap to allow it to expand. It was a common procedure, but timing was critical, and he could not guarantee that Dito would make it. As suddenly as he had entered the waiting room, he was gone, leaving Molly standing alone to wait. She made some phone calls to explain the little bit she knew and ask everyone to pray. Then she sat down to also pray and wait, and wait, and wait.

The doctors cut a round disk out of Dito's skull with a diameter of about three inches. Then they cut a slit in his abdomen in which to put the disk of the skull to keep the bone alive. The doctor said it could take a week or more for the swelling to go down. Praise the Lord, in only three days he had no swelling, and Dito was headed back to the operating room to have the disk removed from his abdomen and returned to his head. It looked like he would be going home earlier than they had expected. That would be a huge relief since they required someone to stay with him at the hospital at all times, day and night. They had set up a rotation between the adults and older teens, but even so, the schedule was getting difficult to keep. Then, when it looked like he would be getting out of the hospital, he got a cellulite infection in his foot, precisely where they had inserted one of his IV tubes. The infection set them back almost a week, and by the time they were bringing Dito back home with the horn honking and children cheering, he had been gone for three weeks.

Thankfully, despite the fact that his injury had been very serious, almost costing him his life, he made a full recovery. Dito still played all his same games and did his favorite things. Molly noted no difference in his seizures either; he neither had more or less, nor were they any stronger or worse. God had healed him completely and graciously, giving them more years with their happy boy. Yet Molly felt like she had now failed him twice, once with the curling iron burn and now by not having two people with him as he bathed and dressed. The young man who had been with him when he fell also felt responsible. Molly didn't know it until much later, but he struggled for years with feelings of guilt for letting Dito fall. Both of them had to come to grips with the truth. They had not purposely planned any malice against Dito, but accidents happen; they are a part of life. God was using them to help care for Dito, but God himself was in charge of Dito's life and his care. God could have prevented any accident; there were probably many more that he had prevented. They needed to realize that Dito was in God's hands, and He knew perfectly well what He was doing, what He would allow, and why. Molly made the necessary precautionary changes and gave Dito back to God's care. It wasn't an instant victory. There were several more "It's my fault, I should have . . ." moments, but she forced herself to just keep giving it back to God.

For years, there was not much change in Dito. His life went on with seizures, new medicines, a few little games, his happy little *uh-huh* sounds, and laughter. Somewhere along the way, he learned to take his pants off, and Molly had to invent a onesie for him that he couldn't get off by having Holly sew long boxer shorts to muscle T-shirts. The onesie made it more difficult for the boys who helped Molly to dress him, but once Dito learned a new talent, he wouldn't let it rest, and Molly wasn't taking any chances with this one that could easily cause an embarrassing situation.

The biggest change in Dito was that he was growing. Molly had long since stopped picking him up because it was giving her back problems. He was still able to walk to the shower, but there was a lot of lifting required with dressing and changing him. All the teen boys took turns helping in this area. All the older girls helped with feeding Dito. It took the whole family working together to care for Dito. Molly was so thankful that her teens had this opportunity to learn compassion, patience, and how to be a servant.

When Dito was about nineteen years old, his doctor put him on a new, promising medicine. It was very expensive and only available in Panama. Fortunately, grown-up Kiffy was now a missionary in Panama and was able to keep Molly stocked up. They began to see an immediate improvement. His seizures were not as strong, and Molly noted that he actually had some seizure-free days, something Molly hadn't seen for years. Molly hoped that his new medicine might be a permanent help for Dito, yet she knew that his nervous system had a history of building up a resistance to medicines to the point that they were no longer effective. Around this same time, Dito stopped saying his uh-huh word. Try as they would, he would not say it. It wasn't until many years later that Molly considered that this might have been connected to his new medicine. They had certainly seen other behaviors end with the introduction of a new drug.

This time, it was not just two years but four years before Dito's seizures worsened. It began with almost an hour of short seizures, separated by five or ten minutes, occurring every evening around the same time. Within a week or two, the evening seizures became longer and stronger, and Molly knew it was time for a change. At the time, Dito was on three medications, and the doctor opted to first change one of the others since Dito had been taking it even longer than the new medicine that had been helping so much. Changing that medication did very little to help control the more aggressive seizures, but his doctor felt that he couldn't make a second medication change so soon, so they learned to deal with the nightly seizure episodes. Unfortunately, the seizures worsened each night. The doctor increased the dose of the most recently added medicine twice, but it was still getting worse. The nightly seizures were shaking Dito violently and lasting longer.

When Molly tried to make another doctor's appointment, she found he was out of the country. In desperation, she took Dito to a different doctor, who simply added a fourth medicine to Dito's growing list. It was obvious to Molly that the medicine that had helped so much was no longer effective. By this time, he was having probably twenty or more seizures throughout the day every day. Molly feared, as had happened many other times, that he would go into a seizure that would not stop and would have to be hospitalized.

As soon as Dito's regular doctor returned, he set up a schedule that would take Dito off the miracle drug in only six days. Molly was concerned. Doctors had always set three or four-week schedules that slowly lowered the old drug and added the new one. She expressed her concern that six days was too fast to remove a drug, but he said Dito was already so bad that the change needed to be made fast, and the new drug would be added just as quickly. Seven days later, Dito went into a seizure that would not stop and was rushed to the emergency room.

Molly was not allowed to choose a hospital. The social medicine system required her to take Dito to the hospital that corresponded to their address. There was another hospital, almost as nearby, that actually had a separate neurology section. Molly was sure they would have dealt with Dito's situation more efficiently, but it was not their region. The hospital that corresponded to them was a general medicine hospital.

First, the doctors gave Dito some emergency medicine that immediately stopped the seizures. Nevertheless, within hours, Molly was already seeing small seizures. The neurologist assigned to emergency that day was ready to release him, but after Molly explained his medicine changes and told him he was already starting to have seizures again, they decided to keep him until they were sure he was stable. Dito did not get stable. By the following day, he was having small, frequent seizures throughout the day again. When Molly questioned the doctor, he just said that they were running tests and had no answers yet. Then, to Molly's surprise, he told her that if she had accepted the brain surgery when he was small, they might not be in this predicament. At first, Molly had no idea what he was talking about; she had totally forgotten the suggestion she had been given when Dito was only five years old. When she remembered, it was obvious that the doctor who had kicked Molly and Dito out of her office had seen Dito's name on the patient list and given a bad report to the doctor who was treating Dito in the hospital. Molly's decision to not operate could not possibly be in some hospital record since it was a ten-minute personal conversation, a suggestion she made between patient and doctor in her private office. From that day on, Molly sensed an indifference in the doctor's attitude toward her.

By the next day, Dito was in an epileptic status. He was having one seizure after another all day long. All the older kids in the home and even many former Lighthouse kids were taking turns being in the hospital with him, only one person was allowed in at a time. Molly had each person who stayed with him record at what time he would have a seizure and how long it would last. On average, Dito was having a seizure every three to five minutes, which would last about a minute or so. Occasionally, he could go for twenty to thirty minutes without a seizure.

Molly took the morning shift, at the time that the doctors made their rounds, yet many days, the doctor never showed up the entire day. Finally, after several days of not seeing the doctor at all, Molly saw him sitting in a hallway with a computer on his lap. Not wanting to be too pushy, she stopped some two yards away and waited for him to look up and notice her. After waiting for more than five minutes, he looked up and told her to stop standing there because he was not attending to patients at the time and would not answer any questions. The cruelty of his manner pierced her heart for Dito's sake. Her precious boy was just a bed number to him.

The epileptic status went on for ten days. Any time Molly could talk to someone, they made her think that everything that could be done was being done and that these seizures might never stop. So many other thoughts went through her mind. Molly remembered how at age twelve, when Dito went from childhood to adolescence, he had gone from a couple of seizure days a month to a few seizures almost every day. She felt sure that this must be the next stage, his transition from adolescence to adulthood. She also remembered that some doctors felt that Dito would only live to be ten or twelve years old. One doctor said that no one died of epilepsy but from the side effects. He felt that Dito could have a heart attack in the middle of a seizure. Now Molly watched time and time again as his heart monitor went crazy with each seizure. It pained her to see his little body being so shaken and taxed all day long. How could it be possible that this would be how Dito's life on earth would end?

Molly told the Lord that she had never imagined such a tragic death for her happy boy. At first, everyone's prayers were that the seizures would stop. As the days went on and no changes were seen, they began to pray that the Lord would have His will in Dito's life. More days passed, and they began to ask the Lord to take Dito home to be with Him. Every time that Molly saw the heart monitor racing, she would whisper, "Now, Lord, it's okay. I give him back to you. Take him, Father. End this trial; don't linger his suffering."

On the tenth day of Dito's epileptic status, a doctor from hospice called Molly in for a private meeting. She clearly said that Dito was dying. She also said that they wanted to start him on a special drug that would allow him to die peacefully. Molly was to give him the drug until he died, but she was not to give him any food. Molly was confused. She said she could not starve him to death; she would have to keep feeding him. The doctor answered that she would not be starving him because he would not feel anything. Then she said they would also be putting him on morphine for the pain. Molly was confused again at how someone who would not be feeling anything would need morphine for the pain. She asked why they were going to give him morphine and was told that it was a precautionary measure since he could not speak and tell them if he was in pain. Molly told her that he cried when he was in pain. They talked some more, and in tears, Molly asked every question she could think to ask. It seemed to her that a drug that would be shutting him down would actually be killing him. When the doctor realized that Molly was unwilling to authorize the medicine, she said that they could start on a very small dose of the medicine and see how he reacted but that the morphine was a must because it looked like maybe the seizures were painful.

Shortly after leaving the private conversation, the neurologist finally came to check on Dito. Molly immediately asked him if it was true that Dito was dying. He was surprised at what the other doctor had said and affirmed what Molly had always been told: the seizures would not kill him. Continuing his explanation, he finally appeared to show a little compassion and explained to Molly that other than the seizures, Dito was healthy, and his heart was still strong. He was not aware that hospice had spoken to her and did not know why she was starting him on the medicines she had mentioned. He said he would check into it. Nevertheless, later that day, Dito received his first small dose.

The following day, Polly was taking the early shift with Dito and Molly the afternoon shift. Around noon, Molly called to get the seizure report from Polly. To her surprise, Polly said she had seen very few seizures and had not seen any for the last two hours. Molly couldn't believe what she was hearing. Polly also said that Dito had squeezed her hand. They had seen no reaction in Dito for ten days. Even if they talked to him, held his hand, or ruffled his hair, he would not respond; the seizures were keeping him knocked out. Molly rushed to the hospital and saw firsthand that the seizures were slowing down, and Dito was waking up.

Molly did not know whether the timing was just a coincidence or not, but it seemed to both her and the medical staff that the medicine that was to allow Dito to die peacefully was stopping the seizures. Suddenly, a whole new set of thoughts went through Molly's mind. This was not the next stage. It was not a transition from adolescence to adulthood in which he would be constantly having seizures. It was not true that the seizures could not be stopped. She thought back to all that had happened. First, she had felt that his regular doctor had changed his medicine much too fast, which had sent him into a seizure that would not stop. Then the doctor in the hospital made several more changes. He changed the only medicine that had not been changed, took him off the medicine his regular doctor had just put him on, left only the medicine he had started some six months prior, and added three totally new, very strong medicines, and all this simultaneously. This was completely opposite of what she had been told for years. Medicines had always been removed and added slowly, and now they just completely dropped the only medicine that had not been changed.

In addition, the doctor said he couldn't change two meds too close together, and now they were making three new changes days after a much-too-quick medicine change. Dito's delicate nervous system could not handle it. That had to be what sent him into an epileptic status on his second day in the hospital. Then they said the seizures couldn't be stopped, but apparently, they could because they had now stopped. Molly struggled to stop overthinking everything. What was done was done. The important thing was there was now a glimmer of hope for recovery.

Dito continued in the hospital for over a week. He was still having probably more than twenty seizures a day but showing small improvements every day. He was becoming alert to things around him. He was aware of the feeding tube that had been in his nose since the first day and was now trying to pull it out. He was responding slightly to those around him and was even allowed to eat small amounts of Jello and mashed potatoes. Although they had taken him off the hospice medicine after only two days on it, the hospice doctor kept insisting that he was dying and that Molly would be taking him home only to care for him during his last weeks of life. Molly believed that she could be right, but at least he would be far better off at home. Now that she had seen doctors and nurses alike stand by and watch as he suffered convulsions, she decided to leave him in God's hands and not freak out if the seizures became more frequent, just to keep him at home and ride it out. She never wanted to take him back to the hospital again.

After three long weeks in the hospital, just like his first hospital stay, Dito came home a very weak, very thin boy. Most of that time, his primary diet had been the nutritional Ensure drink, with very little solid food. All of his ribs were visible, and he was basically skin and bones. They had not removed the feeding tube in the hospital, so he continued trying to remove it himself. Molly was sure she could get him to eat and swallow his pills without it, so she called the family doctor the first morning and got permission and instructions on its removal. She was right; he had no problem swallowing, and they started fattening him up.

Dito was still having daily seizures, but there could be several days in a week where they did not see the larger, yelling, jerking type seizures. Searching the internet, Molly found a couple of supplements she had never heard of that were highly recommended for epilepsy. Within two months she was able to order them, get them to a group that was coming down, and start him on them. Within a month, they saw a clear improvement. There had been probably fifteen days of either no seizures at all or just a few small jumps. In that same month, they had only seen four really bad days, and even those had gone from over an hour of ten to twelve strong seizures to forty-five minutes of six to eight medium seizures. Counting seizures and intensity of seizures became part of their daily routine.

They also started taking Dito off the morphine as soon as he was home. Once off, he began the slow withdrawal process. Dito became very serious as though he were depressed. He didn't act like he was in pain as he could lay still for hours without complaining. But if Molly were to walk past him, talking as she went, he would start to cry. It was like a child who falls and seems to be fine until his mother walks out, and he catches her eye, at which time he starts crying inconsolably. Dito wanted his mother to know that he was not happy. Molly was torn between sneaking by quietly all day long, so as not to upset him, or talking to him anyway just so he would know she was there for him. She decided to sneak by him as often as possible but kneel down and purposely talk to him, hold his hand, and pat his head once or twice a day, even though it made him cry. Sometimes, while sneaking by, someone would ask her a question, and when she answered, he would start crying.

When Molly purposely talked to him, there was no avoiding the tears, but she still felt it was important that she console him. If anyone else tried to talk to him in a kind, consoling manner, they also were answered with sobs. It was two months before they would occasionally get a little smile out of Dito. But if Molly made a big deal out of the smile, it would turn into tears. Most of the crying was gone within four months, but about the time they thought he was recovered, he would have another little crying spell. It was a full seven months before they finally had their happy boy back for good.

Another sad result of Dito's stay in the hospital was that he practically lost all use of his right hand and right foot. He would take no toys in his right hand. They would try to give him his favorite toys, and he would pick them up with his left hand and lay them on the bed next to him. He had no way of playing with them. It was obvious that the continuing seizures for so many days had caused more brain damage. He would never play with his guitar and two Lego pieces again. He also never again laughed when someone sneezed. Although he was now happy and smiled when Molly talked to him, she was saddened that he had lost the ability to do the things that had always made him so happy.

Suddenly, about a month after the crying had stopped, Dito said, "Uh-huh." They had not been able to get him to say his word for over five years. Now, out of the blue, he not only remembered it, but he also wanted to repeat it over and over, sometimes for close to an hour. They were all so very happy to hear the familiar word and went back to their conversations with him and the questions to which they wanted positive answers. It was a great victory.

There were a few other victories in the years after Dito's hospitalization. He had a great appetite and regained the weight he had lost very quickly. Also, as soon as he was strong enough, he was able to sit up on his own and would rock forward and backward for twenty to thirty minutes. Molly called the movement his sit-ups and praised him for doing his exercises. He also began taking his pajama pants off again, with his left hand.

Shortly after Dito's return home, the last of the bigger boys left the home. This meant there were only three boys aged twelve to help with all the lifting, bathing, and changing. Molly felt it was too much for them, but nothing else could be done, as both she and Jerry were facing back problems by then. And so they continued as best as they all could. She had a little makeshift gurney made, thinking it would be easier for them to transport him to the bathroom for his shower. Nevertheless, the boys found it more difficult to use than two of them carrying him by his arms and legs.

God gave Dito a little over three more years of life after leaving the hospital. He was taking four different medications and five different supplements seven different times daily. Molly's chart of which meds and which supplements at which times became much more complicated, especially considering that many of the meds and supplements were repeated two or three times a day. Alarms for the different medicine takes seemed to be going off on her phone all day long.

It became very obvious that Dito was slowly going downhill, but he just kept trudging along. On several occasions, Molly mentioned to Jerry that she didn't believe he would be with them for very much longer. Often, he would go into coughing fits, and at other times, he would struggle to swallow. It seemed like every day, he was doing less. It made Molly sad to see the life draining out of him. She would stroke his head with loving affection and tell him not to worry because things would not always be as they were. She would also talk to him about heaven and Jesus and being made whole, obviously more for her own good than for his. His downward decline lasted probably six months as he just kept hanging on to life.

Even though they realized Dito was getting worse, his final day still took Molly by surprise. Molly and Jerry were in the middle of a three-week trip to the States. Polly and Holly were caring for Dito and the other children. Polly called Molly, very concerned about Dito because he was making noises she had never heard before and having some problems she had never seen. Molly assured her that they were not totally new problems; they were things Molly had been noticing for months. She knew Polly was concerned, but the same things had been a constant concern to Molly for some time, so she didn't think much of it.

One day, Polly called and asked Molly if she wanted her to take Dito back to the hospital if he got worse. Molly told Polly she could have a doctor come to the house and see him but not to take him to the hospital under any circumstances. Molly knew they could do nothing for Dito; so much medicine at such high doses coupled with constant seizures tasking his heart for so many years was taking its toll on his body.

Days later, Molly got a phone message sent to their Home group that said Dito was in heaven. Molly immediately logged into the security cameras and saw Polly call the children into the living room and give them the news. Minutes later, Molly made a video call, talked to the kids, and thanked God for the time that He had given them with Dito. Molly had mixed emotions about not being there when Dito passed, but God knew best. Molly and Jerry remained in the States for another week until the end of their planned trip, giving Molly some quiet time to grieve. His memorial service took place a week after they returned.

Dito's death hit Molly harder than she expected. For some time, she had seen his decline and been willing to let go of him and had actually talked to the Lord about how she longed for the day that he was in Jesus's arms and no longer suffering. But just the same, he had been under her vigilant watch care for twenty-two years, and her heart was intricately linked to him. He had depended on her for everything, and his well-being had always been at the top of her list. It was not a sadness; it was just a powerful feeling. Though she was very happy for him, she found she could not see a picture of him or even just have a thought about him without feeling some kind of strong fluttering somewhere inside. Maybe it was that her heart would beat a tad faster or harder or maybe she breathed a deeper breath; she really couldn't exactly put her finger on it. Yet, it was a definite physical feeling of something that seemed to originate right around where her heart was located.

Chapter 16

Latest Generation

Thuddles

After Ziffy's arrival, although several temporary children came and went, there were no more permanent children for several years. Toodles, Triddles, and Ziffy were the only little ones and became close playmates. Then, came Thuddles. The first time Molly saw Thuddles, he came running and hollering into the church auditorium. He had recently been given to the same missionary family who had brought Ziffy into their lives. It was immediately obvious that he was a live wire, a six-year-old ball of energy. After the church service, Molly noticed that no one was a stranger to him. Like a happy little puppy, he ran from person to person, introducing himself. All his little antics made Molly laugh.

For years now, social services had been offering Molly only problematic teenagers or temporary children, most of whom she had felt needed to be turned down for any number of reasons. She asked the missionary wife what her secret was in getting social services to offer them young, permanent children like Thuddles, mentioning that she would have jumped at the opportunity to have him in their home. She didn't really have an answer for her but called about two weeks later, asking if she was serious about accepting Thuddles into her home. When Thuddles had arrived at the missionary's home, they had already been working with a somewhat hyperactive boy his same age for several years. They felt like the progress they were making with the one boy was going downhill with the addition of the second child, and they really couldn't handle both of them together. They talked to social services, and Thuddles was transferred to the Lighthouse.

Thuddles certainly was a very active little fellow. Molly had never had a child who could wear out a pair of tennis shoes faster than Thuddles. Since his shoes were fairly worn out when he came, the first thing they did was to make him happy with a brand-new pair of sneakers. In less than two weeks, they were totally destroyed, with parts flapping here and there and holes in the soles. How on earth did he do that so fast? They gave him the good old strong furrow-browed lecture on taking better care of his things and bought him a second pair. That pair might have lasted three weeks. Apparently, his favorite bike didn't have brakes, and he needed to use his feet to bring it to a stop. As he grew older, his shoes began to last longer, but they couldn't get more than two months maximum use out of a pair of shoes his whole first year at the home.

From the get-go, Thuddles was a people person. He thrived on entertaining visitors, making friends, and helping wherever needed. Around others, he was always happy, talkative, affectionate, and emotional. In any classroom setting in which the teacher asked questions, he was the first one to offer an answer to every question. Even if he were to answer three questions wrong, he would still be the first to answer the fourth question. That thinking was foreign to most of the other children, who would have been crawling under their seats to hide had they offered even one wrong answer.

Thuddles would also be the one to volunteer for any game at the teen's meeting, no matter how gross or embarrassing while the other teens were hiding so as not to be picked and embarrassed. Sometimes, even his constant volunteering would embarrass them just the same since he was their brother. Yet, though he was so outgoing when visitors were around, among the family, he often kept to himself, quietly working on his many inventions and projects.

Because of his strong desire to captivate any audience, Thuddles's stories needed to be taken with a grain of salt. He was very good at telling tall tales and exaggerating facts. Even Molly heard him adding some fantastic but made-up details to things that had taken place while she was present. She would simply wrinkle her brow and look at him as if to ask from where on earth those details had come. Other staff and kids also came to her and shared his latest tale.

After Jolly had been teaching violin and viola at the home for about a year, she signed the whole gang up for a music seminar at an exclusive private school. Being such a prestigious school, they had dressed as nicely as possible on the first day of the seminar, only to find all the other children in T-shirts and shorts. The rest of the week, Molly let the kids attend in more comfortable clothing like the others. It was an opportunity for them to have individual classes with professional teachers as well as learn to play in string orchestra settings. At the end of the week, there was a talent show for students who had sent in an audition audio file and won the opportunity to participate. Being new to the seminar and playing instruments, none of them participated in the talent show. But when they went back the second year, of course, it was Thuddles who was very vocal about wanting to try out for the big talent show at the end of the week. Naturally, no one else in the home was interested. Jolly helped Thuddles prepare and turn in his audition audio. By this time, he was doing very well on his violin, and nobody was surprised when they picked him to participate in the talent show. He practiced his song all week long, and it sounded great.

Finally, the big day arrived. and off they all went on Friday to watch their brother play in front of all the other students and their parents. As soon as they got out of the car, after an hour's drive to get there, Molly and Jolly were suddenly reminded of a very important little detail about the talent show. The minute they saw a few of the students dressed nicely and a few others carrying nice clothing on hangers, a little light turned on in each of their minds, and they looked at each other in horror. Now they remembered that the year before, the talent show participants had all come in formal attire.

Molly turned to look at Thuddles, who wore black shorts and a bright-colored T-shirt. She asked him to kindly set her mind at ease by telling her that he had brought a change of clothes. He told her that he had forgotten. Triddles quickly corrected him, who said that he had told him at the house that he was supposed to go nicely dressed, but Thuddles didn't care. That made sense. Thuddles was the people person, but Triddles was the person who worried about personal appearance. Together, they'd have made a great team, but Thuddles wasn't going to take advice from his punky little brother. Molly wished Triddles had reminded her and not Thuddles. She told Thuddles to ask around at his classes. Maybe one of his friends would have something more appropriate that he could borrow. At least a pair of long pants and a polo-type shirt would be better. She told him that if he couldn't find anything better to wear, it might be best to tell the teacher he would not be performing. It was, after all, mostly his fault since he was told to dress up but chose not to do so.

Thuddles pleaded with Molly to let him participate. Then, before the show, he came out and told her not to worry. He had a friend who was going to loan him some clothes, and he had taken care of everything. When he was called out to perform, Molly saw that his idea of everything being taken care of and Molly's were quite different. The only thing he had been loaned was a black T-shirt instead of a colored one. Apparently, since most of the boys were in black suits, Thuddles got the idea that dressing in all black was somehow semi-formal.

The minute Molly saw that Thuddles had not found any long pants and was still in his black shorts, another disturbing thought came into her head. Thuddles was one to always just grab two similar socks from the sock basket, without taking time to find exact matches. Hopefully, at least his socks matched. Her eyes quickly glanced down to see her son standing on stage with one black sock and one gray sock. She was starting to have these humbling experiences so often now that she was going to have to start carrying a rock in her purse to pull out and crawl under when necessary. Even so, it's worth mentioning that he played his piece perfectly, but under the circumstances, Molly chose not to holler out from the middle of the auditorium, "That's my boy up there."

It was not the only time that children's appearances in public afforded Molly a crawl-under-a-rock wish. It seemed like with so large a group, they were always too rushed to line the kids up for an inspection before going out the door. The results were often quite scary. Though Thuddles's lack of formal dress was indeed close to the top of the list, the two different socks experience wasn't nearly as embarrassing as the two different shoes experience, which had occurred on a few different occasions. Then there was also the high-water pants, dress shoes, and no socks experience on the day the child's Sunday school class was singing a special. And let's not forget that special feeling when you get to Sunday morning service and find your teenage daughter, who should know better by then, wearing a nice black and white dress with hot pink ankle socks and flip flops.

Thuddles was also a child of many different interests. He was a talented artist, both in drawing and music. He did very well on the violin, learning to play any song by ear and enjoying playing in church services. Other interests included riding a skateboard, playing ping-pong, working on secret "inventions," studying sign language, dabbling with a few other instruments, and brain teaser toys.

Another of Thuddles' favorite pastimes was eating. He became the Home's biggest eater. The cooks would serve him five big serving spoons of rice with his first plate of food, and he would often ask for several more spoonfuls with his second plate full. Once, when they were overloaded with a huge donation of eggs, he asked Molly if he could fry up some eggs for himself and two other boys for a little late-night snack. Molly thought it was taking him quite a while to fry up a few eggs and later found out that after frying one or two for each of the others, he fried up five eggs for himself. Nevertheless, he was as tall and skinny as a green bean. Everyone told him that his eating habits would catch up with him someday when his metabolism changed. They are probably right about that, but it hasn't happened yet.

Scroodles and Scruffy

Shortly after Thuddles came into the home, a government social worker met with Molly. She explained that there were some new regulations and that they would be unable to give the Home any more children unless they became accredited by the government. When Molly asked what all that entailed, they said she would receive monthly government funding. That didn't sound too bad; they had given her a small monthly amount back in the beginning with the first group of children. She then went on to say that they would also be coming in once every month or two to inspect things, interview the children, and tell them what changes needed to be made.

A red flag popped up in Molly's mind. She remembered all the interviews and the demands they had made on Molly when they had removed Poodles from the home. She had been caring for children for over twenty-four years by this time, and though she knew she was constantly making mistakes, she didn't want a twenty-two-year-old social worker who didn't know the Lord and had never cared for children on a twenty-four-hour basis coming in to tell her what she needed to do and not do.

Molly asked what would happen if she chose not to be accredited. She was told that they would not take away the children she already had but would not be able to give her new children. Molly knew that God had already given them many children through churches, grandparents, and other relatives. She knew God could still give them the children He would have in the Home, told the social worker she did not want to be accredited for the time being, and left.

Social services did start calling less often from that time on, but whenever they had a child who was difficult to place anywhere else, the new rules suddenly didn't seem to matter. Thus, there was a nine-year-old girl they gave them for several months and, later on, a brother, six, and a sister, nine, who were with them for six months. Still, it was almost two years after Thuddles's arrival that they finally got a permanent brother and sister. Scroodles came into the Home at age eight and Scruffy at age eleven.

Scroodles was a cute little fellow with straight black hair that stuck up in the air in all directions, giving the impression that he was wearing a motorcycle helmet. He was a quiet, sensitive child by nature who cried his whole first day because he had been in the last government shelter so long that he considered it his home. The "aunts" who cared for them had given him a little goldfish in a plastic bag full of water to cheer him up. Unfortunately, they had not thought to send food or a fish bowl with him. Upon arriving, he clutched the bag tightly in one hand as he wiped the tears from his eyes with the other.

Curiously, the pair had arrived right in the middle of their annual Bible conference, a very difficult time to come into the Home. They were rushed into their rooms to put their things in closets and then ushered immediately to the gym for the services. With close to 150 extra people on the property for the conference, things were too hectic for Scroodles to dwell on his sorrow, and he was soon sitting and talking with the other boys. Later that night, when he finally remembered his little goldfish, they found it lifeless in his closet, not the best ending to his first day.

Scroodles's first couple of years in the Home, they had a few minor problems with him. The first was stealing food, but that was probably how he and his sister had survived for years as small children. The other little problem was his apparent love for killing birds. He had no slingshot but a sharp eye and a fast hand at throwing rocks. Several birds lost their lives before they were able to break him of the habit.

His last two victims were the camp director's pet hummingbirds at children's camp.

Scroodles's early years had been very rough, and he and his sister had suffered extreme abuse. In addition, because of learning difficulties, nobody had ever worked with him in the area of education. School would never be easy for him, but he always kept a good attitude as he slowly advanced through his books. Though he struggled in school, he had several good qualities. Scroodles was a hard worker, actually enjoying manual labor in the yard or shop. He was also a very clean and orderly child, not only maintaining his own things organized but keeping the whole bedroom looking nice. Between him and Triddles, the boys' side of the house was cleaner than the girls' side for the first time in the history of the Home.

Scroodles didn't have a single enemy in the Home. He was Molly's peacemaking child. Even deciding which kids slept in which room and on which side of the room was a struggle because what's his face couldn't get along with what's his name, and so-and-so couldn't leave whoever alone. Scroodles, on the other hand, could be placed on either side of either room because he was the only one who got along with everyone.

Scroodles avoided conflict at all costs. That is not to say that he never fought, but even in disagreements, he was the first one to surrender his right and back away. Unlike all the other boys, he even got along with the girls, which was not an easy feat considering that particular generation of girls who seemed to live in constant competition with the boys.

Scruffy was a special needs child who, like her brother, had hair sticking straight up a mile high in all directions, but unlike her brother, her hair was incredibly curly. Fortunately, they found when they cut it short that it arranged itself in a perfect sort of way around her face, leaving nothing for Scruffy to do in the morning but fluff it a tad with a comb. Also, unlike her brother, she was very happy to arrive at her new home, wore a smile from ear to ear, and hugged everyone as though they were long-lost friends. She would soon become the official children's home greeter, having never met a stranger.

Scruffy's most obvious disability was in the area of speech. She could say individual words that were somewhat understandable but could not say complete sentences. At times, Molly was able to guess what she was trying to say, and other times, she needed to call another child to translate. The kids seemed to understand her better, although sometimes they would start a guessing game of words. They would say word after word while Scruffy shook her head until, finally, they would say the correct word, and Scruffy would smile big and nod her head. She herself did indeed understand everything she was told in Spanish and even thought that she understood everything that was said in English. Whenever visitors arrived from the States, if Polly were telling them something about Scruffy, she would smile and nod her head up and down the whole time to declare that whatever Polly was saying about her was undeniably true.

They hired a speech therapist in the hopes that Scruffy could either learn to form complete sentences or learn sign language, but neither happened. In her mind, she was pronouncing every word exactly as she heard it. She learned a few words in sign language but wouldn't use them, probably because no one else in the house talked like that. Anyway, why would she need to use it if, according to her, she was speaking correctly? There was one miraculous Scruffy situation that happened often and always amazed Molly. A child would come to Molly with a very long, gossipy type story complete with complicated details, and when Molly asked them how they found out about it, they would answer that Scruffy told them. Sometimes, Scruffy was even standing there the whole time, nodding her head in the affirmative.

In school, Scruffy spent her days repeating, time after time, the kindergarten and first-grade books, coloring, cutting, and copying Scriptures. She soon had beautiful printing and participated in their hand-copied family Bible, completing many chapters. She also learned, more or less, the pronunciation of the entire alphabet, and Molly felt that, though far from perfect, her reading was better than her speaking. Math was her most difficult subject, in which she never got much further than just adding and subtracting single-digit numbers.

There were four things that Scruffy liked more than anything else: visitors, jewelry, food, and boys. In the visitor area, as soon as a car pulled up to the gate, she was running to push the button for the electric gate and then dashing outside to run along the car as it slowly pulled up to the house. Before the driver could even come to a full stop, her smiling face was staring at him or her from about two inches away from the glass. If the window happened to be rolled down, her smiling face was actually inside the car.

In the jewelry area, for every Christmas and every birthday, all Scruffy wanted was jewelry, bracelets, necklaces, rings, watches, and earrings. Though she had been given lots of jewelry, she never seemed to have enough. It was common to come home from any church to find Scruffy wearing a new necklace or bracelet that she had conned off some unsuspecting victim by pointing to the object, then to herself, and then looking at them with puppy dog eyes that suggested that she had never had one of those in her whole lifetime. Or she might be holding her arm high in the air, waving goodbye to a visitor driving away, when Molly would glance up and see a new watch on her wrist. Molly knew that people understood she was special, but she also knew that Scruffy should learn that other people like their bracelets and necklaces too, and she needed to respect their personal property.

In the food area, she was another of the best eaters. She liked just about everything except jelly and yogurt. In contrast to many kids, she did not have a big sweet tooth but preferred real food to snacks. She would eat a big plate of food and then get in line with the call for seconds. It was as though she thought eating seconds was a mandatory requirement. Yet more often than not, when cookies were passed out, she gave hers away to others, especially the boys, in an effort to make friends.

Sad to say, she had probably been used to looking for food in garbage cans. Several months after Scruffy's arrival, Molly walked into the dining room to see Scruffy eating well after dinner time. As she approached, Scruffy hid what she was eating. Pressing to see what she had, Molly discovered she was eating chicken bones, and upon reviewing the security cameras, she confirmed she had taken them out of the trash. They also had to watch that she did not eat too much and make herself sick or eat scraps of food off of other people's plates. A few times, she was found sneaking a knife and a couple of tomatoes into the hallway to eat.

In the boy area, Scruffy never met one she didn't like. At every church, in every youth activity, and with every group that arrived from the States, she found new boyfriends. In fact, she had a notebook full of names and phone numbers that she carried everywhere. Any boy who showed any small bit of kindness to her soon found her holding his hand and giving him love letters with huge hearts and his name plus Scruffy's name written in the center.

Although Scruffy had a terrible time keeping her own things in order, she was always willing to help others with chores and cleaning. Whether it was carrying in groceries, washing dishes, bringing things to people, straightening up the living room, or sweeping and mopping floors, she was always eager to help and happy to show others the good job she had done.

Molly tried to be extra cautious with Scruffy in the area of spiritual things since she wasn't sure how much she was capable of understanding. Yet after a few years in the Home, Scruffy came to Molly and indicated that she wanted to talk to her in private. Once they were alone, Scruffy very plainly said the word, "Christ." As Molly began sharing Christ and the gospel with her, she realized that Scruffy did indeed understand. She would ask her yes-and-no questions, and with tears in her eyes, Scruffy would answer correctly. She clearly understood that she was a sinner and needed a Savior. When Molly spoke of Christ dying on the cross for her sins, she began crying uncontrollably.

Molly saw firsthand the difference between the brain and the heart, the mind and the soul. The Holy Spirit was undoubtedly convicting Scruffy's heart and soul of sin and her need for salvation.

That day, simple-minded Scruffy gave her heart to Jesus, and she never forgot or doubted that decision. Molly knew that Scruffy was wiser than many intellectual people who reject God's plan of salvation. The Lord made the gospel easy enough for all to understand.

Twaffy, Twiffy, and Twuffy

About a year and a half after Scroodles and Scruffy arrived, Molly had some sort of an appointment in the social service office. As she waited in the reception area, one of the social workers with whom she had a good rapport came out and happened to glance her way. Even without any type of superpower, Molly undoubtedly saw the gears in her brain turning. She called Molly over and asked if she could stop by her office after her other bit of business. She offered her a group of three sisters, Twaffy, twelve years old, Twiffy, ten, and tiny three-year-old Twuffy. They certainly had room for more children in the home, but Molly reminded her that they were not accredited. Once again, as they had seen before, somehow that suddenly didn't matter; she knew how to take care of that little detail.

The girls had been taken away from the mother for negligence and physical abuse. Though the oldest girl had received the brunt of the abuse, neighbors had reported the mother to the government after they had seen her dragging the middle girl home by her hair. They had been placed with an aunt who lived a good distance from the mother, but that had not prevented her from showing up and causing havoc on a regular basis. Between problems with the girls, the mother, and her own husband, the aunt began to feel too overwhelmed. Then one day, because of strange behavior and comments that Twaffy, the oldest girl, was making at school, social services were called in again, and Twaffy ended up in the psychiatric hospital. By this time, the aunt was on antidepressants, and both she and the social worker felt she could no longer care for the girls. The social worker was now left with the next-to-impossible task of placing three sisters together somewhere, one of which was a troubled preteen. Thus, the rules went out the window as Molly walked in the door.

The two younger sisters, Twiffy and Twuffy, came into the Home a good month before Twaffy, who continued her treatment in the hospital. Twiffy was a bubbly, talkative little girl who was full of all kinds of ideas and opinions. Her optimistic, joyful personality reminded Molly of the fictional character Pollyanna. Nonetheless, within a few weeks, the resemblance to Pollyanna began to fade as her resemblance to Grumpy the Dwarf took its place. It seemed that if things did not go exactly as she wanted, she was mad and stubborn.

The first sign was the day Lolly, the teacher, called Molly up to the school because she was having a problem. She had asked Twiffy to move to a different desk, but the cross look on her face and her folded arms clearly indicated that she was not about to move without a fight. Since Molly had never had a problem with her as of yet, she simply explained that she needed to obey the teacher and reached out to take her arm and escort her to the correct desk. Twiffy lashed out, scratching both of Molly's arms. Somehow, she was able to get her into another unoccupied classroom so as not to continue causing havoc. Once in the adjacent room, she ran to the opposite side of the room and started yelling at Molly not to touch her, that she never wanted to be in a Christian home and a dozen other things. Molly just stood, waiting for her to run out of energy. When she finally did, she explained that for as long as she was in the Home, she would be expected to obey the authorities. In the event that she should choose not to obey, she would have to receive some sort of punishment. Molly then prayed and left the room. By the time Twiffy returned to her class, the only empty desk had been placed right where the teacher had asked her to move.

As the days went on, they found that Twiffy was unable to apologize, to admit she was wrong, or even say that she was sorry. Nothing was ever her fault, and in every argument, she believed she was right. Until she could admit that she was a sinner, she would never have a need for Christ's forgiveness and free gift of salvation. Hence passed the weeks, which turned into months. When things were going her way, she was very happy. When things weren't exactly what she wanted, she would throw a temper tantrum, but it was always someone else's fault, not hers. Finally, one day, many months later, Twiffy crept into Molly's office some hours after a tantrum and whispered into Molly's ear that she was sorry. It was a milestone. Shortly after that time, she accepted Christ as her Savior.

Though Twiffy had a few rough years, Christ made a big difference in her life and, they eventually saw the Pollyanna side of her personality much more often than the occasional Grumpy. She was a hard worker helping with the younger girls, in the kitchen, the school, Sunday school, and anywhere she was needed. She enjoyed finding new recipes on the internet and preparing even the ones that were time-consuming and that others avoided. She was also a hard worker in school, being very dedicated to her studies. Good grades did not come easy for her, but she was always seen studying.

Little Twuffy was a Mommy-pleasing little sweetheart who sat very still on Molly's lap during church services. She was so still and quiet that Molly expected her to be the little girl who would love to play with dolls and would care for them as Molly had cared for her dolls when she was a child. Molly was wrong. She was the rip-all-their-clothes-off-and-stuff-them-in-the-back-of-the-closet-never-to-be-seen-again type of mother. To her credit, she wasn't purposely mean to only her dolls; she honestly did not care for any toys at all. Though she was given puzzles, books, games, stuffed animals, toy dishes, toy doctor sets, toy jewelry, or toy anything else, she was never seen playing with any of it. This, of course, made birthdays and Christmas very difficult as not only could Molly not figure out what to get her, but Twuffy herself had no idea what to ask for either.

When they discovered that Twuffy was more of an outdoorsy type of person, Molly thought maybe she would be good at sports, but not even that interested her. As it turned out, her favorite activities were playing on the monkey bars, swinging, and following others around to watch what they were doing. She was very coordinated and, from a young age, did things on the monkey bars that scared Molly. Even at age four, on the swing, she preferred to go as high as possible in a standing position. Molly tried to slow her down as well as having her sit down, but as soon as no one was watching, she was back to standing and flying high. Also at a very young age, she taught herself to do perfect cartwheels. It seemed to be as easy for her as walking. She could start at one end of the gym and cartwheel herself all the way to the other end without stopping or hesitation.

Twiffy and Twuffy were very close. They were constantly wrestling playfully like boys tended to do but with high-pitched giggling and laughing added. Neither girl was a good eater at mealtimes but could each down over-sized bowls of sugary fruits that Twiffy bought off the fruit and vegetable truck. When Molly argued that they needed a well-balanced diet, they would argue that fruit was healthy. Molly would add that, yes, it was, but in moderation, not in excess. The two also enjoyed watching videos and playing video games together.

Upon their arrival at the Home, Twiffy couldn't wait for Twaffy to get out of the hospital and join them. She worried about her, talked about her, prayed for her, and asked Molly daily if she had heard when she would be coming. Finally, after a month-long wait, Twaffy was reunited with her sisters. Yet in less than three weeks, Twaffy and Twiffy were fighting like cats and dogs. Each one declared that they absolutely could not stand the other. Even after having moved them to separate rooms when they couldn't get along, Molly still had to stop several knock-down-drag-out fights that often ended in bloodshed.

Twaffy's discontentment with her sister probably had roots in jealousy. Both girls agreed that Twiffy had been their mother's favorite. She had been babied by her mother while Twaffy had been mistreated. In addition, Twiffy made friends easily and did well in school, while Twaffy was a shy, nervous wreck who struggled in school. In the first several months of Twaffy's arrival, Molly had to rescue her from school on several occasions because she would start shaking so badly that she could not do her work. Molly would bring her down, make her a calming tea, and try to get her to relax. Fortunately, as Molly had already seen so often, over time, Twaffy began to feel more secure in the Home. Soon, she became close friends with Riffy, who was a quiet girl who avoided fights and problems. Riffy helped her let go of a good deal of resentment that she had held on to for years. Even her relationship with Twiffy changed, and they became close sisters.

In the kitchen, Twaffy became a good helper for both cooks, Dolly and Holly, helping with the tedious jobs of peeling potatoes, cutting up salad makings, and so on. The standing joke was that she liked to help because she could munch on tidbits and taste-test bowls of this and that all morning. By lunchtime, she would declare that she would not be eating because she was trying to lose weight. When she was old enough to be put into the dinner cooking rotation, there were several tragedies before she finally mastered her five or six meals. Among the trials were several "burnt meal" days, several "forgot the salt" days, and then there was the day that all the spaghetti ended up on the floor when she was trying to drain it. But practice makes perfect, and she finally started mastering her meals. Molly's favorite was her Aztec soup.

Several of Twaffy's other idiosyncrasies kept them all in laughter. She was a tad bit clumsy and could not handle carrying several things at once. Rather than carrying smaller amounts, she was determined to master the impossible. Once, when they were putting away the vegetables, she chose to collect all twenty-five large carrots into her arms at the same time instead of making two or three trips. Naturally, on the short journey to the pantry, two carrots fell to the floor. In leaning over to pick them up, three more carrots jumped out of her hands. Then, in reaching to retrieve as many of the carrots as possible, another few toppled to the ground. Molly was too amused to even attempt to lend a helping hand and opted to just watch and see how it all played out. Never thinking to carry some of the carrots to the pantry and come back for the fallen ones, Twaffy continued dropping and picking up carrots for two or three minutes. During most of that time, more carrots were dropping than were being picked up. By now, Molly could no longer suppress her laughter and stood enjoying the show until all the carrots were on the floor. At that point, she told Twaffy to leave the carrots for her to get and to start bringing the cabbages, one at a time, please.

The same incident was repeated several other times with various other fruits and vegetables. Once, Twaffy dropped a whole watermelon and was prohibited from carrying watermelons. On Sundays, Twaffy took over Nuffy's job of being the last one to get on the bus. She would run out with a towel on her head and shoes, brushes, makeup, and other odds and ends in her hands, which she dropped one item at a time at two-feet intervals, as though she were leaving a trail to find her way back home later. One of the other girls would jump off the bus and begin running behind her, picking up the fallen items.

Sometimes, Twaffy had a hard time remembering the names of certain common things. One day, she was, once again, transporting vegetables to the pantry and told Molly that only the broccoli was left on the counter. Since they had not ordered broccoli, Molly went to investigate and found that it was cabbage. Once, she was upset because she had forgotten to order the eggs for her dinner meal. Molly told her the meal didn't call for eggs, and she said she was talking about the green ones. What she meant was avocados. There were many other examples of the same confusion of words. It was hard for Molly to tell if it was just an attention-getting joke or if she was seriously getting her words confused.

In Between

For five whole years, they received only scattered temporary children who stayed anywhere from six months to a year. The most notable of them was a group of four brothers, ages three, five, seven, and eleven, who were all loud and energetic, and though they stayed only six months, they left a lasting impression on everyone. The boys' rooms, which had been winning the cleanliness awards since Scroodles's arrival, suddenly looked like a hurricane had hit them, and they smelled even worse. Although the seven-year-old had a bit of a mean streak, they really weren't rebellious, just hyperactive. Even the smallest one didn't settle down until about 11:30 p.m. but was already up with the rest of them, running around the room, chasing each other when Molly opened the door to wake the boys in the morning.

The mother had been out of the picture for some time, and the boys and a sister were living with a Christian grandmother who had legal guardianship. When the boys became too much for the grandmother, she kept the girl and brought the boys to the Lighthouse. They were very happy and adjusting well when the mother showed up, filed for visitation rights, and began cooperating with the government in hopes of getting her children back. When she was granted the right to visit them, the children were moved to a government home on the other side of the country, closer to the mother. It was hard to let them go as everyone had enjoyed having fun with them. The move hit the oldest boy, who did not want to leave, the hardest. Order was soon returned to the boys' rooms, and life in general settled back down.

Splaffy

Finally, a new permanent child came into the home. Molly received a call from a welfare office in a remote area some distance outside of San Jose. Molly explained that she was not accredited, but they said they could work around that problem. Of course they could; they always could when they really needed help. She was told that Splaffy was a well-behaved little nine-year-old girl who had spent years being passed from one home to another and just needed a stable life. She had spent time in many different government homes, been returned to a grandmother who was really not her grandmother several times, been turned down by her "grandmother" figure, and lastly, her real mother had taken off for Nicaragua with her other siblings, leaving her behind because she didn't want her.

After Splaffy visited the Home and Molly accepted her, they explained that she could occasionally go into a fit of anger and was taking two different medications to calm her down. Molly always marveled at how the government could forbid normal discipline but had no problem prescribing drugs just to calm a child down. How was that not child abuse?

The year was 2021, and the week that Splaffy was to arrive, Molly and Jerry both contracted COVID, delaying her arrival for a couple of weeks. Of the two of them, Molly was hit hardest and was totally out of commission for two weeks. Jerry was somewhat better by the end of the first week, although he still lacked strength. The Home was placed in quarantine, and no helpers dared come near for the first week. That left twenty-one-year-old Riffy in charge of keeping the peace, making sure chores were done, and running the Home in general. Thus, they declared it the weeks of video and video game marathons to keep their young minds occupied and out of trouble.

The whole household was blessed to see a big number of grown former Lighthouse kids step up and divide the meals between themselves, bringing in chicken and rice dishes, pizzas, lasagna, tacos, hamburgers, fried chicken, and so on. The kids were delighted to be getting so many special meals, asked who was covering the next meal, and eagerly awaited each next surprise. Molly and Jerry were the only ones who, without appetites, didn't get to appreciate the scrumptious dishes, although it was a huge relief to know that the children's nutritional needs were met. Although none of the children were diagnosed with COVID during that time, their maintenance man and his wife tested positive a few days after Molly and Jerry. His case was very serious, needing hospitalization and almost costing him his life. It took him several months to fully recuperate.

Splaffy arrived as soon as the quarantine was over and before the patients had fully recovered. It didn't take long to find out that the words "well-behaved" were nothing more than a sales pitch. Molly couldn't remember a child that was more difficult to deal with from the get-go.

On Splaffy's first afternoon in the Home, Molly suddenly heard loud screaming coming from the gym. When she ran outside to see what kind of terrible accident had occurred, she found Splaffy sitting to one side and screaming uncontrollably because someone didn't want to play with her. The periodic screaming continued day after day for several months. At the time, they were still having Sunday evening and mid-week services at the Home because of COVID restrictions. Poor Jerry wouldn't be five minutes into his message before Splaffy would begin some kind of loud scandal over any little nit-picky thing. Every service was interrupted, and if she were sent to the corner, she had to be dragged there, kicking and screaming, and the service was put on pause until her ten-minute prison term in the corner was finished.

Molly had never seen such a wild child. It seemed that she never had even the smallest bit of training. She would lick the floor, suck her big toe, stick tiny pieces of erasers in her ears, and even tore the arm off a big stuffed teddy bear that Molly had bought specially for her arrival to the Home. Holly sewed the arm back on, but within days, she completely killed the bear by pulling out all the stuffing. Everything else she was given was also destroyed within days.

Splaffy also had a bad habit of stealing and destroying the other girls' things. On several occasions, she painted walls, doors, and closets with their nail polish, lipstick, and other items of makeup. It was not the best way to make friends in her new home. Needless to say, they didn't have a whole lot of patience with her. Molly reminded

Twiffy that she, too, had been quite a diamond in the rough when she had come. Twiffy smiled and lightened up somewhat with Splaffy, but sometimes even patience didn't seem to help the situation.

Molly dreaded taking Splaffy to church on Sundays because it always involved some sort of disruptive drama. Due to COVID, they were still transmitting her Sunday school class via Facebook. Molly had to direct her attention to a little phone in front of her at the same time she was trying to control real students sitting in rows on the other side of the phone. Every Sunday morning, she found herself asking the little cell phone that was taping her and the cell phone people who were watching to excuse her several times as she stepped away to deal with problems in some way that didn't get Splaffy's siren of a voice started. The word *frustrated* and all of its 1,000-plus synonyms fell short of describing Molly's feelings.

There were no changes in Splaffy's meds while she adapted to her new home during the first month. Yet, even though they were facing daily battles with her, Molly felt she owed it to Splaffy to at least see if she could live drug-free. After all, she had no physical problem like Dito, which required medication. Therefore, under a doctor's care and recommendations, Molly slowly started to lower the dose of each drug one at a time. When she was finally off both medicines, they really couldn't notice that her behavior was any worse. If anything, she seemed to be doing a little better and starting to adjust to a stable life with set boundaries.

Then, only a few weeks after Splaffy was off all meds, they found themselves facing one of the biggest mysteries in the Costa Rican Lighthouse history. It all started when one of Splaffy's regular tantrums began during tablet time. Some of the girls, eager to show Splaffy how silly she looked, began videotaping her with their tablets. Naturally, this made things worse instead of better. Splaffy ran outside, yelling very ugly things as she went. The kids, running behind her with their tablets in hand, continued taping and began running to Mommy to show her their tapes. In an effort to diffuse the situation,

Molly ordered the kids to stop taping and told Splaffy, who was out of control by then, to go inside and get in the corner. While yelling more very ugly things, Spaffy said she didn't want to live there and started walking toward the entrance gate.

There was positively no way that uncoordinated, heavyset Splaffy was getting out of the tall, heavy electric gate that was closed tightly, so Molly sent the other children inside with their tablets and said she would just sit in the gym and keep an eye on her until she cooled down. Twiffy spoke up and said that since she was going to ride bikes instead of playing video games, she would watch her. Molly very specifically told her not to let anyone open the gate with Splaffy standing near and went inside. As an extra caution, she put the electronic gate opener in her own pocket so that no child could get it and open the gate. About an hour later, Twiffy came running into the house, yelling that they couldn't find Splaffy anywhere.

After a short search for her, Molly called an emergency meeting of the entire family. The boys would search the front of the house and the girls the back side. They were to start against the walls and scan every nook and cranny. She remembered Toodles disappearing and the big open pipe they had found and told them to look for holes in the ground or wall where she might be hiding or through which she might have escaped. They were to look in, on, and under every car and bus.

Meanwhile, Molly checked inside the house, the school, and every apartment. She looked in closets, dryers, and any place big enough for a nine-year-old. When all groups came up with nothing, Molly began to panic. Where on earth could she be? How on earth could she have gotten out? How was Molly going to explain her disappearance to the social workers? Though she was improving little by little, the government was going to tell Molly she should never have taken off her medicine, that it was her fault. If she did get off the property, how? Where would she go? How could she possibly just disappear? They scanned the property again, hollering her name at the top of their lungs.

When Splaffy had been missing for what seemed like forever, they left in two cars to comb the neighborhood. Molly instructed Riffy to stay behind with Scruffy and Twuffy and follow the perimeter of the wall one more time, looking for a hole where she might have escaped. They had been searching in the streets for only about ten minutes when she got a phone call from Riffy that they found her. Molly breathed a sigh of relief and quickly rushed back home. Riffy pointed out to her eight little fingers, grasping the top of the property wall from the opposite side, too high up for Molly to reach. The fingers were about fifty feet away from the closed gate, where she had last been seen.

Apparently, tired of standing by the gate, Splaffy had climbed up into a small tree situated close to the wall. Her being extra big for her age and the branch being extra thin was the perfect recipe for disaster. The minute she sat on the high branch, it snapped and dropped her onto the opposite side of the property wall. The neighbors behind that portion of the wall had constructed extra rooms in almost their entire backyard. All that was left was a one-foot wide band of land across the length of what used to be their backyard. Fortunately for Splaffy, on that side of the wall, the ground was higher up and cushioned with leaves. This not only meant that she didn't fall as far down but also that the leaves cushioned her fall. When she stood, it also allowed her to reach the top of the wall and hang her hands over. She didn't, however, have the strength to pull herself up and over the wall. Even if she could pull herself over, the drop onto the Lighthouse side was at least twice the drop she had already experienced and onto hard ground.

There was a small opening that led into the next neighbor's yard, but when Splaffy glanced around the corner, she saw a doghouse and got frightened. She was not answering when they were hollering her name because she did not want the dog to find her. On the girls' last search around the wall, Splaffy had heard Scruffy talking nearby her, and being so tired and scared by this time, she began softly calling Scruffy's name. That was how they had finally found her.

Molly had to bring a ladder to study the best way to get Splaffy out. Investigating, they found that there was no dog next door, only an empty doghouse. Finally, they were able to convince Splaffy to squeeze through the opening to the neighbor's yard. Once there, they found that the next problem was that nobody was home, and she was now trapped in another backyard. There was one, tall rod iron gate that had places where she could put her feet and climb up and over. When they finally convinced her to climb it, she froze at the top with one leg on either side. There she sat crying for another ten minutes before being convinced to swing her other leg over the gate and make her way down. Molly stood at the bottom, promising to catch her if she should fall.

Deep down, Molly knew that was not going to happen. There was no way she had the strength to catch Splaffy or do anything except maybe break her fall and be the one who ended up in the hospital with broken bones. Thankfully, she safely made her way down with Molly just barely supporting her legs a little. Once her feet were firmly on the ground, everyone began cheering and laughing. The relief that Molly felt wouldn't let her stop laughing. She hugged her and jokingly told her it would probably have been better to stand in the corner for ten minutes because Mommy's punishments weren't as hard as God's punishments. Splaffy nodded her head and went in to change her soiled clothes. She had spent well over an hour trapped on the other side of the wall.

Soon after the incident, Splaffy's attitude slowly began changing. Between learning the Word of God, a stable life, setting boundaries, godly discipline, and a feeling of belonging to a family, they began seeing fewer and less dramatic tantrums. In less than six months' time, Molly told people that she had never in her life seen such a change in a child. It was true. She could still have a couple of small explosions a month, but nothing like before, and they were quickly controlled. Molly couldn't believe that she was the same little girl who daily reminded her that she was getting too old for the role of the mother and kept her wishing she could just step into the old grandmother role.

To her credit, Splaffy never showed any signs of learning problems. When she came at nine years old, she knew most of her letters but couldn't read at all. Molly was afraid school would be difficult for her. Yet by only spending the first hour of the school day in the house studying with Molly, she was reading on her own in less than a month. Molly occasionally asked the teacher how she was getting along, and she had no complaints about her. She quietly worked through each book, meeting all her goals with nice handwriting. Even in Sunday school, once she settled down, they found that she had no problem memorizing Bible verses and answering questions about the Bible stories. Incredibly, when the screaming diminished, they found Splaffy to be a quiet, shy person. She shied away from Christmas dramas, singing specials, large groups of people, and visitors. Her favorite pastimes were watching movies and playing video games.

Smaffy and Smiffy

Being very pleased with Splaffy's progress, the same rural welfare office offered them two more little girls, Smaffy, age eight, and Smiffy, age six. Both girls had been in government homes since before their first birthday. They had never known what it was to live in a family or have someone they called "Mommy." They arrived less than five months after Splaffy. They were both very thin.

Smaffy was also on medication to control her behavior. Though she seemed very happy her first couple of days, soon, they began seeing her temper tantrums as well. Without a doubt, they witnessed firsthand what the modern-day philosophy of not thwarting children's self-expression was doing. Leaving children to themselves with no form of discipline was obviously abuse, while loving correction was true protection and genuine care.

Like Splaffy, after about a month, they began lowering Smaffy's medications until she was off of them. Though they both had temper tantrum problems, their personalities were completely different. Splaffy's tantrums had been based on a "poor me, nobody loves me, everybody's always picking on me" attitude. Once the tantrums were under control, they found a quiet, shy girl behind them.

Smaffy was not at all quiet. She was always talking very loudly and always hungry for attention. She was the "stand right in front of a person, jumping up and down, wildly waving your arms, and making strange faces" attention-getter type. Notwithstanding, she was so cute and forced herself so much into the center of attention that many visitors found themselves delighted with her. Several even commented about wishing they could adopt her. Molly, Polly, Dolly, Lolly, and all the other children would just smile, but as soon as the visitors left, they'd give each other the old "if they only knew" look.

Smaffy's tantrums were defiant, rebellious, in-your-face tantrums. She thought nothing of planting her little fists on her little hips and yelling things like, "You don't tell me what to do," "Mind your own business," "I'm going to hit you right in the face," or any number of other huge, ugly threats. In all of Splaffy's uncontrollable oddities, she had never threatened or disrespected authority. Smaffy's aggressive, brazen defiance was proof of a strong will that needed to be broken and, thus, was harder to handle. Just the same, though the changes came so much slower, using the same biblical principles, Smaffy improved and continues to improve.

[LESSON TO LEARN: We are all nothing more than works in progress, letting Christ work in our lives sometimes and falling flat on our faces spiritually at other times. On a few occasions, while still trying to guide Smaffy into better self-control, older teens who had been in the Home for years and certainly knew better, would lose their cool over any silly little thing and end up in fistfights. "Oh, Father God, save us from allowing our own sinful selves to take control, and teach us to be more like our precious friend and Savior, Jesus Christ."]

Smaffy had what might be considered a selective memory. There were a few important details that she seemed to never forget, like what day a visitor was coming, a party or outing was planned, or a snack was promised. Once she knew of a future event, she couldn't stop talking about it. They finally started making it a point to not announce something until the night before so they wouldn't have to keep hearing about it all day, every day, until the event took place. Sometimes, though, information was leaked, and she would find out just the same. She seemed to have radar ears that heard everything. School facts and Bible verses, on the other hand, couldn't be remembered for anything in the world.

In Sunday school, Smaffy would try her hardest to say the Bible verse and win the piece of candy that came with learning it. Molly could tell she was trying and was purposely picking the shortest verses she could find, but even those were impossible for her to learn. Strangely enough, she could get the first word and the last word but lost everything in between. After they had repeated the verse umpteen times and everyone else had quoted it, Molly would call on Spaffy, who, by that time, was jumping up and down and waving her hand wildly. She would say the first word and follow it with a long pause and a few uumms, and aahhs. When it was obvious she was not going to say anything else, Molly would give her the second word, which she would repeat quickly, followed once again by silence, small noises that gave the idea that she was in deep thought, and a puzzled look on her face. Thus, they would go through the whole verse, telling her each word, one by one, until she blurted out the last word by herself and looked wide-eyed at Molly, believing she had said it well enough to win the candy. Usually, Molly would tell her that she needed to study a little more but that if she behaved in class, she could still win the candy.

Incredibly, behaving during the lesson wasn't at all difficult for Smaffy as she loved hearing Bible stories. Molly marveled that not one of the three newest girls knew any Bible stories. They had all spent years in homes run by nuns but had never heard even the most common stories. They didn't know who Adam and Eve were or Noah, David and Goliath, or Jonah. The thought of that did not compute with Molly, who had grown up in church. How was that even possible? She thought everyone in the world at least knew who Adam, Eve, and Noah were. Yet, the only story they had ever heard, though the details were not all correct, was of baby Jesus and Mary.

Smaffy sat on the edge of her seat; every story was new and exciting to her. For Molly, it was a welcome change from the kids who grew up in church and were constantly interrupting to finish a story, add to the story, or just declare that they already knew that story. Molly was a teacher at heart, and nothing thrills a teacher's heart more than a captive audience hanging onto their every word. Smaffy's interest sparked the fire from Molly's youth, bedded deep in her heart to want to make each story come alive. It made her want to make the exciting parts of each story extra exciting, the sad parts extra sad, and the happy parts extra happy. She would move from one side of the class to the other, acting out parts of the story while closely watching the different expressions of fear, joy, sadness, and anticipation on Smaffy's face. It thrilled Molly to see the expression of worry on her face right before the story's ending suddenly change and turn into joy as right prevailed over evil. She saw in her the exact same joy over a Bible story that the child expressed whenever she found out they were going to have a party. She was certainly an expressive child. No other students in the class responded as she did. In addition, it took about two years, but the Bible verses finally started clicking in her mind. As long as it wasn't very long, she could quote her verses fairly well.

Smiffy's personality was quite different than that of her sister. She was neither hyperactive nor defiant toward authority. She was a frail little girl who was so very thin that Molly wondered how all her bones and internal organs of lungs, kidneys, stomach, intestines, and so on could all squeeze into such a small space.

Though Smiffy was almost two years younger than her sister, she learned much more quickly, which, of course, frustrated Smaffy. Molly tried to teach them to read sitting side by side, but while Smaffy was concentrating on a vowel sound or consonant-vowel combination, Smiffy would blurt out the answer and send Smaffy into a tantrum. When she decided to work with each child separately, Smiffy took off quickly and was reading in no time. Her only struggle in school was her lack of coordination, which was notable in her gross and fine motor skills. She was the kind of child who could turn around and accidentally trip over her own two feet. When she ran, Molly watched on, holding her breath as she teeter-tottered back and forth from one foot to the other, in danger of losing her balance at any minute. In the area of fine motor skills, she could color fairly well but got tired quickly because it was so much work, and she had lots of problems with cutting and writing. Being able to form each letter came very slowly and required great patience on her teachers' part as they tried every method and even invented new ones just to help her. Molly's heart went out to her because she believed that her motor skill problem and a few physical characteristics pointed to a lack of any measures of prenatal care on the part of her birth mother.

Smiffy was not really a hyperactive child, but she was always on the move in her own slow little way. At church, she couldn't stay still. She would pick up Mommy's purse, put it here, move it there, unzip every zipper, re-zip every zipper, set it aside, pick up the Bible, thumb through it, take a pen out of its place in the Bible cover, pick up the purse, put the pen in the purse, set the Bible down, place the purse on the Bible, pick up the hymn book, and on and on. Molly would fold her own hands in her lap and look at her in a gesture for her to do the same. She would do so, and in less than a minute, she would spy a piece of paper on the floor that needed to be picked up or a hymn-book that was not placed just right in the rack.

At school, Smiffy would make quiet little comments all day long. Oftentimes, she was just talking to herself or reflecting on anything taking place around her. Up until this time, the classroom was operated in a quiet library-type setting. Smaffy and Smiffy turned their silent library of a schoolroom into a circus as each one of their comments would set all the other students to laughing.

Smiffy also had a hard time accepting the fact that any of her answers were wrong. Should she fall into a wrong answer rut, and it could take her an hour or more to escape. She would insist that it had to be the teacher who was wrong. Then she would take her booklet back to her desk, pout for a couple of minutes, and without correcting anything, take it back up to be graded again with the hope that the wrong answers would somehow be right this time or maybe that they had corrected themselves. When her answers were still wrong, she would take them back, mumbling, mad, and crying. Then she would erase the wrong answers, rewrite the same wrong answers, and turn in the work a third time, once again, hoping for the best. The teacher would point her to exactly where she could find the right answer but wouldn't give it to her if she herself wasn't even trying. By this time, she would be sufficiently upset to make huge holes in her booklet by erasing so hard. Eventually, the booklet was taken away for a while so she could chill, and she was given something else on which to work.

Disagreements and fights with the other children were also things Smiffy could not get past. She would explain the problem time and time again, going in circles about how she was right or how she had been mistreated and stressing every minute detail of what happened. Molly would call a meeting, listen to all sides, find a solution, administer correction if necessary, have everyone forgive one another, pray, and send them off to go play without fighting. Then upon turning around, there would be little Smiffy, still standing there, and she would immediately start explaining the problem as if it were fresh news and Molly had not yet heard what happened.

Of all the problems that Smiffy could not let go of, the poor chicken recipe topped the list. Holly had a delicious sweated chicken leg quarter recipe that was one of almost everyone's favorites. Upset Smiffy, however, could not get past the idea of eating sweaty chicken. She asked endless questions about why they had purchased sweaty chickens instead of clean chickens, what the chickens had done to get so sweaty, and why the chickens had not bathed. She simply could not bring herself to eat anything so disgusting. Many people explained many times that it was a way of cooking the chicken and wasn't really sweat at all, but every time it was served, the whole sweaty chicken conversation had to be repeated. They could never get her to eat more than just one small tidbit of the scrumptious poultry. Then one day, after years of abstaining from sweaty chicken, Molly noticed that Smiffy was eating a plate full of rice drowning in the broth from the chicken. Molly questioned Smiffy, and she explained that though she still didn't like the sweaty chicken, she had recently discovered that she did like the armpit sauce.

Spoodles

Only four months after Smaffy and Smiffy's arrival, the government asked Molly to take in one more child, a ten-year-old boy named Spoodles. That was perfect; the girls' side of the house was overflowing while there was plenty of room on the boys' side ever since the fearless four had left. They were well aware that they had not been forthright about Splaffy and Smaffy's behavior and made a point of repeating several times that Spoodles was well-behaved and loved by all. When Molly came right out and said that she had heard the word *well-behaved* before, the social worker got an embarrassed look on her face and told her it was really true this time. The home he was in hated to see him go, but it was only for young children, and he was getting too old.

She was right. Spoodles was indeed a breath of fresh air. He was happy and friendly and a good sport when the older boys teased him or roughed him up a little in a playful manner. Similar to Twuffy, he had no favorite toys or games to play. The toys he received at Christmas and on his birthday sat in his closet untouched. Once, the whole gang went to a toy store in the mall to spend some birthday money that everyone had been given. He carried his basket from aisle to aisle, trying to decide what he wanted. He would put something in it, being sure that was what he wanted, and then take it back to the shelf where he had gotten it and begin to look for something else. Molly, who was trying to help everyone, noticed that every time she saw him, he had something different in his basket.

Soon, everyone else had made their purchases and were standing in the mall with their bags, looking in the display window at Spoodles, who continued walking down each aisle, trying to decide on something. Since Molly had promised them ice cream at the end of the shopping trip, their faces grew more and more serious as they watched and waited. When he finally chose something, everyone sighed a sigh of relief. He took his gift home, played with it for an hour or so, and set it in his closet next to all his other untouched toys, taking it out occasionally to lend it to other boys who asked to borrow it.

Spoodles preferred people over toys and would follow Scroodles or Triddles around, doing whatever they were doing. He did enjoy playing games on his tablet, but even that was more fun if several of the kids were involved in playing the same game. Sometimes, he would even set his own tablet aside to sit next to Scroodles and watch him play. He was definitely another people person, but maybe even more so than Thuddles in that he enjoyed being with the other family members as well as visitors. He was also happy to help anyone in the Home, bringing them this or that and lending them a hand with their chores.

Spoodles had absolutely no problem with any of the authorities being a very respectful child. There was the slight curiosity that the volume knob on his vocal cords seemed to be stuck on the highest setting. He could not talk in a quiet voice. If he was asked to lower his voice, he would get an embarrassed look on his face, close his mouth, and remain completely silent for several minutes. Then, when he finally opened his mouth to speak, it was once again at full volume.

Equally odd was the fact that though he was eager to help others, he couldn't for the life of him remember to make his own bed or pick up his things. Apparently, in his former home, there were employees in charge of the cleaning, and the children didn't have even the tiniest bit of responsibilities. Therefore, his dirty clothes would lay precisely where he had taken them off to shower. Sometimes, he would even leave a perfectly spaced trail that would start in his room and lead to the shower, first the shoes, then the socks, followed by the shirt, the shorts, and lastly, the underwear right in front of the shower. Each item would stay right where it was dropped as though it were invisible. Boys could walk back and forth past the items with no thought that they might not be in the correct spot. They would not be moved until some adult entered the room and reminded Spoodles why there was a laundry hamper in the corner of the bathroom. The boys who had recuperated their clean room award had once again gone from fantastic to mediocre. The only reason the boys still remained ahead of the girls was because the three new girls were worse at cleaning than Spoodles.

Spoodles was a very intelligent child. His biggest problem in school was that he was not accustomed to individual learning and had a hard time concentrating on his own work while being keenly aware of everything that everyone else was doing. Nevertheless, in Sunday school, he excelled in the class. His former home had been taking the children to a Baptist church on Sundays, and unlike the girls, he knew all the Bible stories. He also had a keen memory and learned Scripture verses one after another with little effort. Maybe it was his great memory that helped him learn English so fast, or maybe he just had a knack for languages. Normally, a new child wouldn't begin speaking English for at least two years. Spoodles was making himself understood, howbeit with many grammatical errors, in less than a year. Whereas most children shied away from speaking English when they were first learning, Spoodles had no problem with lancing out and putting together whole sentences. It didn't bother him to be laughed at or corrected, which proved to be the fastest route to conquering a new language.

[LESSON TO LEARN: Each child who came into the Home was complex and unique in his or her miraculous way. Each was a beautiful creative expression of their Almighty Creator, who makes us all distinct individuals, different from each other in so many different ways. In addition, each of them, like each of us, had their own particular weaknesses and strengths, their own set of victories and defeats. Psalm 139:14 says, "I will praise thee; for I am fearfully and wonderfully made: marvelous are thy works; and that my soul knoweth right well."
Yet, all of us are identical in our sinful condition and need for Christ. We all have the same need and God has the same goal for all of us. Our need is to recognize our complete inability to save ourselves and trust Christ solely and completely for salvation. The goal that God has for all of us, which should be ours as well, is found in Romans 8:29, "For whom he did foreknow, he also did predestinate to be conformed to the image of his Son, that he might be the firstborn among many brethren." Thus, our need is to look to Christ for forgiveness, a new life in Christ, and a home in heaven. Our goal is to strive to show Christ to the world, that their need be satisfied as well, and they may be saved also.]

Author's Final Thoughts

I hope that some of our stories have brought a bit of joy or laughter into your life. They are the funny moments that most stand out in my mind, but judging from the way everyone gets to laughing at family gatherings, many more books could be written by other family members. They all seem to have their own set of noteworthy memories.

On the serious side, maybe you can relate to some of the same trials and struggles that we have been through, and it has reminded you of God's faithfulness to sustain us. These memories are a treasure chest of joys and tears. Above all, I hope that you have seen the hand of God at work in our lives and in your own and have given your heart to Jesus Christ, who died to pay for your sins.

Wouldn't it be wonderful if I could write in conclusion that every child who has passed through our doors and started his or her own life has been faithful to the Lord? I can't. Each person controls their own heart's desires, and sadly, many have loved the world and made poor choices. Though God has given us so much laughter, we have also experienced almost all the many heartbreaks and then some that sinful decisions on the part of grown children bring to Christian parents. Those most difficult trials and bad decisions are not even worth mentioning. Many times, I have questioned whether or not I would have even wanted to start a children's home had I known ahead of time all the sorrow it would include. No wonder God has arranged for us to live only one day at a time and keeps the future to Himself as one of His hidden treasures.

Nevertheless, that question is nothing more than a fleeting thought because I am immediately reminded of the fifteen or more sons and daughters who might never have known Christ but now continue in the Lord's work. Some are in full-time Christian service, and others serve faithfully in various ministries of the churches they attend. I think of their children who are being raised in the ways of the Lord. I think of the countless souls who have come to Christ through their testimonies and ministries. They have made it worth every effort and every heartache.

I am also reminded that the seed has been planted. Isaiah 55:10–11 says, "For as the rain cometh down, and the snow from heaven, and returneth not thither, but watereth the earth, and maketh it bring forth and bud, that it may give seed to the sower, and bread to the eater: So shall my word be that goeth forth out of my mouth: it shall not return unto me void, but it shall accomplish that which I please, and it shall prosper in the thing whereto I sent it." Some eighteen years after an angry Maffy left the home and the ways of the Lord, the seed sprouted, the Word of God took root, and she returned. She has been instrumental in the salvation of her husband and two children, and as a family, they are attending faithfully and serving in a local church.

At age twelve, Doodles talked about preaching someday and was already translating for Brother Neff in several different churches. Later, as a young adult, he had a "friend" who bought him some alcohol and got him started down a wrong path. After years of riotous living, the prodigal son hit bottom and returned to his loving heavenly Father. He came by the Home and asked for verses that would help him grow in the Lord. I gave him two of the key ring collections of verses he had grown up quoting. He came back the following week, praising the Lord for how the verses were helping him. He began quoting them to me, slowly, phrase by phrase, with feeling, explaining them to me with such enthusiasm and asking me if I understood how wonderful each truth was. I smiled and nodded my head. He acted as though it was the first time he had ever seen them. Praise God, I believe it truly was.

Author's Final Thoughts

We shall continue to pray for every family member whom God, in His wisdom, brought our way. We pray that those who are close to the Lord will remain strong and faithful. We pray that those who have strayed will return. We pray that those who are still in the home and just starting their Christian life will make wise decisions. In the words of my favorite author:

"Be guided, only by the healer of the sick, the raiser of the dead, the friend of all who were afflicted and forlorn, the patient Master who shed tears of compassion for our infirmities. We cannot but be right when we put all the rest away, and do everything in remembrance of Him . . . There can be no confusion in following Him, and seeking for no other footsteps, I am certain!" —Charles Dickens

I would love to hear from you!
email: sselfaro@gmail.com
tel.: (352) 684-1679
WhatsApp number: 506 8415-8182

Milton Keynes UK
Ingram Content Group UK Ltd.
UKHW031617231124
451036UK00003B/30